HOMEOWNERSHIP AND AMERICA'S FINANCIAL UNDERCLASS

Why are Americans so obsessed with the concept of homeownership? Why do cash-strapped Americans who have no savings and unstable jobs continue to believe that buying a home is in their best interest? Why do parents continue to put their children at an educational disadvantage by buying homes in neighborhoods with low-performing schools just so they can claim to be homeowners? More importantly, when will America's leaders admit that homeownership is now risky for many Americans and that far too many financially struggling Americans are being encouraged to buy homes because home sales are good for the U.S. economy and for the powerful moneyed constituent groups who support U.S. political leaders?

After describing homeownership's myths, assumptions, and flawed premises, Mechele Dickerson explains why the economic conditions America's financial underclass face make it impossible for them to reap the benefits associated with homeownership. Dickerson specifically links housing choices to educational choices and demonstrates that Americans who are poorly educated will always struggle to become and remain homeowners. Dickerson also exposes the ongoing risks of "home buying while brown or black" and argues that remaining traces of racial discrimination in housing and mortgage markets combined with certain demographic features make it especially challenging for blacks and Latinos to receive homeownership's promised benefits. Given the dire economic conditions facing America's financial underclass, the author admonishes U.S. leaders to reassess current housing policies and develop new ones that make it easier for Americans to have affordable housing, whether it is rented or owned.

Mechele Dickerson is the Arthur L. Moller Chair in Bankruptcy Law and Practice at the University of Texas at Austin School of Law. She is a frequent speaker at legal and judicial conferences throughout the United States and has delivered lectures and conducted workshops on bankruptcy and over-indebtedness in Brazil, Canada, and Tobago. She is a former Associate Dean for Academic Affairs at the University of Texas Law School and previously taught on the law faculty of William & Mary Law School. She is the author of more than thirty articles, essays, and book chapters on consumer debt and bankruptcy, and her writings have appeared in the *Atlanta Journal-Constitution*, the *Boston Review*, the *Austin American-Statesman*, and a variety of leading law reviews and journals.

Homeownership and America's Financial Underclass

FLAWED PREMISES, BROKEN PROMISES, NEW PRESCRIPTIONS

MECHELE DICKERSON
University of Texas at Austin School of Law

CAMBRIDGE
UNIVERSITY PRESS

32 Avenue of the Americas, New York, NY 10013-2473, USA

Cambridge University Press is part of the University of Cambridge.

It furthers the University's mission by disseminating knowledge in the pursuit of education, learning, and research at the highest international levels of excellence.

www.cambridge.org
Information on this title: www.cambridge.org/9781107663503

First published 2014

Printed in the United States of America

A catalog record for this publication is available from the British Library.

Library of Congress Cataloging in Publication data
Dickerson, Arletrice Mechele, 1962–
Homeownership and America's financial underclass : flawed premises, broken promises, new prescriptions / Arletrice Mechele Dickerson.
pages cm
Includes bibliographical references and index.
ISBN 978-1-107-03868-4 (hardback) – ISBN 978-1-107-66350-3 (paperback)
1. Home ownership – United States. 2. Mortgage loans – United States.
3. Housing – United States – Finance. I. Title.
HD7287.82.U6D53 2014
333.33'808900973–dc23 2014002248

ISBN 978-1-107-03868-4 Hardback
ISBN 978-1-107-66350-3 Paperback

To my parents, Warner and Arcola Dickerson

Contents

Acknowledgments		*page* ix
1	Chasing the American Dream	1
2	The Happy Homeownership Narrative	19
3	U.S. Support for Homeowners	38
4	The Homeownership Crisis	64
5	Homeowner Harm and the Blame Game	85
6	Flawed Premises	114
7	The Burden of Home Buying While Black or Latino	145
8	The Benefits of Home Buying While Black or Latino	179
9	Homeownership: Educational Disparities	206
10	Homeownership: Income Disparities	231
11	Outlook and Prescription for the Future	252
Index		275

Acknowledgments

I have been thinking about homeownership for almost a decade and have had numerous formal and informal conversations with people about the ideas presented in this book.

I especially wish to thank the following group of people who have offered advice and editorial assistance over the last year. Jolyn Piercy read and critiqued the entire manuscript (multiple times) and also input revisions to earlier drafts. I also thank Jane O'Connell both for reading chapters and for providing magnificent research support. Finally, I thank the copy editors and anonymous reviewers who worked on behalf of Cambridge University Press, and Wendy Wagner for initially encouraging me during our many lunches over Skype to turn my ideas into a book.

I am grateful to a large group of friends, family, and colleagues, including Dorothy Brown, John Dzienkowski, Frank Fernandez, Tina Fernandez, Henry Hu, Joan Leavell, and Bob Peroni, who offered helpful comments on individual chapters, and to Melissa Bernstein who continued to provide research support even after she left the University of Texas School of Law. I also thank student research assistants Fermin Diego Gonzalez, Grant O'Hickey, Alex Martin, Brionna Ned, and Imaeyen E. Nsien for editorial and reference help.

I owe thanks to my former institution, William & Mary Law School, for providing financial support during the early stages of this research. This book would not have been completed without the support of my current institution, the University of Texas, and specifically the Arthur L. Moller Chair in Bankruptcy Law and Practice, which provided funding and the year-long sabbatical leave I used to write the first draft of the book.

I am most indebted, however, to my sons, John and Joshua, for their willingness to share their often-distracted and sometimes cranky mother with piles of research materials and an ever-present laptop.

1

Chasing the American Dream

Home Sweet Home. There's no place like Home. Home is where the heart is. Home is where you hang your hat. A man's Home is his castle. A house is not a Home. Mi casa es su casa. Few things have captivated the heart, mind, and soul of the American public as much as the concept of homeownership. Living in the home you own is viewed as a basic American privilege and a core component of the American cultural norm of what it means to be a success.

The vast majority of Americans, whether renters or homeowners, have long believed that owning a home is a better financial strategy than renting a home is. Indeed, homeowners and renters of all races and income groups continue to believe that owning a home is the safest long-term investment they can make. Americans continue to hold on to this belief, even though millions of Americans have low (or no) savings, stagnant (or declining) income, and unstable (or no) employment. Indeed, not even the worst economic slowdown since the Great Depression, skyrocketing foreclosure rates, and plummeting home prices could convince most Americans that becoming a homeowner is not low-cost, low-risk, or easily attainable. For example, more than two-thirds of the people polled in a 2010 Fannie Mae survey felt that homeownership is preferable to renting because homeownership gives you more space for your family, more control over your living space, and is a better investment than renting.[1]

While U.S. housing policies have focused on increasing homeownership rates since President John Quincy Adams extolled the concept of sea-to-shining-sea continentalism, the U.S. government did not make homeownership the centerpiece of U.S. housing policies until Franklin D. Roosevelt's New Deal programs in the 1930s. Since then, U.S. political leaders have gone to great lengths to convince Americans that homeownership is low-risk,

[1] Fannie Mae National Housing Survey (2010–2011).

low-cost, and a guaranteed way to increase their household wealth. Sadly, these premises are no longer true for lower- and middle-income Americans. And they have *never* really been true for some Americans.

FINANCIAL BENEFITS

Since the Depression, U.S. housing policies have focused on giving Americans incentives to buy houses and finding ways to increase and maintain high homeownership rates. U.S. housing policies are premised on the assumption that homeownership makes Americans more financially stable, that owning a house provides economic security for homeowners and their families, and that homeowners are more responsible, concerned, and involved citizens than renters are. Deciding to buy your own home is said to instill good financial habits in the potential owner, and becoming a homeowner is said to almost magically transform renters into thrifty, financially responsible individuals. Although no longer true, historically these premises were borne out in reality.

During the recent housing boom, lenders allowed renters to qualify for a mortgage loan and buy a house even if they put little (or no) money down. Historically, however, homeownership served as a forced savings device because everyone who wanted to become a homeowner had to have at least *some* financial capital because they needed money for a down payment or they would never qualify for a mortgage loan. During the first few decades of the twentieth century, a buyer needed to make a down payment of almost 50 percent of the home sales price before a lender would approve his mortgage loan application. After the United States intervened in the housing finance markets in the 1930s to stem the tide of foreclosures triggered by the Depression, a potential home buyer could make a smaller down payment, usually 20 percent of the home price. Even though U.S. housing policies made it easier for some borrowers to buy a house with a low-cost, self-amortizing, government-insured private mortgage, borrowers were still forced to exercise financial restraint and save enough for the down payment. Until lenders all but abandoned their traditional underwriting standards in the recent housing boom, renters who failed to save enough money to make a 20 percent down payment could not buy a home with a long-term, government-insured, prime interest rate loan unless they purchased expensive private mortgage insurance (PMI).

For most of the twentieth century, homeownership served as a forced savings device even *after* borrowers saved enough money to make a down payment and pay their loan closing costs, because the terms and structure of government-insured, fixed-interest rate mortgage loans forced homeowners to be financially responsible. Government-insured, prime interest rate mortgage loans have fixed-interest rates, relatively long repayment periods (typically fifteen or thirty years), and are self-amortizing. Because homeowners had to save enough money each month to make a full payment of principal plus interest for an extended period of time, they were forced to either exercise long-term fiscal restraint or risk losing their homes and the investment they made in those homes.

Buying a home did more than just instill the financial virtues of thrift and saving in homeowners. Homes have historically been sound, stable, long-term investments, and being a homeowner has been a relatively safe way for many Americans to increase their net worth. Overall housing prices during the late 1990s and early 2000s housing boom increased by more than 50 percent, and housing prices in some regions increased annually by more than 10 percent.[2] For a while, homeownership seemed like an almost guaranteed way to increase household net worth, and some homeowners seemed to conclude that homeownership was a low-cost, risk-free way for them to increase their net worth *and* increase their spending.

Skyrocketing housing prices during the recent housing boom made homeowners "feel" rich, and many responded to this feeling of wealth with incessant buying. Overall U.S. consumer debt levels skyrocketed during the housing boom, and some homeowners appeared to believe that no matter how much they increased their spending, they could always dig themselves out of debt with their platinum shovel: the equity in their ever-appreciating Home Sweet Home. Of course, they (wrongly) assumed that housing prices would always rise, interest rates would never rise, home equity loans would always be available, and there (always) would be an available buyer for their homes. While homeowners were feeling house-rich during the housing bubble, renters panicked and feared that they were throwing away their hard-earned dollars by paying rent to their landlords and squandering valuable tax benefits by not owning a home. Watching everybody else buy expensive homes and still spend, spend, spend thanks to the platinum shovel made renters even more determined to become homeowners.

The government uses tax incentives to encourage renters to buy homes. Indeed, one of the largest and most expensive tax expenditures in the U.S. Tax Code is the mortgage interest deduction. People who itemize their tax deductions (instead of taking the standard deduction) can reduce their tax burden by deducting the interest they pay on mortgage loans (including home equity loans and lines of credit) on their primary and secondary homes up to

[2] S&P/Case-Shiller, *National Composite Index of Home Prices, available at* http://us.spindices.com/indices/real-estate/sp-case-shiller-us-national-home-price-index.

a certain dollar amount. Itemizers can also deduct the state and local real property taxes they pay for their homes and, if they sell their home and buy a more expensive one, they can shield some of the profits from the sale from federal income taxes. While these homeownership benefits are used only by the small percentage of high-income homeowners who itemize their deductions, *all* homeowners receive an implicit tax break. That is, each month homeowners make a mortgage payment, they are paying themselves the equivalent of rent. Unlike landlords, however, owner-occupants are not taxed on this imputed income, and this untaxed income has recently accounted for more than 8 percent of the U.S. gross domestic product.[3]

HOMEOWNERSHIP HAS ITS PRIVILEGES

In addition to valuable financial benefits, there are powerful social benefits, privileges, and legal rights associated with homeownership, and property owners have always had a higher social and political status than renters. A homeowner makes a financial investment when he buys and then maintains (or improves) his home and his decision to buy the house indicates his intent to be a long-term resident in his neighborhood. Because of this investment and commitment, the homeowner is viewed as having a greater stake in his community than a renter does. To reward homeowners for their commitment to their communities, U.S. housing policies give homeowners the right to control or influence how land near them will be used and who should be allowed to live in their neighborhoods. For decades, both public (i.e., zoning and subdivision laws and policies) and private (i.e., restrictive property covenants) land use laws have allowed homeowners to exclude property uses and people from their neighborhoods. Local land use policies and regulations give homeowners the ability to essentially veto requests for zoning changes in their neighborhoods and fence out activities if they deem the proposed uses to be undesirable, or if they think the activities might be dangerous or pose threats to their neighborhoods.

Homeowners aggressively protect their Not In My Backyard (NIMBY) rights, and their stakeholder mentality makes them think that their views are superior to the views of renters or nonresidents and should prevail in any public policy decision involving how properties in their neighborhoods should

[3] J. Comm. Tax'n., *Present Law and Background Relating to Tax Treatment of Household Debt* (Jul. 11, 2011); Jordan Rappaport, *The Effectiveness of Homeownership in Building Wealth*, Federal Reserve Bank of Kansas City Economic Review (2010), *available at* https://www.kansascityfed.org/publicat/econrev/pdf/10q4Rappaport.pdf.

be used or developed. Thus, whenever a local or state governing authority attempts to place a public project homeowners find undesirable (like a hazardous waste facility, junkyard, halfway house, or homeless shelter) in their neighborhoods, homeowners frequently organize and lobby to try to keep the project out. Likewise, if another property owner seeks to use his property in a way that is not authorized by existing zoning rules, homeowners often band together and object to the request for a variance if the homeowners find the proposed use objectionable.

For almost a century, exclusionary zoning laws have permitted homeowners to fence out more than just undesirable commercial uses. Generally speaking, exclusionary zoning laws protect homeowners from "undesirable" housing (and neighbors) by fencing out structures, including homes that might pose dangers or cause the value of homes to fall. These laws fence out multifamily or other affordable housing based on the view that this type of housing will lower the value of single-family homes or destroy the stability and social order of the neighborhood. Exclusionary zoning laws fence out affordable housing (and, thus, lower- and moderate-income residents) by, for example, requiring builders to construct large homes on large lots. These laws are consistent with the general rhetoric surrounding the American Dream of owning a home. Together with housing policies that allow homeowners to control how their neighborhoods develop, exclusionary zoning laws have helped emboldened homeowners and convinced many that they have the right to live in the "right" neighborhood with the "right" sorts of people.[4]

Of course, allowing homeowners to protect their property interests by excluding certain property uses is not necessarily a bad thing, and *no one* wants undesirable projects to be located near them. But whereas no one wants to live near these projects, *everyone* understands that most of these projects are societal necessities. All homeowners ostensibly have these stakeholder control rights, but only *some* homeowners have been able to use their stakeholder powers effectively and consistently to fence out public, societally beneficial projects or affordable housing. Higher-income homeowners have been much more successful at excluding property uses and residents they deem undesirable. Successful lobbying efforts by higher-income homeowners usually result in them protecting their property values from any potential harm that might

[4] Indeed, merely saying the names of certain cities or neighborhoods triggers a vision of the type of person most likely to live there. Examples of racially or economically branded areas include Harlem, Key West, Detroit, Chevy Chase, Westchester County, Aspen, Martha's Vineyard, South Beach, Beverly Hills, and the like, even if those areas might have transitioning populations. See Sam Roberts, *New York City Losing Blacks, Census Shows*, N.Y. TIMES (Apr. 3, 2006), at A1.

ensue from being located near societally beneficial but undesirable public projects. But these public projects must be sited somewhere. So, while excluding these undesirable uses from their high-income and predominately white neighborhoods helps these politically strong homeowners, their effective lobbying efforts impose costs on the neighborhoods that are forced to house these projects or housing developments.

The neighborhoods that are most often forced to accept these projects are, not surprisingly, lower-income ones. And, like the residents most likely to be fenced out of the higher-income neighborhoods, the homeowners or neighbors who are often forced to live near these undesirable, albeit useful, projects are often black or Latino. As explained in more detail in later chapters, letting higher-income homeowners fence out property uses (and certain types of people) and forcing lower-income and minority homeowners to live near these properties has, over time, almost guaranteed that homeowners in lower-income white, black, and Latino neighborhoods do not reap the same financial homeownership benefits that the owners of homes in higher-income, predominantly white neighborhoods receive.

SOCIAL BENEFITS

U.S. housing policies support and subsidize home purchases because homeownership purportedly provides positive benefits for owners, neighborhoods, and communities. Specifically, housing policies favor homeownership based on the assumption that homeowners are more involved in their communities and actively participate in homeowners' associations and other local civic organizations. In the Happy Homeownership Narrative, homeownership is good for all property owners who live in owner-occupied neighborhoods because homeowners take good care of their homes and ensure that their neighborhoods remain safe and desirable. Because people are more likely to take better care of the things *they* own than the things they use but *others* own, homeowners should be expected to repair, improve, and perform routine maintenance on their homes.

U.S. housing policies are correct to assume that actual and potential homeowners are affected by how homes are maintained in a neighborhood and the types of amenities the neighborhood has. Appraisers assess the value of surrounding properties when calculating the value of a home. Thus, appropriately maintained homes generally have higher property values. Just as they lobby to fence out undesirable uses, actively involved homeowners frequently lobby local governments to ensure that they have high-quality amenities (like new roads and improved schools) in their neighborhoods and communities.

In addition to enjoying these neighborhood amenities while they remain in their homes, existing homeowners benefit from living near well-kept homes in desirable neighborhoods when they decide to sell their homes, because when potential homeowners consider whether and where to buy a house, they evaluate the amenities in the house *and* in the neighborhood. Potential buyers consider things like: Who are the other neighbors? How well do they maintain their homes? Are the schools and other community facilities and services of high quality?

U.S. housing policies also encourage and subsidize homeownership because of the belief that being a homeowner makes you happy and is good for school-age children. Homeowners regularly report that owning their own home makes them feel good, that they believe that owning a home is better emotionally and psychologically for their households, and that they derive pleasure from living in their particular home or neighborhood. Renters with young children are especially likely to aspire to become homeowners because of the belief that children who live in rented housing are deprived of valuable educational and societal benefits that automatically flow to homeowners' children. Although inconclusive, most studies do show that homeownership provides social, psychological, and emotional benefits for homeowners' children that renters' children do not receive, and data confirm that homeowners' children perform better in school and on standardized tests than renters' children. Studies further suggest that owner-occupied housing generally is a happier and healthier environment in which to rear children.[5]

While some of these myths and assumptions are true, not all are. Neighborhoods that consist of homeowners are neither necessarily nor always "better" than a primarily renter-occupied neighborhood. Furthermore, homes in owner-occupied neighborhoods are not guaranteed to have higher market values than homes in neighborhoods that consist primarily of renter-occupied housing. Likewise, renters can obviously be just as responsible and involved in their communities as homeowners can. Whether the assumptions and myths associated with homeownership are valid or not is largely irrelevant. Since the Depression, U.S. political leaders have justified enacting and protecting housing policies that encourage and heavily subsidize homeownership because of the financial and positive external benefits that purportedly flow to neighborhoods and communities when people own their own homes. Given that

[5] Donald R. Haurin et al., *The Impact of Homeownership on Child Outcomes* 10 (Joint Ctr. for Hous. Studies, Harvard Univ., Working Paper No. LIHO-01.14, 2001), *available at* http://www.jchs.harvard.edu/sites/jchs.harvard.edu/files/liho01–14.pdf.

most Americans also continue to believe that homeownership is better than renting, no one really seems interested in examining whether the myths and assumptions about homeownership are actually true.

BENEFITS TO THE U.S. ECONOMY

Homeownership might not provide the financial and psychological benefits portrayed in the Happy Homeownership Narrative. But, it is undeniable that homeownership has positive economic spillover effects and significant economic benefits for the U.S. economy. Indeed, the strength of housing markets has long served as a bellwether for the general strength of the U.S. economy. And, as the recent Great Recession demonstrated, weak housing markets create volatility across the spectrum of credit markets both in the United States and abroad. Until the recession (which started in December 2007 and officially ended in June 2009), consumer spending accounted for 70 percent of all economic activity in the United States and housing-related revenue *alone* regularly accounts for almost a quarter of the U.S. economy.

A robust housing market where people buy and sell houses and repay or refinance mortgage loans is good for builders, realtors, banks, and home improvement stores. Builders must purchase construction materials and homeowners must furnish their new homes, so having a robust housing market increases overall demand for consumer goods and services. Because people are needed to design, construct, and rehabilitate homes, an active residential real estate market also helps boost local employment rates. Localities welcome builders of single-family housing, *especially* expensive homes, because the housing sector invigorates other economic activity. Additionally, cities encourage and recruit potential owners to houses in economically depressed neighborhoods that are being revitalized or gentrified because of their desire to invigorate those neighborhoods. Given these overall benefits to the economy, national, state, and local leaders not surprisingly support laws that encourage and subsidize home sales. As discussed in more detail in later chapters, however, U.S. housing policies now seem more focused on boosting the economy and ensuring the financial well-being of the real estate and the financial services industry than supporting the people who are being encouraged to buy houses.

MORTGAGE INNOVATION TO THE RESCUE

As discussed in greater detail later in Chapter 3, starting in the 1970s, housing prices soared and housing price appreciation made some homeowners, especially the ones who owned homes in high-income communities, house-rich. Since the 1970s, however, wages for all but the most highly paid have been stagnant, real median household income has declined, and the savings rate has hovered at or below zero. By the late 1990s, housing price increases created a housing unaffordability problem, and many low- and moderate-income (LMI) renters who wanted to become homeowners found that they simply could not afford to buy a house because of the combination of stagnant wages, no savings, and escalating housing prices. LMI buyers found themselves priced out of most housing markets, *especially* high-appreciating markets, and many could not qualify for a traditional fixed rate mortgage (FRM) because their financial profiles did not match the profile envisioned in the Happy Homeownership Narrative.

Increasingly, LMI renters had no money to make a down payment. Their stagnant or declining income did not give them enough monthly disposable income to repay a fixed rate, fifteen- or thirty-year mortgage loan, and their crushing debt levels prevented them from satisfying lenders' debt-to-income ratio requirements. Americans were sorted into the housing haves and the housing have-nots who would never buy a home and experience the benefits promised by the Happy Homeownership Narrative.[6]

The U.S. government became concerned that homeownership was becoming unaffordable and, again, intervened in the housing finance market. To address this unaffordability crisis, the Clinton and George W. Bush administrations, as well as members of Congress, developed strategies and initiatives to make it easier for people to buy homes. The U.S. government explicitly encouraged lenders to "innovate" their mortgage products to create new loans that would make it easier for buyers to purchases houses. The innovated products helped increase home sales, but ultimately did not help renters become long-term homeowners.

The lending industry created and extensively marketed a wide array of nontraditional mortgage products. As discussed in more detail in later chapters, these innovations succeeded in causing overall homeownership rates to increase in the late 1990s and then skyrocket to reach a record high of 69 percent by 2005.[7] The nontraditional (also called exotic or alternative) mortgage products renters used to buy homes during the housing boom would

[6] The president of the National Association of Realtors testified before Congress that the affordability crisis had created a nation of "housing haves" (who purchased homes before the price explosion) and "housing have nots" (who were forced to "scale down their expectations and make lifestyle sacrifices to afford adequate shelter"). *Hearing before the Committee on Banking, Housing, and Urban Affairs of the U.S. Senate, on Increasing Minority Homeownership, and Expanding Homeownership to all Who Wish to Attain It*, 108th Cong., 1st Sess. (Jun. 12, 2003) (prepared statement of Cathy Whatley, President of The National Association of Realtors).

[7] U.S. Census Bureau, *Housing Vacancies and Homeownership*, tbl. 14, *available at* http://www.census.gov/housing/hvs/data/histtabs.html.

have been unrecognizable to lenders in the 1940s–1970s. Until recently, the only borrowers who could qualify for low-cost, low-risk fifteen- to thirty-year FRMs were people who had good credit, consistent income, and made a down payment on the home purchase. To keep homeownership rates and home sales high, lenders essentially abandoned the underwriting criteria they had used for most of the twentieth century and approved mortgage loans for borrowers with bad credit or borrowers who could not (or would not) document their income and assets. Additionally, borrowers were approved for loans to buy a house even if they made low (or no) down payments. In fact, lenders innovated mortgage products to keep the initial monthly loan payments low enough to allow borrowers with unsteady or stagnant income and no savings to qualify for a mortgage and become homeowners.

Even though homeowners in the Happy Homeownership Narrative are thrifty savers, the very structure of these innovated loans discouraged households from being thrifty or financially responsible. Historically, cash-strapped renters had an economic incentive to be thrifty savers because they needed money for a down payment in order to qualify for a mortgage loan and then needed to save enough money from their paychecks to make fixed monthly payments on that mortgage loan. During the "innovation" phase of the housing boom, though, lenders effectively discouraged borrowers from exercising thrift and financial responsibility when they created exotic mortgage products that did not require borrowers to make down payments. In addition, because many of these products had adjustable-interest rates with low initial "teaser" payments that sometimes covered only the interest on the loans, borrowers had no incentive to save or be financially prudent, even though monthly payments on these exotic loans would increase, sometimes dramatically, when the initial teaser interest rates reset.

Mortgage innovation seemed to "fix" the unaffordability problem by allowing cash-strapped renters to buy their homes. Even though the exotic mortgage products were high-cost and high-risk, homeowners assumed that home values would keep rising and lenders would always refinance the loans. As long as housing prices rose but interest rates remained low, this was a reasonable assumption. So, at least for a while, becoming a homeowner helped households increase their net worth, and this mortgage fix helped perpetuate the myth that homeownership remained attainable and financially advantageous for all potential buyers. Unfortunately, homeowners' assumptions about their high-cost, high-risk exotic loan products and their miscalculations about U.S. housing markets were fatally flawed.

When interest rates reset, monthly payments increased – often dramatically – on these loans. By the time the housing market started to collapse in the mid-2000s, borrowers faced the greatest risk a homeowner could ever face – the risk of foreclosure and losing an entire economic investment. Much to the chagrin of homeowners who felt rich and had borrowed against their houses during the housing boom, the lenders who had aggressively marketed and eagerly approved the exotic loans that let them become homeowners (or borrow against their homes) refused to let them refinance their high-cost, high-risk loans. Because many homeowners had little (or no) equity in their homes, they were trapped: they could not afford their monthly mortgage payments; lenders refused to refinance their high-cost loans; and a depressed housing market made it impossible for homeowners to sell their homes for an amount that would let them repay their mortgage loans.

HOMEOWNERSHIP: THE CRISIS

There is no single cause for the housing crisis or the recent recession that the crash helped trigger. Generally speaking, the housing market collapsed because house prices stopped appreciating and started to depreciate, interest rates rose, and borrowers defaulted in record numbers on their mortgage loans. While homeowners from all income groups defaulted on loans and lost homes in the recent recession, black and Latino households were particularly hard hit, in large part because of their household income. Black and Latino workers have lower overall household income than white workers, and LMI workers of all races have faced sobering economic statistics for almost thirty years. Household income for LMI Americans has been stagnant since the 1980s, and these workers continue to have fewer higher-wage job opportunities than they had up until the 1970s. By the mid-2000s, unemployment levels and stagnant wages, especially for middle-skilled workers, had risen, and households found themselves with too much debt and not enough money to pay those debts. Unemployment levels were – and remain – especially high for blacks, Latinos, and workers who do not have a college degree.

The toxic combination of stagnant income, rising unemployment and interest rates, and depressed housing values caused record numbers of homeowners to default on their mortgage loans. Default rates were particularly high for people who bought their homes using high-cost, high-risk exotic lending products. Additionally, people whose homes were worth less than the outstanding mortgage debt (i.e., upside-down homeowners) defaulted in record numbers. In fact, even after government officials declared that the recession was over, one in seven homeowners had outstanding mortgage debt that exceeded the value of their still-depreciating homes. That is, of the approximately 45 million outstanding mortgages in 2011, more than 12 million were underwater. By the end of 2011, there were almost 2.7 million delinquent mortgages and 2.2 million homeowners involved in foreclosure proceedings.[8]

RACE AND HOMEOWNERSHIP

Homeownership has never been easy, low-cost, or low-risk for blacks and Latinos, and their path to homeownership has *always* been obscured by obstacles and barriers in the mortgage and residential housing markets. Despite this, blacks and Latinos have always placed a high priority on becoming homeowners and experiencing the same sense of pride, stability, and security that whites feel when they buy homes. Many of the obstacles blacks and Latinos historically faced when they tried to buy homes, such as racially restrictive covenants, steering, and redlining, are now illegal. Nonetheless, race continues to be an obstacle for black and Latino homeowners. For example, a recent lawsuit revealed that mortgage loan officers used racially derogatory language when referring to black borrowers, routinely referring to them as "mud people" who did not pay their bills. Loan officers also called black neighborhoods "slums" and the "hood," and they called the loans that they were pushing on borrowers in black neighborhood "ghetto loans." This racist conduct was the norm during the early part of the twentieth century, and these negative stereotypes about blacks were common well into the 1960s before state and federal governments enacted anti-discrimination and fair housing laws. Sadly, the bank officers who referred to blacks as mud people and called black neighborhoods slums worked for Wells Fargo *in the 1990s and 2000s*, and the loans that were being "pushed" on black borrowers were high-cost, subprime loans that were "innovated" to make homeownership more accessible and affordable to black and Latino homeowners.[9]

Private actors were not the only ones who made it harder for blacks (and, later, Latinos) to achieve the American dream of homeownership. For

[8] Octavio Nuiry, *Strategic Default "Only Choice" for Some* (Jan. 18, 2012), *available at* http://www.realtytrac.com/Content/news-and-opinion/strategic-default-only-choice-for-some-6989; Realtytrac, *2011 Year-End Foreclosure Report: Foreclosures on the Retreat* (Jan. 9, 2012), *available at* http://www.realtytrac.com/content/foreclosure-market-report/2011-year-end-foreclosure-market-report-6984.

[9] Declaration of Tony Paschal, Mayor of Baltimore v. Wells Fargo Bank, 677 F. Supp. 2d 847, No. 1:08-cv-00062-JFM, Doc. 176–2 (2010), *available at* http://www.relmanlaw.com/docs/Baltimore-Declarations.pdf; Declaration of Doris Dancy, City of Memphis v. Wells Fargo Bank, No. 2:09-cv-02857-STA, Doc. 29–1 (W.D. Tenn. May 4, 2011), *available at* http://www.relmanlaw.com/docs/Declarations-Memphis.pdf; Declaration of Elizabeth M. Jacobson, Mayor of Baltimore v. Wells Fargo Bank, 677 F. Supp. 2d 847, No. 1:08-cv-00062-JFM, Doc. 176–1 (2010), *available at* http://www.relmanlaw.com/docs/Baltimore-Declarations.pdf.

decades, the U.S. government aided and abetted these private actors by either actively participating in or willingly condoning programs and policies that discriminated against racial minorities. For example, the Federal Housing Administration (FHA) embraced a racist lending system commonly known as "redlining." With redlining, all-white areas received the highest (blue) rating. In contrast, black neighborhoods received the lowest (red) rating, which led to the use of the term redlining. Neighborhoods that bordered black neighborhoods received a green rating, which was only slightly higher than redlined neighborhoods. The FHA refused to provide insurance for loans to blacks or to anyone who wanted to buy homes in redlined neighborhoods. Once the FHA deemed non-white neighborhoods risky, private lenders were discouraged from making traditional, low-cost loans to blacks (or anyone) who tried to buy homes in black neighborhoods.[10]

In addition to making it more expensive for blacks to buy homes *anywhere* and for *anyone* to buy a home in a black neighborhood, cities across the United States enacted and enforced racially discriminatory zoning laws mandating that neighborhoods be segregated by race. Even after the Supreme Court found those laws to be unconstitutional, racial segregation in neighborhoods remained because state and federal courts enforced racist real property covenants that prevented white homeowners from selling their homes to non-whites. These racially restrictive property covenants made it virtually impossible for blacks and Latinos to buy higher-appreciating homes in white neighborhoods, *especially* suburban neighborhoods. Then, even after the U.S. Supreme Court struck down racially restrictive property covenants, realtors continued to steer minorities (especially blacks) to non-white urban neighborhoods that had older and generally smaller homes with fewer amenities. Finally, even though federal laws ultimately banned this form of housing discrimination, federal housing agencies, realtors, and lenders continued to exhibit negative racial biases against blacks and continued to engage in informal steering.

Blacks and Latinos continued to face discrimination in the mortgage lending markets, and they were unable to buy homes using low-cost, low-risk, government-insured mortgage loans, even though the 1968 Fair Housing Act and the 1974 Equal Credit Opportunity Act made it illegal for lenders to engage in discriminatory lending practices. Because this discrimination continued to occur after these federal laws prohibited it, Congress enacted the 1975 Home Mortgage Disclosure Act (HMDA), which requires lenders

[10] Douglas S. Massey, *Origins of Economic Disparities: The Historical Role of Housing Segregation*, in SEGREGATION: THE RISING COSTS FOR AMERICA 69 (James H. Carr & Nandinee K. Kutty eds., 2008).

to publish data that show how they distribute credit to potential borrowers. As the recent abhorrent conduct of Wells Fargo loan officers vividly displays, however, blacks and Latinos continue to face barriers in housing and lending markets despite these laws, and the racial homeownership gap still has not closed. Indeed, because of years of racist public laws and policies, as well as the private discriminatory acts of realtors, sellers, and hostile neighbors, neighborhoods in many U.S. cities remain racially segregated.

For reasons discussed in greater detail in later chapters, lower homeownership rates combined with the vestiges of mortgage and real estate market discrimination have created a racial wealth gap. In general, homes in white neighborhoods have higher appreciation values than homes in non-white neighborhoods. Because blacks and Latinos have lower homeownership rates and generally own homes that are less valuable in housing markets, there has always been a racial housing wealth gap between whites, blacks, and Latinos. Federal and state officials have tried for more than twenty years to find ways to increase black and Latino homeownership rates. But even when the United States encouraged lenders to "fix" the housing unaffordability problem and make homeownership easier for blacks and Latinos, blacks and Latinos ended up paying more for houses that were valued less in the housing market.

During the housing boom and especially after lenders innovated new loan products, blacks and Latinos received a disproportionate share of higher-cost loans. Specifically, blacks and Latinos were more likely to pay higher interest rates relative to white borrowers whether the loans were prime or subprime. Less than 20 percent of home purchase loans issued to white borrowers were high-cost loans. In contrast, more than 50 percent of all loans blacks used to purchase homes, and 40 percent of the loans Latinos used, were subprime loan products. These subprime loans had higher fees and riskier payment options. While these lower initial payments made it possible for cash-strapped borrowers to qualify for a mortgage loan and to make (at least initially) small monthly payments, these loans negatively amortized. This negative amortization caused the borrower's principal loan balance to *increase* each month, even if the borrower made the "full" monthly payment. Blacks and Latinos were also more likely than whites with similar risk factors to be forced to purchase expensive PMI or to buy homes with loans that carried prepayment penalties.[11]

Studies conducted during and after the housing boom consistently found that blacks and Latinos disproportionately paid more to buy homes and that these higher costs were not justified by the borrower's likely risk of default.

[11] Debbie Gruenstein Bocian et al., *Race, Ethnicity and Subprime Home Loan Pricing*, 60 J. ECON. & BUS. 110, 110–11 (2008); National Fair Housing Alliance, *The Crisis of Housing Segregation: 2007 Fair Housing Trends Report* (2007).

Despite the higher costs, these loan products *did* make it easier for blacks and Latinos to buy homes, and their overall homeownership rates increased more during the housing boom than white homeownership rates. However, these high-cost mortgage products saddled black and Latino households with higher overall mortgage debts relative to whites, and the loans' adjustable rates and other exotic loan features placed blacks and Latinos at a higher risk of defaulting on their loans and losing their homes to foreclosure.

When housing prices plummeted, interest rates rose, and unemployment rates soared, these risks became realities: blacks and Latinos had significantly higher foreclosure rates than whites, and the recent recession essentially wiped out the gains to black and Latino homeownership rates. Thus, rather than smoothing the road to homeownership, recent attempts to make homeownership easier and more accessible made the path toward homeownership for blacks and Latinos even rockier.

In addition to wiping out the increases in black and Latino homeownership, the recession also wiped out years of accumulated wealth for black and Latino homeowners. For example, between the years 2005 and 2009, median net worth for white households fell 16 percent. In stark contrast, median net worth fell 53 percent for black and 66 percent for Latino households. Median wealth for white households is now twenty times that of black households and eighteen times that of Latino households. The vast majority of the losses in median net worth are related to housing (i.e., foreclosures or housing price depreciation).[12]

While blacks and Latinos have been treated abominably at times by both private and public actors in lending and housing markets, historical and current lending and housing discrimination does not fully explain why homeownership is particularly risky for blacks and Latinos, why clinging to the homeownership myth is especially dangerous for them, and why they have faced and will continue to face stumbling blocks on their road to homeownership. Blacks and Latinos have not received and will never receive the full economic benefits associated with homeownership due to certain demographic factors. Overall, blacks and Latinos are less educated and more poorly educated than whites, and this racial educational gap makes it more likely that they will have lower-skilled jobs, lower household income, lower overall savings rates, and higher unemployment rates and job instability relative to whites.

These stark demographic disparities may be the logical and natural consequences of years of racial discrimination against blacks and Latinos.

[12] Pew Research Ctr., *Wealth Gaps Rise to Record Highs between Whites, Blacks and Hispanics* (2011).

Or these disparities may be caused by lifestyle choices these groups have made and continue to make. Whatever the cause, though, these demographic realities combined with lingering vestiges of discrimination in housing markets increase home buying costs for blacks and Latinos and shut them out of the more desirable U.S. housing markets. Until something changes, the dream of homeownership will continue to elude most blacks and Latinos.

GOING FORWARD: RETHINKING HOMEOWNERSHIP

The severity and length of the recent housing market crash and the almost complete failure of all recent legislative initiatives to jump-start the U.S. economy failed to cause the country's elected leaders to seriously reassess the purported benefits of homeownership. To be sure, recent programs and initiatives that were created to try to stem soaring foreclosure rates and mortgage loan defaults did indeed help some borrowers renegotiate their mortgage loans and helped some homeowners lower the monthly payments on their loans. These programs have been of limited use to the vast majority of financially struggling homeowners, though, because U.S. politicians have completely avoided answering a crucial question: Is it sound public policy to make homeownership the centerpiece of U.S. housing policies given the economic realities many homeowners are facing? Similarly, no one seems willing to deliver the somber news that homeownership is not a low-risk, low-cost, high-return, surefire deal if you are black, Latino, or an LMI American. Rather than examining U.S. housing policies to find ways to make housing – and not just homeownership – more affordable, Congress, President Obama, and federal agencies continue to respond to the "foreclosure crisis" by launching programs, plans, and policies to keep cash-strapped Americans in homes they cannot afford and often could not afford when they bought them.

Because housing spending plays such a critical role in the growth of the U.S. economy, the U.S. government has an obvious incentive to create and subsidize programs and initiatives that make it easier for renters to buy houses and for existing homeowners to remain in their houses. Individual political leaders have another reason to encourage home sales, though: buying and selling houses is profitable for home builders (and the stores that sell them supplies), realtors, banks, and other members of the financial services industry. Given the political and financial influence of these powerful, moneyed constituent groups, elected leaders have a political incentive to create, encourage, and subsidize home purchases *even if* those programs might not be in the best interests of the people who are being encouraged to become and remain homeowners.

OVERVIEW

This book examines our country's love affair with homeownership and dissects the myths, narratives, flawed premises, and broken promises associated with owning a home in the United States, especially for America's financial underclass. Chapters 1 and 2 present the promises of homeownership and describes the financial and psychological myths most commonly associated with homeownership. I collectively call these myths and assumptions "the Happy Homeownership Narrative." Chapter 3 then documents how U.S. housing policies have helped shape housing markets and have helped lower the cost of buying a house. While overall homeownership rates have steadily increased since the Depression, housing policies in the United States have encouraged and condoned laws that privilege existing homeowners at the expense of renters and often black, Latino, and LMI home buyers.

Chapters 4–6 present the flawed premises behind homeownership and the actual realities many homeowners now face. Homeownership is an easy, low-cost, low-risk but high-return venture only if the renter can afford to become a homeowner before he starts the home buying process. Households with no savings, stagnant income, and unsteady employment do not fit the profile of the homeowner in the Happy Homeowner Narrative and can no longer realistically expect to benefit from the promises of homeownership.

Chapters 7 and 8 expose the risks of "home buying while brown or black." This part shows how the same governmental policies that made it easier for whites to buy homes easily and cheaply made it harder and more costly for blacks and Latinos to buy homes. As a result, the financial and psychological myths associated with homeownership have never really been true for blacks and Latinos. Racism alone does not explain why blacks and Latinos have lower ownership but higher foreclosure rates, why they own homes that fail to appreciate at rates similar to the homes white buyers' purchase, and why owning a home is more costly and risky for them than it is for white households. Without blaming the victim, Chapters 9 and 10 show that black and Latino households tend to have lower educational levels, lower overall household income, less inherited wealth, lower marriage rates, and higher unemployment rates than white households. These demographic factors virtually guarantee that they will pay more for homes in neighborhoods that will have lower rates of appreciation than homes located in predominately white neighborhoods. And buying homes in higher-poverty neighborhoods virtually guarantees that their children will go to higher-poverty/lower-quality schools.

The book ends by urging policymakers, housing advocate groups, and politicians alike to abandon their relentless and reckless campaigns to perpetuate the outdated myths associated with homeownership. The U.S. government should, of course, continue to play a role in housing markets. But Congress and federal regulatory agencies should reevaluate all current housing policies and discontinue ones that encourage Americans to make irrational borrowing decisions. Moreover, U.S. leaders should develop new housing policies and initiatives that ensure that Americans of all races and income groups have greater access to affordable housing, whether rented, owned by one person, or owned communally, and that acknowledge the ways that housing decisions affect the educational opportunities of homeowners' children.

2

The Happy Homeownership Narrative

Americans love the idea of Home Sweet Home. A statement, written more than thirty years ago by a trade association for savings and loans banks, continues to capture this nation's virtually unconstrained adoration of homeownership:

> A family's home is much more than shelter. A home signifies the family's accomplishments in life, eloquently expresses its personality, establishes its place in the community, and defines the perimeter of its private and personal stake in society. Indeed, the American dream traces its origins to the very beginning of this country, to the quest of those first colonists for the freedom to rule over their own domain, no matter how small, no matter how meager. This is a dream shared by those who have come to this country, and it is the rightful heritage of all Americans.[1]

Even after enduring the worst housing crisis since the Great Depression, homeownership still remains enormously popular among Americans of all ages, races, and incomes.

For decades, U.S. housing policies have reinforced this rhapsodic view of homeownership. Indeed, for almost eighty years, the U.S. government has provided significant subsidies for people who want to rule over their own domain. U.S. leaders staunchly defend these subsidies based on assumptions and beliefs that collectively form what I will call the "Happy Homeownership Narrative." In the Happy Homeownership Narrative, homeownership brings out the best in people. It makes them more involved as citizens, and it strengthens the moral and economic fiber of the country. Homeowners are viewed as being noble, hardworking, responsible, and financially stable and secure. In stark contrast, renters are viewed as weak and financially vulnerable. In the Narrative, homeownership creates stronger neighborhoods and improves

[1] James W. Christian et al., *Homeownership: The American Dream Adrift*, Econ. Dep't United League of Savings Association 11–12 (1982).

society overall. *Every* citizen should strive to become a homeowner. Renting, on the other hand, is a parasitic state that people should aspire to flee from as soon as they possibly can.[2]

Many of these assumptions are no longer true. Some were never totally accurate. Still, Americans obsessively aspire to claim their rightful place as homeowners. The prevalence and staying power of the Happy Homeownership Narrative continues to encourage renters to buy homes and gives U.S. policymakers a plausibly valid reason to provide enormously generous financial benefits to homeowners.

POWERFUL PROPERTY OWNERS VERSUS PITIFUL RENTERS

Even before the United States declared its independence from England, colonial leaders started to enact laws and create norms that marginalized renters and privileged homeowners. Thomas Jefferson relied heavily on the Virginia Declaration of Rights when he drafted the U.S. Declaration of Independence. The Virginia Declaration of Rights lists the "means of acquiring and possessing" property as an inherent right of every American. Although acquiring and possessing property was ultimately not listed as an inalienable right in the Declaration of Independence, owning property has long been associated with economic autonomy and prosperity, and property owners have always enjoyed elevated social and political status.

Since the pre-revolutionary era, citizens who own property have been viewed as stable and powerful. Property owners were accorded enhanced political and economic privileges largely based on the assumption that owning land gave them a greater economic stake in society. For example, until the middle of the nineteenth century, only property owners (the white, male ones) were allowed to vote and hold political office. Consequently, landowners (but not renters) were able to influence the laws that would determine how their communities would form and how the properties in those communities would be used.[3]

Renters, in stark contrast, have always been viewed as unstable, economically dependent, or presumptively subservient to their landlords. Because renters lacked property "stakes" in their communities, they were presumed

[2] *Resolution Recognizing National Homeownership Month and the Importance of Homeownership in the United States*, H. Res. 477, 110th Cong., 1st Sess. (Jun. 11, 2007); Office of Management and Budget, Press Release announcing Obama administration support for *American Homeownership and Economic Opportunity Act of 2000*, H.R. 1776, 106th Cong. (1999–2000), *available at* http://www.whitehouse.gov/omb/legislative_sap_106-2_hr1776-h.

[3] Jayne Allen, Jefferson's Declaration of Independence (1998); Pauline Maier, American Scripture: Making the Declaration of Independence (1997).

too transient to really care about how their communities developed. Given this presumption, renters and non-property owners were not allowed to vote or hold elected offices, and even when they were allowed to vote, they were not allowed to vote in private for most of the nineteenth century. Because of this pro-landowner bias, renters were largely deprived of the ability to influence the laws that would be used to govern them and the future of their communities.[4]

In addition to allocating voting rights to landowners but not renters, U.S. housing laws and policies have had implicit and explicit biases in favor of owner-occupied housing. For example, a 1926 U.S. Supreme Court decision considered whether municipalities could enforce zoning laws that excluded apartment buildings from residential districts that had been designed for detached housing. Apartments were viewed unfavorably and held in disdain in part because of the Court's view that they monopolized "the rays of the sun which otherwise would fall upon the smaller homes."[5] The Court characterized renter-occupied housing as a nuisance and viewed both multiunit housing and its dwellers as parasites that brought disturbing noises and increased traffic to neighborhoods. The Court ultimately concluded that cities had the right to segregate single-family homes from multiunit housing (and thus, renters) to ensure that homeowners would not be forced to live in close proximity to renters, who would deprive homeowners of the "free circulation of air" and deprive their children "of quiet and open spaces for play."[6]

Renters are no longer viewed as parasitic nuisances who are weak and unconcerned about their communities. Similarly, renters are now allowed to vote, although they may be prevented from voting in specialty districts, such as water districts.[7] Nonetheless, homeowners' associations, which are private quasi-governments, have the authority to prevent owners from turning their owner-occupied homes into rental property. Moreover, U.S. laws and policies continue to view homeowners as more responsible than renters, and prevailing social norms view living in a home you own as preferable to living in a house you rent. In the minds and hearts of most Americans, only owned houses are generally thought of as *homes*. The view that a house is not necessarily a home

[4] William A. Fischel, *The Evolution of Homeownership, reviewing* The Unbounded Home: Property Values beyond Property Lines, 77 Chic. L. Rev. 1503 (2010).

[5] Euclid v. Ambler Realty, 272 U.S. 365 (1926).

[6] *Id.*

[7] For example, the U.S. Supreme Court, in Salyer Land Co. v. Tulare Lake Basin Water Storage Dist., 410 U.S. 719, 730–35 (1973), validated a state statute that allowed only landowners to vote in a water storage district election.

is perfectly captured in a statement made by a former Secretary of Housing and Urban Development, who stated that homeownership

> takes a family out of the second-class citizenship that poverty so often inflicts upon people ... gives them a chance to be in control of their own financial lives, and as such, to really rise in the way that America has for so many others provided that kind of opportunity.[8]

Of course, the housing crisis that preceded and precipitated the 2007–2009 Great Recession vividly demonstrates that homeowners are not always in control of their financial lives. Nevertheless, as discussed in greater detail in later chapters, homeownership has been the focal point of U.S. housing policies since the 1930s.

THRIFT AND FISCAL RESPONSIBILITY

The Happy Homeownership Narrative assumes that once renters buy a house and elevate themselves from their second-class renting status, homeownership will magically convert them from being unstable and economically vulnerable renters into thrifty and financially responsible homeowners. Having a nation of thrifty, financially responsible savers has been deemed good for the country. Political leaders have justified giving federal subsidies and tax benefits to homeowners because they believe that homeownership has transformative qualities. It is possible, of course, that the mere thought of obtaining the elevated status of homeownership converted profligate, irresponsible renters into financially thrifty and responsible homeowners. It is more likely, however, that the lending and loan underwriting standards that financial institutions historically applied when they evaluated mortgage loan applications *forced* potential and existing homeowners to alter their saving and spending habits.

Whether by choice or by force, for years renters could not become and then remain homeowners unless they were thrifty savers. That is, until lenders relaxed underwriting criteria during the 1990s housing boom to increase home sales, renters could not become homeowners unless they saved money to make down payments, convinced loan officers that they were financially stable, and put aside enough money each month to make ongoing mortgage payments for an extended period of time. In effect, to preserve their first-class homeownership status, owners/borrowers were forced to exercise long-term

[8] *Hearing before the Committee on Banking, Housing, and Urban Affairs of the U.S. Senate, on Increasing Minority Homeownership, and Expanding Homeownership to All Who Wish to Attain It*, 108th Cong. 1st Sess., at 15 (Jun. 12, 2003) (statement of Mel Martinez, U.S. Department of Housing and Urban Development Secretary).

fiscal restraint. Homeowners who honored the pledge to become and remain thrifty and responsible savers would, according to the Happy Homeownership Narrative, receive the reward of long-term housing security once they paid off their mortgage loan. Additionally, if for some reason a homeowner wanted (or needed) to sell a home or move to a different home before paying off the mortgage, the Happy Homeownership Narrative posited that the sales price would provide the homeowner with enough money to pay off the existing mortgage, return all savings (the equity accumulated in the home as the mortgage debt was paid down), and provide a tidy profit (the appreciated value of the home minus the outstanding mortgage balance).

The belief that renters would be forced to be and remain thrifty if they wanted to buy a home was largely accurate for decades. Until the Clinton administration encouraged lenders to relax their underwriting criteria to make it easier for people to buy homes, borrowers generally would not qualify for a low-cost mortgage loan unless they had saved enough money to make at least a 20 percent down payment. As discussed in greater detail in Chapter 3, since the Depression, the most common mortgage loan product has been fixed-interest rate, self-amortizing loans guaranteed by the U.S. government. These loans were popular with homeowners for many reasons.

The fixed rates of interest made monthly payments predictable, which made it easier for homeowners to budget. Additionally, the U.S. government's financial guarantees made the loans low-risk for lenders and, subsequently, low-cost for borrowers. Renters who lacked savings would not be approved for these über-desirable loans unless they were willing to buy private mortgage insurance (PMI), which was often quite expensive and largely did not exist until the 1960s. Historically, therefore, the terms and requirements associated with mortgage lending gave renters incentives to become and remain thrifty savers.[9]

The aspect of the Happy Homeownership Narrative that suggests that being a homeowner magically transforms renters into financially responsible individuals probably developed from mortgage loan underwriting practices and policies that applied from the 1930s until the 1980s. Key among those policies was an almost refusal to approve a low-cost mortgage loan for renters who lacked savings. While lenders significantly relaxed underwriting standards during the late 1990s–early 2000s housing boom, until then they imposed rigorous borrowing requirements on renters who wanted to buy homes using traditional mortgage loans. These requirements helped to prevent homeowners from reverting to their spendthrift renter habits after they had saved enough

[9] Richard K. Green & Susan M. Wachter, *The American Mortgage in Historical and International Context*, 19–4 J. Econ. Persp. (Fall 2005).

money to make a down payment and had survived the loan approval process. As explored in greater detail in the next chapter, traditional, government-backed, fixed rate mortgage (FRM) loans were long-term (typically fifteen or thirty years). Because of these longer terms, even after they saved money to make a down payment, borrowers were forced to save enough money each month to ensure that they could make equal monthly payments of principal and interest for fifteen–thirty years. If borrowers exercised financial self-restraint and made their payments, they would repay their loans in full and, after making their last payment, own their home.[10]

While the view that homeowners had to be (and remain) more financially responsible than renters was largely true for most of the twentieth century, by the early 2000s, the Happy Homeownership Narrative could no longer accurately claim that homeownership automatically transforms profligate renters into thrifty, responsible savers. During the housing boom in the early 2000s, lenders stopped carefully scrutinizing borrowers' income, assets, and debts to make it easier for people to qualify for mortgage loans and buy houses. These relaxed lending standards allowed renters who had no savings to be approved for loans even though they made a small (or no) down payment, and borrowers were allowed to buy homes even though they could not afford the monthly mortgage payments.

Many of the loans people used to buy homes during the housing boom had variable interest rates, allowed the borrower to essentially choose the monthly payment amount, and required the borrower to make only interest (not principal) payments each month during the initial months of the loan. Additionally, because housing prices were soaring, homeowners were encouraged to refinance their mortgage loans frequently and roll the costs into a new thirty-year loan, even though doing so increased the balance of the loan and extended the homeowners' loan obligation into the future. Although lenders tightened credit during the subsequent recession, homeownership could no longer be viewed as a forced savings device.

[10] Allen J. Fishbein & Patrick Woodall, *Exotic or Toxic? An Examination of the Non-Traditional Mortgage Market for Consumers and Lenders*, Consumer Fed'n of Am. 28 (2006), *available at* http://www.consumerfed.org/elements/www.consumerfed.org/file/housing/Exotic_Toxic_Mortgage_Report0506.pdf; William E. Nelson & Norman R. Williams, *Suburbanization and Market Failure: An Analysis of Government Policies Promoting Suburban Growth and Ethnic Assimilation*, 27 Fordham Urb. L.J. 197, 226–31 (1999); Eric Belsky & Joel Prakken, *Housing Wealth Effects: Housing's Impact on Wealth Accumulation, Wealth Distribution and Consumer Spending* (Joint Center for Housing Studies of Harvard University, Working Paper No. W04–13, 2004), *available at* http://www.jchs.harvard.edu/sites/jchs.harvard.edu/files/w04-13.pdf.

STABILITY AND SECURITY

In the Happy Homeownership Narrative, buying a home makes homeowners financially independent and secure and gives them stable housing for the rest of their lives. Owning rather than renting gives homeowners the comfort of knowing that they can remain in their homes as long as they want and never worry that someone else (like a landlord) will make them move. Of course, they must remain thrifty savers who honor the pledge to repay their mortgage loans and pay for the other expenses associated with owning a home. Assuming they honor that pledge, though, homeowners can generally expect to have relatively stable and predictable monthly housing expenses and can remain in their homes for the rest of their lives.

With the possible exception of renters who live in properties that are protected by rent-control laws, renters generally have little long-term housing security or stability. While renters are no longer disenfranchised or politically or socially controlled by their landlord, their housing tenure nonetheless remains linked to their landlord. Even renters who have rented a house or apartment for a long time, have made rent payments on time, and have timely and fully complied with all lease terms still cannot predict whether they will be allowed to remain in the same housing unit on a long-term basis. U.S. real property laws have never allowed renters to prevent a landlord (the property owner) from exercising the right to decide how to use the property, including the right to decide whether to allow renters to remain in the house or apartment once the lease expires.

Although somewhat curtailed by prevailing market rates, the property owner/landlord also has the right to determine the amount of renters' future housing mortgage costs. As a result, renters cannot reliably forecast their long-term monthly housing expenses, because the landlord can unilaterally decide to increase their rent at the end of the lease term. Even worse, whether renters have housing security often depends on whether their landlord is financially responsible. As many renters painfully discovered in the recent housing crisis, they can be forced to move if their landlord fails to pay taxes or if the landlord defaults on the mortgage debt on the rental property. If their landlord/property owner loses the property in a foreclosure proceeding, renters can be evicted even if they have been responsible and have always paid the rent on time.

While renters cannot predict whether their landlord will increase their monthly rent, monthly payments on a traditional, fixed-interest rate, government-backed mortgage loan do not change. Thus, if a homeowner purchases a home using a traditional, fifteen- to thirty-year FRM loan, he or she can easily expect that the monthly mortgage payments will remain the same each month for the entire fifteen- to thirty-year repayment period. Because the loans are self-amortizing, homeowners also can predict how long it will take to pay off the loans and have debt-free housing.

Of course, homeowners can choose to increase their mortgage debt by taking out home equity loans or second mortgages (as many did during the housing boom). They can also increase the debt and extend the length of the initial loan repayment term if they choose to refinance the mortgage loan to take advantage of lower interest payments (as many also did during the housing boom). Assuming, however, that a borrower does not extend the initial mortgage loan term or increase the monthly mortgage payments, the Happy Homeownership Narrative correctly portrays homeownership as a way for homeowners (but not renters) to budget for their fixed housing expenses (i.e., the mortgage payment) and ensure that they set aside enough money to pay other reasonably predictable housing expenses (e.g., property taxes and routine maintenance costs).

Homeownership is also touted as a way to have lifetime housing security. That is, once young homeowners repay their mortgage loan, they can generally have the security of assuming that – absent an unexpected disaster – they can remain in their home for the rest of their lives. As discussed in greater detail in later chapters, U.S. household income for all but upper-income earners has stagnated over the last thirty years, household savings rates have declined, and employer-provided pensions have dwindled or disappeared. Given these economic changes, the potential to have rent-free, long-term shelter as their income shifts from wages to a pension has become even more important to older Americans. Even though millions of homeowners lost their homes and many older Americans remain at risk for losing their homes because they cannot afford to pay property taxes or pay for routine maintenance, the idea of having fixed monthly housing expenses for fifteen to thirty years and then only ongoing maintenance expenses for the rest of their lives remains a significant selling point for homeownership.

FINANCIAL FLEXIBILITY

The Happy Homeownership Narrative touts the financial flexibility that having equity in a house gives homeowners. Even renters who have lived in the same house or apartment for years do not accumulate equity or otherwise develop a permanent financial stake in the rented property unless the property owner agrees to apply some portion of the rental payments as a down payment on the home. In contrast, owners accumulate equity when they pay down their mortgage debt and their homes appreciate in value. Homeowners with equity in a house (or who own a home outright) can sell it and buy other things – including another home. Additionally, with built-up equity, homeowners can reduce their monthly loan payments by refinancing their current mortgage loan if interest rates are falling. When homeowners refinance a loan for an amount that is lower than the value of the home (but greater than the existing mortgage), they can get cash that they can then use to retire other debts, purchase goods or services, or invest. Having equity in a house also lets a homeowner who wants to start a new business (and needs capital) or a homeowner who needs to pay for college pledge the house as collateral for a bank loan to start the business or pay for college.

The ability to borrow against a home gives owners an asset that they can use if they unexpectedly find the need to supplement or augment their monthly income. That is, a financially stressed owner who loses a job, encounters unexpected expenses, or is otherwise hit with an economic setback can take out a home equity loan and use the proceeds from the loan to pay for monthly living expenses until other financial opportunities arise. Likewise, a homeowner who needs to quickly and permanently downsize can sell the home, use some of the proceeds to retire any existing mortgage debt, and then use the rest to pay ongoing bills (including, potentially, a new mortgage on a smaller home). A homeowner who loses a job can also lower monthly housing expenses by refinancing the mortgage and lowering the monthly mortgage payments, while a renter who loses a job cannot "refinance" rental payments or otherwise lower monthly rental payments without the landlord's permission. Finally, older homeowners can take out what is known as a "reverse mortgage," which lets them remove equity from their home to supplement their retirement incomes.

THE BEST INVESTMENT YOU CAN MAKE

In the Happy Homeownership Narrative, homes are safe and secure investments that always appreciate in value. Even though owners generally place greater faith than renters do in the strength of the housing markets, most Americans believe that buying a house is the best investment a household can make. Likely because of the perception that home prices only go up and also because of the favorable tax benefits associated with buying a home, housing equity consistently constitutes the bulk of U.S. household wealth. This has been especially true for lower-income households. For example, while the value of the family home consistently accounts for almost 30 percent of assets for U.S. households overall, home equity generally represents more than 50 percent of total wealth for lower- and middle-income households. Most Americans, except for the highest earners, choose housing as their primary investment device and prefer housing investments to investing in stocks, bonds, bank deposits, or even their own retirements.[11]

For homeowners who bought homes located in favorable housing markets using low-cost mortgages, homeownership historically has been a fairly safe and relatively low-cost way for them to increase their household wealth. As discussed in more detail in Chapter 4, home prices in the 1950s and 1960s increased at rates that lagged inflation rates and also lagged increases in median family income. Thus, during this period, household income generally increased more than housing prices rose. This economic climate made housing prices reasonable and made homeownership a particularly sound investment for renters who were able to buy homes using low-cost, government-insured, fifteen- to thirty-year mortgages.

By the 1970s, it became somewhat less affordable to buy homes because housing prices were increasing while household income had started to stagnate. Housing prices appreciated in the 1970s largely because of the increased demand for single-family, detached houses. Demand for this type of housing soared during this decade when renters who were born between the years of 1946 and 1964 (i.e., the post–World War II baby boomers) began forming their own households. This increased interest in single-family housing drove up land prices and ultimately caused housing prices to increase by approximately 10 percent in the 1970s and 5 percent in the 1980s. While these increases made it harder for renters to become homeowners, higher home values made homeownership a great investment for existing owners.[12]

A change in U.S. tax laws in 1976 made homeownership significantly more financially advantageous to certain taxpayers. Specifically, before 1976, U.S. taxpayers could deduct interest on most consumer loans. Since 1976, however, taxpayers have been allowed to deduct interest on mortgage debt but not on other consumer debt. This gives renters a tax incentive to buy homes and, as discussed in more detail in Chapter 5, gives homeowners an incentive to take out second mortgages against their homes and use the mortgage loan proceeds to pay down credit card debts, because they cannot deduct interest on non-mortgage consumer debt.

Strong housing markets since the 1940s and favorable tax benefits for mortgage debt helped perpetuate the belief that housing is a safe and secure

[11] Joint Ctr. for Hous. Studies, Harvard Univ., *The State of the Nation's Housing* (1997), *available at* http://www.jchs.harvard.edu/sites/jchs.harvard.edu/files/son_97.pdf; Jesse Bricker et al., *Changes in U.S. Family Finances from 2007 to 2010: Evidence from the Survey of Consumer Finances*, Federal Reserve Bulletin (2012).

[12] Edwin S. Mills & Ronald Simenauer, Homeownership as an Investment: Recent Trends and the Outlook for the 1990s (1991).

long-term investment. By the mid-1990s, home prices started soaring and, in some regions, home prices increased by as much as 10 percent each year from 1996 to 2001. Housing prices increased by more than 130 percent from roughly 1996 to 2006, and this soaring home price appreciation ultimately led to the early 2000s housing bubble and the 2007–2009 Great Recession. Before the bubble popped, though, homeownership was the best investment option for most U.S. households.[13] Moreover, even with skyrocketing foreclosure rates, plummeting housing prices, and a sluggish market for residential home sales, recent polls show that most Americans continue to believe that buying a home is the best and safest long-term investment they can make and the best way to achieve their long-term financial goals.[14]

Although the belief that all homes appreciate in value and homeownership is low-risk is no longer true for many Americans, owning a home may remain the best overall long-term investment for some Americans. However, as later chapters in the book will show in greater detail, homeownership is not the best short- or long-term investment strategy for owners who cannot obtain low-cost financing, who have unsteady income, who reap no homeownership tax benefits, who are not likely to remain in a home long-term, or whose homes are located in neighborhoods that have low appreciation rates.

BLISSFUL HOMEOWNERS

U.S. housing policies have long preferred homeowning to home renting in part because homeowners in the Narrative are viewed as being happy, although, it is obviously not possible to quantify "feeling good." Still, homeowners regularly report that they enjoy owning their homes, and even though the social and political plight of renters has improved greatly over the last 300 years, with the exception of those struggling to pay their mortgages, homeowners are more likely than renters to feel that they are in control of the daily events in their lives. Additionally, renters and homeowners believe that owning a home provides intangible emotional and psychological benefits that renting does not.

[13] Karl E. Case, et al., *Wealth Effects Revisited: 1978–2009* (Nat. Bur. Econ. Research, Working Paper No. 16848, Mar. 2011); Karl E. Case, *Land Prices and House Prices in the United States*, in Housing Markets in United States and Japan 30, 31 (1994); S&P/Case-Shiller, *National Composite Index of Home Prices, First Quarter 1996 to First Quarter 2006, available at* http://us.spindices.com/indices/real-estate/sp-case-shiller-us-national-home-price-index.

[14] Pew Research Ctr Poll (Apr. 2011) (citing earlier polls); Harris Interactive Poll, conducted for the Nat'l. Ass'n. Realtors, *American Attitudes about Homeownership* (Oct. 6–20, 2010 & Jan. 19, 2011); Meredith Corporation Survey, *Homeowner Attitudes and Behaviors* (Oct. 31, 2011), *available at* http://meredith.mediaroom.com/index.php?s=2311&item=77869.

Surveys have shown that both renters and homeowners are likely to label homeowners as more financially secure, stable members of their communities than renters.[15] Homeowners also report feeling healthier and in better physical shape than renters, and they believe that they have less psychological distress than renters. Homeownership appears to make people feel that they have succeeded in life. Buying a home is said to boost the homeowner's self-confidence and self-esteem partially because the owner thinks that buying a home is a signal that the owner has achieved greater success in life than someone who cannot afford to buy a home.

Given that Americans often define themselves by what they have, owning a home makes people happy simply because their homes are tangible – and can be quite large. The mere fact that the home is *their home* gives owners a sense of pride that they likely would not have even if they were to rent the same house from someone else. In effect, homeownership serves as a visible reflection of the owner's worth, and this reflection may be one reason why owning a home makes people happy.[16]

Homeownership also makes owners feel emotionally secure. That is, homeowners relish the thought that they have a place they can live in and change in whatever way suits their interest: that place called home. Because renters do not own the homes that they occupy, many of the personal choices that they might want to make – such as owning a pet, painting their bedroom hot pink, or letting friends or distant relatives live with them – may be constrained by the terms of their leases with the landlords. Although local zoning regulations or homeowners' associations' rules might prevent homeowners from painting the exterior of their homes pink and green or having a chicken coop in their backyards, homeowners' personal choices about their homes generally are not limited by third parties, and neither public nor private land use regulations dictate what they can do to the interior of their homes.

Perhaps because of the lingering stigma associated with being a renter, homeowner surveys and social sciences literature regularly find that homeowners of all ages, races, and genders from all geographic regions are happier

[15] The George H. W. Bush White House enacted Homeownership and Opportunity for People Everywhere (HOPE) and noted that "homeownership instills pride, improves neighborhoods, enhances independence, and encourages stable and intact families." George Bush & Jack Kemp, *Homeownership and Opportunity for People Everywhere*, U.S. Dep't of Hous. and Urban Dev. 4 (1990).

[16] Pew Research Ctr Poll, *supra* note 14; Harris Interactive Poll, *supra* note 14; Meredith Corporation Survey, *supra* note 14; Eighth Quarterly Allstate-National Journal Heartland Monitor Poll (2011); Marianne B. Culhane, *No Forwarding Address: Losing Homes in Bankruptcy*, in HOW DEBT BANKRUPTS THE MIDDLE CLASS 133 (Katherine Porter ed., Stanford University Press) (2012).

and more satisfied with (the physical space and condition of) their homes and their neighborhoods than renters are. They are also more likely to report that they like their homes and derive comfort from the fact that they live in those homes. Homeowners also report that they perceive their communities as safer and more stable than renter communities. These homeowner perceptions are bolstered by empirical studies that find neighborhoods with owner-occupied homes have higher-quality K–12 schools, lower dropout rates, lower crime rates, and better and more stable social conditions than neighborhoods with renters.[17]

Even though homeowners report being happier and more satisfied than renters, it is unclear whether homeownership itself causes the happiness or whether homeowners are happy because of the demographic differences between people who own and people who rent homes. As a group, homeowners tend to be employed, have more money, and be married. These characteristics generally are positively correlated with greater happiness. Moreover, although homeownership consistently evokes powerful positive emotions, the level of homeowners' satisfaction with their homes or neighborhoods does appear to decrease if the neighborhood is changing. Examples of changes that cause homeowners to be unhappy include increasing crime rates, a transition in the racial composition of their neighbors, or a rise in the undesirable commercial or residential use of properties within the neighborhood. Still, regardless of *why* homeownership makes owners happy, it is fair to say that the Happy Homeownership Narrative accurately portrays people who own homes as generally happier than people who rent homes.[18]

BLISSFUL FAMILIES

In the Happy Homeownership Narrative, homeownership is good because it provides "[d]ecent, affordable, and stable housing [that] promotes family

[17] Meredith Corporation Survey, *supra* note 14; Pew Research Ctr Social & Demographic Trends Survey (Oct. 3–19, 2008), *available at* http://www.pewsocialtrends.org/2009/02/19/even-as-housing-values-sink-theres-comfort-in-homeownership; Fannie Mae Foundation, African American and Hispanic Attitudes on Homeownership: A Guide for Mortgage Industry Leaders 15 (1998); U.S. Dep't. of Hous. and Urban Dev., *American Housing Survey for the United States: 2009* (Mar. 2011).

[18] Harris Interactive Poll, *supra* note 14; Pew Research Ctr Social & Demographic Trends Survey, *supra* note 17; Peter H. Rossi & Eleanor Weber, *The Social Benefits of Homeownership*, 7–1 Housing Pol'y Debate (1996); William M. Rohe et al., *The Social Benefits and Costs of Homeownership: A Critical Assessment of the Research* 4 (Joint Center for Housing Studies of Harvard University, Working Paper No. LIHO-01.12, 2001); Robert D. Dietz, *The Social Consequences of Homeownership* (2003).

stability and creates a positive environment for raising children."[19] U.S. parents strive to become and remain homeowners because they believe that neighborhoods with owner-occupied homes are better, safer, and more stable than neighborhoods with primarily renter-occupied housing. Neighborhoods with mostly owner-occupied, single-family detached homes are viewed as preferable to renter neighborhoods in part because those neighborhoods tend to have more open space, more privacy, and better educational and social opportunities than neighborhoods with multiunit housing.[20]

Research corroborates the view that homeownership creates happier, smarter, and more secure children who have social, psychological, and emotional advantages over renters' children. That is, some studies show that the children of homeowners score higher on academic achievement tests, have fewer behavioral problems in school, are less likely to become high school dropouts, and are more likely to graduate from high school than the children of renters. Data also indicate that the children of homeowners are more emotionally stable and are much less likely to be arrested or become teenage parents than renters' children. Homeowners' children are also more likely to buy homes as adults and to have more household wealth (in part because they own homes).[21]

In general, housing stability helps children perform better in school. Studies have shown that children who are forced to move or otherwise change their living environments typically switch to lower-performing schools and that displaced children perform worse academically and are involved in fewer extracurricular activities than children who are not involuntarily displaced from their living environments. Moreover, research indicates that even children who are displaced but are *not* forced to change schools appear to perform worse academically in school and to have more behavioral problems. This research certainly is consistent with the Happy Homeownership Narrative

[19] Bipartisan Millennial Hous. Comm'n, *Meeting our Nation's Housing Challenges* (2002), *available at* http://govinfo.library.unt.edu/mhc/MHCReport.pdf.

[20] Fannie Mae Foundation, African American and Hispanic Attitudes on Homeownership: A Guide for Mortgage Industry Leaders 13 (1998); Rolf Pendall et al., *Demographic Challenges and Opportunities for U.S. Housing Markets*, Bipartisan Policy Ctr. (Mar. 2012).

[21] William M. Rohe & Leslie S. Stewart, *Homeownership and Neighborhood Stability*, 7–1 Housing Pol'y Debate (1996); Donald R. Haurin et al., *The Impact of Homeownership on Child Outcomes* 10 (Joint Center for Housing Studies of Harvard University, Working Paper No. LIHO-01.14, 2001), *available at* http://www.jchs.harvard.edu/sites/jchs.harvard.edu/files/liho01–14.pdf; Rossi & Weber, *supra* note 18; Dietz, *supra* note 18; Thomas P. Boehm & Alan M. Schlottmann, *Does Home Ownership by Parents Have an Economic Impact on Their Children?*, 8 J. Hous. Econ. 217 (1999); Thomas P. Boehm & Alan M. Schlottmann, *Housing and Wealth Accumulation: Intergenerational Impacts*, in Low-Income Homeownership: Examining the Unexamined Goal 407 (N. P. Retsinas and E. S. Belsky eds., 2002).

that living in a home long-term is beneficial to children whose parents own homes.[22]

Just as it is unclear whether it is homeownership itself (and not the demographic characteristics of owners) that makes homeowners happy, it is also unclear whether the children of homeowners fare better than renters' children because of their parents' demographic characteristics. That is, studies indicate that homeowners' children perform better in school and have fewer disciplinary problems than renters' children, but it is possible that this is because of the homeowners' parenting skills or the level of their involvement in their children's educational development. Homeowners' children might also perform better in school than renters' children because homeowners' overall higher incomes, wealth, and employment stability allow them to provide more cognitively stimulating and emotionally supportive home environments than renters can.

While the studies that purport to show that homeownership is beneficial for children are inconclusive and have been criticized for having statistical flaws, data consistently show that renters (especially married renters) with school-age children are statistically more likely to buy homes than childless renters and that homeowners are more likely to remain in their homes if they have school-age children. Again, whether accurate or not, the Happy Homeownership Narrative seems to have convinced renters that they must remove themselves *and their children* from that second-class status to ensure that their children are not deprived of the valuable educational and societal benefits that purportedly flow to children who live in homes that their parents own.[23]

Finally, in addition to the benefits that homeownership gives children while they live with their parents, homeownership also gives children benefits well after they move away from their parents' home. Homeowners, unlike renters,

[22] Hazel L. Morrow-Jones, *Black-White Differences in the Demographic Structure of the Move to Homeownership in the United States*, in OWNERSHIP, CONTROL, AND THE FUTURE OF HOUSING POL'Y 52–56 (R. Allen Hays ed., 1993); Donald Krueckeberg, *The Grapes of Rent: A History of Renting in a Country of Owners* 10–1 HOUSING POLICY DEBATE 9–30 (1999); Vicki Been et al., *Does Losing Your Home Mean Losing Your School?: Effects of Foreclosures on the School Mobility of Children*, 41 REGIONAL SCIENCE AND URBAN ECONOMICS 407 (2011); Eric Rodriguez, *Assessing the Damage of Predatory Lending by Countrywide: The Fallout for Latino Families: Hearing on Examining Lending Discrimination Practices and Foreclosure Abuses of the Senate Committee on the Judiciary* (Mar. 7, 2012); Jennifer Comey & Michel Grosz, *Smallest Victims of the Foreclosure Crisis: Children in the District of Columbia*, Urban Inst. (2010); JANIS BOWDLER ET AL., THE FORECLOSURE GENERATION: THE LONG-TERM IMPACT OF THE HOUSING CRISIS ON LATINO CHILDREN AND FAMILIES (2010).

[23] Dietz, *supra* note 18; Anna Maria Santiago et al., *The Experiences of Low-Income Homebuyers*, in FAIR AND AFFORDABLE HOUSING IN THE U.S.: TRENDS, OUTCOMES, FUTURE DIRECTIONS (Robert Mark Silverman & Kelly L. Patterson eds., 2011).

have the comfort and pride in knowing that they can leave their homes – and their memories – to their children after they die. Although the ability to bequeath wealth does not give owners financial benefits during their lifetime, the Happy Homeownership Narrative reminds homeowners that owning a home lets owners make their families happy – even if they are no longer around to witness that happiness.[24]

THE POWER AND BENEFITS OF BEING STAKED IN (AND TO) A HOUSE

In the Happy Homeownership Narrative, homeownership creates stable, involved citizens who care for their homes and their neighborhoods. Except for speculators who buy rundown homes with the goal of repairing them quickly and then selling them for a profit (i.e., flipping), the decision to buy a home generally signals that a homeowner has made a commitment to a house, a neighborhood, and a community. Owners are naturally more vested in and have a greater stake in their homes and neighborhoods for several reasons.

First, people typically take pride in the things they own and generally take better care of their own property than property others own. Homeowners have a particular reason to keep their homes in good condition and to make improvements to their homes. For better or worse, most people care about what other people think of them, and a home's appearance is a status symbol: *no one* wants to own the worst looking home on the street. So, in addition to their desire to enjoy the present benefits of living in a well-kept home and their desire to increase the market value of their homes, pride (or vanity) also causes homeowners to repair, improve, and perform routine maintenance on their homes.[25]

In addition to pride in ownership, homeowners typically have a deeper commitment to their homes than renters do because it is harder for homeowners to move quickly and cheaply. The time and costs associated with selling a house, moving to another area, and buying a new house makes homeowners less mobile. Data consistently confirm that homeowners are less likely to be planning to move than renters and that neighborhoods that consist primarily of owner-occupied homes generally are more stable and have fewer turnovers. The one exception, as discussed in more detail later in Chapter 7, is that white

[24] Fannie Mae National Housing Survey, *Understanding America's Homeownership Gaps* (2003).

[25] LeeAnn Lands, The Culture of Property: Race, Class, and Housing Landscapes in Atlanta, 1880–1950 (2009); Rohe & Stewart, *supra* note 21; Dietz, *supra* note 18. Data indicate, though, that homeowners will decrease the amount of their housing maintenance expenditures if they think that the racial composition of their neighborhoods is changing.

homeowners are likely to move out of their neighborhood if they perceive that the racial composition of the homeowners in their neighborhood is becoming predominantly more brown or black. Still, regardless of whether they are motived by a commitment to their community or by high transaction costs, homeowners are less mobile than renters, and this immobility gives them a greater incentive to invest in their homes and communities and to participate in activities that protect the value of their homes and neighborhoods.[26]

In addition to pride in ownership and higher transaction costs, owners have an incentive to maintain their homes in order to protect their long-term financial investments. Homes that are well-maintained and located in desirable neighborhoods will be worth more than under-maintained homes or homes in dangerous neighborhoods. Because owners will want to sell their homes for a profit whenever they decide (or need) to move, they have an economic incentive to keep their homes in good condition to ensure that they can at least recoup the financial investments they made in their houses.

Studies confirm that homeowners are more likely than renters to maintain their homes, maintain gardens, do (or pay for) lawn work, and make routine and major repairs to their homes. Owners are especially likely to perform home repairs to remediate conditions that pose health risks and they also are likely to make repairs that, if left unabated, would harm the market value of their houses. Because owner-occupied homes provide both present (use) and future (investment) benefits, homeowners often make improvements to their homes that might not increase the house's value in the real estate market. For example, homeowners install swimming pools and make extravagant kitchen or bathroom upgrades, even though real estate surveys consistently show that owners rarely recoup the value of those improvements when they sell their homes. Because they know they can enjoy the improvements while they live in the house, homeowners are willing to pay for these improvements even if the improvements do not increase their home's market value.[27]

In addition to keeping their homes in good (and marketable) condition, in the Happy Homeownership Narrative, homeowners are said to participate in activities that help preserve and improve the overall stability, safety, and desirability of their neighborhoods. Because they expect to be in their communities

[26] David K. Ihrke & Carol S. Faber, *Geographical Mobility: 2005 to 2010: Population Characteristics*, U.S. Census (Dec. 2012).

[27] William A. Fischel, The Homevoter Hypothesis: How Home Values Influence Local Government Taxation, School Finance, and Land-use Policies (2001); Rohe & Stewart, *supra* note 21; Dietz, *supra* note 18; Denise DiPasquale & Edward L. Glaeser, *Incentives and Social Capital: Are Homeowners Better Citizens?* 11 (Nat. Bur. Econ. Research, Working Paper No. 6363, 1998).

for a longer time than most renters are, homeowners have an incentive to participate in activities that enhance their ability to enjoy their home's features and their neighborhood's amenities. Studies show that homeowners in all income groups and from all educational levels appear to have higher levels of community involvement in activities that protect the value of their homes and neighborhoods than renters with similar socioeconomic characteristics.

For example, because the quality of public schools, community centers, and other high-quality neighborhood services are capitalized into the prices of homes in those neighborhoods, existing homeowners have a financial incentive to be active and involved citizens who preserve their present quality of life and ensure the ongoing desirability of their neighborhoods. Homeowners protect their neighborhoods by lobbying local governments for long-term, high-quality community services, such as new or improved roads, neighborhood schools, or community amenities (like swimming pools or parks). In addition, homeowners are also said to protect the value of their homes and the quality of life in their neighborhoods by remaining vigilant, being observant, and reporting criminal or suspicious activities.[28]

One way that homeowners protect their housing value and their neighborhoods is through private, quasi-government entities known as homeowners' associations (HOAs). HOAs wield power over how owners can use their properties and what types of properties can be sited in a particular neighborhood. As discussed in greater detail in Chapter 3, owners whose homes are governed by an HOA have the right to participate in that HOA. When HOAs (or individual owners) perceive that an actual or proposed activity *might* threaten the security of their neighborhoods or the value of their homes, HOAs often galvanize their members to help rid their neighborhoods of those unwelcome activities. HOAs also encourage their members to participate in local politics and to vote for particular institutions or politicians that they perceive will protect the safety and security of their neighborhoods and communities. Given that political leaders are more responsive to informed citizens who are politically active, HOAs are often quite effective.

[28] Shannon Van Zandt & William M. Rohe, *The Sustainability of Low-Income Homeownership: The Incidence of Unexpected Costs and Needed Repairs Among Low-Income Home Buyers*, 21–2 HOUSING POL'Y DEBATE 317 (2011); *Subprime and Predatory Lending: New Regulatory Guidance, Current Market Conditions, and Effects on Regulated Institutions: Hearing before the Subcommittee on Financial Institutions and Consumer Credit of the House Committee on Financial Services*, at 8 (Mar. 27, 2007) (statement of Harry H. Dinham, on behalf of the National Association of Mortgage Brokers); Christopher E. Herbert et al., *Homeownership Gaps Among Low-Income and Minority Borrowers and Neighborhoods*, U.S. Dep't of Hous. and Urban Dev. (2005).

In the Happy Homeownership Narrative, having vigilant, involved neighbors who work to ensure that neighborhoods are safe and have desirable services provides positive external benefits for all residents (be they homeowners or renters). While most homeowners are not actively involved in HOAs, homeowners are generally more likely than renters to vote, especially in local elections, and surveys indicate that homeowners are more likely to participate in the political process and are generally more involved in local political groups and civic organizations than renters.[29]

However, despite the empirical support for the view that homeowners are more civic-minded and take better care of their property than renters, the data are thin and appear to vary depending on the homeowners' income, socioeconomic status, and educational attainment. Moreover, because people with higher levels of formal education and those with higher incomes are generally more likely to be homeowners, to vote, to volunteer, and to be involved in their communities, it is unclear whether homeowners vote because they own homes or because of their income or educational attainment levels. Likewise, it is unclear whether renters – especially lower-income renters – are less involved in community affairs because they are less civic-minded or because they simply have less free time, have less flexible work hours, and face greater transportation challenges relative to (higher-income) homeowners.[30]

Again, whether homeowners are in fact more civic-minded and involved than renters is largely irrelevant, just as it largely does not matter whether the Happy Homeownership Narrative's assumptions about the financial benefits homeownership provides are factually accurate. The dominant view is that homeownership transforms renters into financially secure owners and then transforms them into stable, less transient and more actively involved citizens. And, as long as this is the prevailing societal view, U.S. housing policies will continue to subsidize homeownership.[31]

[29] Rohe & Stewart, *supra* note 21; Rossi & Weber, *supra* note 18; Dietz, *supra* note 18; DiPasquale & Glaeser, *supra* note 27.

[30] Richard J. Colley & Andrew Sum, *Fault Lines in Our Democracy; Civic Knowledge, Voting Behavior, and Civic Engagement in the United States*, Educational Testing Service (Apr. 2012), *available at* http://www.ets.org/s/research/19386/rsc/pdf/18719_fault_lines_report.pdf.

[31] Stephanie M. Steen, *Reassessing the Citizen Virtues of Homeownership*, 100 COLUM. L. REV. 101 (2011); Ingrid Gould Ellen & Margery Austin Turner, *Does Neighborhood Matter? Assessing Recent Evidence*, 8 HOUSING POL'Y DEBATE (1997); Amanda Moore McBride et al., *Civic Engagement among Low-Income and Low-Wealth Families: In Their Words*, 55–2 FAMILY RELATIONS (Apr. 2006); Fannie Mae National Housing Survey, *supra* note 24; Karla Hoff & Aruit Sen, *Homeownership, Community Interactions, and Segregation*, THE AMERICAN ECONOMIC REVIEW 1167 (2005).

3

U.S. Support for Homeowners

For years, U.S. political leaders and governmental agencies have supported campaigns that were designed to educate renters about the value of homeownership and the benefits of living in a single-family home. Even though the U.S. government has encouraged and extolled homeownership since the eighteenth century, the federal government's role in the housing market was largely passive until the twentieth century, and the United States did not actively participate in mortgage finance markets until the Great Depression. The economic consequences of the Depression, including widespread bank failures, skyrocketing unemployment rates, and record foreclosures caused the government to intervene in the private housing finance market with the explicit goals of stimulating home sales, reducing the risk of borrower default, protecting the stability of banks, and keeping home sales high. The government has continued to subsidize homeownership by guaranteeing private mortgage loans, buying private mortgage loans in the secondary market, and providing tax benefits for people who buy and occupy houses. In addition to these financial subsidies, the United States increases the attractiveness of homeownership by giving homeowners the power to exclude certain types of property uses – and frequently certain types of residents – from their neighborhoods.

HOUSING FINANCE: THE EARLY YEARS

The complex mortgage loan products that people used to buy homes during the early 2000s housing boom bore little resemblance to the mortgages borrowers used to buy homes during most of the twentieth century. As discussed in Chapter 2, in the Happy Homeownership Narrative, buying a home converts a profligate renter into a financially responsible and thrifty owner. This aspect of the Narrative was largely true until the 2000s housing boom, because most people who sought to buy a home in the United States had to satisfy fairly rigid mortgage underwriting standards, and those standards forced renters to save, likely for years, if they wanted to buy and then remain in their homes.

For example, before the Depression, most mortgages required borrowers to make significant down payments of as much as 50 percent of the value of the home. Because of this requirement, mortgages had relatively low loan-to-value (or LTV) ratios, often less than 50 percent. While the down payment requirement made mortgage lending secure and largely risk-free for lenders, the requirement made it harder for renters to buy a home early in life. But once the renter managed to save enough for the down payment, there was a strong incentive to be thrifty and repay the mortgage loan, because a foreclosure would wipe out the significant financial investment the renter had made in the home.

In addition to having high down payment requirements, pre-Depression loans had relatively short repayment periods. While a common repayment period was five–ten years, repayment periods could be as short as three years. Principally because of these short repayment periods, pre-Depression mortgage loan products did not self-amortize. While a few lenders (mostly building and loan societies) offered long-term, fully amortizing mortgage products before the Depression, the mortgage loan products that most banks, life insurers, and private individuals offered during this time were not fully amortizing. Because these loans did not fully amortize, a borrower would not own the home even after making a substantial down payment and timely payments on the mortgage loan.

A homeowner who "bought" a home with a non-amortizing mortgage loan product would not own the home outright until after making a final "balloon" payment, and this payment often was substantial. Once the balloon payment came due, the homeowner could keep the home only if he or she had (or could borrow) cash to pay the final principal balance in full or could convince the lender to renegotiate the remaining loan balance. Few people had enough spare cash to make the balloon payments. Additionally, homeowners could not qualify for a new loan from another lender to finish buying a home that was already encumbered by an outstanding mortgage loan. As a result, most pre-Depression borrowers either had to work with their existing lenders to find a way to refinance their mortgage loans or they would lose their financial investment (and their homes) once the balloon payment came due.[1]

Although fixed rate mortgage (FRM) loans are now the norm in mortgage lending, until the Depression most mortgage loan products had adjustable

[1] Richard K. Green & Susan M. Wachter, *The American Mortgage in Historical and International Context*, 19–4 J. ECON. PERSP. (Fall 2005).

rates of interest. After the initial payment period (now commonly referred to as a "teaser" period) ended, the interest rate on the mortgage loan would reset to a figure generally determined relative to a financial index (e.g., the rate for U.S. Treasury bonds). Adjustable rate mortgage (ARM) loans posed higher risks for borrowers because their future monthly loan payments would increase if interest rates rose. ARMs were also risky for home buyers because fluctuating interest rates made it hard for them to accurately gauge the amount of the final balloon payment. ARMs and their unpredictable fluctuating rates made it virtually impossible for a homeowner to engage in any type of reliable, long-range financial planning.

Because of federal regulator standards governing bank solvency, before the Depression banks rarely approved loans with terms longer than five years or loans that had LTV ratios of less than 50 percent. In addition to the banking regulations, lenders were unwilling to originate long-term, fixed-interest rate loans because of their concern that they would be locked into receiving lower returns on these long-term loans, even if interest rates soared during the loan term. Similarly, lenders avoided residential mortgage loans with terms longer than five years because of the difficulty of predicting whether a borrower might default twenty years into a thirty-year loan. Furthermore, lenders avoided longer-term or fixed-interest rate loans because of their legitimate concern that they might face a liquidity crisis if they found themselves forced to pay higher interest rates to their local customers (whose short-term savings account deposits funded long-term mortgages) but received lower interest rates from homeowners who repaid longer-term FRMs.[2]

While low LTV ratios, short repayment periods, and adjustable-interest rates protected banks and made mortgage lending relatively low-risk for them, these loan features made homeownership high-risk and high-cost for most potential home buyers. Even though few borrowers could afford to make their final balloon payments, these risks appeared to be negligible because most lenders were willing to renegotiate mortgage loans, provide additional financing, or otherwise extend mortgage loan terms to allow borrowers to remain in their homes until the Great Depression.

THE GREAT DEPRESSION

Although the U.S. Departments of Labor and Commerce engaged in campaigns to encourage citizens to better their lives and become homeowners in the 1910s and 1920s, the United States had a limited role in mortgage finance

[2] *Id.*

markets until the Depression.[3] During the Depression, businesses – including a significant number of banks – failed in record numbers. Banks faced a severe liquidity crisis because a significant number of borrowers, both businesses and individuals, defaulted on their loans. While borrowers defaulted, the bank's "lenders" (i.e., depositors) panicked and rushed to remove their deposits from the banks. The combination of these events caused widespread bank failures during the Depression.

Due to the record number of business failures, unemployment rates soared during this period. With no jobs, no income, and little savings, homeowners defaulted on their mortgage loans in record numbers. Unemployed homeowners could not afford to make their monthly mortgage payments, *much less* their final balloon payments. Massive mortgage loan defaults ultimately caused foreclosure rates to soar, and a glut of homes flooded the real estate market. This glut then made it impossible for struggling homeowners to sell their homes for anywhere near the pre-Depression values.

During the Depression, even the banks that did *not* fail suffered catastrophic financial losses and were unsure of their own futures. Because of these concerns, banks dramatically restricted lending and were not willing to renegotiate or refinance financially struggling homeowners' mortgage loans. Home values plummeted and, ultimately, the U.S. housing market collapsed. Homeowners were stuck: they could not afford to keep their homes, they could not sell those homes, and banks were unwilling to renegotiate their mortgage loans. To stem the catastrophic financial losses that banks, real estate developers, and homeowners suffered during the Depression, the federal government intervened in the mortgage finance market. This massive intervention ultimately created mortgage finance programs that would forever change the U.S. housing finance market.[4]

THE HOLC, FHA, FANNIE, FREDDIE, AND GINNIE

In order to stimulate home sales (for developers), create jobs in the construction industry, and stem foreclosures (for lenders and homeowners), the United States created the Home Owners' Loan Corporation (HOLC). The HOLC

[3] Vincent J. Cannato, *A Home of One's Own*, NAT'L AFF. (Spring 2010). While the most significant changes to U.S. housing markets occurred during the New Deal, many were set in place during the Hoover administration. For example, in 1931 President Hoover convened a White House Conference on Home Building and Home Ownership to respond to the housing crisis. The real estate industry attended the conference, and they shared Hoover's vision of increasing the government's participation in the housing finance market JEFFREY M. HORNSTEIN, A NATION OF REALTORS®: A CULTURAL HISTORY OF THE TWENTIETH-CENTURY AMERICAN MIDDLE CLASS 147–48 (2005).

[4] Cannato, *supra* note 3.

was authorized to buy residential mortgage loans that were in default (or were likely to default) and then refinance those loans with lower-cost, longer-term, government-backed mortgages. Lenders were eager to sell their loans to the HOLC because, with the HOLC-backing, they faced little risk that they would not be repaid. This mortgage relief made it possible for homeowners whose loans were eligible for HOLC refinancing to remain in their home and make new and lower payments on their government-backed mortgages. The HOLC was not designed, however, to buy all defaulted loans, nor was it designed to refinance private mortgage loans that *might* go into default in the future.

To spur home sales and reinvigorate the U.S. economy, lenders needed to approve more mortgage loans. But lenders were unwilling to free up credit for financially precarious borrowers because of concerns that looser lending would trigger a liquidity crisis. Lenders also wanted assurances that their risk of loss from loans they approved for these borrowers would be minimal. Given the limitations of the HOLC program and the ongoing need to further stabilize the housing market and calm the nerves of lenders and real estate developers, the United States realized that it had to do more than just refinance a limited number of at-risk mortgage loans. To help restore liquidity and stability in the financial system and increase the availability of funds that banks could use to originate residential mortgage loans, Congress created the Federal Home Loan Bank system. Generally speaking, the Federal Home Loan Bank system gave banks access to additional funds, which increased the bank's liquidity and decreased the likelihood that banks would lack sufficient cash reserves to fund larger, longer-term, lower-interest rate mortgages.[5]

Even with access to additional funds, though, banks were reluctant to approve lower-cost, longer-term mortgages to borrowers because of the increased default risks associated with these loans. Record-high business failures and unprecedented unemployment rates during the Depression made banks unwilling to significantly increase their mortgage loan origination volume because they had little reason to believe that financially beleaguered homeowners could afford to repay the loans. While there was a small third party private mortgage insurance (PMI) market that would guarantee payments if the borrower defaulted, during the Depression the PMI industry vanished (and essentially remained dormant until the 1970s). With little reason to believe that homeowners would repay their mortgage loans and with a now nonexistent PMI market, lenders remained unwilling to approve mortgage loans unless borrowers made significant down payments or agreed to other pro-lender loan terms.

[5] *Id.*

The United States attempted to assuage these worries by enacting the National Housing Act of 1934 (Housing Act), which created the Federal Housing Administration (FHA). To encourage lenders to approve longer-term, lower-cost mortgage loans, the FHA guaranteed that lenders would face no risk of loss for loans that the FHA insured. Generally speaking, the FHA assumed the risk of borrower default by placing funds they received from borrowers in a reserve fund that would be used to indemnify lenders if a borrower defaulted on an FHA-insured mortgage loan. Because of these guarantees, lenders became willing to approve longer-term loans. These guarantees made the loans lower-cost and lower-risk to banks because they now knew that any risk that a borrower would default and not repay a loan would be covered by the government insurance. With the promise that the government would pay if borrowers did not, lenders were finally willing to relax their lending restrictions and approve more home mortgage loans that had rates that were more favorable to borrowers.

To further help stabilize the housing finance market and give banks another incentive to increase the volume of their loan originations, the United States created a number of agencies to provide additional liquidity in the mortgage market. That is, in 1938 the United States established the Federal National Mortgage Association (now known simply as Fannie Mae). The United States ultimately decided to split Fannie Mae into two entities and assign many of Fannie Mae's loan guarantee operations to the Government National Mortgage Association (Ginnie Mae) in 1968. Ginnie Mae is a wholly owned U.S. government corporation that is part of the Department of Housing and Urban Development (HUD). The United States also created the Federal Home Loan Mortgage Corporation (now known as Freddie Mac). While Ginnie Mae remains an agency of the U.S. government, Fannie Mae and Freddie Mac are no longer units of the U.S. government and instead are now known as "government-sponsored enterprises" (GSEs) whose stock is publicly traded. Since their creation, these GSEs have provided liquidity in the mortgage market by buying private mortgage loans using funds generated from bonds they issued in the capital markets.

Initially, Fannie Mae could only purchase FHA-insured or Veterans Administration (VA)-guaranteed mortgages. Since 1970, though, both Fannie Mae and Freddie Mac have been permitted to purchase conventional mortgages that were not backed directly by the United States. Still, until the housing boom, the GSEs did not purchase high-risk, residential mortgage loans and would not purchase loans if the lenders did not impose relatively rigid lending standards that confirmed the borrowers' creditworthiness. These "conforming loans" were required to charge prime interest rates, to have a relatively low

LTV ratio, and could not exceed a certain principal amount. To keep the LTV ratio low, a borrower was required to make a 20 percent down payment. Until the housing boom, the GSEs would not buy high LTV mortgages unless the borrower purchased PMI which was costly and could increase the homeowner's annual borrowing costs by $1,000 for each $100,000 borrowed depending on the borrower's credit standing.[6]

Finally, the GSEs generally would not buy mortgage loans unless borrowers could prove that they could afford to repay the loan. For example, borrowers had to show that even after putting 20 percent down, they had adequate savings to cover two months of loan payments. Similarly, to ensure that homeowners could afford to repay the mortgage loan, the GSEs initially would not purchase the loan if homeowners' monthly payments exceeded 28 percent of their pre-tax monthly income or if the loan forced them to spend more than 36 percent of their pre-tax income on total mortgage and revolving (e.g., automobile loan, credit card, etc.) debt. While Congress ultimately permitted the GSEs to buy subprime and other high-risk, nonconventional residential mortgages, for most of their existence the GSEs were selective in the loans they bought and would purchase only "safe" conforming loans.[7]

The GSEs, FHA, and later the Veterans Administration (VA) mortgage program (which was created after World War II as part of the GI Bill) have played crucial roles in stabilizing housing markets and giving banks an economic incentive to increase their mortgage loan originations. Because FHA and VA loans allowed eligible borrowers to buy homes with less than a 50 percent down payment, these loan programs helped boost overall homeownership rates. Just as the FHA has insured the vast majority of all FRMs, Fannie Mae and Freddie Mac have consistently been the largest buyers of mortgages on the secondary market. Because lenders knew they could originate loans (that the FHA would then insure) and then sell those government-backed mortgages to the GSEs in the secondary market, private lenders had an incentive to approve more residential housing loans and then use the sale proceeds to originate more loans.

The government's intervention in the mortgage finance market caused overall U.S. homeownership rates to increase from approximately 44 percent in 1940, to more than 53 percent in 1950 and almost 62 percent by 1960. With

[6] The GSEs would only purchase loans that met the following criteria: the borrower had to have a FICO score of at least 620; the loan value could not exceed $417,000; and the loan had to have an LTV of no more than 80 percent. Loans that failed these criteria could only be sold to private investors.

[7] Robert W. Kolb, The Financial Crisis of Our Time 2–4 (2011); 16–92A Powell on Real Property § 92A.04 (Michael Allan Wolf ed., LexisNexis Matthew Bender).

the federal government bearing the risk of default for these private mortgage loans, qualified borrowers could *finally* purchase homes at lower costs and with less risk. While federal mortgage loan guarantees and increased liquidity in the mortgage lending markets made it easier for renters to buy homes, perhaps the most significant post-Depression government intervention involved the creation of the fixed-interest rate mortgage.[8]

FIXED RATE MORTGAGES

The programs that the government created after the Depression made low-cost mortgages more readily available for qualified borrowers and created a secondary mortgage market. The most long-lasting intervention, though, was the role the United States played in creating the amortizing, long-term, FRM. Before Congress created the FHA, federal regulations made it virtually impossible for banks to approve residential mortgage loans that had high LTV ratios and long repayment periods. To jumpstart home sales, stem foreclosures, and calm nervous lenders, the United States revised federal banking regulations to allow banks to approve larger loans that self-amortized, even though borrowers made down payments – typically 10 percent – that were significantly lower than pre-Depression amounts. This smaller down payment requirement made it easier for a broader group of borrowers to purchase homes and also made it possible for renters to buy a home earlier in life because they no longer had to save for years to accumulate enough money to make a 50 percent down payment.[9]

Because most pre-Depression mortgage loans were non-amortizing ARMs, monthly payments were often unpredictable and borrowers faced large balloon payments even after they finished repaying the mortgage loan. The newly created FRMs had longer payment terms, generally fifteen–thirty years. This gave the homeowner more time to repay the loan and also lowered the monthly mortgage payments. Because the loans amortized, FRMs were less risky for borrowers because they knew that once they had made monthly mortgage payments of interest and principal for fifteen to thirty years, they would own their home outright. Because interest rates were fixed, homeowners no longer had to fear that their monthly payments would unexpectedly skyrocket at some point during the loan repayment period.

Since their creation, FRMs have been enormously popular with borrowers. Because of their longer repayment terms, traditional fifteen- to thirty-year

[8] Cannato, *supra* note 3.

[9] Kolb, *supra* note 7.

FRMs are more affordable in the short-term, even though the loans could cost more over the long-term if interest rates were to fall and the borrower was to remain locked into a higher rate of interest. Despite potentially higher long-term costs, FRMs have dominated the mortgage finance market since their creation principally because their simple, understandable terms make it possible for borrowers to easily calculate and comprehend the size of their monthly payments and long-term borrowing costs before they sign the loan document. Today, financial calculators (and the Internet) make it possible for borrowers to calculate their total home buying costs almost instantaneously, and the predictable payments of a self-amortizing FRM have always made it easy for homeowners to create a long-term budget that includes the (equal) monthly loan payments they must make to be sure that they own their homes outright in fifteen to thirty years.

The U.S. government's massive intervention in the housing markets after the Depression was enormously successful in increasing homeownership rates and, consequently, housing sales. In addition, as discussed in greater detail in Chapter 7, the FHA underwriting standards favored new, suburban, single-family homes, which facilitated the expansion of suburban neighborhoods and transformed the residential landscape in most cities. However, the same U.S. housing policies that made homeownership easier and cheaper for borrowers who qualified for FHA-insured loans forced homeowners who could *not* qualify for these loans (and this included virtually all borrowers who were not white) to buy homes with loans that had the same risks and costs that borrowers faced before the massive government intervention. Likewise, as discussed in more detail in Chapter 8, the housing policies that favored suburban communities fenced blacks and Latinos out of those communities and contributed to the decline of predominately black urban housing markets.[10]

SECURITIZATION: THE EARLY YEARS

Fannie Mae and Freddie Mac have consistently been the largest buyers of mortgages on the secondary market, a fact which ultimately caused them to be placed in a conservatorship in 2008 during the recent housing crisis. Because lenders knew they could originate loans (that the FHA would then insure) and then sell those government-backed mortgages to the GSEs in the secondary market, private lenders had an incentive to approve more residential housing loans then use the sale proceeds to originate more loans.

[10] Adam Gordon, *The Creation of Homeownership: How New Deal Changes in Banking Regulation Simultaneously Made Homeownership Accessible to Whites and Out of Reach for Blacks*, 115 Yale L. J. 186 (2005).

Since 1970, though, both Fannie Mae and Freddie Mac have been permitted to purchase conventional mortgages that were not backed by the United States.

As will be discussed in greater detail later in the next Chapter, starting in the 1970s housing prices outpaced inflation, household income stalled, and households stopped saving. By the late 1990s, low- and moderate-income (LMI) renters could not qualify for a traditional mortgage loan because their financial profiles failed to match the profile envisioned in the Happy Homeownership Narrative: they had no money to make a down payment, they had stagnant or declining income, and their crushing debt burdens prevented them from satisfying lenders' debt-to-income ratio requirements. The U.S. government became concerned in the 1990s that homeownership was becoming unaffordable and, again, intervened in the housing finance market.

Even though the GSEs ultimately bought subprime and other high-risk, nonconventional residential mortgages they initially did not purchase high-risk residential mortgage loans unless the lenders imposed relatively rigid lending requirements that confirmed the borrowers' creditworthiness. To respond to the housing unaffordability crisis, Congress set goals that required Fannie Mae and Freddie Mac to increase the number of loans they bought that were made to LMI borrowers. Requiring GSEs to purchase more mortgages issued to LMI borrowers would, Congress correctly assumed, give lenders an incentive to originate more of these loans. As discussed in more detail in Chapter 4, lenders dramatically loosened their lending standards and increased the volume of loans they approved for LMI borrowers. These loans lacked most of the financial safeguards (low LTV, down payment requirements, fixed-interest rates) that had been in place since the United States intervened in the mortgage finance market in the New Deal. As a result, the loans were not low cost to borrowers, were far from low-risk, and ultimately proved to be toxic for borrowers, lenders, and the entities that invested in the loans once they were packaged and sold as securities.

In addition to providing liquidity in the domestic housing market, the government's involvement in the secondary market fueled mortgage loan securitizations and made mortgage-backed securities (MBS) popular and enormously profitable. In its simplest form, lenders originate mortgage loans, charge the borrower interest (e.g., 4 percent), then sell the loans and the right to receive monthly payments from borrowers on the pooled mortgage loans to another entity (often a trust). This entity then bundles the loans and creates mortgage-backed (also called asset-backed) securities. MBSs are backed by the income stream from borrowers' monthly loan payments. The entity sells the bonds to private investors and agrees to provide a rate of interest lower than the homeowners' mortgage loan (e.g., 3 percent) to the investors who, again, are paid from the income stream of the monthly loan payments of borrowers whose loans are in the pool.

While the GSEs kept some of the loans they bought, they packaged and securitized many of these loans into pools and used the pool of loans as collateral for a tradable bond/security that they sold to private investors. Freddie Mac and Fannie Mae were the first major securitizers of mortgage loans. Ginnie Mae (which does not originate or purchase mortgage loans or sell, or issue MBSs) has been the principal financing entity for government mortgage products. Ginnie Mae agreed that, in exchange for a fee, it would guarantee the timely payment of principal and interest for government-insured private mortgage loans that have been pooled into residential MBSs (often by Freddie or Fannie). Because Ginnie Mae is wholly owned by the U.S. government, its MBSs are backed by the full faith and credit of the U.S. government. Because of the implicit promise that the United States would honor the GSE's obligations, Fannie Mae and Freddie Mac MBSs were enormously popular with private investors.

Until the housing boom, the GSEs dominated the MBS market. By the late 1970s, investment banks and other private entities started to securitize mortgage loans and issue private-label mortgage-backed securities (PLS). The securitization process for PLSs was similar to the process the GSEs used, though PLS did not guarantee borrowers' loan payments. As was initially true with government-backed MBS, investing in a PLS was a fairly low-risk activity because a large percentage of the mortgages in the private label MBS conformed to the GSE underwriting guidelines. By the 1990s, the PLS became riskier. Because of their relatively higher yields, the overall share of PLS in the MBS market started to increase toward the end of the 1990s and smaller percentages of the loans in the PLS market were nonconforming loans. As discussed later in the book, during the housing boom the PLS packaged a significantly larger percentage of high-risk subprime loans that were made to borrowers who simply could not afford to repay those loans.[11]

SECURITIZATION: SHIFTING INCENTIVES

As noted earlier, during and immediately after the Depression, lenders would not approve low-cost, long-term FRM loans because they worried that their customers' short-term demand deposits would not be sufficient to adequately

[11] For an excellent discussion and explanation of the mortgage loan securitization, see KOLB, *supra* note 7, at 16–37.

fund these long-term mortgages. Just as the liquidity Fannie Mae and Freddie Mac provided in the secondary mortgage market encouraged lenders to increase the volume of their loan originations, securitization gave lenders incentives to approve residential mortgage loans – especially conforming loans that Fannie and Freddie could purchase and securitize. Lenders realized that they could originate and quickly sell residential mortgages in the now-robust secondary mortgage market because securitizers could profitably package, securitize, and sell those loans to investors who were eager to invest in PLS – especially those backed by high-cost, high-yield, subprime loans. Once lenders understood the profitability of approving and then selling high-cost, subprime loans, they willingly offered mortgages to an increasingly large numbers of potential home buyers – even if those borrowers had blemished credit. Similarly, because the GSEs reaped enormous profits from the fees they received to securitize FHA or VA mortgages, they also had a financial incentive to package a greater number of high-cost loans – even though they knew (or should have known) that many of those loans were high-risk and made to borrowers with bad credit.[12]

Starting in the 1990s, an increasing percentage of loans in PLS were Jumbo loans (loans to prime borrowers with principal balances that are larger than the GSE-conforming limits), Alt-A loans (loans made to borrowers with good credit who may have too much debt or may be unable to document income), and, eventually, subprime loans. Borrowers with bad credit are most likely to buy homes using subprime mortgage loans and, for this reason, these loans typically have higher risks of default. To protect themselves against these risks, lenders charge higher interest rates and impose greater fees for subprime loans. Because borrowers pay more for subprime loans, these loans are enormously profitable both for the loan originator and for investors in MBSs. This profitability fueled an almost insatiable demand for these high-risk loans, and this demand ultimately caused lenders to abandon the "originate-to-keep" model in favor of the "originate-to-sell" model.

Many subprime loans were sold even before the first loan payment was due, and most were privately securitized and then sold primarily to large institutional investors, including hedge funds and pension funds. By the end of the 1990s, the PLS market was flooded with securitized pools of high-risk loans. During this period, the GSEs legitimized the largely unregulated and, until then, largely stigmatized subprime lending market. GSEs started to purchase nonconforming subprime mortgage loans and to invest in the PLSs that

[12] Jonathan McCarthy & Richard W. Peach, *Monetary Policy Transmission to Residential Investment*, Econ. Pol'y. Rev. 139–58 (2002).

bundled these loans. Indeed, during the height of the housing boom, GSEs were the primary investors in subprime MBSs, even though an increasing percentage of those securities were backed by the income streams from nonconforming loans approved for high-risk borrowers who made small (or no) down payments, had relatively low credit scores, and would never have qualified for a conforming loan.[13]

The voracious demand for subprime loans in the secondary market dramatically changed lenders' financial incentives. From the time the United States intervened in the housing finance market after the Depression until the early 2000s, mortgage loans were not particularly risky to either the lender or the borrower because lenders scrutinized the borrowers' creditworthiness and typically approved only financially sound loans. Indeed, despite the changes over time to the structure of the mortgage finance industry and the increased role of the U.S. government in the housing finance market, until recently core aspects of the Happy Homeownership Narrative remained true.

First, borrowers were required to invest in their housing purchases by making a down payment. This requirement gave them a strong incentive to be thrifty savers who engaged in responsible financial behavior to ensure they could make the monthly loan payments and protect their equity in their homes. Second, financial institutions had incentives to carefully scrutinize borrowers' incomes, assets, and debts because banks kept and serviced many of these loans and, thus, faced the risk of nonpayment if they approved loans for borrowers who were not creditworthy.

As discussed in greater detail in Chapter 6, once subprime lending dominated the MBS market and the mortgage finance market shifted from a loan-to-keep to a loan-to-sell model, lenders no longer retained any of the risk of nonpayment. Because lenders did not bear the risk of loss if borrowers defaulted, they had minimal incentives to engage in careful underwriting. During the housing boom, lenders approved increasingly large numbers of mortgage loans for borrowers with blemished credit who could not afford to repay the mortgage loans. After originating these risky loans, lenders sold them, securitizers packaged them, and investors bought them. These securitized subprime loan pools often had terms and structures that were so complex that investors could not grasp the risks they were assuming. The profitability of these securitized pools, though, caused virtually everyone – originators,

[13] Adam B. Ashcraft & Til Schuermann, *Understanding the Securitization of Subprime Mortgage Credit*, Fed. Res. Bank N.Y. Staff Reps. (Mar. 2008); Richard J. Rosen, *Too Much Right Can Make a Wrong: Setting the Stage for the Financial Crisis* (Fed. Res. Bank Chi., Working Paper No. 18, 2009).

securitizers, rating agencies, and investors alike – to turn a blind eye to the risks associated with MBSs.[14]

HOMEOWNERSHIP HAS ITS BENEFITS: TAX DEDUCTIONS AND EXCLUSIONS

In addition to participating in housing finance markets either directly or through GSEs, the United States encourages homeownership by providing direct subsidies and incentives, mostly to people who buy houses. The United States provides limited financial assistance to renters, and this assistance largely consists of low-rent public housing projects, rental housing vouchers for lower-income renters, and investor tax credits for low-income housing developments. For at least three decades, the United States has reduced its financial support for low-income rental housing and, since the late 1970s, the vast majority of U.S. housing subsidies have been given to people who are buying (or have bought) homes.

Tax subsidies are the most significant and most often touted incentive the United States gives to encourage renters to buy houses. Since 1913, the U.S. Tax Code has allowed taxpayers who own and occupy residential housing to deduct the interest they pay on mortgage loans. The mortgage interest deduction (MID) has always benefited a small segment of taxpayers who own homes, and it was taken by only a small percentage of taxpayers until homeownership rates began to increase after World War II. Although most Americans continue to believe that owning a home would be less attractive if the MID were repealed, there is no indication that the initial justification for the MID was to encourage or subsidize homeownership, and Congress gave no explicit rationale for the consumer home interest deduction when it originally agreed that taxpayers could deduct interest on all consumer loans.

Until 1986, taxpayers could deduct interest they paid on credit cards or other loans they used to purchase consumer goods – not just mortgage loans. Congress revised the interest deduction provisions in the Tax Reform Act of 1986 to limit the consumer interest deduction to home mortgages.[15] While taxpayers can no longer deduct *non*-mortgage interest on high-interest consumer loans (like payday loans) or credit card debt, members of Congress have consistently rejected virtually all proposals to limit (or eliminate) the

[14] Giovanni Dell'Ariccia et al., *Credit Booms and Lending Standards: Evidence from the Subprime Mortgage Market* (Int'l Monetary Fund, Working Paper No. WP/08/106, 2008), *available at* http://www.imf.org/external/pubs/ft/wp/2008/wp08106.pdf.

[15] Cong. Budget Off., U.S. Cong., *The Tax Treatment of Homeownership: Issues and Options* (1981).

MID. In reaffirming its continued support for the MID, Congress recently espoused the Happy Homeownership Narrative's mantra that homeownership should be encouraged because it fosters "neighborhood stability, promote[s] civic responsibility, and improve[s] the maintenance of residential buildings."[16]

Because of this steadfast support for homeownership and the MID, U.S. taxpayers can deduct interest payments they make on mortgages that allow them to buy or build their first *and* second homes up to a maximum of $1 million of mortgage debt. Taxpayers can also deduct interest they pay on home equity loans (HEL) or lines of credit (HELOC) up to a maximum of $100,000 of such debt, even though these loans do not help taxpayers become or remain homeowners. Finally, U.S. tax laws encourage people to buy houses by letting homeowners deduct state and local real estate taxes from their income.[17]

The limited federal income tax exclusion for gains from home sales also subsidizes homeownership and encourages renters to buy houses. Taxpayers who purchase homes can sell their homes as frequently as every two years and avoid paying capital gains taxes on up to $500,000 of the profits they make on the sale if they are married taxpayers filing a joint return (or $250,000 if they are unmarried). Taxpayers are entitled to this tax benefit even if they are short-term homeowners or real estate speculators. Congress initially justified this benefit as a way of protecting homeowners from uncontrollable and unpredictable circumstances, including the need to move because of a new job or because the taxpayer's family increased in size. By 1981, though, members of Congress suspected that this exclusion was no longer consistent with the Happy Homeownership Narrative because it is not limited to taxpayers who plan to live in their homes or neighborhoods long-term.

A Congressional Budget Office report discussing this deduction noted that while it

> may still be valid if homeownership is viewed as primarily a consumption decision ... [w]ith the tremendous appreciation of home prices in the last decade...a growing number of households have come to view their homes as investments as well. To the extent that this is so, homeowners receive a significant tax benefit, since capital gains from investments in other assets are taxed when realized.[18]

[16] J. Comm. Tax'n., *Present Law and Background Relating to Tax Treatment of Household Debt* (2011).

[17] *Id*; IRS, U.S. Dep't Treasury, *Tax Topics – Topic 503 Deductible Taxes* (2013), *available at* http://www.irs.gov/taxtopics/tc503.html.

[18] Cong. Budget Off., *supra* note 15.

Regardless of whether the tax benefits encourage Americans to buy home, all serious discussions to repeal the MID and other homeownership tax benefits have been thwarted because the MID, like social security, is an enormously popular government benefit. Surveys show that renters are keenly aware of the existence of the MID. Despite the disturbing disconnect between the ability of many financially struggling Americans to afford to buy houses, 75 percent of homeowners and 60 percent of renters feel that it is extremely or very important that the MID remain in place. Given this public support, politicians have no political incentive to eliminate any of the homeownership tax benefits despite their significant costs, despite the fact that these benefits encourage people to buy large homes and more than one home (i.e., vacation homes), and despite data that show that the MID encourages homeowners to finance non-housing purchases (or borrow against their homes to pay for non-housing debts) because they can no longer deduct interest on non-mortgage consumer loans.[19]

The homeownership tax benefits are massive. For example, in 2012 the cost for the MID tax expenditure was more than $68 billion, the cost of the property tax deduction was more than $24 billion, and the cost of the capital gains exclusion on home sales exceeded $22 billion.[20] Most politicians and the vast majority of taxpayers likely view these massive tax expenditures as warranted because of the benefits that homeownership purportedly provides for society. Average Americans probably fail to realize, though, that fewer than half of all homeowners and only about 30 percent of all U.S. taxpayers itemize their deductions and claim these benefits. Moreover, the taxpayers who receive these enormous homeownership tax benefits are disproportionately high-income and disproportionately white.[21]

Finally, U.S. taxpayers who own homes receive another significant tax benefit that is rarely discussed outside of tax policy debates: untaxed, imputed rental income. Generally speaking, the U.S. Tax Code forces owners to pay taxes on income generated by the assets they own. For example, owners of rental property are taxed on the income their rental property generates but

[19] Fannie Mae Foundation, African American and Hispanic Attitudes on Homeownership: A Guide for Mortgage Industry Leaders 13 (1998); Harris Interactive, conducted for the Nat'l Ass'n. Realtors, *American Attitudes about Homeownership* (2011).

[20] In general, tax expenditures are measured by calculating the difference between the existing tax liability and the tax liability that would result if the current tax deduction did not exist (assuming there was no change in taxpayer behavior if the deduction was repealed). See Off. Mgmt. Budget, Exec. Off. President, *Analytical Perspectives: Fiscal Year 2012 Budget of the U.S. Government* 242 (2012), *available at* http://www.whitehouse.gov/sites/default/files/omb/budget/fy2012/assets/spec.pdf. (Table 17–1, Estimates of Total Income Tax Expenditures for Fiscal Years 2010–2016).

[21] IRS, U.S. Dep't. Treasury, *Individual Income Tax Returns 2008: Publication 1304* (2008), *available at* http://www.irs.gov/pub/irs-soi/08inalcr.pdf.

can deduct the expenses associated with earning this income (like mortgage interest payments and property taxes) from gross income. Because of the bias U.S. housing policies have in favor of homeownership, homeowners are not required to pay taxes on the imputed rental income they receive from themselves each month when they essentially pay themselves rent. Although they are not taxed on this income, they are allowed to take some of the same deductions that owners of rental housing take.[22]

If homeowners who live in the houses they own were treated the same way that homeowners who rent their houses are treated, owner-occupied households would be taxed on the imputed income (i.e., rent) they would have received had they rented their home to a renter. This homeownership tax benefit is rarely discussed by anyone other than tax policy analysts, but the U.S. government is aware of the costs associated with this benefit because it calculates a value for the benefit and includes this amount in the U.S. gross domestic product (GDP) as part of personal consumption expenditures. This benefit, like the other homeownership tax benefits, is massive and has in recent years accounted for roughly 8 percent of the country's GDP. Stated differently, the cost to the United States for the income exclusion of imputed rent for owner-occupied housing was estimated to be $41 billion in 2010 and $46 billion in 2011.[23]

THE POWER TO EXCLUDE: PRIVATE LAND USE RESTRICTIONS

In addition to being attracted to homeownership's financial benefits (both wealth accumulation and government tax subsidies), renters are drawn to homeownership because of the powerful political privileges homeowners have. As discussed in the last chapter, homeowners have always been accorded a higher social and political status than renters have. Over time, this has caused homeowners to develop and adhere to an ownership ideology that makes them think they are better than renters. Homeowners also seem to believe that their status gives them the right to decide what happens in their

[22] Owners of rental housing do receive some benefits that homeowners do not. For example, the owners of rental housing – but not homeowners – are allowed to deduct maintenance expenses or depreciation.

[23] Generally speaking, the United States uses what is generally referred to as the "rental equivalent method" to calculate the market value of what the owner would have to pay as rent for living in their home or would earn from renting a similar home. The benefit is calculated by subtracting the house's expenses (depreciation, maintenance, taxes, and mortgage interest) from this imputed rental value. See Bureau Econ. Analysis, U.S. Dep't Com., *Concepts and Methods of the U.S. National Income and Product Accounts* 5 (2011); Robert Poole et al., *Treatment of Owner-Occupied Housing in the CPI*, Bureau of Labor Statistics (2005); Off. Mgmt. Budget, *supra* note 20.

neighborhoods and who should be allowed to live near them. While renters are no longer prevented from voting or becoming elected officials, land use laws and regulations continue to marginalize them and keep them weaker and politically less powerful than homeowners.[24]

As discussed in greater detail in Chapter 7, racially restrictive covenants that provided that neither an owner nor his or her heirs would sell, lease, or give their property to blacks were historically used to prevent white property owners from selling their land to blacks. The U.S. Supreme Court declared these covenants to be unconstitutional in 1948, but homeowners can still use private deed covenants to control how other property owners can use properties in their neighborhoods. In general, private deed covenants let homeowners prevent their neighbors from making major alterations to their homes without prior approval, and these covenants often dictate lot size and whether a multifamily unit can be built on the property. Although these covenants are private contractual agreements between landowners, local governments often refuse to approve new housing developments unless the developer includes land covenants for the properties they sell. These private agreements are often difficult to enforce, though, because individual landowners must sue the breaching landowner and then must rely on courts to force the landowner to comply with the terms of the covenant.

Because of these enforcement difficulties, the most common form of land restrictions now are the ones imposed on homeowners who purchase property that is located in a community that is regulated by a homeowners' association (HOA). HOAs are private quasi-governments that can restrict how homeowners use their property and can prohibit activities that the HOA deems to be inconsistent with the HOA rules and regulations. Once homeowners decide to purchase a home that is bound by an HOA, they must abide by the HOA regulations and covenants. HOAs have the authority to enforce their rules and regulations, and these regulations ostensibly are designed to protect a neighborhood's aesthetic and character. An HOA also has the authority to modify those regulations and covenants, often with less than unanimous consent of the homeowners. Because HOAs are vested with the authority to interpret existing covenants and modify or remove existing regulations or covenants, they can be quite powerful.

[24] Donald A. Krueckeberg, *The Grapes of Rent: A History of Renting in a Country of Owners*, 10 Hous. Pol'y Debate 9 (1999); *Preserving the American Dream: Predatory Lending Practices and Home Foreclosures: Hearing before the Senate Committee on Banking, Housing, and Urban Affairs*, 110th Cong. 10 (2007) (statement of Harry H. Dinham, on behalf of the National Association of Mortgage Brokers) ("No merchant, no government and no company should superimpose their own moral judgments on what is a basic American privilege of homeownership").

In addition to dictating lot sizes and the design of homes that owners can build on their property, HOA regulations in private covenanted subdivisions often bind owners to rules that dictate where owners can park their cars; where trash cans or recycling bins must be kept; the types of sheds owners can build; whether owners can demolish or otherwise modify structures on their property; and even what types of lawn or fences the landowner can have. Some HOAs reserve the right of first refusal to purchase an owner's home, while other HOAs prevent owners from selling a home governed by the HOA unless the other property owners approve of the sale.

Of course, homeowners can avoid being governed by these quasi-governments by not purchasing homes in communities that are regulated by HOAs. But, despite the burdens associated with HOA regulations and the accompanying restrictions imposed on a homeowner's property rights, many homeowners prefer to live in covenanted communities because the rules and restrictions imposed by the covenants let them control what their neighbors can do to (and on) their land. HOA regulations essentially provide a form of private property insurance that lets private owners have a general sense of how their neighborhood likely will develop over time and what (and who) will be in their neighborhood. Indeed, as shown in the following sections, many homeowners continue to prefer covenanted communities in urban and suburban neighborhoods because the covenants give them the right to exclude undesirable housing and, ultimately, undesirable people from their neighborhood.[25]

PUBLIC LAND USE LAWS: FENCING OUT THINGS AND PEOPLE

Public land use laws, the most common being zoning ordinances, also restrict how landowners can use their private property. As briefly mentioned in Chapter 2, U.S. cities have had land use laws since the early 1900s. The U.S. Department of Commerce's Advisory Committee on Zoning developed a model state zoning ordinance in 1922 to ensure that public land use regulations would protect owners from "unreasonable injury by neighbors who would seek private gain at his expense."[26] Once the committee developed this model law, municipalities rapidly enacted comprehensive zoning laws, and in 1926 the U.S. Supreme Court ruled that localities can legally enforce comprehensive zoning laws. The plaintiffs in *Euclid v. Ambler Realty* challenged

[25] Lee Anne Fennell, The Unfounded Home: Property Values beyond Property Lines (2009).

[26] Advisory Committee on Zoning of the Housing and Building Division, *The Zoning Law and Its Benefits* (1922), *available at* http://query.nytimes.com/mem/archive-free/pdf?res=F20613FC355B11728DDDAC0A94DE405B828EF1D3.

municipal zoning ordinances that prevented private owners from building apartments in the same vicinity as single-family, detached houses.[27]

In *Euclid*, the Supreme Court ruled that municipalities have the authority to enact and enforce a zoning ordinance if the ordinance is needed to ensure that the community develops in an orderly manner. The Court concluded that municipalities need to have the authority to enforce zoning ordinances to preserve the public health, safety, morals, and general welfare of the community. The opinion in *Euclid*, consistent with the Happy Homeownership Narrative, treated homeownership as more socially beneficial than renting. Apartments and their dwellers (i.e., renters) were undesirable and needed to be segregated from single-family, detached housing because:

> the coming of one apartment house is followed by others, interfering by their height and bulk with the free circulation of air and monopolizing the rays of the sun which otherwise would fall upon the smaller homes, and bringing, as their necessary accompaniments, the disturbing noises incident to increased traffic and business, and the occupation, by means of moving and parked automobiles, of larger portions of the streets, thus detracting from their safety and depriving children of the privilege of quiet and open spaces for play, enjoyed by those in more favored localities – until, finally, the residential character of the neighborhood and its desirability as a place of detached residences are utterly destroyed.[28]

In expressing its bias in favor of single-family, owner-occupied housing, the Supreme Court observed that, unless municipalities could control how private land in their communities was used, nothing prevented developers from placing apartment houses or other projects in open green space near single-family homes. According to the Court, municipalities needed to exercise their police powers to eliminate impediments to the development of single-family housing and to keep single-family homes separate from multifamily housing.

Early zoning ordinances primarily focused on commercial and industrial properties, like slaughter houses, fertilizer factories, and smelting plants, and they were designed to keep those uses away from residential neighborhoods. Homeowners fought to exclude those properties from their communities by arguing that they were nuisances that posed health risks to the residents in the neighborhoods. Early zoning laws also were used to exclude nonresidential but not industrial buildings like schools, churches, and mental hospitals from residential neighborhoods. Some neighborhoods sought to exclude these socially beneficial but nonresidential uses because "[c]hildren are noisy

[27] Euclid v. Ambler Realty, 272 U.S. 365 (1926).
[28] *Id.*

and sometimes mischievous"; because "private families are disturbed by the practicing of music" at churches; and because of "the depressing effect of [mental] institutions on the surrounding inhabitants."[29]

By ruling that comprehensive zoning laws are constitutional, the Supreme Court gave municipalities the power to favor and protect neighborhoods that had detached, single-family housing. *Euclid* also gave cities the right to exclude renter-occupied apartments, commercial uses, and – eventually – other undesirable uses from single-family neighborhoods, *even* if those undesirable uses had socially beneficial purposes. Once land became scarce, municipalities found it harder to exclude all objectionable industrial facilities and properties from residential areas, even though they continued to enact and use zoning ordinances to stabilize neighborhood property values and preserve the residential nature of neighborhoods. Municipalities were the first entities to use zoning laws to promote or preserve the integrity or character of existing neighborhoods, but property owners now use zoning laws to prevent other landowners from using their properties to site socially beneficial activities, like homeless shelters and halfway houses. Because homeowners have the right to notice and to be heard whenever a public zoning board conducts a hearing to consider a request for a land use variance, homeowners use public land use laws to fence out undesirable property uses and undesirable neighbors.

Socially beneficial but politically unpopular land uses, such as homeless shelters and halfway houses, do not necessarily pose health or safety risks like smelting plants or slaughterhouses did. Nonetheless, owners of single-family houses and HOAs routinely seek to fence these properties and residents out of their neighborhoods if the proposed use does not strictly conform to existing land use laws. Existing owners of single-family houses typically argue that one or more of the following undesirable consequences will result if the zoning board grants the rezoning request: property values will drop; there will be increased neighborhood traffic; existing homes will have blocked aerial views or increased shadows; neighborhood schools will become overcrowded; or there will be overall negative changes in the ambience or aesthetic appeal of the neighborhood.[30] If existing property owners can convince the zoning board that the socially necessary, albeit unpopular, project might pose a health or safety risk or cause property values to decline, they can prevent the owner or municipality from siting the project in their neighborhood.

[29] EDWARD M. BASSETT & KATHERINE MCNAMARA, ZONING: THE LAWS, ADMINISTRATION, AND COURT DECISIONS DURING THE FIRST TWENTY YEARS (Russell Sage Foundation ed., 1948).

[30] Krueckeberg, *supra* note 24.

Courts rarely agree that residents of halfway houses or homeless shelters are nuisances *per se*. Still, existing homeowners seek injunctions to exclude these properties by arguing that the residents of such houses and shelters will engage in criminal acts and that these potential neighbors pose safety risks to existing homeowners, their families, and the neighborhood. Like the property owners in *Euclid*, property owners argue that allowing any property uses other than single-family, detached housing in their neighborhoods should be prohibited because of the negative external harm the homeowners will suffer if those socially beneficial projects are placed in their neighborhoods. Homeowners also seek to exclude homeless people or parolees from their neighborhoods by arguing that having them as neighbors will have a depreciative effect on the value of their homes. Courts typically refuse to exclude these property uses from residential neighborhoods based *solely* on homeowners' speculative fears and intangible worries. Still, individual property owners and their HOAs are vigilant in their efforts to prevent attempts to place undesirable but societally beneficial properties in their neighborhoods, and they often succeed in excluding the undesirable properties (including the residents) from their neighborhoods.[31]

Individual homeowners, especially upper-income owners, feel that their status in the community gives them the right to decide how the community will develop and what activities will be allowed in their community. They also believe that they have the right to ignore whether a proposed property use (be it conforming or nonconforming) will have socially beneficial uses for the entire community. Instead, individual owners vigorously oppose zoning variances that would allow these properties to be sited in their neighborhoods if they think that the societally beneficial use will cause *their* property value to decrease and, thus, impose personal costs on *them*. In effect, public land use laws (including planning laws, subdivision standards, and zoning restrictions) have helped create and perpetuate the Not in My Backyard (NIMBY) syndrome.

Homeowners' fears that they will be harmed if an undesirable property use is placed in their neighborhoods are often unfounded and incorrect. Their determination to oppose these proposed developments is not surprising, though, because most people are risk-averse and unwilling to wait and see whether the undesired property that is proposed to be sited in their neighborhood will actually result in the harms they fear. But, homeowners' fears about how the presence of certain properties or neighborhood amenities and features will affect their homes are not totally irrational. Housing

[31] Nicholson v. Connecticut Half-Way House, Inc., 218 A.2d 383 (Conn. 1966).

research consistently shows that certain desired features (like parks and high-performing schools) increase the values of homes that are near those amenities, just as undesired neighborhood features (like high crime rates and low-performing schools) decrease housing values. Because the actual or perceived quality of life in a neighborhood is often capitalized into the value of a property, homeowners have reason to be anxious when municipalities or developers attempt to place certain undesirable properties or activities in their neighborhoods.[32]

FENCING OUT PEOPLE

Homeowners no longer view schools and churches as nuisances, and current land use policies and ordinances no longer assume that apartments and renters pose health or safety risks to children or destroy the character of owner-occupied neighborhoods. Still, the owners of single-family, detached houses regularly attempt to block developers' attempts to place multifamily units, high-rise apartments, small houses, and public or low-income housing in their neighborhoods. When individual homeowners use zoning laws to exclude property uses (or residents) from their neighborhoods to protect *their* private property interests or the character of their neighborhoods, though, they do more than just fence out a use or activity. Powerful and politically savvy homeowners and their HOAs often use public zoning and nuisance laws to also fence out lower-income residents.

Because local zoning laws give existing owners the privilege of being notified of requests to rezone properties in their neighborhoods, homeowners armed with numbers, their HOAs, and often a lawyer frequently organize and lobby to block rezoning requests that might place apartments, multifamily, or other affordable housing in their neighborhoods. Zoning laws and private covenants give homeowners the right to influence who can live near them and homeowners (especially those in higher-income neighborhoods) generally prefer to have neighbors who share their values about the neighborhood aesthetic and character. For example, homeowners and their HOAs lobby to make sure public land use laws will force builders to construct homes in ways that have the effect of excluding certain types of residents. Indeed, although existing homeowners ostensibly lobby to exclude certain types of *properties* from their neighborhoods, their lobbying efforts also exclude certain types of

[32] FENNELL, *supra* note 25. For a recent attempt by an organized neighborhood group to prevent a rezoning that would allow new homes to be built in a densely populated area of New York that was accessible to public transportation, see Roderick J. Hills, Jr. & David Schleicher, *Balancing the "Zoning Budget,"* 63 CASE WEST. L. REV. (2011).

people whom the homeowners have concluded have different values from the existing neighbors.

Based on what they perceive to be their privilege as property owners, homeowners routinely object to proposed zoning changes, even if the objection has the discriminatory effect of excluding people based on their race or socioeconomic status. Just as homeowners have always argued that allowing certain property uses (like slaughterhouses or schools) to be sited near them would change the character of their neighborhood, homeowners who lobby against multiunit or low-income housing essentially are arguing that certain *people* would not suitably blend into their neighborhood. Most homeowners will not admit that they want to exclude apartment dwellers or renters based on their fears about renters' socioeconomic class and race. Instead, homeowners disguise their elitist and racist beliefs by using neutral language. So, rather than saying that they do not want to live near blacks, Latinos, or poor people, white suburban homeowners make veiled references to "those people" and argue that having the children of apartment dwellers attend neighborhood schools will lower the academic rating and performance of the schools.

Similarly, urban homeowners oppose rezoning requests that would allow smaller and more affordable homes to be built based on arguments that the new housing would make a densely populated area (that was desirable to lower-income residents because it was accessible by public transportation) even more overcrowded.[33] Homeowners, especially wealthy ones, have successfully wielded their rights as stakeholders to fence out renters, poor people, and racial minorities. As a result, the mere mention of certain U.S. neighborhoods, cities, and counties (like South Central Los Angeles, Westchester County, Key West, or Martha's Vineyard) spontaneously invokes visual images of the people most likely to live in those locations.

Recently, homeowners have raised environmental concerns to fence out low-income residents from desirable upper-income suburban neighborhoods. While the "green" environmental movement generally is associated with progressive, left-wing politics, residents have used "open space" zoning laws to stop developers from building new affordable housing developments on suburban green spaces. Existing owners, relying on local land use laws and federal and state environmental laws, raise environmental concerns and often stall or thwart efforts to build moderate-income housing by arguing that the real estate developer did not consider the environmental impact of the private development on the community at large.

[33] LeeAnn Lands, The Culture of Property: Race, Class, and Housing Landscapes in Atlanta, 1880–1950 (2009); Hills & Schleicher, *supra* note 32.

Attempts to preserve green space and slow real estate development in areas where land is scarce are laudable from an environmental perspective. By restricting land that can be developed, however, these movements (alternatively referred to as anti-growth, no-growth, slow-growth, managed growth, or smart-growth) and the laws they have spawned have the (un)intended consequences of making developable land scarce, increasing land prices, and generally making it harder for low-income buyers to move into suburban or less dense urban communities. Of course, some property owners may not realize that "green" movements fence out lower-income residents. Arguments to restrict development in order to protect Mother Earth certainly sound less elitist or racist than arguments that seek to fence out property uses because the residents dislike a particular type of housing or resident. Despite the merits of restrictive zoning arguments based on environmental concerns, however, the fact remains that allowing existing homeowners to fence out socially desirable property uses makes it harder for lower-income renters to live in neighborhoods that may have higher-quality schools and other desirable community facilities.[34]

A recent land use controversy involving the wealthy community of Marin County, California, shows the power, and sometimes folly, of an HOA's attempt to fence out an undesirable property use (and its residents). Decades ago, Star Wars director George Lucas built a movie production company in Marin County and for years this production studio peacefully co-existed with the multi million dollar homes in the county. When Lucas tried to expand the facility, though, a recently resurrected (and until then defunct) HOA lodged vehement objections to his zoning request. The HOA objected to the proposed project because of the "threat" to the "nature" of the community and because of the light pollution. Lucas abandoned the proposed expansion, but – to the horror of the homeowners – then sold the entire property to a developer to build affordable housing in Marin County. This, of course, prompted homeowners to bemoan that Lucas had declared class warfare and was attempting to force them to live with drug dealers and "lowlife."[35]

It is fairly easy for existing homeowners and their HOAs to organize and lobby against a request for a zoning variance or to attempt to fence out undesirable property uses and residents because their individual property interests are clearly identifiable. In contrast, the owners of not-yet-built, low-income houses or the potential residents of halfway houses or homeless shelters are unknown, and these unknown renters or proposed residents cannot easily form a group

[34] William A. Fischel, *An Economic History of Zoning and a Cure for Its Exclusionary Effects*, Urban Studies (Feb. 2004).

[35] Norimitsu Onishi, *Lucasfilm Retreats in Battle with Wealthy Neighbors*, N.Y. Times (May 21, 2012).

to lobby in favor of the rezoning. While there may be merits to allowing individual homeowners to protect their individual property interests, letting private citizens use public laws to protect their property values essentially gives them the functional equivalent of publicly funded home-value insurance. Although these public laws let individual homeowners protect their private interests, renters and property owners in other neighborhoods receive no benefits for this de facto public insurance.

Moreover, as discussed in Chapter 8, allowing politically powerful property owners to fence out potentially harmful activities from their neighborhoods imposes negative externalities on people who rent or own homes in neighborhoods whose homeowners are not politically powerful or savvy. And, as is true with most conflicts between Powerful versus Powerless Americans, these undesirable but socially beneficial property uses are almost always placed – and affect the values of homes located in – lower-income and black or Latino neighborhoods.[36]

[36] Bassett & McNamara, *supra* note 29; Fischel, *supra* note 34.

4

The Homeownership Crisis

U.S. housing prices soared in the 1990s and early 2000s. This was very good for the United States because a strong housing market has historically been a bellwether for the overall strength of the U.S. economy. House price appreciation was also good for existing homeowners, especially because most household wealth is concentrated in housing. Unfortunately, home appreciation was not good for the financially strapped renters who were struggling to become the homeowners envisioned in the Happy Homeownership Narrative. To ensure that Americans continued to buy homes, the United States intervened yet again in housing finance markets. Like the government's massive intervention after the Great Depression, changes in the mortgage finance market during the 1990s and early 2000s succeeded in helping cash-strapped renters buy homes. Unlike the post-Depression interventions, however, these recent fixes were short-lived primarily because the government's attempt to solve the problem of stalled homeownership rates mischaracterized the actual problem Americans faced: far too many people simply cannot afford to be homeowners.

STALLED HOMEOWNERSHIP RATES, SOARING APPRECIATION RATES

As shown in Figure 4.1, even though overall homeownership rates now exceed 60 percent, less than 40 percent of U.S. households owned homes before the turn of the twentieth century. During the first few decades of the twentieth century, homeownership (mostly farm-ownership) rates remained relatively stable. Rates dipped only slightly in the first few years of the twentieth century as the United States shifted from a farming to a nonagrarian economy. Non-farm-ownership rates continued to have modest increases until the 1930s, when rates stalled and then fell because of the Great Depression.

Homeownership rates in the United States and in many countries in Western Europe started to soar in the 1940s largely because of the dramatic

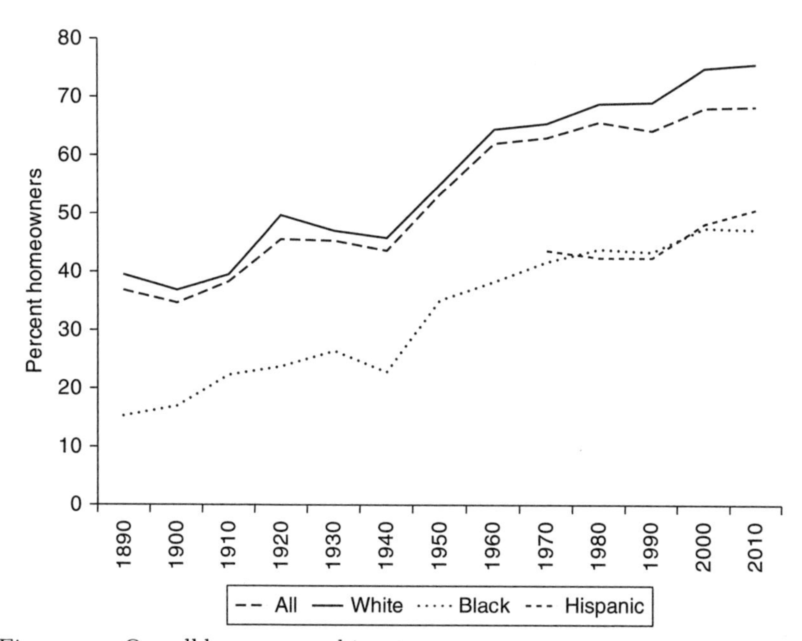

Figure 4.1. Overall home ownership rates.
Source: U.S. Census Bureau, Historical Census of Housing Tables.

demographic changes to the American family after World War II, most notably the explosive birth rates that created the Baby Boomers. Homeownership rates also increased because of sustained economic growth and prosperity during that period and because of the government's increased involvement with and interventions in the housing markets. Homeownership rates continued to grow during the 1970s when the large group of Baby Boomers started to form their own households. Rates then stalled starting in the 1980s as the Boomers' households shrank and later as they aged, sold their larger homes, and moved to rented housing or to live with family members.[1]

The Happy Homeownership Narrative accurately describes homeownership as one way Americans can increase household wealth. As shown in Figure 4.2, from 1940 to 2000 U.S. home values (adjusted for inflation) almost quadrupled. Housing price appreciation rates were fastest in the 1970s due

[1] Hous. and Household Econ. Statistics Div., U.S. Census Bureau, *Historical Census of Housing Tables: Homeownership* (2011), *available at* http://www.census.gov/hhes/www/housing/census/historic/owner.html; Vincent J. Cannato, *A Home of One's Own*, NAT'L AFF. (Spring 2010), at 72; Jón Rúnar Sveinsson, *Housing in Iceland in the Aftermath of the Global Financial Crisis*, in HOUSING MARKETS AND THE GLOBAL FINANCIAL CRISIS 60 (Ray Forrest & Ngai-Ming Yip eds., 2011).

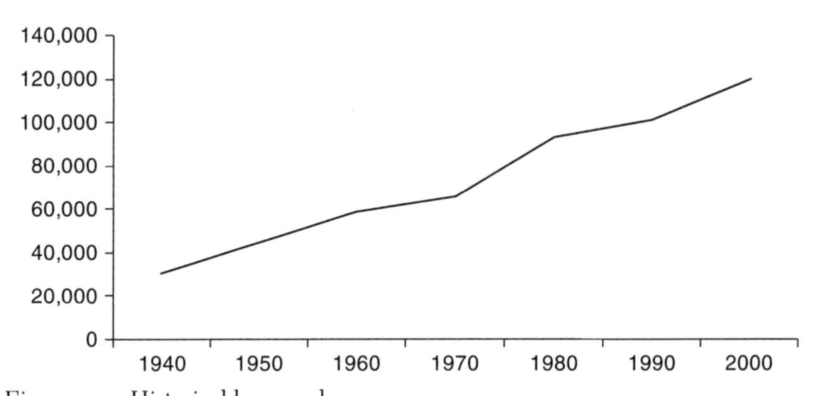

Figure 4.2. Historical home values.
Source: U.S. Census Bureau, Historical Census of Housing Tables: Home Values.

largely to the Boomers' increased demand for single-family houses. Rates then slowed during the 1980s once the largest wave of Boomers had moved into their own households. Rates rose by more than 40 percent during the 1970s (from $65,300 to $93,400, adjusted to 2000 dollars) but rose only 8.2 percent (from $93,400 to $101,100, adjusted to 2000 dollars) during the 1980s. Although homeownership rates stalled in the 1990s, home prices continued to rise and then soared during the housing boom. Between 2003 and 2007, home prices rose by more than 60 percent in some U.S. cities before they plummeted when the recession started in 2007.[2]

NO SAVINGS AND UNSTEADY INCOME

As noted in Chapter 3, renters historically needed to save enough money to make a 20 percent down payment if they wanted to buy a home with an FHA-insured, fixed rate mortgage (FRM) loan. Lenders would approve these favorable loans for borrowers who did *not* make a 20 percent down payment only if the borrowers bought private mortgage insurance (PMI), which guaranteed that the loan would be repaid.[3] In addition to protecting lenders from an increased risk that a borrower would default and not repay the mortgage loan, the down payment requirement helped instill the values of thrift and financial

[2] Edwin S. Mills & Ronald Simenauer, Homeownership as an Investment: Recent Trends and the Outlook for the 1990s (1991).

[3] Depending on the borrower's credit standing, private mortgage insurance can increase the monthly housing costs by $70–110 monthly for every $100,000 borrowed. See Joint Ctr. for Hous. Studies, Harvard Univ., *The State of the Nation's Housing* (2012), *available at* http://www.jchs.harvard.edu/sites/jchs.harvard.edu/files/son2012.pdf.

Figure 4.3. Personal saving rate.
Source: Bureau of Economic Analysis.

responsibility in borrowers by forcing them to save to buy their homes and then save to repay their mortgage loans over a fifteen- to thirty-year period. Forcing borrowers to make a down payment also helped them lower their total borrowing costs, because the down payment reduced the amount homeowners needed to borrow in order to buy their home. Furthermore, forcing borrowers to make a down payment helped them start building equity in their home as soon as they moved in.

While people who owned homes in the 1990s and early 2000s profited handsomely from house price appreciation, skyrocketing prices created an unaffordability problem for low- and moderate-income (LMI) Americans. By 2000, median home prices exceeded median household income fourfold in most U.S. markets. During this period, most renters who started to purchase homes but did not complete the purchase cited affordability as the reason they did not complete the purchase.[4] Since the 1980s, renters increasingly have been unable to save enough money to prepare for an income shock (e.g., reduced working hours or losing a job), an expenditure shock (e.g., uninsured medical expenses, college tuition), or a down payment on a house.

Thus, as shown in Figure 4.3, the U.S. savings rate rose to almost 11 percent in 1982 but dropped to less than 2 percent in 2005. Savings have declined for all ages, genders, and household types (married, single, with and without children), although some evidence suggests that homeowners saved even less

[4] Joint Ctr. for Hous. Studies, Harvard Univ., *The State of the Nation's Housing* (2006), *available at* http://www.jchs.harvard.edu/sites/jchs.harvard.edu/files/son2006.pdf; Joint Ctr. for Hous. Studies, Harvard Univ., *The State of the Nation's Housing* (2001), *available at* http://www.jchs.harvard.edu/sites/jchs.harvard.edu/files/son2001.pdf.

than renters because they viewed the value of their appreciating homes as a reliable source of savings. By the end of the 1990s, many households essentially had a *negative* savings rate: they saved less than they spent on goods and services.

In addition to having little in savings, LMI renters who wanted to buy a home in the 1990s had shrinking income. The homeowners in the Happy Homeownership Narrative have a reliable source of funds that allows them to save enough money each month to pay constant, equal monthly payments on their self-amortizing, fixed-interest rate loan. Since the 1980s, though, U.S. household income has been unsteady and stagnant for all but the highest paid workers. Until the end of the 1970s, earnings for workers at the bottom of the wage scale actually grew at faster rates than income growth for top earners. Since the 1990s, however, wages and total household income for LMI workers have been flat, have not kept pace with inflation, and have significantly lagged the income increases higher-paid workers have received.

Overall household income increased in the 1980s, but much of this increase was a result of the huge influx of Baby Boomers who joined the workforce. In a similar pattern, overall household incomes rose at the end of the 1990s as the Baby Boomers approached their peak earning years. Household income also increased during the 1980s because a large influx of women joined the workforce as more wives left home to work in the labor market. Except for this brief period in the late 1990s, however, wages for LMI workers have essentially been stagnant since the 1970s.[5]

While income has been stagnant for LMI workers, income for highly paid workers has soared, and the income gap between the highest and lowest income groups in the U.S. has grown dramatically since the 1970s. For example, while overall median wages for male workers increased by approximately 8 percent during the early 1980s, the increase for the top 10 percent (40 percent) dwarfed the increase for the bottom 10 percent of earners (5 percent). Similarly, while overall median wages for female workers increased by 37 percent, the increase for the top 10 percent of women was significantly larger (70 percent) than the increase for the bottom 10 percent of female workers (8 percent). The largest income growth, though, went to the group made famous by the Occupy Wall Street protestors in 2011–2012: the top 1 percent.[6]

Income for the top 1 percent of earners grew by 275 percent between 1979 and 2007. The next highest earners (top 80–99 percent) also saw their incomes

[5] Rolf Pendall et al., *Demographic Challenges and Opportunities for U.S. Housing Markets*, Bipartisan Policy Ctr. (Mar. 2012).

[6] Cong. Budget Office, U.S. Cong., *Trends in the Distribution of Household Income between 1979 and 2007* (2011).

soar by 65 percent, although this rate obviously pales in comparison to the top 1 percent of earners. The remaining 80 percent of the population had income increases over this period that ranged from 40 percent (for the middle class) to 18 percent (for the bottom 20 percent of earners). Ninety-five percent of all income gains went to the top 1 percent of earners in 2010, when the economy still had not recovered from the recession.

In addition to having the largest absolute income increases, the *share* of total income for the higher-income earners increased, while the share accruing to middle- and lower-income households decreased. That is, in 1979 the top 1 percent of earners received 8 percent of total income. By 2007, that share had increased to more than 17 percent. The rest of the top 20 percent of earners received substantially the same share of income in 1979 (35 percent) as they did in 2007 (36 percent). Middle-income workers were the biggest losers: they received 50 percent of total income in 1979 but only 43 percent in 2007. People in the bottom 20 percent, who only had 7 percent of total income in 1979, had an even smaller share (5 percent) by 2007.[7]

While top earners may still fit the profile of the owner portrayed in the Happy Homeownership Narrative, it has become increasingly harder for the rest of American workers to reasonably predict that their income will increase while they repay a mortgage loan over fifteen to thirty years. And, as discussed in the next sections, it is increasingly difficult for lower-skilled workers to even predict whether they will have jobs or what those jobs might be.

THE TRANSFORMATION OF THE U.S. WORKPLACE

LMI workers cannot afford to buy a home, and the wage inequality gap between them and top earners has expanded, largely because many of the lower-skilled but higher-wage jobs that existed in the 1970s disappeared. For decades, the unionized U.S. manufacturing sector provided full-time jobs that paid relatively high wages for less educated, middle-skilled workers. Since the 1970s, though, the number of high-wage, low-skilled manufacturing jobs has declined.

Job security for lower- and middle-skilled workers has been weakened in large part because of technological advances. Specifically, the increased use of factory robots and other computerized machinery has eliminated many of the higher-wage, repetitive-skilled production manufacturing jobs that existed in the 1970s. Additionally, computers and other computerized devices have reduced jobs in a number of middle-skilled professions outside the manufacturing sector, such as travel agents, professional photographers,

7 *Id.*

and proofreaders. Technological demands continue to threaten the number of repetitive, middle-skilled jobs in other professions (like accountants, office managers, secretaries, office assistants, and paralegals) that have been core to the U.S. middle class. The loss of these jobs has made it significantly harder for LMI workers to become and remain homeowners.

Technology has done more than just permanently eliminate jobs or replace workers with technology. Even though the U.S. economy has continued to create jobs, the labor market is no longer dominated by the unionized manufacturing sector. Instead, much of the new job creation has taken place in the lower-skilled, lower-paid, non-unionized service sector (e.g., the retail trade, food, cleaning, and personal services industries). Technology has dramatically changed the distribution of earnings in the United States because many of the jobs that are being created pay low wages and are low-skilled or pay high wages but require workers to have higher technology skills.

Technology has made some U.S. workers virtually unemployable outside of the service sector, and job opportunities for U.S. workers are increasingly polarized by skill level. Although there are significantly fewer high-wage jobs for lower- and middle-skilled workers, the number of lower-skilled, lower-wage jobs (especially in the service sector) for workers who lack a college degree has remained stable. In addition, while there have been significant reductions in the high-wage, low-skilled labor market and in the middle-skilled sales, administrative, and clerical workforce, since the 1980s job opportunities have expanded for college-educated, highly skilled workers who hold professional and managerial positions.[8]

Finally, over the last thirty years, the United States lost its global dominance in educational attainment. With a less educated workforce relative to other countries, even college-educated U.S. workers now compete with people abroad for middle-skilled jobs that historically would have been performed by workers in the United States. Because of changes to the U.S. workforce and because of technological advances, many jobs that historically were performed in the United States can now be performed almost anywhere. Since the 1980s, global competition for jobs and overall changes in the U.S. workforce have made it increasingly difficult for lower-skilled, lower-wage workers to save for a down payment, qualify for a low-cost mortgage loan, and then repay the loan and remain in their home.

[8] Philip Moss & Chris Tilly, Stories Employers Tell: Race, Skill, and Hiring in America (2001); Cong. Budget Office, U.S. Cong., *Changes in the Distribution of Workers' Hourly Wages between 1979 and 2009* (2011); David Autor, *The Polarization of Job Opportunities in the U.S. Labor Market: Implications for Employment and Earnings* (2010); Harry J. Holzer & Marek Hlavac, *An Uneven Road and Then a Cliff: U.S. Labor Markets since 2000*, Project U.S. 2010 (2011), *available at* http://www.s4.brown.edu/us2010/Data/Report/report4.pdf.

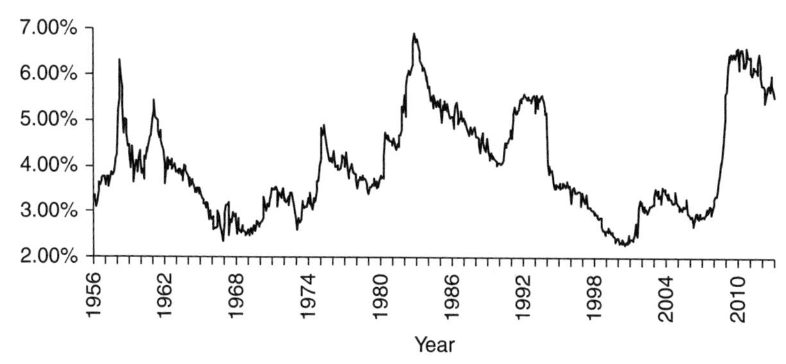

Figure 4.4. Percentage of workforce involuntarily employed part-time.
Source: Bureau of Labor Statistics.

UNEMPLOYMENT AND UNDER EMPLOYMENT

Even though official U.S. unemployment rates were fairly low until the recent recession, income for all but the highest-paid, highest-educated workers has been unsteady and unpredictable since the 1970s because many employers have eliminated full-time jobs and replaced those jobs with temporary or part-time jobs. To save costs, employers have reduced the average weekly hours for full-time workers and have replaced many full-time employees with temporary, part-time workers. As shown in Figure 4.4, this has caused an increasing number of U.S. workers to be involuntarily under employed. Involuntarily employed, part-time workers prefer to work full-time but cannot because those jobs no longer exist or are simply harder to find.

Many of the manufacturing jobs that provided retirement and medical benefits in the 1970s have disappeared. Increasingly, jobs that are created in the service sector are temporary, pay low wages, and provide few (or no) benefits. Many of these jobs pay wages that are so low that it is virtually impossible for the workers who hold these jobs to live above the poverty level. Indeed, the drastic decrease in the number of Americans who have employer-provided pensions is one reason household savings have declined since the 1970s. Fewer unionized workplaces, growing disparities in earnings (and power) between workers and managers, corporate layoffs, restructurings, and downsizings have become the new norm for U.S. workers. This new financial norm has made it harder for many American workers to afford to buy a house.[9]

[9] For example, between 1979 and 2009 the share of employees who were covered by a union collective bargaining agreement fell from 27 percent to 14 percent with unions in the private manufacturing or construction sector seeing the greatest decline in membership. See Cong. Budget Office, *supra* note 6.

THE BUBBLE: MORTGAGE INNOVATION TO THE RESCUE

Because so many Americans in the 1980s had stagnant or unpredictable income, many renters found it increasingly hard to qualify for a traditional, fixed rate, fifteen- to thirty-year mortgage loan. The U.S. government took a number of steps in the 1990s and early 2000s to respond to this housing unaffordability crisis. For example, in response to stalled housing sales, Congress enacted the Federal Housing Enterprises Financial Safety and Soundness Act of 1992 (the GSE Act).

The GSE Act imposed housing goals that required Fannie Mae and Freddie Mac to increase the number of mortgages they bought that provided housing for LMI households and households that live in areas traditionally underserved by the mortgage market, which included most black and Latino neighborhoods. Requiring GSEs to purchase nonconforming and often subprime mortgages issued to lower-income borrowers would, Congress correctly assumed, give lenders an incentive to originate more of these loans. As discussed in Chapter 8, though, some have argued that this Act forced lenders to originate riskier mortgage loans and that this requirement played a major role in the housing crash.

In response to the housing affordability crisis, the Clinton White House launched *The National Homeownership Strategy: Partners in the American Dream* in 1995. This *Strategy* proposed that the Secretary of HUD (then, Henry G. Cisneros) work with nonprofit organizations, local government leaders, and the housing industry to find ways to make buying a house more affordable, to make financing more readily available, and to simplify the home buying process. The explicit goal of the *Strategy* was to increase homeownership rates by 8 million families between 1995 and 2000. The George W. Bush administration also made homeownership a key part of its agenda, finding that "[h]omeownership remains the largest and best investment a family can make for the long term."[10] Like the Clinton administration, the Bush administration also sought to increase overall homeownership rates.

As was true when the United States intervened in mortgage finance markets after the Depression, when housing sales stalled in the 1990s, the U.S. government viewed itself as being in a partnership with realtors, home builders, and mortgage bankers to increase homeownership rates, especially for black and Latino Americans. Rather than reevaluate whether it remained good public policy to encourage cash-strapped renters to buy houses, both the

[10] The White House, *Homeownership: The President's Agenda to Expand Opportunities to Homeowners* (2007), *available at* http://georgewbush-whitehouse.archives.gov/infocus/homeownership.

Clinton and Bush administrations responded to the unaffordability problem, stalled homeownership rates, and sluggish home sales by encouraging mortgage originators to use creative financing methods to innovate new mortgage products to help cash-strapped renters buy homes. And they did, indeed, create products that were virtually unheard of in the mortgage industry.[11]

TECHNOLOGY AND THE STREAMLINED LOAN APPLICATION PROCESS

Since the Depression, the overwhelming majority of all home mortgage loans have been FRMs. Despite their popularity, affordability, and predictability, applying for a traditional, self-amortizing FRM was a burdensome, time-consuming process. Borrowers could qualify to purchase a home with these low-cost mortgage loans only if they participated in a rigorous and detailed application process. At a minimum, borrowers were forced to visit the bank, meet face-to-face with a loan officer, and complete a detailed loan application. The loan officer would then review the application and verify the accuracy of the borrower's stated income, assets, and debts. The lender, aided by a real estate appraiser, would then confirm that the house the borrower wanted to buy was worth at least as much as the total amount of the mortgage loan. Only after the bank confirmed this information and determined a borrower's creditworthiness and likely risk of default would the lender approve the borrower's mortgage loan application.[12]

Starting in the 1990s, Fannie Mae and private lenders made technological improvements that significantly streamlined the mortgage application loan process. Because of automated underwriting systems, the time it took to evaluate and approve mortgage loans and the lenders' transaction costs to approve those loans decreased drastically. Gone were the days where the borrower

[11] *Hearing before the Subcommittee on Housing and Community Opportunity of the House Committee on Financial Services*, 108th Cong. 1 (2003); *Hearing before the Committee on Banking, Housing, and Urban Affairs of the U.S. Senate, on Increasing Minority Homeownership, and Expanding Homeownership to All Who Wish to Attain It:*, 108th Cong. 1st Session (Jun. 12, 2003) (statement of Mel Martinez, U.S. Department of Housing and Urban Development Secretary); William E. Nelson & Norman R. Williams, *Suburbanization and Market Failure: An Analysis of Government Policies Promoting Suburban Growth and Ethnic Assimilation*, 27 FORDHAM URB. L.J. 197, 226–31 (1999) (tracing the history of government intervention in the housing markets to expand homeownership by loosening financial requirements).

[12] Richard K. Green & Susan M. Wachter, *The American Mortgage in Historical and International Context*, 19–4 J. ECON. PERSP. (Fall 2005); Christopher L. Foote et al., *Why Did So Many People Make So Many Ex Post Bad Decisions? The Causes of the Foreclosure Crisis*, Fed. Res. Bank of Boston Policy Paper Discussion Series (2012); Allen J. Fishbein & Patrick Woodall, *Exotic or Toxic? An Examination of the Non-Traditional Mortgage Market for Consumers and Lenders*, Consumer Fed'n of Am. 28 (2006), *available at* http://www.consumerfed.org/pdfs/exotic_toxic_mortgage_report0506.pdf.

was forced to appear physically in a bank to provide detailed asset and debt information on documents that a loan officer would then personally evaluate. Borrowers no longer were forced to wait for one to two months to be approved for the mortgage loan. Technological changes in the mortgage application process let homeowners apply for a loan online and be approved for the mortgage within moments after the applicant clicked the word "submit."

Another dramatic change to the loan approval process involved lenders' increased reliance on commercial, automated credit scoring devices. Although they were widely used by mortgage originators during the housing boom, these devices were developed to be used to approve credit cards. Credit scoring devices were *never* designed to predict whether borrowers would be able to repay a long-term mortgage or whether they would have the capacity to repay (or refinance) an adjustable rate mortgage (ARM) once the interest rates increased. Because those scoring devices could not verify a borrower's income, lenders protected themselves from the increased risk of default by charging borrowers higher interest rates. As a result, while technological advances may have made the loan application process quicker and may have allowed more borrowers to qualify for loans, these loans were higher-cost and higher-risk. These "easy" loans looked nothing like the mortgage loans that emerged after the homeownership crisis during the Depression or the loans envisioned in the Happy Homeownership Narrative.

DOCUMENTING INCOME

Renters who wanted to purchase a house with an FHA-insured mortgage loan historically needed to document that they could afford to repay the loan. Specifically, before the housing boom, borrowers needed to confirm their employment status and show that their payment-to-income ratio (for the mortgage loan) did not exceed 28 percent and their debt-to-income ratio (for all consumer loans) did not exceed 36 percent. They also were required to show that they would have savings that equaled at least two monthly mortgage payments *after* paying closing costs. In effect, before the boom, renters would not be approved for a mortgage loan to buy a house unless they could prove that they were the financially responsible homeowners envisioned in the Happy Homeownership Narrative.[13]

During the housing boom, banks, mortgage originators, and even the U.S. government essentially abandoned the presumption that potential homeowners would be denied a mortgage loan if they failed to show that they

[13] Robert W. Kolb, The Financial Crisis of Our Time 2–4 (2011).

were thrifty and financially responsible. To make it easier for cash-strapped borrowers to qualify for a mortgage, lenders approved loans without verifying the accuracy of the income the borrower stated in the loan application. These loans later came to be referred to as "no doc" (no documentation) or "low doc" (low documentation) loans because borrowers were not required to document their income. These loans were pejoratively labeled "liar" loans because borrowers sometimes fraudulently inflated their incomes, while mortgage originators sometimes encouraged borrowers to lie about their income or altered the borrowers' income to ensure they qualified for the mortgage loan.[14]

Approving a mortgage loan without requiring a borrower to document his or her income *might* be justified if the borrower is a high-income worker who can afford the monthly payments but might prefer not to disclose that income. Waiving the requirement also might be reasonable for a self-employed or seasonal worker who may have high income but cannot verify that income. But lenders approved "liar" loans for borrowers from all income groups. As discussed in Chapter 5, many of the borrowers who purchased homes during the housing boom could not afford the loans either when they applied for the loans or when they later defaulted on those loans. Although no-doc loans existed in the 1990s, they were rarely approved before the 2001–2005 housing boom. By 2005, though, these loans accounted for more than 10 percent of all subprime loan originations, and by 2006 more than 35 percent of newly originated subprime loans were either low- or no-doc loans.[15]

ABANDONING THE DOWN PAYMENT REQUIREMENT

Historically, borrowers were required to make a down payment, even if it was smaller than the 20 percent requirement that lenders imposed after the Depression. As noted earlier, banks generally refused to approve high

[14] These loans were issued globally and had a number of variations. Some were "no income, no asset" (NINA) loans, which did not require a borrower to document their income or assets and could be approved based on the borrower's stated employment, credit history, the property value, and the down payment (if any). Other variations included "no income, no asset, no employment" (NINANE) loans (where the borrower did not have to disclose income, assets, *or* employment) and ratio loans (where the borrower did not have to list income, employer's name, or debt-to-income ratio). *Frenzy of Risky Mortgages Leaves Path of Destruction*, N.Y. TIMES (May 8, 2007); Kenneth R. Harney, *The Lowdown on Low–Doc Loans*, WASH. POST (Nov. 25, 2006), at F01.

[15] Joint Ctr. for Hous. Studies, Harvard Univ., *The State of the Nation's Housing* (2005), *available at* http://www.jchs.harvard.edu/publications/markets/son2005; Andrew Haughwout et al., *Real Estate Investors, the Leverage Cycle, and the Housing Market Crisis*, Fed. Res. Bank N.Y. Staff Reps. (Sep. 2011); Gene Amromin et al., *Complex Mortgages* (Nat. Bur. Econ. Research, Working Paper No. 17315, 2011), *available at* http://www.nber.org/papers/w17315.

loan-to-value (LTV) loans because they worried that borrowers who made a relatively low down payment were more likely to strategically default on their mortgage loan (i.e., to choose to default because they lacked equity in their home), even if they could afford to make the monthly payments. In addition to the borrowers' potentially higher risk of default, lenders avoided high LTV loans because they could not sell those loans to the GSEs on the secondary mortgage market, and the GSEs generally would not securitize those loans.

It was possible for people to buy homes with less than a 20 percent down payment before the housing bubble. Until the 1980s, however, more than 60 percent of home buyers put at least 20 percent down on their homes. Fewer than 20 percent of home buyers made down payments that were smaller than 10 percent before the housing boom. While only a small percentage (4 percent) of homeowners made down payments of 5 percent or less in 1990, that percentage soared to 16 percent by 2000. Similarly, while the median down payment for a mortgage loan was 9 percent in 2000, by the mid-2000s more than 20 percent of all home buyers put zero down on their homes. By the time the housing market collapsed, almost 30 percent of all borrowers bought homes but made no down payment.[16]

Because the U.S. savings rate started to drop and potential homeowners lacked funds to make a down payment, it became harder for borrowers to be approved for a government-backed loan. Before the housing boom, borrowers could be approved for an FHA-insured loan only if they purchased PMI. Even though the PMI market largely evaporated during the Depression, it reappeared in the 1970s, and a robust PMI market made it possible for some cash-strapped borrowers to buy homes when homeownership rates initially stalled in the 1990s. To make it even easier for borrowers to buy a house, make no down payment, but avoid purchasing expensive PMI, lenders during the housing boom created a new dual loan system commonly referred to as "piggyback" loans.

The piggyback loan system lets a borrower take out a first mortgage (typically for 80 percent of the value of the home) and then a simultaneous second mortgage (or line of credit) for the remainder of the sales prices of the home. Piggyback loans initially were marketed to lower-income borrowers who lacked the savings to make a down payment and did not want (or could not afford) to buy PMI. Although borrowers could always cancel the PMI if they repaid enough of the loan to reduce the remaining loan balance (typically to

[16] Joint Ctr. for Hous. Studies, Harvard Univ., *The State of the Nation's Housing* (2002), *available at* http://www.jchs.harvard.edu/sites/jchs.harvard.edu/files/son2002.pdf; Bipartisan Millennial Hous. Comm'n, *Meeting Our Nation's Housing Challenges* (2002), *available at* http://govinfo.library.unt.edu/mhc/MHCReport.pdf; United League of Savings Institutions, *Homeownership: Celebrating the American Dream* (1984); Kolb, *supra* note 13.

equal 90 percent of the home's value), piggyback loans were marketed as being cheaper than PMI. During the housing boom, lenders began to aggressively market these loans to higher-income borrowers as "smart" financial products that let borrowers choose whether to invest money in their home (in the form of a down payment) or to put their money in another investment vehicle. Whether a borrower is high- or low-income, and regardless of whether the piggyback system is a wise investment strategy, having two mortgage obligations increases the risk that the homeowner will default on one of those loans and lose the home. Moreover, the increased use of low-doc, no-doc, and piggyback loans gave borrowers no incentive to be the thrifty, financially responsible savers envisioned in the Happy Homeownership Narrative.[17]

SUBPRIME LENDING

Before the housing boom, cash-strapped households that lacked savings and made no (or very small) down payments also would not qualify for a traditional low-cost, low-risk mortgage loan because their debt-to-income ratio was too high and they could not satisfy lenders' underwriting criteria. Borrowers who lacked savings, had stagnant income, and had high debt loads could only qualify for a high LTV or piggyback loan. These loans posed higher default risk to lenders, so to protect themselves, lenders charged the borrowers who accepted those loans higher rates of interest. These and other subprime mortgage products fueled the housing boom and ultimately led to the housing bust.

Subprime mortgage products are designed to be offered to borrowers who are at a higher risk of defaulting on their payments. Typically, this includes borrowers with limited credit histories, those who have filed for bankruptcy or defaulted on loans, those with high debt ratios, and those who have low credit scores. To compensate lenders for the extra risks associated with lending to a less creditworthy borrower, subprime loans carry higher interest rates and costs. Borrowers generally pay more in the form of points than prime loans, and subprime loans often impose prepayment penalties on borrowers who attempt to refinance their loan to take advantage of lower interest rates.

While subprime loans can have fixed-interest rates, the bulk of the loans homeowners used to buy homes during the housing boom were

[17] Louise Story, *Home Equity Frenzy Was a Bank Ad Come True*, N.Y. Times (Aug. 14, 2008); *Calculated Risk: Assessing Non-Traditional Mortgage Products: Hearing before the Subcommittee on Housing and Transportation and the Subcommittee on Economic Policy of the Senate Committee on Banking, Housing, and Urban Affairs*, 109th Cong., at 6 (Sep. 20, 2006) (statement of William A. Simpson on behalf of the Mortgage Insurance Companies of America).

ARMs. Adjustable rate mortgages pose higher risks of default for borrowers, because once the initial "teaser" rates expire and interest rates reset upward, a low initial monthly payment can dramatically increase based on the new, higher, "fully indexed" interest rate. The risk of a substantially higher monthly loan payment made these products substantially similar to the pre-Depression loans that had unaffordable balloon payments that borrowers often could not pay, *especially* if they were employed.

For most of the twentieth century, GSEs could neither purchase nor securitize subprime loans. Because lenders could not quickly sell these subprime loans in the secondary market and only private issuers could securitize these loans, lenders were unwilling to significantly increase the volume of loans they originated for borrowers who lacked enough savings to make a down payment. This all changed in the 1990s once the United States allowed GSEs to purchase riskier, high LTV loans made to borrowers with blemished credit. By the end of the 1990s, the subprime mortgage monster was born.

Subprime mortgage lending accounted for less than 9 percent of all mortgage originations in the 1990s. By the height of the 2001–2005 housing boom (once GSEs could purchase these higher-risk loans), however, more than 20 percent of all mortgage originations were subprime. Subprime mortgage originations rose from $160 billion in 2001 to more than $600 billion in 2005 and 2006.[18] These loans made it easier for cash-strapped renters to buy a house, but they are not the low-cost, low-risk mortgages envisioned in the Happy Homeownership Narrative. Moreover, as will be discussed in greater detail in Chapters 8 and 9, much of the increase in subprime lending was concentrated in lower- and moderate-income neighborhoods and, as has now been exposed in settlements between the United States and state Attorney Generals, both large lenders and smaller mortgage originators disproportionately pushed these high-cost, high-risk loans on black and Latino borrowers.

[18] See Kolb, *supra* note 13; Fed. Res. Bd. of Governors 0, *Consumer Handbook on Adjustable-Rate Mortgages* 7 (2006); *Subprime and Predatory Lending: New Regulatory Guidance, Current Market Conditions, and Effects on Regulated Institutions: Hearing before the Subcommittee on Financial Institutions and Consumer Credit of the House Committee on Financial Services*, 110th Cong. 8 (2007) [hereinafter *Subprime and Predatory Lending*] (statement of Shelia C. Bair, on behalf of the Federal Deposit Insurance Corporation); Joint Ctr. for Hous. Studies, Harvard Univ., *The State of the Nation's Housing* (2004), *available at* http://www.jchs.harvard.edu/sites/jchs.harvard.edu/files/son2004.pdf.

THE RETURN OF THE NON-AMORTIZING LOAN

Self-amortizing mortgage loans have been the norm since the Depression. In 2003, during the early stage of the housing boom, more than 95 percent of residential mortgages were fully amortizing, long-term FRMs or ARMs that had initial interest-rate periods of five–seven years. As more borrowers struggled to buy homes during the 2000s, though, they increasingly turned to non-amortizing and even *negative* amortization loans to finance their home purchases. By 2005, almost 30 percent of residential mortgages were nontraditional mortgage products that were either non-amortizing or had high interest rates. Once the housing bubble popped in 2008, however, the percentage of these high risk loans relative to all mortgage loan products dropped to less than 2 percent.[19]

The most common type of non-amortizing loan that borrowers used to buy homes during the housing boom was the Interest Only (IO) mortgage. An IO mortgage loan gives a borrower the option of making a monthly payment that includes only accumulated interest – not principal – over an initial ("teaser") period. Interest rates on IO loans are higher because of their higher risks, but initial loan payments on these mortgages are lower than the monthly payments for amortizing, government-backed FRMs. Initial monthly payments are lower because borrowers are not required to make full principal plus accrued-interest payments. The IO mortgage becomes a fully amortizing loan after this initial teaser period ends, and the unpaid interest and principal is added to the principal loan balance.

Unlike the non-amortizing loans borrowers used to buy homes before the Depression, IO loans *negatively* amortize because the unpaid principal and interest that is added to the principal loan balance cause the loan to increase (not decrease), even though the borrower makes monthly payments. Initially, IO loans were marketed primarily to creditworthy, high-income borrowers who were willing to accept the higher risks associated with a loan whose payments would soar after the teaser period because these borrowers anticipated future income increases and anticipated that their houses would appreciate in value. Eventually, though, lenders approved IO mortgages for borrowers whose income was not sufficient to make the mortgage payments once the loan fully amortized.

Another non-amortizing mortgage product that lenders introduced during the housing boom to increase home sales was the payment option ARM loan. Like IO loans, option ARMs have low initial interest rates and do

[19] Amromin et al., *supra* note 15.

not require borrowers to make a full amortized payment (of principal plus interest). Option ARMs let borrowers choose the amount of the monthly loan payment from a range of payment options, which include interest only, amounts less than interest, or in some instances "zero" because option ARMs give borrowers the option of skipping a monthly payment altogether. Of course, the unpaid principal and interest is added to the principal balance, which makes option ARMs (like IO loans) negatively amortizing loans. While less than 1 percent of borrowers used IO or negative amortization loans to purchase a home in 2003, by 2005 almost 37 percent of ARMs were IO loans. Similarly, although payment option loans were largely nonexistent before the housing boom, by 2006 almost 10 percent of all ARMs were payment option loans.[20]

Finally, lenders introduced a mortgage product during the housing boom that essentially turned homeowners into renters. Specifically, lenders created loan products with extended maturity periods that gave owners as long as forty–fifty years to repay their mortgages. While these extended maturity loans lowered monthly mortgage payments, these loans essentially converted what was meant to be a fifteen- to thirty-year house buying process into what was essentially a long-term rent-to-own arrangement with a lender. These extended maturity loans and the other exotic, nontraditional loans that lenders approved during the housing boom bore little resemblance to the traditional self-amortizing FRM that the U.S. government encouraged lenders to use after the Depression. Moreover, these loans were most decidedly not the low-cost, low-risk ones envisioned in the Happy Homeownership Narrative.

While borrowers from the end of the Depression until the 1980s assumed that their mortgage applications would either be approved or denied, mortgage market innovations during the housing boom created a new approval category: approved but with higher costs and higher risks. Despite the higher costs and risks associated with the innovated loan products created during the housing boom, the streamlined approval process, relaxed lending standards, and low interest rates helped borrowers with weak credit histories and little or no savings get approved for a mortgage loan. Moreover, the nontraditional mortgage products that lenders innovated at the behest of the U.S. government succeeded in increasing home sales and increasing homeownership rates for lower-income home buyers. In 2004, homeownership rates hit an all-

[20] Kolb, *supra* note 13; Urban Inst., *Housing in the Nation's Capital* 32 (2009); Joint Ctr. for Hous. Studies (2006), *supra* note 4.

time high of more than 69 percent, and these innovations can be credited with helping cash-strapped renters buy homes and remain in those homes ... at least for a while. Because, however, LMI households continued to have stagnant wages and unstable employment, the higher-default risks associated with the high-cost, nontraditional loan products soon pushed them out of their homes.[21]

THE BUBBLE POPS

During the housing boom, houses appreciated at rates that far exceeded the modest increase in overall household income. Organizations, including both neutral, well-respected housing groups and groups funded by the banking industry, understood the risk that surging home prices and unstable household finances might cause the housing market to crash. For example, the prestigious Harvard Joint Center for Housing Studies observed in a 2002 report on the State of the Nation's Housing that "[w]hile surging home prices have sparked fears of a housing market collapse, widespread price declines are unlikely because home prices in most areas have increased in line with income growth." The 2002 report went on to ominously note, however, that

> job losses have forced more mortgage borrowers into foreclosure, increased the number of homeowners spending half or more of their incomes on housing, and softened some rental markets. In addition, expansion of mortgage credit to borrowers with past payment problems has elevated foreclosure risks. Finally, increased mortgage debt levels and growing shares of homebuyers with high loan-to-value ratios have raised concerns about the amount of debt carried.

The Joint Center, like U.S. leaders, minimized the troubling disconnect between stagnant income and home prices by focusing on *overall* income growth during the housing boom.

While U.S. incomes increased during the boom, as noted earlier in this chapter, almost 95 percent of the income gains between 1979 and 2007 went to the top 1 percent of earners. The Joint Center also minimized the risk of a housing crash by stressing that

> thanks to lower interest rates, owners have been able to increase their debt loads without necessarily adding to their monthly payments. In addition,

[21] Pendall et al., *supra* note 5; Joint Ctr. for Hous. Studies, Harvard Univ., *The State of the Nation's Housing* (2011), *available at* http://www.jchs.harvard.edu/publications/markets/son2011/son2011.pdf.

> strong home price appreciation has increased home values, providing fully 88 percent of mortgage borrowers with equity of 20 percent or more in 2001.[22]

The housing bubble would not pop, everyone assumed, because home prices would continue to increase and homeowners would always be able to afford their unaffordable mortgages and pay their other expenses by refinancing those mortgages and using their extracted home equity to pay their bills.

While housing appreciation helped increase overall household wealth, soaring appreciation rates during the housing boom were often the result of housing speculation. That is, housing prices soared in many regions because of the large number of investors and speculators who could pay cash for expensive homes. Bidding wars became commonplace during the housing boom because of cash-only buyers, and these wars drove up already high housing prices and made housing even more expensive for noninvestors (i.e., homeowners). Nervous renters who worried that they might never be able to buy homes joined the bidding wars and were willing to pay prices that far exceeded the seller's initial asking price for totally nondescript homes – especially if those homes were in markets that had limited available housing. Potential homeowners willingly paid astronomical prices for nondescript homes because they assumed that they could get mortgage financing and because they mistakenly believed that the houses would continue to appreciate in price.

Home prices reached an all-time high at the beginning of 2007, but by December 2007, the market crashed. By 2008, the United States was in what has come to be known as the Great Recession, which the National Bureau of Economic Research determined to be the period beginning in December 2007 and continuing through June 2009. This housing collapse had all the characteristics of a classic boom and crash.

During the bubble, demand for single-family housing increased at a frenzied pace, and this demand caused housing prices to skyrocket. Lenders significantly relaxed their standards and financed these housing purchases. This easy credit discouraged thrift and financial responsibility and instead gave buyers an incentive to engage in risky, speculative, and often reckless behavior. Then – predictably – housing sales slowed, housing appreciation stalled, foreclosures increased, banks tightened lending standards, the housing bubble popped, and the market crashed. Cash-strapped homeowners who faced a housing unaffordability problem in the 1990s found themselves facing an even

[22] Joint Ctr. for Hous. Studies, Harvard Univ., *The State of the Nation's Housing* (2003), *available at* http://www.jchs.harvard.edu/sites/jchs.harvard.edu/files/son2003.pdf.

worse problem after the bubble popped in the mid-2000s: housing that was suddenly *too* affordable because homes started depreciating in value.

When home prices soared, the share of equity homeowners had in their houses increased. When home prices plummeted, homeowner equity and household wealth plunged as well. For example, while U.S. households had $13.5 trillion in home equity at the beginning of 2006, this number plummeted to $5.3 trillion by the beginning of 2009. In addition to having significantly less in home equity, many homeowners also had crushing mortgage debt when the housing market crashed because they had increased their mortgage debt during the housing boom through cash-out refinances, second mortgages, and home equity lines of credit. Once housing prices started to fall and lenders refused to refinance the high-cost mortgages they had approved during the housing boom, homeowners of all ages, races, and income groups started defaulting on their mortgages.[23]

The total number of prime mortgage loans that went into default exceeded the number of subprime ARMs largely because the subprime loan market has always been smaller than the prime mortgage loan market. However, subprime loans (be they FRM or ARM), negative amortization loans, and high LTV loans had the highest delinquency and default rates, foreclosed more quickly, and constituted a disproportionately large share of overall foreclosures. These high-cost, high-risk loans had higher default rates in part because some lenders made little attempt to verify whether borrowers could actually afford these loans when they approved them during the housing boom. By the spring of 2007 there was more than $1 trillion outstanding in subprime mortgages, and by March 2008 approximately one in eleven subprime mortgages were either past due or in foreclosure. Likewise, at various times during the recession, subprime ARM loan foreclosures accounted for more than half of total foreclosure filings, even though they were never more than 15 percent of all outstanding mortgages before the housing crash.[24]

In general, homeowners defaulted on the mortgage payments because they could not afford the payments. Other borrowers, especially investors and speculators, chose to strategically default on their mortgages and not even attempt to repay their loans, even if they had the funds to do so. Borrowers were especially likely to default if the mortgages were "underwater" (i.e., the value of

[23] Rajashri Chakrabarti et al., *Household Debt and Saving during the 2007 Recession*, Fed. Res. Bank N.Y. Staff Reps., No. 482 (Jan. 2011).

[24] Fed. Res. Bd. of Governors, *The U.S. Housing Market: Current Conditions and Policy Considerations* (2012); Kenneth P. Brevoort & Cheryl R. Cooper, *Foreclosure's Wake: The Credit Experiences of Individuals Following Foreclosure*, (Fin. & Econ. Discussion Series, Fed. Reserve Bd., Working Paper No. 2010–59, 2010).

their homes was lower than their mortgage balances). Indeed, although it was inconsistent with the assumptions and premises underlying the Happy Homeownership Narrative, homeowners increasingly started to view their homes as debts – not assets – and some chose to simply walk away from their housing debt and their homes rather than even attempt to repay the loans. Housing prices stopped dropping by 2013 and home sales increased in some U.S. housing markets, but four years after the recession was declared officially over, many homeowners continue to struggle to remain in their Home Sweet Home.[25]

[25] Of course, even though homeowners may view their houses solely as a debt, they technically cannot walk away from the debt (unless they have a non-recourse loan), because they are still liable for the mortgage debt even after the lender repossesses the house.

5

Homeowner Harm and the Blame Game

The recent housing slump had a more devastating effect on the economy than any U.S. housing crisis since the Depression. Homeowners with no savings, no jobs, and stagnant income (assuming they were employed) found themselves trapped in homes they could not afford and could not sell. Much to the dismay of homeowners, the same lenders who aggressively marketed and eagerly approved the exotic high-risk loans that let them buy homes during the housing boom were unwilling to let them refinance those high-cost, high-risk loans. The short- and long-term harms that the recent recession has had on U.S. households have been catastrophic, and every entity that participated in the housing boom shares part of the blame for causing the housing crash. Everyone – lenders, borrowers, and the U.S. government – had unrealistic and unsustainable expectations about continued house price appreciation. And each participant engaged in risky behavior because of those expectations.

HARM: BY THE NUMBERS

By 2005, lenders and investors began to lose confidence in the value of subprime mortgages and mortgage-backed securities (MBS). Lenders became less willing to lend to struggling homeowners (or to the entities who had invested in these high-risk MBSs). Lenders set higher thresholds for borrowers to qualify for mortgage loans, and by 2011 even the Federal Housing Administration (FHA) approved fewer loans to borrowers with low credit scores. Because of these more restrictive lending requirements, the percentage of high loan-to-value (LTV) mortgage loans to borrowers who made less than a 10 percent down payment dropped from 30 percent in 2007 to 7 percent by 2009.

Because of tighter lending standards, fewer homeowners were able to continue treating their homes like ATMs. As a result, while the proportion of cash-out refinances (where homeowners borrowed against their homes to remove equity) to total mortgage loan refinances was 70 percent in 2006, the proportion was cut in half (to 35 percent) by the end of 2009. With little equity in their homes, high unemployment rates, and no way to refinance their unaffordable mortgages, homeowners were trapped. They could not afford to repay their mortgage loans, they could not refinance those loans, and they could not sell their homes.[1]

As briefly noted in Chapter 4, subprime and prime mortgage loan defaults, foreclosure filings, and actual foreclosure sales reached record highs during the recession and then continued to increase even after the recession ended in June 2009. For example, almost 2.9 million homes were involved in some form of foreclosure activity in 2010. While the foreclosure activity slowed and increased by a smaller amount (2 percent) between 2009 and 2010, the total amount of foreclosure activity in 2010 had increased by 20 percent since 2008 and by more than 120 percent since 2007 (when the recession began). Since 2009, there have been disproportionately more prime mortgage loans in foreclosures relative to subprime foreclosures largely due to lenders' tighter lending standards and rising unemployment rates. Even homeowners in higher-income neighborhoods were involved in foreclosure proceedings after they lost their jobs and could not afford to pay their mortgages. Because of high unemployment rates and a sluggish economy, even six months after the recession officially ended in June 2009, almost 25 percent of all residential mortgages were underwater and that number remained at slightly more than 21 percent in 2012, three years after the recession had ended.[2]

The increased number of foreclosures and the continued sluggish U.S. economy caused overall homeownership rates to fall to 65 percent in 2010, down from the all-time high of more than 69 percent. Overall homeownership rates had not been this low since 1995, and they would have been lower than the official rates calculated based on census data if those rates had excluded negative equity homeowners (who are essentially renters). Because of high unemployment rates and because many buyers cannot qualify for

[1] Rajashri Chakrabarti, et al., *Household Debt and Saving during the 2007 Recession*, Fed. Res. Bank N.Y. Staff Reps., No. 482 (Jan. 2011); Office of Management and Budget, Executive Office of the President, *Budget of the U.S. Government, Fiscal Year 2012*, at 242, table 17–1 (2012) *available at* http://www.whitehouse.gov/sites/default/files/omb/budget/fy2012/assets/spec.pdf.

[2] Daren Blomquist, *A Record 2.8 Million Properties Receive Foreclosure Notices in 2009, available at* http://www.realtytrac.com/landing/2009-year-end-foreclosure-report.html?a=b&accnt=233496; RealtyTrac, *Record 2.9 Million U.S. Properties Receive Foreclosure Filings in 2010 Despite 30-Month Low in December, available at* http://www.realtytrac.com/content/foreclosure-market-report/record-29-million-us-properties-receive-foreclosure-filings-in-2010-despite-30-month-low-in-december-6309.

mortgage loans, homeownership rates dropped the most for younger renters – the households who are most likely to be first-time buyers. Contrary to the Happy Homeownership Narrative, fewer young renters are now forming their own households and becoming homeowners. Even more startling, increasing numbers of older homeowner households are losing their homes and returning to renter status.[3]

By 2013, the rate of foreclosure sales finally started to slow down. Many of those sales, though, were replaced by short sales (also known as pre-foreclosure sales). In general, homeowners who choose to sell their homes in a short sale do so because they are delinquent on their mortgage payments, cannot qualify for a loan refinancing, or cannot sell their home at a price that equals the mortgage debt. Foreclosures represented 11.5 percent of home sales in October 2012, down from 17.3 percent in October 2011 and well below the 30 percent level that they reached during the recession. At the end of 2012, short sales increased to 10.4 percent (up from 8.1 percent the year before). While short sales are obviously better for both the lender and the borrower and these sales impose fewer negative externalities on neighboring homes, short sales occur only because the owner has an underwater mortgage. Thus, the recent increase in short sales indicates that many homeowners remain in financial distress and have yet to fully recover from the devastating impact of the recent recession.

Housing sales started to increase in 2013 and, in many regions, homes were being sold for well over their asking price. However, another dire indication that homeownership remains unaffordable to many Americans is the fact that an unusually large percentage of home buyers since 2010 have been investors, and not owner-occupiers. In fact, since the end of 2010, the share of all-cash homes sales (which are generally an indication that an investor and not owner-occupant is the purchaser) has averaged 30 percent. Because investor sales ordinarily account for 10 percent of housing sales, their increased involvement in recent housing sales suggests that there has been no significant improvement in household finances for low- and moderate-income (LMI) Americans and that LMI households still cannot afford to buy homes. In fact, by 2013 the increased presence of all-cash buyers/investors made it harder for first-time buyers (who generally rely on mortgage loans) to buy homes, because all-cash

[3] Federal Reserve researchers have argued that the effective homeownership rate (actual homeowners minus negative equity owners) differs from the official rates released by the U.S. Census Bureau and that the "homeownership gap" between effective and actual rates exceeded 20 percent in some hard-hit markets during the Great Recession. Andrew Haughwout et al., *The Homeownership Gap*, 15–5 CURRENT ISSUES IN ECONOMICS AND FINANCE (May 2010), *available at* http://www.newyorkfed.org/research/current_issues.

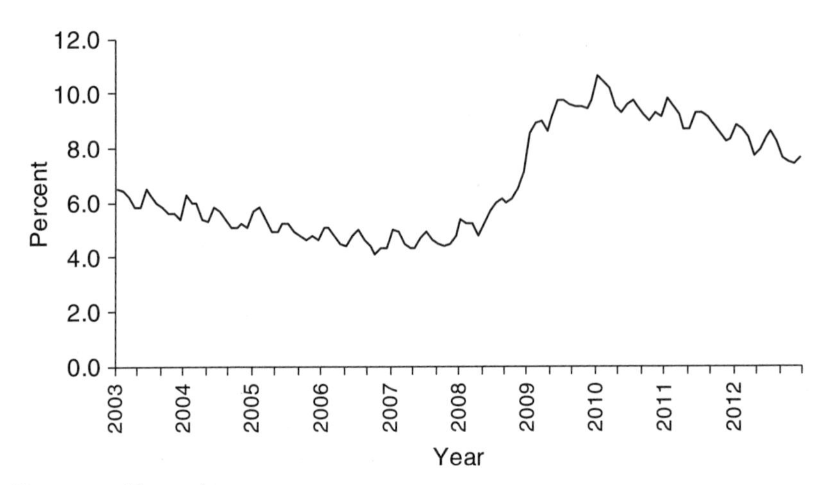

Figure 5.1 Unemployment rate.
Source: Bureau of Labor Statistics.

buyers can complete home purchases much more quickly than borrowers can be approved for mortgage loans.[4]

Foreclosure rates soared and have remained high, home purchases by owner-occupiers (rather than investors) have remained low, and lenders have refused to loosen their underwriting standards largely because U.S. workers continue to have stagnant income and high unemployment rates. As noted in Figure 5.1, overall unemployment rates rose to more than 10 percent after the recession ended in June 2009 but finally dipped below 8 percent by the end of 2012.

While the unemployment rate dipped to 7.5 percent by mid-2013, it still remains higher than it has been for almost twenty-five years. Even unemployed workers who found new jobs experienced increasingly longer periods of unemployment relative to workers who lost jobs in previous U.S. recessions. Many Americans have simply stopped looking for work. Other workers who lost jobs during the recession now hold permanent, part-time positions that do not provide benefits or any of the other perks that workers (especially those in the manufacturing economy) historically received. Moreover, many workers who did not lose their jobs during the recession now earn less than they did before the recession because so many employers have reduced their labor costs by reducing workers' hours and essentially converting their full-time workplace into a mostly part-time one.

[4] Robert Dietz, *What Happens to the Housing Market When the Investors Leave?*, U.S. News & World Report (May 3, 2013).

RETIREMENT HOUSING (IN)SECURITY

In the Happy Homeownership Narrative, older Americans have the highest homeownership rates but the smallest amount of mortgage debt. Because seniors live rent-free in the Narrative, they can pay their remaining living expenses with their retirement income. Historically, this has been true, and people over the age of fifty continue to have higher homeownership rates than younger Americans. Since 1989, though, older homeowners have significantly increased their mortgage debt.

For example, while slightly more than 21 percent of homeowners between the ages of sixty-five and seventy-four had mortgage debt in 1989, almost 41 percent had mortgage debt by 2010. And, while slightly more than 6 percent of homeowners over the age of seventy-five had mortgage debt in 1989, more than 24 percent had mortgage debt in 2012. Older Americans also have had the largest relative increases in debt. Since 2000, the amount of secured debt held by older Americans almost doubled (from roughly $25,000 to $50,000). The median overall debt level for households headed by someone over the age of 65 rose by almost 120 percent (from approximately $12,000 to $26,000) from 2000 to 2011, and most of that increase can be attributed to a rise in mortgage debt. Older Americans increased their mortgage debt primarily by taking out second mortgages and reverse mortgages.[5]

Generally speaking, with a reverse mortgage a homeowner aged sixty-two or older borrows against the equity in the home and receives a lump sum payment, a monthly payment, or a line of credit. The homeowner is required to pay property taxes, maintenance, and insurance but otherwise lives in the home rent-free for the rest of his or her life. Assuming the owner makes these payments, the loan itself does not need to be repaid until the owner dies or stops using the home as a primary residence. Because interest on the reverse mortgage and any insurance premium for the mortgage are added to the loan balance, reverse mortgages negatively amortize, which is one reason few owners (or their heirs) can afford to repay these loans. The U.S. government subsidizes reverse mortgages, because virtually all of these mortgages are insured through the FHA. Like most mortgages, reverse mortgages have been securitized since 2006. Lenders ultimately developed a loan-to-sell model (like the model lenders used when they increased their subprime loan originations during the housing boom), and this may be one reason these loan products are now so aggressively marketed to senior Americans.

[5] Lori A. Trawinski, *Nightmare on Main Street: Older Americans and the Mortgage Market Crisis*, AARP Public Policy Institute (2012).

Reverse mortgages were originally marketed to older seniors as a way for them to get money to make major home repairs, pay for unexpected medical expenses or long-term care assistance, or take a once-in-a-lifetime vacation. While the average homeowner age for reverse mortgages was seventy-seven in 2000, that number dropped to just over seventy-one in 2012. Since 2000, however, younger seniors (e.g., under the age of sixty-five) have been draining equity from their homes, and many younger seniors are using the lump-sum proceeds from a reverse mortgage to refinance an existing mortgage on their home. Others use the lump-sum payment to pay their pre-retirement living expenses or to pay down other consumer debt (including credit card debt).

Younger seniors have used the proceeds from reverse mortgages to pay off their non-mortgage debts, even though borrowing at a younger age reduces the amount of equity they can extract from their homes, drains equity they may need in the future for long-term care, and generally exacerbates their financial predicament. Because senior homeowners – like all Americans – now enter retirement after years of having stagnant income and unsteady employment and have less secure retirement income than retirees had thirty years ago, many seniors face retirement burdened with significantly higher levels of mortgage and non-mortgage consumer debt that they cannot afford to repay.[6]

Younger homeowners continue to have higher mortgage loan delinquency rates (which include mortgages that are ninety days or more delinquent and loans in foreclosure) than older homeowners. For the last decade, however, the mortgage delinquency rate on mortgage loans for senior homeowners rose, and by the end of 2011, approximately 3.5 million loans held by Americans over the age of fifty were underwater. More than 600,000 older Americans were in foreclosure two years after the recession ended, and another 625,000 mortgage loans were seriously (ninety days or more) delinquent. Between the time the recession officially started in 2007 and 2011 (more than two years after the recession officially ended), more than 1.5 million older Americans lost their homes. Moreover, delinquency rates for older homeowners significantly outpaced rates for younger homeowners, and these delinquency rates continued to soar even after the recession ended.

The serious delinquency rates for all loans (prime and subprime) for homeowners over the age of fifty increased from 1.1 percent in 2007 to 6.0 percent in 2011. As is true for all borrowers, the foreclosure rate for prime loans of older homeowners was lower than the rate for subprime loans. Nonetheless, the foreclosure rate for prime loans for older homeowners rose at a level that vastly outpaced the rate for subprime delinquencies. That is, by 2011, the delinquency

[6] Consumer Fin. Prot. Bureau, *Report to Congress on Reverse Mortgages* (Jun. 2012).

rate for prime loans for older homeowners was 23 times the 2007 rate, increasing from almost zero (.1 percent) to 2.3 percent, while the foreclosure rate for subprime loans increased from 2.3 percent in 2007 to almost 13 percent in 2011.

While the post-Depression federal interventions in the housing finance market created the low-cost and low-risk, fixed rate mortgage (FRM) product that was designed to help homeowners buy and keep their homes, older Americans are now losing their homes in record numbers, even though many purchased those homes with prime loans. Moreover, older Americans have borrowed against their homes using reverse mortgage products and recent research reveals that many older homeowners simply do not understand the true risks or the often high fees associated with these products.[7]

RETIREMENT INCOME (IN)SECURITY

The main reason so many older Americans have little retirement *housing* security is because American workers increasingly lack retirement *income* security. As noted in Chapter 4, the savings rates for all ages, genders, and household types have been low since the 1990s. While the overall savings rate increased somewhat during the recession as households deleveraged, since the recession many Americans have stopped saving for retirement and household income for people nearing retirement has become even more unstable. Since the recession, U.S. workers increasingly borrowed against their employer-controlled retirement plans and drained funds from their private 401(k) accounts to pay for current household expenses. Americans raided their retirement funds without seeming to fully comprehend (or accept) that borrowing money from an employer-controlled retirement plan or removing money from a private 401(k) retirement account is an expensive form of credit that has significant long-term consequences.

Generally speaking, 401(k) retirement accounts allow workers to save for their retirements tax-free because they are not taxed on the amounts they place in those accounts until they remove the funds, presumably when they retire and are in a lower tax bracket. Because these tax-favored investment vehicles are meant to encourage employees to save more for their retirement, a taxpayer who makes an early withdrawal from a 401(k) account faces significant tax penalties. In addition to a 10 percent early withdrawal penalty, the funds withdrawn from the account are treated as income that is immediately taxable at the taxpayer's current tax rates, which is likely higher than it would be when the worker retires.

[7] Trawinski, *supra* note 5.

Despite these stiff monetary penalties, high unemployment rates, stagnant income, and high health care costs caused almost 40 percent of American workers to withdraw funds from their retirement accounts during the recession, and almost 25 percent of households raided their retirement plans to pay for their household expenses, including their mortgages. A recent study found that in 2010 U.S. workers withdrew almost $60 billion in cash, which is about half the total amount employers contributed to 401(k) plans for employees that year. Even though some workers did increase their retirement account contributions, workers overall reduced their retirement savings in amounts that were almost twice as large as the amounts people contributed to retirement savings. The retirement income for lower-income households was especially harmed during the recent crisis, and they disproportionately depleted their retirement income. Recent data show that people who earned less than $50,000 annually represented 30 percent of the people who withdrew retirement funds, while less than 8 percent of workers who earned more than $150,000 raided their retirement savings.[8]

While older homeowners in the Happy Homeownership Narrative live carefree and rent-free, they now find themselves with higher mortgage debt and lower retirement savings. There is nothing carefree about the housing and income security many older Americans now face. Given the cultural significance of homeownership and the fact that most people are loss averse and value avoiding present losses (like losing their home) more than they value future gains (like having retirement income), it is not surprising that homeowners drained their retirement incomes to try to keep their homes.

Removing money from a retirement account to try to save your house is not, of course, a wholly irrational short-term strategy, just as it is not wholly irrational to take out a second mortgage to pay for college expenses or other debts (or to take out a high-interest payday loan to pay for immediate household expenses). While raiding retirement savings has the short-term benefit of stalling a scheduled foreclosure, this strategy (like taking out a payday loan) works only if the borrower will be able to replenish the retirement savings (or repay the payday loans). Many LMI homeowners have not been able to replenish their retirement income and they may be unable to do so anytime soon because of persistently high unemployment rates and stagnant income.[9]

[8] Chakrabarti et al., *supra* note 1.

[9] Gregory Elliehausen, *Regulation of Consumer Credit Products*, Federal Reserve Board (2010); Debbie Borie-Holtz et al., *No End in Sight: The Agony of Prolonged Unemployment* (May 2010). Data recently reported by the Federal Reserve Bank of New York also indicates that by 2013 student loan debt grew faster for adults over the age of sixty than for recent college graduates. Loan default rates for those groups are also increasing and, as a result, many retirees have had their social security checks garnished.

NEGATIVE NEIGHBORHOOD EXTERNALITIES

In the Happy Homeownership Narrative, living in a neighborhood with people who own their own homes has positive external benefits for the neighborhood. Homeowners are said to be more responsible, to take better care of their homes, and to be more active, concerned, and civic-minded citizens than non-property owners. Living in a neighborhood that consists of owner-occupied homes increases the value of all homes in the neighborhood, and neighborhoods with owner-occupied homes have been found to be safer and to have better amenities, like schools and parks, than neighborhoods with renter-occupied houses. As the recent housing crisis made painfully clear to homeowners throughout the United States, however, living in neighborhoods with people who are losing their homes to foreclosure imposes *negative* external costs on all other residents in those neighborhoods. For the last several years, homeowners who did *not* have risky mortgages, who were *not* in default on those mortgages, and who did *not* behave recklessly have been forced to stand by silently and watch their home values plummet because they lived near neglected and abandoned homes.

Living in a neighborhood with homeowners who are in financial distress harms neighbors who are not in financial distress largely because of the way distressed homeowners typically treat their houses. Owners who have defaulted on their mortgage or who have an underwater mortgage might reasonably assume that they are going to lose their home. Owners who perceive that they will soon lose their financial stake in their house have no economic incentive to take care of that house. So, although homeowners generally keep their homes in better condition than renters, homeowners who know or suspect they are going to lose their home and unemployed or otherwise cash-constrained homeowners are more likely to treat their home like rental property and, as a result, are less likely to perform or pay for routine maintenance on their house.

The presumption that owners who are facing foreclosure will not properly maintain their homes is largely borne out by reality. Homes that are sold in a short sale or a foreclosure sale commonly have overgrown lawns, are in a visibly deteriorated condition, and may sit abandoned until the bank completes the foreclosure process or new owners buy them. In addition, neighborhoods with a high percentage of foreclosed homes have higher rates of crime (including arson, prostitution, and looting), and abandoned homes attract criminal activity (and sometimes wild vermin), all of which depress the value of neighboring homes.

In addition to the external harm of living near an unkempt house, homeowners who live in neighborhoods with owners who are losing their homes to foreclosure or short sales are harmed by the market value of those homes. That is, homes that are sold in a foreclosure or short sale are almost always sold at a discount, and these lower sales prices harm neighboring owners who may be trying to sell their homes or take out a second mortgage against the home. This is because appraisers assess the value of homes based partially on recent sales of comparable homes in the neighborhood. If a neighboring home sells for a low price, this depresses the market values and selling prices of all homes located near that property, even if the owners who live in those homes have been responsible and have taken care of and maintained their homes.[10]

Foreclosure sales also decrease the value of other homes because the sales increase the supply of available homes. Home prices hit historic lows during the recent recession, and prices remained low for almost three years after the recession ended, in large part because of the increased supply of foreclosed homes or homes that were sold in short sales. Homes started to appreciate again by 2013, but prices remained 28 percent lower than they were at the 2006 pre-recession peak and were at roughly 2003 prices. The depressed value of these homes made it hard for owners to sell their homes at anything other than distressed sale prices, and as stated earlier in this section, lower appraised values made it harder for homeowners who had not defaulted on their mortgage loans to refinance those loans. Foreclosure sales and the resulting depressed home values did more than just harm individual homeowners. Lower home values have also hurt municipalities.[11]

Any increase in foreclosure properties imposes costs on the cities where the properties are located. For example, in the recent housing crisis, municipalities lost both real estate tax revenue (which accounts for about 75 percent of local tax revenue) and real estate transfer taxes. In addition, in an attempt to curtail the harm to neighbors from abandoned properties, many cities chose to demolish uninhabitable abandoned properties, to pay maintenance costs for habitable properties, and to provide additional police, fire, and other public safety services to these vacant properties. With lower tax revenues, however, municipalities often could not afford to provide upkeep for abandoned properties.

Because of the loss of tax revenue, some municipalities sued lenders to recoup the costs they incurred due to the increased number of vacant homes

[10] W. Scott Frame, *Estimating the Effect of Mortgage Foreclosures on Nearby Property Values: A Critical Review of the Literature*, Fed. Res. Bank of Atlanta (2010); Dan Immergluck & Geoff Smith, *The External Costs of Foreclosure: The Impact of Single-Family Mortgage Foreclosures on Neighborhood Crime*, 21 Housing Studies 851–66 (2006). "Investors" who recently purchased foreclosed homes at rock-bottom prices in one U.S. city turned the homes into indoor marijuana grow houses. Norimitsu Onishi, *Foreclosed Houses Become Homes for Indoor Marijuana Farms*, N.Y. Times (May 5, 2012).

[11] Mark Niquette & Tim Jones, *Foreclosure Deal May Help States Prop Up Budgets, Raze Homes*, Wash. Post (Feb. 13, 2012); Shelia Dewan, *A City Invokes Seizure Laws to Save Homes*, N. Y. Times (Jul. 29, 2013).

in their cities. In fact, some municipalities that have been particularly hard-hit by foreclosures have now threatened to use their eminent domain powers to seize underwater mortgages. Cities have threatened to reduce the principal loan balance and then resell the reduced mortgages to new investors (or refinance the now lower amount with a government-backed loan) if the investors who own the mortgages refuse the city's offer to buy the loans at an amount that roughly equals the fair market value of the home.[12]

HIDDEN HARMS: UNHEALTHY AND IN DESPAIR

As noted earlier in Chapter 2, homeownership as portrayed in the Happy Homeownership Narrative makes owners and their families happy. In the Narrative, homeowners feel secure and good about themselves and believe that their families are more stable and generally better off living in homes they own rather than rent. Homeownership is portrayed as good for children in the Narrative, and studies indicate that the children of homeowners perform better at school than renters' children.

Homeowners view their homes as a link to their community, their children's schools, and their past. They will do almost anything to avoid a foreclosure because of their desire to preserve the roots and memories they established in those houses and to give their children (and grandchildren) a place to return to visit. The Narrative fails to mention, however, that just as being a homeowner makes you happy and makes you feel good, the process of losing your home makes you sad and can make you sick.

People who are under severe economic stress, including homeowners who are involved in foreclosure proceedings, have an increased risk of depression and are at a greater risk of having insomnia, chest pains, heart attacks, and ulcers. Losing a home is particularly stressful because the foreclosure process is long, unpredictable, and virtually guaranteed to be emotionally and physically unpleasant. In most cases, homeowners do not lose their homes immediately. Instead, the homeowners will struggle to make monthly loan payments, fall behind and miss several payments, and then will likely be hounded by the lender or debt collectors. If the homeowners fail to convince the lender (or debt collector) to let them stay in the home, they must endure the foreclosure

[12] Ian Urbina, *Foreclosures Prompt Cities to Make Plea for Aid*, N.Y. TIMES (Jan. 24, 2008); Lee Anne Fennell & Julie A. Roin, *Controlling Residential Stakes*, 77 U. CHIC. L. REV. 143 (2010); Creola Johnson, *Fight Blight: Cities Sue to Hold Lenders Responsible for the Rise in Foreclosures and Abandoned Properties*, 3 UTAH L. REV. 1169 (2008). Some states indicated that they would use some of the funds they received as part of the national foreclosure settlement against lenders to demolish abandoned and dilapidated homes. Niquette & Jones, *supra* note 11; Dewan, *id.*

itself and the disruption to their household that being displaced from a home entails. While the time to complete a foreclosure sale varies by state, if the state authorizes a non-judicial process to foreclose on a home, it can take up to one-and-a-half years to complete the process.

This long and unnerving process can make homeowners feel helpless. Indeed, many homeowners report that they feel helpless well before they actually lose their homes and sometimes feel helpless if they even *suspect* that they will be involved in a foreclosure process. The stress of a foreclosure can cause homeowners to have depression-related symptoms, especially because homeowners often blame themselves for losing their homes. That is, homeowners often view the foreclosure – and their return to the dreaded second-class status of renter – as a visible sign that they have failed in life, and many report experiencing a profound sense of loss when they are forced to become renters again.[13]

Not surprisingly, recent interviews of homeowners who lost their homes in a bankruptcy or a foreclosure sale showed that many of these homeowners had high levels of tension and that the economic stress caused several married couples to contemplate divorce.[14] Moreover, although it is not yet clear whether the economic downturn was the primary factor, recent research conducted by the Centers for Disease Control and Prevention found that between 1999 and 2010 there was a significant increase in the suicide rate for middle-aged Americans (aged thirty-five to sixty-four) and that suicide rates for some groups increased by 40 percent during that period.[15]

People who are financially stressed or facing foreclosure are also more likely to face what public health researchers commonly refer to as the holy trinity

[13] A recent study by a California health department indicates that even renters who live in foreclosed properties have higher rates of stress, depression, and anxiety. Viji Sundaram, *Study Finds Unhealthy Effects of Foreclosures*, The Bay Citizen (Sep. 2010), *available at* https://www.baycitizen.org/news/housing/study-finds-unhealthy-effects/. In addition, homeowners who have defaulted on their loans but had no contact with the lender report being stressed out because of the uncertainty involving when the lender *might* start the eviction process. See Susan Saulny, *When Living in Limbo Avoids Living on the Streets*, N.Y. Times (Mar. 3, 2012).

[14] Marianne B. Culhane, *No Forwarding Address: Losing Homes in Bankruptcy*, in How Debt Bankrupts the Middle Class 132 (Katherine Porter ed., Stanford University Press, 2012). Dramatic housing price fluctuations also influence marriage and divorce rates because, when housing prices drop, unhappily married couples who have an underwater mortgage on a house that they cannot sell and cannot afford to maintain separately are often forced to stay together in the house. Conversely, fewer couples who want to form a happy household do so when housing prices skyrocket because they cannot afford to buy a home. Ronald, Richard & Kees Dol, *Housing in the Netherlands before and after the Global Financial Crisis*, in *Housing Markets and the Global Financial Crisis* 106 (Ray Forrest & Ngai-Ming Yip eds., 2011); John Leland, *Breaking Up is Harder to Do after Housing Fall*, N.Y. Times (Dec. 29, 2008).

[15] Ctr. for Disease Control and Prevention, *Suicide among Adults Aged 35–64 Years – United States 1999–2010*, *available at* http://www.cdc.gov/mmwr/preview/mmwrhtml/mm6217a1.htm?s_cid=mm6217a1.

of risks: smoking, drinking, and eating. People who lose their jobs, face foreclosures, or otherwise are stressed out because they cannot pay their bills frequently increase their tobacco use and drink more alcohol, often in excess. In addition, public health research reveals that financial stress often causes or exacerbates eating disorders. While some financially stressed homeowners try to console themselves by eating (often overeating), others appear to lose their appetites and refuse to eat. And, while they are smoking more, drinking too much, or eating too much (or not enough), financially stressed people are less likely to visit doctors for routine preventive care. Moreover, to save costs they often stop taking medicines and avoid getting prescriptions filled, or they substitute a cheaper generic or over-the-counter medication for a prescription because they cannot afford to pay for the more expensive drugs.[16]

Children who live in a household that is enduring (or has endured) a foreclosure also face increased health and emotional risks. Studies have shown that children who are displaced and forced to change schools typically attend schools that are of lower quality than the schools they attended before their parents lost their homes. Displaced children perform worse academically and often feel disconnected from their new schools, because the displacement often makes it impossible for them to continue participating in extracurricular activities. Displaced students frequently get into fights with kids at their new schools and face the emotional stress of having to make new friends, while missing their old friends.[17] Additionally, because teachers do not know them or their particular educational needs, displaced students may not be properly grouped or, worse, may be improperly labeled as having a learning disability. Although children who are forced to change schools are at the highest risk for having behavioral problems, even children who are forced to change residences but are *not* forced to change schools fare worse academically in school and have more behavioral problems.[18]

[16] Susann Rohwedder et al., *Pooled Assets: Three Ways for Coping in Hard Times*, RAND REVIEW (Spring 2010), *available at* http://www.rand.org; Associated Press Poll, *AP-GfK Poll* (Jul. 2011); Gary Bennett et al., *Will the Public's Health Fall Victim to the Home Foreclosure Epidemic?*, PLoS MEDICINE (Jun. 2009), *available at* http://www.plosmedicine.org; Craig Evan Pollack & Julia Lynch, *Health Status of People Undergoing Foreclosure in the Philadelphia Region*, 99–10 AM. J. OF PUB. HEALTH 1833–39 (Oct. 2009); Lauren M. Ross & Gregory D. Squires, *The Personal Costs of Subprime Lending and the Foreclosure Crisis: A Matter of Trust, Insecurity, and Institutional Deception*, 92–1 SOCIAL SCIENCE QUARTERLY (Mar. 2011).

[17] Although they are perhaps unquantifiable, there are costs to students who have to make new friends each year, learn the social mores of a new school, and learn how to "fit in" with kids in the new school.

[18] Vicki Been et al., *Does Losing Your Home Mean Losing Your School?: Effects of Foreclosures on the School Mobility of Children* 41 REGIONAL SCIENCE AND URBAN ECONOMICS 407–14 (2011); Eric Rodriguez, *Assessing the Damage of Predatory Lending by Countrywide:*

Homeowners who are evicted usually have blemished credit, and homeowners who have lost their homes because of unemployment find it particularly difficult to find affordable housing. Because of this, people who lose their homes are often forced to move multiple times before they can find permanent, suitable (and affordable) rental housing. Thus, in addition to the psychological changes homeowners and their households endure when they face a foreclosure sale, foreclosures disrupt the household physically, because the homeowners and their families must move once they are evicted. Many families who lost their homes in the recent recession were lucky to be able to move in with friends or other family members. This temporary doubling up, however, often creates cramped, overcrowded, and tense household conditions, and these living conditions have negative effects on children's academic achievement.[19]

THE BLAME GAME

Many culprits can be – and have been – blamed for the housing crash. Banks and other financial institutions have been blamed for recklessly approving loans for high-risk borrowers, for misleading borrowers, for using lax underwriting practices, and for engaging in outright fraud. Homeowners have been blamed for buying houses they knew, or should have known, they could not afford. The government has been blamed for enacting and pushing housing policies that gave lenders an incentive to approve loans for borrowers who could not afford to buy houses and for failing to regulate lenders and bond rating agencies. All these culprits helped create the crisis. The government's role is particularly problematic, though, because U.S. housing policies now

The Fallout for Latino Families: Hearing on Examining Lending Discrimination Practices and Foreclosure Abuses of the Senate Committee on the Judiciary (Mar. 7, 2012); Jennifer Comey & Michel Grosz, *Smallest Victims of the Foreclosure Crisis: Children in the District of Columbia*, Urban Inst. (2010), *available at* http://www.urban.org/publications/412220.html; Janis Bowdler et al., *The Foreclosure Generation: The Long-Term Impact of the Housing Crisis on Latino Children and Families* (2010). When parents try to keep their children in their old schools until the school year ends, they often exacerbate their financial plight. That is, unless the school district agrees to provide transportation, parents who move to a neighborhood that is not zoned for the children's prior school often increase their transportation costs by driving their children to/from their old school. While the McKinney-Vento Homeless Assistance Act gives parents the right to insist that the school district provide transportation to their previously zoned school if they become homeless or are forced to live in shared housing because of economic hardship, it is likely that few parents know they have this right, and school districts have no financial incentive to inform parents of this option, given their strained budgets.

[19] Dalton Conley, *A Room with a View or a Room of One's Own? Housing and Social Stratification*, 16–2 SOCIOLOGICAL FORUM (2001).

appear to encourage people to buy homes for reasons that have little to do with their financial or emotional well-being or with the rhetoric associated with the Happy Homeownership Narrative.

GREEDY, IRRESPONSIBLE LENDERS

Lenders have been blamed for causing the housing crash because they approved too many subprime loans for renters who could not afford to buy houses. Lenders increased the volume of subprime loan originations during the housing boom partially because of the intense competition for borrowers and their need to continue to originate mortgage loans. The market for prime mortgage loans was already saturated because most creditworthy and higher-income borrowers had already bought homes and relatively few of them needed to use home equity loans to pay for their ongoing expenses. The only way to keep loan originations high was to turn to the pool of untapped borrowers: young renters and existing homeowners with blemished credit. A dwindling pool of borrowers, combined with the U.S. government's challenge to make housing more affordable for LMI borrowers, gave lenders just the incentive they needed to "innovate" mortgage products and increase their mortgage loan originations.

As discussed in Chapter 4, during the housing boom lenders drastically relaxed the criteria they historically used to approve mortgage loans. To make it possible for cash-strapped renters to buy homes, lenders approved loans for borrowers who had characteristics that historically would have deemed them too high-risk. Because of the virtual disappearance of the down payment requirement, the overall denial rate for mortgage loans dropped during this period, and lenders increased the LTV and DTI ratios they used to approve subprime loans. As a result, lenders approved larger loans to borrowers with blemished credit and used what were referred to as risk-layering practices.

In general, risk-layering occurs when a mortgage originator approves a loan that combines a number of nontraditional features. For example, during the housing boom lenders approved adjustable rate mortgage (ARM) loans that let the borrower choose the amount of the monthly payment from a menu of options. Lenders approved these option ARMs, even though the loan often did not require the borrower to provide proof of income or wealth (i.e., a no-documentation, or "no doc," loan). Lenders also increased the number of high LTV, no-doc loans they would approve for borrowers who did not (or could not) make a down payment.

During the housing boom lenders also created a new loan system, commonly referred to as "piggyback" loans. A piggyback loan transaction allowed borrowers to avoid paying for private mortgage insurance (PMI) by letting borrowers take out a first mortgage (typically for 80 percent of the value of the home) and then a simultaneous second mortgage (or line of credit) for the remainder of the sales price of the home. Even though the piggyback loan system allowed borrowers to avoid paying PMI, the system burdened borrowers with two mortgage obligations and, thus, increased the amount of the mortgage debt and the risk that the homeowners would default and lose their home.

Of course, none of these individual loan features forced homeowners to default on their mortgages. But layering multiple default risks in one loan transaction virtually guaranteed that cash-strapped borrowers would default on their loan payments and lose their homes *unless* interest rates remained low, mortgage credit remained available, housing price appreciation continued to soar, and borrowers had stable or rising income.[20]

Before the housing market collapsed, lenders had a strong incentive to ignore the risks inherent in lending to borrowers who had no savings and no documented income or assets because of skyrocketing housing price appreciation, because the United States bought, guaranteed, or securitized higher risk loans during the boom, and because of the almost insatiable investor demand for high-return MBSs. Indeed, as long as the value of the home exceeded the amount of the outstanding mortgage debt, even high-risk subprime loans looked safe.

From the lender's perspective, even if the borrower defaulted, the lender faced little risk because the United States would repay the loan (if it was a "conforming" mortgage) or the lender could seize the collateral (the ever-appreciating house) and sell it to satisfy the mortgage debt. Moreover, lenders generally discounted the risk of default when they approved these high-risk loans because they knew they could quickly sell these loans in the secondary mortgage market. In fact, the presence of a robust secondary market for high-yield loans (regardless of the quality or creditworthiness of the borrower) gave lenders strong financial incentives to originate a higher volume of loans *regardless of the risks* because lenders knew they could sell the loans and that someone else – the investor/purchaser of the loan – would bear the cost of any future default.[21]

Neither the banks that originated high-risk subprime loans nor the investment bankers who participated in the private label securities (PLS) market carefully considered the individual borrower's risk of default, and mortgage

[20] ROBERT W. KOLB, THE FINANCIAL CRISIS OF OUR TIME (2001).

[21] Giovanni Dell'Ariccia et al., *Credit Booms and Lending Standards: Evidence from the Subprime Mortgage Market*, 44 J. OF MONEY, CREDIT AND BANKING 367 (Mar.–Apr. 2012).

securitizers did not seem to understand (or did not care about) the risks these loans posed to the ultimate investor/owner. To make matters worse, after these high-risk subprime loans were packaged into securities, rating agencies either misjudged or ignored the likelihood that these loans would go into default.

Unlike the prime mortgages that were purchased, guaranteed, or securitized by Fannie Mae, Freddie Mac, or other GSEs, subprime loan securitizers did not guarantee borrowers' loan payments so investors should have investigated the creditworthiness of the borrowers. Investors, especially cash-rich foreign investors, generally knew nothing about the creditworthiness of the borrowers in the securitized pools and may not even have read the prospectus. These investors seemed to assume that the PLSs were safe because these securities often received favorable ratings by reputable rating agencies. Moreover, investors eagerly bought these PLSs without carefully examining the risks associated with the subprime loans in the securitized pools because the rapidly appreciating housing prices made these high-yield (albeit high-risk) securitized loans appear to be relatively safe bets. Indeed, as long as housing prices kept appreciating, mortgage originators, investment banks, rating agencies, and investors seemed unconcerned about the value or risks associated with the MBSs and PLSs, nor did they seem interested in determining whether the borrowers had the ability to repay the high-cost loans.[22]

In addition to greed, irresponsibility, and willful blindness, some lenders and mortgage brokers engaged in outright fraud. Even before the recession, civil rights and housing advocacy groups claimed that smaller independent mortgage brokers had engaged in outright fraud by artificially inflating home values, falsifying loan documents and tax returns, and misrepresenting or intentionally inflating borrowers' incomes.[23] Recent lawsuits and settlements show, however, that fraud was widespread and that large institutional mortgage lenders also engaged in fraudulent lending practices. The most

[22] Atif R. Mian & Amir Sufi, *Household Leverage and the Recession of 2007 to 2009*, 58 IMF Economic Review, 74–117 (2010); Adam J. Levitin & Susan M. Wachter, *Information Failure and the U.S. Mortgage Crisis*, in The American Mortgage System: Crisis and Reform (Susan M. Wachter & Marvin Smith eds., 2011). A recent paper written by analysts at the Boston Federal Reserve relates the story of two hedge fund managers who profited handsomely by anticipating the housing crash and betting against future housing price increases. These managers were *not* housing insiders. Instead, they reached their investment decisions (and profited handsomely) the old-fashioned way: by painstakingly reading complicated prospectuses. Christopher L. Foote et al., *Why Did So Many People Make So Many Ex Post Bad Decisions? The Causes of the Foreclosure Crisis*, Fed. Res. Bank of Boston Policy Paper Discussion Series 18–19 (2012).

[23] Vikas Bajaj & Miguel Helft, *The Loan that Keeps on Taking*, N.Y. Times (Sep. 25, 2007), at C1.

egregious allegations of lender fraud during the housing boom involved black and Latino borrowers.

As discussed in greater detail in Chapter 7, in lawsuits filed against lenders, municipalities, black, and Latino plaintiffs argued that lenders discriminated against blacks and Latinos by charging them higher fees and by steering them toward costlier higher-interest rate subprime loans than the loans the lenders offered to white borrowers with similar credit risks. Evidence disclosed in these cases (virtually all of which ultimately settled) also showed that some mortgage loan originators encouraged borrowers to misrepresent credit information on loan applications, while others altered or inserted erroneous financial information in borrowers' loan applications in order to qualify borrowers for loans they could not afford. Other brokers or loan officers fraudulently altered the borrowers' financial information to ensure that they would *not* qualify for prime loans and, instead, would only qualify for higher-cost subprime loans. Lenders also deceived borrowers by telling them, for example, that costly pre-payment penalties could be waived (which was never true) or by encouraging borrowers to increase their mortgage debt by refinancing loans that were less than two years old (even though this violated the lenders' own underwriting standards).[24]

Since the crash, the U.S. Departments of Justice (DOJ) and Housing and Urban Development (HUD), federal agencies (including the FHA, the Board of Governors of the Federal Reserve System, and the Federal Trade Commission), and most state Attorney Generals sued mortgage servicers for wrongfully foreclosing on homes, often without ever verifying the accuracy of foreclosure filings. The first major settlement occurred in February 2012 and another followed in 2013 when a group of lenders and mortgage servicers agreed to pay $8.5 billion to settle claims that alleged they mishandled mortgage loan modifications and wrongfully evicted borrowers who were either current on their payments or had made timely but reduced monthly payments.[25] This settlement has been controversial, and many argue that it falls short of providing meaningful relief to homeowners.

[24] Declaration of Tony Paschal, Mayor of Baltimore v. Wells Fargo Bank, 677 F. Supp. 2d 847, No. 1:08-cv-00062-JFM, Doc. 176–2 (2010), *available at* http://www.relmanlaw.com/docs/Baltimore-Declarations.pdf; Declaration of Doris Dancy, City of Memphis v. Wells Fargo Bank, No. 2:09-cv-02857-STA, Doc. 29–1 (W.D. Tenn. May 4, 2011), *available at* http://www.relmanlaw.com/docs/Declarations-Memphis.pdf; Declaration of Elizabeth M. Jacobson, Mayor of Baltimore v. Wells Fargo Bank, 677 F. Supp. 2d 847, No. 1:08-cv-00062-JFM, Doc. 176–1 (2010), *available at* http://www.relmanlaw.com/docs/Baltimore-Declarations.pdf.

[25] Anna Maria Santiago et al., *The Experiences of Low-Income Homebuyers*, in FAIR AND AFFORDABLE HOUSING IN THE U.S.: TRENDS, OUTCOMES, FUTURE DIRECTIONS (Robert Mark Silverman & Kelly L. Patterson eds., 2011).

A host of problems make this settlement controversial. First, only $3.3 billion was designated to be used to actually compensate homeowners who were evicted in 2009 and 2010. More than 3.8 million foreclosure sales took place during that two-year period, and all homeowners were entitled to recover compensation from the fund, even though the consulting firm that was selected to pay claims from the fund did not require proof that the foreclosure was procedurally defective or that the former homeowner was harmed by the bank's conduct during the foreclosure proceeding. Moreover, rather than have an independent consultant review the claims and determine whether homeowners were entitled to relief, the settlement allowed the mortgage companies – the same ones who mishandled the mortgage loan modifications or improperly evicted homeowners – to determine how to distribute the settlement funds.

Not surprisingly, given how this settlement fund was structured, payment problems have plagued the settlement process. The consulting firm that was selected to pay claims has been accused of taking too much time to tell borrowers how much they were owed based on the settlement's payment rubric. In addition, some of the settlement checks that borrowers received bounced, some borrowers received checks in the wrong amount, some checks were sent to incorrect addresses, and some checks were mailed to dead people.

While the banks and mortgage servicers obviously cannot be blamed for the consulting firm's actions, banks *can* be blamed for their part in delaying payments to homeowners whom they victimized during the housing boom. For example, Bank of America (BOA) agreed in 2012 to pay some borrowers between $1,000 and $5,000 after it was accused of improperly foreclosing on the borrowers' homes. BOA has since resisted efforts to pay victims by asking homeowners to provide documentation that was not required by the settlement agreement (which is, in fact, illegal), and by failing to compile a list of the victims who were eligible to be paid out of the settlement more than a year after the settlement was reached. Similarly, Wells Fargo agreed to compensate up to 10,000 borrowers after the Federal Reserve found that it had improperly steered borrowers into subprime loans even though they qualified for better mortgages. Although this settlement was reached in 2011, by 2013 no borrowers had received money from the settlement.[26]

Finally, even some of the states who sued the lenders have failed to use the settlement funds to provide relief to financially struggling homeowners (or ex-homeowners) who were victimized by the lenders. The states received

[26] Danielle Douglas, *Behind the Mortgage Settlements from the Housing Crisis*, N.Y. TIMES (May 19, 2013).

$2.5 billion from the settlement, but by the end of 2012 most had not used the money to assist distressed homeowners. Moreover, while the states intended to use $1 billion of the funds to help distressed homeowners, $1 billion of the settlement funds were actually designated to be used to help close state budget gaps. States relied on language in the settlement language that provided that they should use the money "to the extent practicable ... for purposes intended to avoid foreclosures" in order to justify their decision to use that money to close budget gaps.[27]

GREEDY, IRRESPONSIBLE HOMEOWNERS

Homeowners also have been blamed for causing the housing crash. Recent research has revealed that during the housing boom sellers, developers, and borrowers in some markets regularly conspired with appraisers to inflate home prices in order to circumvent the lenders' loan requirements. In a typical transaction, the parties would agree to a loan amount (e.g., $275,000) that exceeded the actual value of the home ($250,000). As part of the agreement, the seller or developer would agree to make a side transfer of goods worth $25,000 (money, cars, etc.) to the buyer. In addition to defrauding individual lenders who were never informed of the side transfer, inflating the loan amount to provide a side payment to the borrower effectively forced lenders to fund the down payment that it had required borrowers to make from savings. Moreover, these fraudulent appraisals artificially inflated housing prices, because legitimate appraisers rely on the sale price of comparable homes when determining the market value of homes for sale in any given market, and artificially higher prices harm all potential buyers by increasing their home buying costs.[28]

While only a limited number of homeowners appeared to actively participate in fraudulent conduct, most homeowners can be blamed for naïvely embracing the Happy Homeownership Narrative premise that buying a home is risk-free and that homes always increase in value. Homeowners never seemed to consider whether, despite their rhapsodic views about owning their own home, renting might actually be a better financial decision. Instead, they bought homes, even though they did not have enough money to make a down payment and even if they knew (or should have known) they could not afford the fully amortized loan payment. They accepted high-cost and high-risk mortgage products without realistically considering what they would do if they lost their jobs, their homes stopped appreciating, or lenders tightened credit standards.

[27] *States Shift Foreclosure-Suit Funds*, WALL ST. J. (Oct. 18, 2012), at A7.

[28] Itzhak Ben-David, *Financial Constraints and Inflated Home Prices during the Real Estate Boom*, 3 AM. ECON. J.: APPLIED ECON. 55–87 (Jul. 2011), *available at* http://www.aeaweb.org/articles.php?doi=10.1257/app.3.3.55.

During the housing boom, homeowners acted as if they would never actually have to repay the high-cost ARMs (that they knew they could not afford) because they would always be able to refinance those ARMs once interest rates increased. Whether because of greed, stupidity, or naïveté, many homeowners who bought homes never seemed to grasp that if housing appreciation stalled, interest rates rose, and foreclosure rates soared, lenders might refuse to refinance their high-risk and high-cost loans.

Because homeowners seemed convinced that they would reap the benefits associated with homeownership and that those benefits would far exceed the costs, many disregarded the actual costs associated with homeownership. Homeowners either ignored or were totally unaware of the need to set aside money for utilities, routine maintenance, major repairs, taxes, or property insurance. Moreover, rather than making sure they saved or earned enough money to reduce their mortgage debt and increase their home equity, homeowners increased the debt on their homes and essentially treated their homes like they were ATMs. Homeowners kept borrowing against their homes because, like lenders and investors in MBSs, it never seemed to occur to them that their homes might not rise in value. Indeed, even as the housing market was crashing, a survey showed that homeowners were more optimistic that their homes would continue to increase in value than they had been in the 1990s (before the housing boom).[29]

Homeowners during the housing boom found themselves in the same predicament homeowners faced during the Depression: they had no savings and could not afford to repay their mortgage loans; they lacked equity in homes they could not sell; and their lenders refused to renegotiate the terms of their unaffordable loans. The fact that so many homeowners succumbed to greed and made irresponsible decisions and gross financial miscalculations is not terribly surprising given the generally low levels of financial literacy in the United States.

Even though high school and college graduation rates have increased in the United States over the last thirty years, many Americans do not manage their money effectively, and many lack the basic skills and knowledge to make informed, rational financial decisions. For example, studies show that Americans consistently fail to save enough for retirement and often choose

[29] Paul Taylor et al., *As Home Prices Cool Down, Homeowners Temper Their Optimism*, Pew Research Ctr. (2006); Telis Demos, *Leading Indicators*, FORTUNE (Sep. 17, 2007), at 30; Mark Wiranowski, *Sustaining Home Ownership through Education and Counseling* 10 (Joint Ctr. for Hous. Studies, Harvard Univ., Working Paper No. W03–7, 2003); *Remarks by Governor Susan Schmidt Bies at the National Credit Union Administration 2007 Risk Mitigation Summit* (Jan. 11, 2007), at 6.

risky or higher-cost investment options and credit products. Borrowers without college degrees, lower-income borrowers, and minority borrowers seem especially likely to make unwise financial decisions and to accept loan products they do not understand. These groups are also the least likely to be informed of other lending options, and their generally lower levels of financial literacy cause them to consistently make irrational and costly homeownership decisions.

Research shows that lower-income homeowners who do not have college degrees are less likely to attempt to refinance higher-interest rate mortgages when interest rates are falling even if a refinancing would help lower their overall homeownership costs. People with lower levels of financial or debt literacy routinely pay more for credit cards (in the form of fees and penalties) and are disproportionately more likely to use high-cost, high-risk, short-term credit products, such as payday or car title loans. Additionally, borrowers with low levels of financial literacy generally are not aware of the availability of less expensive credit products, and even when those borrowers *are* aware, research shows that they often fail to choose the best financial option.[30]

Just before the housing market crashed, Congress created a Financial Education and Literacy Commission to respond to consumer financial illiteracy in the United States. Among other things, the Commission created a web portal that is designed to teach people the basics about buying a home and retirement investing. U.S. political leaders knew that potential home buyers, especially lower-income and minority buyers, often make unwise financial decisions in their zeal to buy a house. A Latina member of Congress observed during a hearing on the need for housing counseling services that many home buyers get

> caught up in the excitement of purchasing their first home [and] are often ill-informed or misinformed about the loan agreement they are signing. As a result, they end up with mortgage payments they cannot afford and, with alarming frequency, face default or foreclosure.[31]

[30] Gopi Shah Goda et al., *Does Understanding the Relationship between Retirement Contributions and Future Monthly Income Encourage Savings?, Insight*, Financial Literacy Ctr. (Feb. 2012), *available at* http://www.rand.org/content/dam/rand/pubs/working_briefs/2012/RAND_WB113.pdf; *Hearing before the U.S. Senate Committee on Banking, Housing, & Urban Affairs, on Housing Finance Reform: Continuation of the 30-Year Fixed-Rate Mortgage* (Oct. 20, 2011) (testimony of Paul S. Willen, Senior Economist and Policy Advisor, Federal Reserve Bank of Boston); Ross & Squires, *supra* note 16; Annamaria Lusardi & Peter Tufano, *Debt Literacy, Financial Experiences, and Overindebtedness* (Nat. Bur. Econ. Research, Working Paper No. 1480, Mar. 2009), *available at* http://www.nber.org/papers/w14808.

[31] *Successful Homeownership and Renting through Housing Counseling; Hearing before the Subcommittee on Housing and Community Services of the House Committee on Financial Services* (Mar. 18, 2004) (statement of Rep. Nydia M. Velazquez).

Of course, not all borrowers were greedy, naïve, or irresponsible during the housing boom. Still, many of the borrowers who defaulted on loans they could never really afford to repay seemed genuinely shocked when they could not sell their homes and could not refinance their mortgage loans.

Even though they used an irrational decision-making process, their decisions are not surprising; in fact, they were quite predictable. Behavioral research shows that people are overly confident when they participate in credit transactions and that this confidence causes them to underestimate how much they will use (or abuse) credit. This overconfidence bias causes people to overestimate their ability to repay their debts in the future. Research also shows that consumers have a tendency to agree to credit transactions that may pose risks in the future because of their limited ability to gauge the likelihood of negative future events, like whether their property will decrease in value or whether they will lose their job or be forced to take a cut in pay. Finally, behavioral research shows that people often consider noneconomic factors (like values, emotions, and events they experienced earlier in their lives) when making financial decisions and that those factors may cause them to make irrational financial choices.

Although homeowners with no savings and unstable income bought homes with high-risk loans, many of them probably never believed that they would not be able to repay the loans in the future. Also, while homeowners had utterly unrealistic expectations about how much their homes would increase in value in the future, neither homeowners, investors, lenders, *or even the U.S. government* accurately gauged the magnitude of the recession that caused so many homeowners to default on their loans and lose their homes. Because so many Americans blindly accepted the rosy views portrayed in the Happy Homeownership Narrative and because U.S. housing policies encouraged renters to leave their second-class status and become homeowners, it is not surprising that so many homeowners bought homes they could not afford.[32]

IT'S THE GOVERNMENT'S FAULT

The federal government has also been blamed for causing the housing crisis, in part because of a law that was designed to make credit more available to LMI borrowers. The Community Reinvestment Act (CRA) of 1977 and the GSE Act were designed to give banks an incentive to meet the credit needs

[32] Oren Bar-Gill, *Bundling and Consumer Misperception*, 33 U. Chic. L. Rev. 45 (2006); Oren Bar-Gill, *Seduction by Plastic*, Nw. U. L. Rev. 1373 (2004); Ren S. Essene & William Apgar, *Understanding Mortgage Market Behavior: Creating Good Mortgage Options for All Americans*, Joint Ctr. for Hous. Studies, Harvard Univ., 18 (2007).

of borrowers in LMI areas by requiring regulators to monitor the banks' lending performance in those areas. In addition, when homeownership rates stalled in the 1990s, the GSE Act required Fannie Mae and Freddie Mac to purchase more mortgages that provided housing for LMI households and mortgage loans that borrowers who lived in areas traditionally underserved by the mortgage market used to buy a home. While the GSEs originally were urged to set aside 40 percent of their total purchases for loans made to underserved populations, by 2008 more than 55 percent of the loans GSEs purchased were made to LMI households. Even though neither of these laws requires lenders to engage in reckless lending, critics nonetheless have argued that these federal mandates forced lenders to engage in unsound and high-risk lending practices.[33]

In response to these criticisms, Federal Reserve analysts examined the loan performance data for subprime mortgages that were made in LMI neighborhoods. Their research found that CRA loans performed as well as, if not better than, other subprime loans made in middle- or higher-income areas. Researchers also examined a loan program that helped lenders comply with the CRA and found that the loans lenders made to comply with the CRA had prime loan features and lower default risks than loans made in non-CRA areas. Moreover, unlike most subprime loans, these CRA loans did not have prepayment penalties, did not have mortgage broker involvement or the costs (and abuses) associated with some non-CRA subprime loans, and did not have adjustable-interest rates. While the government's housing policies can be blamed for overemphasizing the benefits of homeownership, this research suggests that if there had been *more* CRA lending, there might have been fewer mortgage broker-initiated subprime ARMs. Moreover, rather than causing the housing crisis, more CRA lending might have allowed more homebuyers (especially lower-income, black, and Latino borrowers) to avoid being pushed into higher-risk, higher-cost subprime loans.[34]

The U.S. government can, however, be blamed for failing to scrutinize the GSEs' increasingly risky investments in subprime mortgages. The GSEs were

[33] Jonathan Spader & Roberto G. Quercia, *Community Reinvestment Lending in a Changing Context: Evidence of Interaction with FHA and Subprime Originations*, 14–4 J. REAL ESTATE FINAN. & ECON. 505–25 (2012); Peter J. Wallison, *Dissent* from the Majority Report of the Financial Crisis Inquiry Commission, Washington, D.C., American Enterprise Institute for Public Policy Research (2011), *available at* http://www.huduser.org/portal/datasets/gse.html.

[34] Glenn Canner & Neil Bhutta, *Memo* to Sandra Braunstein, *Staff Analysis of the Relationship between the CRA and the Subprime Crisis* (Nov. 21, 2008), *available at* http://www.federalreserve.gov/newsevents/speech/20081203_analysis.pdf; Roberto Quercia & Janneke Ratcliffe, *The Community Reinvestment Act: Outstanding, and Needs to Improve*, in REVISITING THE CRA: PERSPECTIVES ON THE FUTURE OF THE COMMUNITY REINVESTMENT ACT (2009).

the first to securitize mortgages, but by the height of the housing boom in 2005 private entities had a larger share of the securitization market than the GSEs. Faced with a loss of market share and potentially lower profits (and disgruntled shareholders), Fannie Mae and Freddie Mac started to purchase and securitize riskier subprime loans – some of which were no-doc loans. In addition to failing to anticipate the risks associated with buying mortgage loans that the borrowers could not afford to repay, the U.S. government can also be blamed for failing to acknowledge that the housing crisis was, indeed, a crisis. As late as August 2007, the leaders of the Federal Reserve were still convinced that the housing crisis was not widespread, that the United States would not enter a recession, and that the crisis was limited to the subprime mortgage market.

Federal regulators initially downplayed the severity of the housing crisis, even though consumer debt levels had been at unsustainable rates since at least 2005, mortgage defaults and foreclosure rates had begun climbing by 2006, and housing prices had started to decline at the beginning of 2007. State officials, in contrast, were worried well before the recession that the housing crisis would be widespread, and some states sought to regulate many of the high-risk mortgage products and lending practices that eventually caused the housing market to collapse. Rather than support these proposed regulations, however, the Office of the Comptroller of the Currency thwarted the states' attempts to regulate those lending practices and instead blamed subprime borrowers for the crash.

While many state officials blamed lenders for behaving recklessly and all but abandoning historical underwriting criteria, federal leaders insinuated that the increased rate of mortgage defaults and foreclosures were caused by irresponsible, greedy, or outright fraudulent borrowers. Rather than accept that the housing crisis was widespread and that far too many mortgage loans had been approved due to lax underwriting and lending policies in general, U.S. politicians seemed content to blame the collapse on homeowners and a handful of rogue brokers or smaller financial institutions.[35]

Even though the housing crisis had spread globally by March 2008, the United States remained unwilling to provide comprehensive mortgage relief for homeowners. The United States had, however, adopted the "too big to fail" policy to provide massive financial relief to prevent financial institutions that were deemed crucial to the U.S. economy from failing. For example, the United States brokered a deal with one investment bank (J. P. Morgan) to prevent another investment bank (Bear Stearns) from becoming insolvent

[35] See Fed. Res. Bd. of Governors, 2007 *Transcripts, available at* http://www.federalreserve.gov/monetarypolicy/fomchistorical2007.htm.

and filing for bankruptcy. The United States then proceeded to bail out or otherwise shield from financial ruin a series of financial institutions that were involved in the housing crisis (Citigroup Bank, the American International Group, and IndyMac) before placing the then nearly insolvent Fannie Mae and Freddie Mac into conservatorships under the direction of the Federal Housing Finance Agency (FHFA). By December 2008, the Federal Reserve was authorized to purchase GSE debt and to invest in MBSs in order to support mortgage lending and stimulate housing markets. By December 2010, the government had purchased $1.25 trillion in GSE MBSs and $172 billion of GSE debt.

Consumer advocates and populist critics responded to these bailouts by arguing that the United States provided corporate handouts to the very entities that banking regulators – most notably the Federal Reserve (the primary financial regulatory agency before the bust) – failed to oversee during the housing boom and that better oversight might have prevented the housing crisis.[36] Critics also noted that while the government was willing to fully guarantee high-risk, reckless investment deals and to shift the costs of those risky ventures onto U.S. taxpayers, the government has never been willing to force lenders or mortgage servicers to permanently write down the principal balance of mortgage loans or to otherwise bail out struggling homeowners who cannot afford to repay their loans or who have lost their homes in record numbers. The Consumer Financial Protection Bureau has recently adopted rules that limit fees for some mortgage products and curb some of the most abusive practices that occurred during the housing boom. Still, the government's primary response to pleas for relief for struggling homeowners has been a series of programs designed to help homeowners modify their mortgage payments, remain in their homes, and continue repaying their restructured mortgage debt.[37]

One of the earliest responses to the foreclosure crisis was the 2008 Hope for Homeowners program. This program was acknowledged to be an almost

[36] Congress responded to those criticisms by passing the 2010 Dodd–Frank Wall Street Reform and Consumer Protection Act. Office of Management and Budget, Executive Office of the President, *supra* note 1.

[37] For example, the CFPB recently announced a revised "Ability-to-Repay rule" that generally requires lenders to determine the consumer's ability to repay a loan's full amortized principal and interest, not just whether the borrower can afford the initial "teaser" loan payments. This rule also prevents lenders from offering no-doc or low-doc ("liar") loans. While lenders are not banned from making these high-risk loans, the Consumer Financial Protection Bureau strongly discourages borrowers from having total debt payments (including credit cards, student loans, and mortgage loans) that exceed more than 43 percent of their annual income, a much higher debt-to-income level than the previous 33 percent suggestion.

unmitigated failure largely because its success depended on a lender's agreement to voluntarily reduce a homeowner's mortgage debt to 90 percent of the home's value. If the lender agreed to reduce the debt, the lender would then refinance the mortgage into a new FHA-backed loan. Of the 400,000 homeowners projected to benefit from this program, a grand total of 764 actually received relief by the time this program ended in 2011. One of the first major programs of the new Obama administration that could be deemed a success was the Housing Affordability and Stability Plan (HASP), which included the Making Home Affordable (MHA) program.

The MHA was designed to help stem the losses that were flowing from the foreclosure crisis in general, to stimulate the U.S. economy, and to keep homeowners in their homes. The MHA included programs that provided for FHA refinance and loss mitigation programs, loan forbearance programs, housing counseling programs, and foreclosure alternative programs. The primary subprogram was the Home Affordable Modification Program (HAMP). Even though HAMP was not as disastrous as earlier programs, it also was destined to fail because of its single-minded focus on maintaining high homeownership rates and protecting home values for existing homeowners rather than addressing why so many homeowners could not afford to pay for their homes.

HAMP also relied on the voluntary participation of loan servicers. Servicers who were willing to participate in HAMP were required to lower the interest rates on mortgage loans in exchange for receiving certain government subsidies. But HAMP, unlike the Hope for Homeowners program, was a pure loan restructuring program. It was not designed to require *or even to request* that lenders forgive any of the balance remaining on the homeowner's mortgage loan.

For a whole host of reasons (including poor communication, foot-dragging, and weak regulatory oversight), HAMP faltered from the start. The Treasury Department and loan servicers reported numerous problems during the implementation phase. Moreover, HAMP consistently failed to provide meaningful relief to homeowners because it was overly complex, ill-designed, and (many concluded) hurriedly put in place within the first few months of the Obama administration.

The Home Affordable Refinance Program (HARP) was enacted in 2009 and was also designed to keep homeowners in homes by allowing them to restructure and then repay their mortgage loans. HARP's goal was to lower monthly loan payments for creditworthy homeowners who had underwater mortgage loans insured or owned by Fannie Mae and Freddie Mac. Despite repeatedly being modified to give lenders greater incentives to refinance mortgage loans, HARP (like HAMP) also failed to provide meaningful relief to the millions of homeowners who could not pay their mortgages and could not sell their homes.[38]

The HUD's Neighborhood Stabilization Program (NSP) was another attempt to provide relief to homeowners who were being harmed by the foreclosure crisis. The goal of the NSP, which was created in 2008, is to help cities deal with the problems caused by abandoned, deteriorated homes in their communities and to help ameliorate the harm those homes inflict on other homes in the neighborhoods. Cities that receive NSP grants can use those funds to buy land or houses, to demolish or rehabilitate abandoned properties, or to provide down payment or closing cost assistance to LMI families who seek to purchase the rehabilitated homes. Despite this program's noble goals, its limited funding has prevented it from providing significant assistance to cities with large numbers of abandoned homes.

Whether because of design flaw or the fact that so many homeowners had unaffordable and often underwater mortgages, by March 2012 most of the early attempts to provide relief to financially struggling homeowners had clearly failed. Because of their negative equity stake and because home prices in some areas still had not returned to pre-recession levels, by 2013 many underwater homeowners were not able to take advantage of the governmental programs and instead lost their homes to foreclosure. And, despite record low interest rates, millions of homeowners have not been able to refinance their mortgage loans because of their precarious financial states. To be sure, these recent housing initiatives helped some borrowers renegotiate some of the loan terms, such as interest rates, and helped them lower their monthly payments. But even federal officials have acknowledged that the government's response to the housing crisis failed to revive the economy in ways that were typical after most U.S. recessions.[39]

[38] *Foreclosure Prevention: Is the Home Affordable Modification Program Preserving Homeownership? Hearing before the House Committee on Oversight and Government Reform* (Mar. 25, 2010) (statement of Office of the Special Inspector General for the Troubled Asset Relief Program); *Foreclosure Prevention, Part II: Are Loan Servicers Honoring their Commitments to Help Preserve Homeownership, Hearing before the House Committee on Oversight and Government Reform* (Jun. 24, 2010) (statement of David Friedman, President and CEO of American Home Mortgage Servicing, Inc.).

[39] For example, the Federal Reserve noted that even three years after the recent recession ended, growth in the real gross domestic product (GDP) averaged only 2.2 percent annually. In contrast, for the three-year time spans following the previous ten U.S. recessions, average GDP growth was more than double (4.6 percent) the annual rate for the period following the most recent recession. Speech by Janet L. Yellen (Vice Chair of the Federal Reserve), *A Painfully Slow Recovery for America's Workers: Causes, Implications, and the Federal Reserve's Response*, at the A *Trans-Atlantic Agenda for Shared Prosperity* conference, sponsored by the AFL-CIO, Friedrich Ebert Stiftung, and the IMK Macroeconomic Policy Institute, Washington, D.C. (Feb. 11, 2013).

That these programs have failed is not surprising, because the programs – by design – skirt the issue of whether it remains sound policy to continue to encourage cash-strapped Americans with stagnant and declining wages to buy homes based on flawed premises that no longer reflect their economic reality. Indeed, the worst kept secret during the current housing crisis is that the U.S. government's attempts to solve the foreclosure crisis have been unsuccessful, and mortgage relief programs have failed because too many homeowners simply cannot afford to be homeowners.

The U.S. government's adamant refusal to seriously question whether the American Dream of homeownership remains a goal worth pursuing continues to have disastrous consequences for financially struggling American homeowners. Although polls indicate that most homeowners continue to believe owning a home is a good investment, Americans are increasingly skeptical of the government's role in promoting homeownership.[40] Indeed, many now believe that the U.S. push to get renters who lacked savings and steady income into homes did not create more stable citizens or communities. On the contrary, these flawed efforts destabilized neighborhoods and decimated the finances of renters who had unstable employment and high debt loads but were nonetheless encouraged to buy homes they could not afford.[41]

[40] Eighth Quarterly Allstate-National Journal Heartland Monitor Poll (2011).

[41] Michael Powell & Andrew Martin, *Foreclosure Aid Fell Short, and Is Fading*, N.Y. Times (Mar. 29. 2011); *The Obama Administration's Response to the Housing Crisis: Hearing before the Subcommittee on Insurance, Housing and Community Opportunity of the U.S. House of Representatives Committee on Financial Services* (Oct. 6, 2011) (written testimony of Carol Galante, Acting Assistant Secretary for Housing/Federal Housing Commissioner U.S. Department of Housing and Urban Development (HUD)); Joint Ctr. for Hous. Studies, Harvard Univ., *The State of the Nation's Housing* 11 (2011), *available at* http://www.jchs.harvard.edu/sites/jchs.harvard.edu/files/son2011.pdf; *Hearing on New Ideas for Refinancing and Restructuring Mortgage Loans before the U.S. Senate Committee on Banking, Housing, and Urban Affairs* (Sep. 14, 2011) (testimony of Mark Zandi, Chief Economist and Co-Founder of Moody's Analytics) *available at* http://www.ots.treas.gov/_files/490069.pdf; Fed. Res., *The U.S. Housing Market: Current Conditions and Policy Considerations* (Jan. 4, 2012).

6

Flawed Premises

In 2003, Franklin Raines, then Chair of Fannie Mae, declared that "[t]he American Dream of homeownership has never been a more powerful lure, nor has it ever been so achievable." According to Raines,

> [i]n almost every respect, 2003 was the greatest year for housing in America's history. Housing sales were at all-time highs. Mortgage interest rates dropped to their lowest level since the late 1960s. Mortgage originations were up more than 40 percent from just the year before, coming in at a remarkable $3.7 trillion, as consumers bought homes or refinanced their existing mortgage.[1]

Because interest rates were lower than they had been in almost forty years and housing prices had soared, homeowners "felt" wealthy and they refinanced their mortgages to cash out some of this perceived wealth. The year 2003 was definitely a banner year for housing sales and housing financing: corporate profits for the financial services sector and for the real estate industry soared. The year 2003 was not, however, a banner year for the cash-strapped customers who were being lured into buying homes or refinancing their mortgages in order to tap into their housing wealth.

The dramatic disconnect between soaring corporate profits and sinking household finances should have been a warning sign that something was amiss with the Happy Homeownership Narrative. But because U.S. leaders ignored the warning signs, the disconnect between the boardroom and the living room persists to this day. Political leaders still refuse to admit or accept that the Happy Homeownership Narrative is based on flawed premises and

[1] Fannie Mae National Housing Survey, *Understanding America's Homeownership Gaps* (2003).

assumptions that are no longer valid for many low- and moderate-income (LMI) Americans. Political leaders may refuse to acknowledge the disconnect between the premise and the reality, but those considering buying a home must understand that they are being encouraged to do so not for their own financial well-being but for the good of the U.S. economy and moneyed constituent groups who support U.S. political leaders.

ALL RENTERS CAN AFFORD TO BE HOMEOWNERS

U.S. housing policies are based on the assumption that most renters can afford to buy homes. These assumptions are no longer true for most LMI renters. Generally speaking, renters who are debating whether to buy a house must evaluate a number of factors. First, renters need to be sure that they have enough money to make a down payment. Second, they need to have relatively stable income and must be willing to remain thrifty for fifteen to thirty years while they repay the mortgage loan. Third, they need to gauge realistically whether they will be able to afford the other costs associated with homeownership, including maintenance costs (both routine and major repairs), insurance, and real property taxes for the rest of their lives. Finally, they need to consider the "what ifs": How will they make the monthly mortgage payments and pay for the other costs associated with owning a home if they lose their job or if they get hurt and are temporarily unemployed?

Even homeowners whose homes appreciate in value will need to have a reliable source of funds to pay for ongoing housing expenses (i.e., utilities, taxes, and routine maintenance). These expenses can be significant even if the home was new when the homeowner bought it. If the homeowner does not perform routine maintenance on the home, the home will not appreciate and likely will lose value. Moreover, an owner who remains in the same house for a long period of time will inevitably need to make major home repairs (like replacing a roof or electrical/mechanical systems) even after retiring the mortgage debt.

Routine maintenance is crucial, especially for older homes, and the cost to maintain homes increases with the age of the home. For example, some data indicate that the owner of an older home will pay .7 percent of the value of the home in annual routine maintenance, while owners of homes that are less than five years old pay less than .2 percent annually. Homes that are not maintained can drop as much as 3 percent in value annually, while performing routine maintenance may add as much as 1 percent of value to the home. Owners who purchased a home in a low-performing market especially need income to pay for routine maintenance, because keeping the house in good condition may be the only way they can reasonably expect to accumulate and maintain equity in the home.[2]

The buyers in the Happy Homeownership Narrative have stable and steadily increasing income over their working life. Today's home buyers can no longer assume that their household income will remain stable or that their income will increase during the fifteen- to thirty-year loan repayment period. While overall income stopped declining by 2013 (four years after the recession ended), household income actually fell more (6.7 percent) in the two years *after* the recession officially ended than it did (3.2 percent) during the 2007–2009 recession. Indeed, while overall income started to slowly rise in 2013, recent data show that the 2013 inflation-adjusted minimum wage is essentially the same as it was in the 1980s.[3]

Household income is especially fragile for senior Americans. Overall household income for all ages in June 2012 (three years after the recession ended) was about 5 percent lower than it was in 2009. Overall income for Americans aged fifty-five to sixty-four, however, was almost 10 percent less than it was in June 2009. Similarly, while overall household income fell 7.2 percent between 2007 and 2009, income for households between the ages of fifty-five and sixty-four fell by 9.7 percent. Recent evidence indicates that because retirement savings for so many Americans plummeted in value during the recession, more and more people nearing retirement age cannot afford to stop working because their depleted savings would not provide sufficient income to support them for the rest of their lives.

Almost 40 percent of the people who recently raided their retirement savings to pay current debts were over the age of fifty. These workers will almost certainly have to postpone their retirement in order to repay their debts, especially their secured (mostly mortgage) debts. Just as older Americans cannot continue to assume that their future earnings will be enough to pay for their reasonably foreseeable non-mortgage housing expenses (e.g., property taxes, insurance, and maintenance costs), stagnant income and high unemployment rates for all but the top earners now make it unreasonable for younger Americans to realistically expect that they can afford to buy a home using a traditional mortgage loan.[4]

[2] Shannon Van Zandt & William M. Rohe, *The Sustainability of Low-Income Homeownership: The Incidence of Unexpected Costs and Needed Repairs Among Low-Income Home Buyers*, 21–2 HOUSING POL'Y DEBATE, 317–41 (2011).

[3] Rolf Pendall et al., *Demographic Challenges and Opportunities for U.S. Housing Markets*, Bipartisan Policy Ctr. (Mar. 2012); Annalyn Kurtz, *A History of the Minimum Wage since 1938*, CNN (Feb. 14, 2013), *available at* http://economy.money.cnn.com/2013/02/14/minimum-wage-history/?iid=SF_E_River.

[4] Jessica Silver-Greenberg, *A Risky Lifeline for Seniors Is Costing Some Their Homes*, N.Y. TIMES (Oct. 14, 2012); Lori A. Trawinski, *Nightmare on Main Street: Older Americans and the Mortgage Market Crisis*, AARP Public Policy Institute (2012).

During the recent recession, the top 20 percent of workers received 53 percent of total income. Stated differently, the top one-fifth of workers received more than 50 percent of total income, leaving the remaining 80 percent of U.S. workers to share less than 50 percent of total income. The top earners also had larger wage increases. While overall male wages have increased by approximately 8 percent since 2000, wages increased more for the top 10 percent of earners (40 percent) than for the bottom 10 percent of earners (5 percent). Likewise, the wage increase for the top 10 percent of female earners was dramatically larger (70 percent) than the increase for the bottom 10 percent of female workers (8 percent).

As discussed in greater detail in Chapter 9, college-educated workers fared much better during the recession than workers who lacked college degrees. Although their income also fell during the recession, workers with college degrees had lower unemployment rates, more job security, and higher overall earnings than lower-educated workers. Indeed, the wage decline for workers who recently completed college was 50 percent lower than wage declines for workers who did not attend or complete college.[5]

By 2013, unemployment and underemployment rates had fallen from the heights they reached during the recent recession. Still, as discussed in Chapter 5, unemployment rates remain higher than they were before the 2007 recession started, and the gap between the highest earners and the rest of American workers continues to grow. The income gap between the highest and lowest earners continued to spread both during and after the recession, and now the only U.S. workers who can safely assume that they can afford to buy homes are higher-paid and higher-educated workers.

Whereas the homeowner portrayed in the Narrative is thrifty, financially responsible, and saves money to make a 10–20 percent down payment, many U.S. households have been drowning in debt since the mid-1990s. The ratio of household debts to personal income grew astronomically in the 1990s and 2000s. As Figure 6.1 shows, debt-to-income ratios grew modestly (and often fluctuated) until the early 1990s. By the early 1990s, however, debt levels started to rise and soared to a record high in 2007.

[5] Cong. Budget Office, U.S. Cong., *Trends in the Distribution of Household Income between 1979 and 2009* (Oct. 2011); Rebecca Blank, *Economic Change and the Structure of Opportunity for Less-Skilled Workers*, in Changing Poverty (Maria Cancian & Sheldon H. Danziger eds., Russell Sage Press, 2009); Harry J. Holzer & Marek Hlavac *An Uneven Road and Then a Cliff: U.S. Labor Markets since 2000*, Project U.S. 2010 (2011), *available at* http://www.s4.brown.edu/us2010/Data/Report/report4.pdf. College-educated women are especially likely to have more stable and higher-paid jobs relative to lower-educated male and female workers.; Pew Econ. Mobility Project, *How Much Protection Does a College Degree Afford? The Impact of the Recession on Recent College Graduates*, The Pew Charitable Trusts (2013), *available at* http://www.pewstates.org/uploadedFiles/PCS_Assets/2013/Pew_college_grads_recession_report.pdf.

Figure 6.1. Household debt-to-income ratio.
Source: Federal Reserve Board.

Ironically, one of the reasons debt levels soared during the housing boom was *because* of homeownership. Household wealth for homeowners increased during the housing boom. But this wealth increase masked homeowners' soaring debt levels and the fact that many cash-strapped renters used their homes to pay for other consumer debts. During the boom, renters dramatically increased their debt loads to buy homes that had escalated in value at the same time as existing homeowners borrowed *against* their appreciating homes to pay down credit card debt, pay college expenses, or pay for other household expenses. Many homeowners ultimately had mortgage debts on their homes that exceeded the market value of those homes. Although U.S. housing statistics include this group as homeowners, they essentially became renters because lenders actually owned more of their homes than they did.[6]

In addition to soaring mortgage debt, credit card debt levels also started to increase in the 1990s and have remained high. As shown in Figure 6.2, while average household credit card debt was approximately $2,100 in 1989, that number had almost quadrupled to approximately $8,200 by the 2007 recession. Credit card debt rose and has remained high, in part because of stagnant household earnings. Many U.S. households essentially viewed their credit card limits as replacement income for the wage increases they were not receiving.

[6] Atif R. Mian, & Amir Sufi, *Consumers and the Economy, Part II: Household Debt and the Weak U.S. Recovery*, FRBSF Economic Letter (Jan. 18, 2011); Reuven Glick, & Kevin J. Lansing, *Consumers and the Economy, Part I: Household Credit and Personal Saving U.S. Household Deleveraging and Future Consumption Growth*, FRBSF Economic Letter (January 2011).

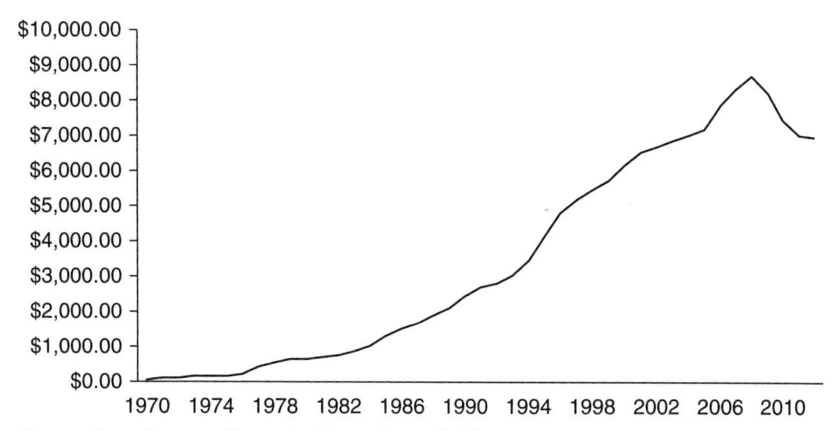

Figure 6.2. Average household credit card debt.
Source: U.S. Census Bureau, Federal Reserve Board.

U.S. households generally prefer to make ends meet by using credit cards rather than other forms of borrowing (like payday loans) because cardholders can use their credit cards to buy small household items or to pay for larger and more expensive goods or services (e.g., medical expenses) depending on the card's credit limit.

Ironically, the recession caused U.S. households to start saving again, and the U.S. savings rate actually peaked at more than 8 percent during the recession. By the end of the recession, Americans had started to pay down credit card and other household debt, and by 2010 the number of families who borrowed against their homes had dropped significantly. A number of reasons may explain why consumer spending slowed and why U.S. households increasingly deleveraged (i.e., reduced their debt loads) during and just after the recession. It is possible, of course, that consumers chose to save more and spend less because they rediscovered the virtues of thrift and frugality and decided to be more financially responsible. Similarly, consumers may have become more cautious and chose to spend less because persistently high unemployment rates made them wary about the future.

Although self-restraint could be the reason consumers deleveraged, it seems likely that many U.S. households were *forced* to deleverage because lenders tightened consumer credit after the housing crash, causing a significant decrease in the availability of consumer credit. As noted in Chapter 4, lenders increased the supply of mortgage credit during the housing boom by dropping historical lending criteria to make it easier for renters to buy homes and for owners to borrow against their homes. Once the housing market crashed and the recession started, however, lenders severely restricted consumer credit, especially for potential borrowers who already had defaulted on mortgages and for people with low credit scores. So, while some Americans may have chosen to be thrifty and spend less, other cash-strapped households were forced to deleverage because they did not have savings, may have been unemployed (and thus lacked income), and no longer had easy access to credit.

For whatever reason, despite low interest rates, U.S. households deleveraged during the recession, and by the end of 2011, household debt levels had dropped to mid-1990 levels. Deleveraging was good for individual households. But household deleveraging was bad for the U.S. economy because the economy depends so heavily on consumer spending. In fact, financial analysts uniformly concluded that consumers' unwillingness to borrow and spend slowed the recovery of the U.S. economy. Fortunately (for the U.S. economy, at least) overall consumer debt levels started to increase in 2012, and by March 2013 some economists concluded that the bulk of U.S. household deleveraging was over and that the U.S. economy was finally in a consistent state of recovery.[7]

While many households deleveraged during the recession, Echo Boomers (i.e., the generation of adults born between the years 1980 and 1995, the oldest of which were thirty-three in 2013) were financially devastated by the recession and found it harder to deleverage and regain their financial stability. Echo Boomers are the generation of Americans who should be starting to form households and buy homes. Instead, they are now the first generation of Americans who are delaying home purchases.

In sharp contrast to the Baby Boomers who flooded the single-family housing market in the 1970s when they married and formed households, Echo Boomers are continuing to live at home with their parents or with friends. For example, the number of Americans between the ages of eighteen and thirty-four who live at home with their parents rose between 2006 and 2010, and by the end of the recession, one in three members of this age group lived at home with their parents. The age group that is slightly older than the Echo Boomers also faces a grim financial future. Generation Xers (roughly the generation born between 1966 and 1975 and who were between the ages of thirty-eight and forty-seven in 2013) lost almost half of their wealth from 2007 to 2010.[8]

Finances for younger Americans remain precarious, principally because real income growth for them has barely increased. Four years after the end

[7] Annie Lowrey, *Rise in Household Debt Might Be Sign of a Strengthening Recovery*, N.Y. TIMES (Oct. 26, 2012); Associated Press, *Consumers Raised Debt in March*, N.Y. TIMES (May 7, 2012).

[8] Because female Echo Boomers are more likely to attend college and work outside the home and all Echo Boomers are remaining single longer and having children later than Baby Boomers, these factors may dramatically change housing markets and depress future homeownership rates.

of the recession, unemployment rates remain high. Echo Boomers and Gen Xers have relatively higher credit card and student loan debt loads than other demographic groups, and they have higher debt levels than Baby Boomers did at similar ages. While Echo Boomers are more likely to have college degrees than their Baby Boomer parents, they are now at considerably higher risks of living in poverty and many of them are forced to live in someone else's household just to be able to live above the poverty line.[9] Americans – whether they are young Echo Boomers, middle-aged Gen Xers, or Baby Boomers have good reason to worry about their economic futures. Given the current economic conditions, many Americans simply cannot assume that hard work and high hopes are enough to help them achieve the American Dream.[10]

EVERYBODY *SHOULD* BUY A HOME

In the Happy Homeownership Narrative, buying is *always* more economically and emotionally beneficial than renting. However, just because renters can afford to buy a house does not necessarily mean that they *should* buy one. Once renters determine that they can afford to make a down payment, to pay housing maintenance costs, and to repay the mortgage loan over fifteen–thirty years, they should still compare the relative value of buying over renting and should buy a house only if being homeowners provides the best financial return for them. At a bare minimum, before buying a house renters should determine how much it would cost to rent a house that is comparable to the house that they intend to buy (i.e., the price-to-rent ratio). Then, before buying a house to take advantage of the homeownership tax benefits, they should be sure that they will actually be eligible to make use of those benefits.

[9] Bipartisan Policy Ctr., *supra* note 3; Joint Ctr. for Hous. Studies, Harvard Univ., *The State of the Nation's Housing* (2012), *available at* http://www.jchs.harvard.edu/sites/jchs.harvard.edu/files/son2012.pdf; Pew Charitable Trusts, *Retirement Security across Generations: Are Americans Prepared for Their Golden Years?* Echo Boomers have higher mobility rates than earlier generations. They are less likely to put down roots in a community and to purchase a home because they have less job security than the Baby Boomers. When Echo Boomers are ready to buy homes, though, it will be harder for them to find suitable housing. The homes built for the Baby Boomers in the 1970s are larger in size than many single, childless Echo Boomers need, and the square footage of homes has consistently increased since the 1970s. Echo Boomers who may want to become homeowners do not have the same incentives to buy a home as earlier generations did because they are more likely to be single and less likely to have children. Consequently, they may find it particularly challenging to find houses that fit their needs because the glut of homes were built for married couples with children.

[10] Robert Pear, *Recession Officially Over, U.S. Incomes Kept Falling*, N.Y. TIMES (Oct. 9, 2011); Pew Research Ctr., Pew Charitable Trusts, *The Lost Decade of the Middle Class: Fewer, Poorer, Gloomier* (Aug. 22, 2012).

Assuming rents are high relative to mortgage payments and the renters earn enough money to take advantage of the homeownership tax benefits, renters then need to estimate the *reasonably likely* return on their housing investment. Of course, owners in the Happy Homeownership Narrative buy homes that *always* appreciate in value. But, as discussed in more detail later in this chapter, not all homes appreciate in value. Moreover, even if a house is likely to appreciate in value, renters must consider whether it is likely that they will remain in the house long enough to recoup their home buying costs. Owners who purchase a house in a widely appreciating housing market might be able to sell the home for a profit even if they remain in the house for a very short period of time. However, most buyers need to remain in their home for at least three years just to break even and recoup their purchase and sales costs.[11]

Before buying a house, renters also need to consider whether they are likely to receive the noneconomic benefits associated with homeownership. As noted in Chapter 2, homeowners have always had more political, economic, and social privileges than renters, but not all homeownership benefits are evenly distributed through all neighborhoods. Homeowners overall are more politically powerful than renters, but some owners are more powerful than other owners, and power tends to be concentrated in upper-income, white neighborhoods.

Not all homeowners can successfully lobby to prevent unwanted (though potentially socially beneficial) properties from being placed in their neighborhoods. Moreover, not all homeowners can protect the long-term quality of their neighborhood schools, parks, and other community amenities, or guarantee that their neighbors will always take care of their homes and otherwise engage in activities that protect the value of all the homes in the neighborhood. Only homeowners who live in neighborhoods with low foreclosure rates and whose residents have stable income can feel confident that they have the ability to protect the long-term quality of their communities. Thus, in addition to comparing the relative economic benefits of owning versus renting, before renters make a financial commitment to a neighborhood, they must try to gauge whether the neighborhood is likely to remain one that will provide long-term noneconomic benefits.

Finally, renters also need to consider the opportunity costs of using funds to invest in a house rather than in an alternative investment. Few potential homeowners likely view the decision to buy a home as a choice between competing investment devices. But when renters spend money to buy the house

[11] Andrew Haughwout et al., *The Homeownership Gap*, 15–5 Current Issues in Economics and Finance (May 2010), *available at* http://www.newyorkfed.org/research/current_issues; William M. Rohe & Leslie S. Stewart, *Homeownership and Neighborhood Stability* 7–1 Housing Pol'y Debate 43 (1996).

they intend to occupy, they are also making a decision to use money to invest in a house rather than place that money in another investment vehicle. Thus, in addition to making the short-term economic decision to pay either rent or a loan payment, when renters decide to use money to pay for a house over a fifteen- to thirty-year period, they are also making a longer-term investment decision. The investment decision to buy a house (and earn profits from the anticipated appreciation) is not necessarily related to the decision to consume a particular type of housing. But the consumption decision (to live in a certain type of house in a particular neighborhood) is often influenced by whether a buyer thinks that owning that particular house is more profitable in the long run than putting money in another investment vehicle.

Most renters probably do not consider whether they *should* buy a home once they have concluded – or the lender has told them – that they can afford to buy a home. Buying a home is not always wise financially, as evidenced by the catastrophic losses in the recent housing crash. Because homeownership may not be economically and emotionally satisfying long term due to future changes in the local housing market, renters should stop assuming that they *should* buy a home simply because they *can* buy one.

ALL HOMEOWNERS RECEIVE TAX BENEFITS

The ability to deduct mortgage interest payments and real estate taxes on federal income tax returns is the largest, best advertised, and likely most popular homeownership benefit. Overall housing costs for homeowners (mortgage payments, taxes, insurance, and maintenance expenses) often exceed what they would pay to rent similar housing. Federal tax benefits are designed to help offset these potentially higher ownership costs and to encourage Americans to buy houses. As a result, homeownership is more financially beneficial than renting for some taxpayers because, as discussed in detail in Chapter 3, tax benefits allow homeowners who itemize their deductions to reduce their tax liability and thereby increase their income. Homeowners also receive tax benefits when they sell their houses because they can avoid paying capital gains taxes on up to $500,000 on the profits from the sale, assuming they wait two years between home sales. In the Happy Homeownership Narrative, these tax benefits make buying preferable to renting for *all* renters.

The Happy Homeownership Narrative never mentions that most taxpayers (70 percent) take the standard deduction and do not itemize their deductions or that most itemizers are higher-income taxpayers. LMI households are less likely to benefit from the mortgage interest deduction (MID) in part because they have lower homeownership rates. Moreover, even when they *do* own homes, their homes typically are smaller, less expensive, and require smaller mortgage loans. With smaller mortgage interest payments, these households are significantly less likely to itemize their deductions and are more likely to take the standard deduction.

While homeowners may not realize who reaps the benefits of the homeownership tax subsidies, Congress has known for at least thirty years that higher-income taxpayers disproportionately benefit from the MID. In 1981, when less than 40 percent of all homeowners claimed the MID, a Congressional Budget Office report observed that

> higher-income taxpayers are more likely to own homes – in particular, more expensive homes with larger mortgages and correspondingly larger interest payments. Higher-income taxpayers also receive a disproportionate share of the tax savings because many lower-income homeowners do not itemize deductions.[12]

This trend has continued since the CBO released this report because, while the vast majority of LMI taxpayers take the standard deduction, more than 98 percent of *high-income* taxpayers are itemizers. Similarly, while 60 percent of higher-income taxpayers take the MID, only 10 percent of lower-income taxpayers take the MID.[13]

While most Americans (be they renters or owners, or upper-, lower- or moderate-income) enthusiastically support these homeownership tax subsidies, they probably do not realize (and the Happy Homeownership Narrative certainly never mentions) that this tax subsidy benefits only a small percentage of taxpayers and drains approximately $90 billion in revenue from the U.S. Treasury for the MID, but forces *all* taxpayers to subsidize large, expensive homes. As noted in the 1981 CBO report and a report prepared thirty years later by the Joint Committee on Taxation, housing tax subsidies distort housing choices by giving higher-income taxpayers an economic incentive to buy larger homes (with larger mortgages) than they would buy absent the subsidies.

Buying a larger and more expensive home with a larger mortgage loan allows taxpayers to deduct the interest and property taxes they incur, and, as a result, reduces their overall tax burden. These tax incentives then increase the demand and cost of *all* homes by potentially creating bidding wars that would not take place without the subsidy. These regressive tax subsidies are then capitalized into the price of all housing, increase housing prices generally,

[12] Cong. Budget Off., U.S. Cong., *The Tax Treatment of Homeownership: Issues and Options* 11 (Sept. 1981).

[13] J. Comm. Tax'n, *Present Law and Background Relating to Tax Treatment of Household Debt* (Jul. 11, 2011).

and unfairly redistribute income from renters and LMI homeowners (who do not generally benefit from the subsidy) to existing higher-income homeowners (who disproportionately benefit from the subsidy).[14]

ALL HOMES APPRECIATE IN VALUE

The Happy Homeownership Narrative never discloses that the biggest gamble an owner makes when buying a house is whether or not the house will appreciate in value. Generally speaking, a home will not appreciate unless the owner buys the *right* house at the *right* time and in the *right* location. The Happy Homeownership Narrative largely ignores these factors and for years has convinced naive renters that buying a home is a surefire investment, that homes always appreciate in value, and that they will be able to sell their homes for a profit regardless of the location or the demographic makeup of the residents in the neighborhood. Of course, no one can predict with 100 percent accuracy whether a given house or neighborhood will be in high demand or appreciate in value. Still, it is possible to make a few generalizations about when houses are likely to increase in value.

Housing prices appreciate when there is an increased demand for housing. As was true when the Baby Boomers started to buy homes in the 1970s, when a large cohort group in a population starts to form households, there will be a greater demand for housing, and this increased demand will drive up prices. Similarly, increased housing demand (and price appreciation) often occurs when new workers migrate to a region because of a strong labor market. Housing prices are especially likely to increase if the workers who move to the area are higher-income or if the households include school-age children. Conversely, as is evident in the current economic crisis, housing prices generally decline when a region experiences an overall economic downturn.

Additionally, the scarcity of land typically drives up the value of the remaining land, especially if the region is experiencing strong economic growth and an influx of workers. Construction costs also affect the price of housing and, as the home building industry regularly asserts, burdensome or excessive regulations or zoning laws often increase the costs of residential housing development and construction.[15] For example, zoning regulations in single-family

[14] Eric Toder, *Mortgage Interest Deduction: Background Information*, Tax Policy Center (Jul. 28, 2011); Consumers Union, *Rich House, Poor House: The Two Faces of Home Equity Lending* 3 (1997), *available at* http://www.consumersunion.org/finance/home-tx2.htm; Lee Anne Fennell, *Homes Rule*, 112 YALE L. J. 617 (2002).

[15] For example, the cost to build homes in California soared during the late 1960s and early 1970s after state and federal environmental regulations restricted the supply of developable land.

neighborhoods regulate lot sizes in ways that make it harder to build smaller, more affordable homes. These lot size regulations reduce the supply of land that can be used to build multifamily units. If there is a high demand for homes in an area that has a small supply of developable land, housing demand and prices for houses will increase. This likely explains why appreciation rates for homes in neighborhoods with exclusionary zoning laws tend to be higher than appreciation rates in areas that have more inclusive zoning.[16]

The types of houses and amenities found in neighborhoods also affect the demand for the housing and the housing appreciation rates. Households with school-age children prefer to live in single-family housing in neighborhoods with high-performing schools. Because there is a modest supply of single-family housing on the rental market, households with school-age children prefer to be homeowners rather than renters. Parents' desire to buy single-family housing in neighborhoods that have higher-ranked schools then causes those homes to appreciate more than homes in neighborhoods with academically deficient schools. Similarly, homes in neighborhoods that have developed a positive reputation because of the perceived quality of the neighborhood amenities (including schools) generally have higher appreciation rates because community amenities are capitalized into the price of housing.

National policies unrelated to housing can also influence the price of U.S. housing. For example, after the terrorist attacks on 9–11, the U.S. Federal Reserve kept interest rates artificially low to spur economic growth. Similarly, the Federal Reserve kept interest rates low during the housing boom (and recent recession) to encourage people to buy houses.

During the housing boom, lower interest rates succeeded in boosting housing sales and keeping the U.S. economy strong, but they also encouraged borrowers to buy homes they could not afford. In fact, mortgage innovation and the increased availability of credit created two unintended but predictable consequences: soaring housing price escalation and bidding wars.

Even though well-maintained, single-family homes historically have had higher rates of appreciation, during the housing boom, renters and homeowners seemed to think that *all* houses were a safe, reliable way to build wealth.

[16] For example, during the late 1980s, there were housing booms in California, New York, Seattle, and Boston. During these volatile booms, housing appreciated in these places at rates that ranged from 30 to more than 110 percent, while appreciation rates nationally ranged from 14 to 28 percent. Karl E. Case, *Land Prices and House Prices in the United States* 40 (1984); *Hearing before the Subcommittee on Housing and Community Opportunity of the House Committee on Banking and Financial Services*, 106th Cong., 1st sess., at 83 (Sep. 15, 1999) (testimony of Antone Giodano on Behalf of the National Association of Home Builders); Urban Policy Brief, *Homeownership and Its Benefits*, No. 2 (Aug. 1995), *available at* http://www.huduser.org/publications/txt/hdbrf2.txt [hereinafter *Homeownership and Its Benefits*];

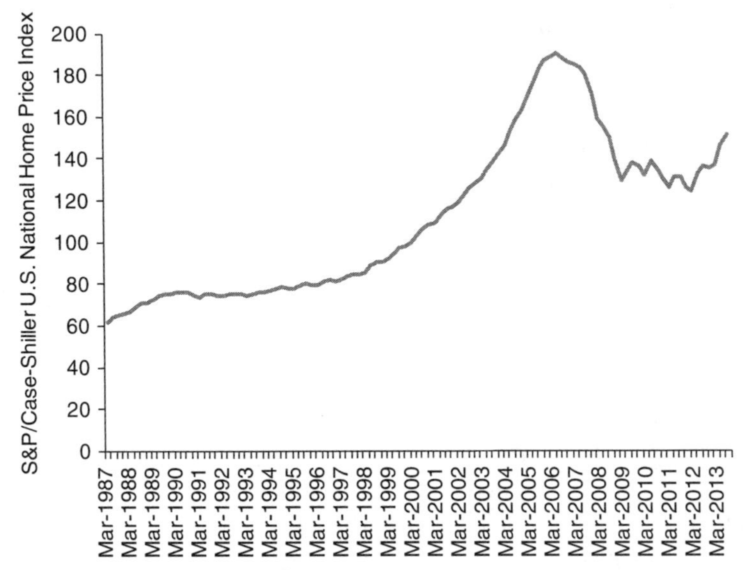

Figure 6.3. Home price trends.
Source: S&P.

Stated differently, while everyone has heard that "location, location, location" is the key to making sure that a house appreciates in value, when housing prices were increasing at astronomical rates during the housing boom, buyers seemed to believe the Happy Homeownership Narrative that homeownership was a guaranteed way to build wealth and that all homes (regardless of type or location) appreciate in value. House prices rose by approximately 40 percent between 2003 and 2007, and house prices in some U.S. metropolitan areas rose by more than 60 percent during the housing boom. As shown in Figure 6.3, housing prices started to decline in 2007 and fell by more than 25 percent between 2007 and 2009. Prices did not start consistently rising in most U.S. markets until 2013.[17]

The recent housing bust is a painful reminder that, before renters decide to buy a house, they must realistically assess the type of financial return they think they will receive from the house. If a renter buys a house that does not appreciate or if the increase does not exceed the total costs associated with homeownership (purchase costs, mortgage interest, taxes, utilities, maintenance, and comparable rental costs), the renter may forever regret the decision to buy rather than rent.

[17] Karl E. Case et al., *Wealth Effects Revisited: 1978–2009* (Nat. Bur. Econ. Research, Working Paper No. 16848, Mar. 2011); Case-Shiller, *U.S. National Home Price Index 1987–2011*, *available at* http://macromarkets.com/csI_housing/.

HOMES ARE JUST USED FOR SHELTER

In the Happy Homeownership Narrative, Americans want a safe and secure shelter that they can call home. Notwithstanding this premise, homeowners do not view their houses as places to enjoy and occupy solely because of the comfort they give to the owner in the present. Even though many home buyers made no down payments during the housing boom and some had loan balances that were increasing each month (i.e., the loans negatively amortized), owners viewed their homes as investments that would provide future financial benefits. Rather than treating their heavily mortgaged homes as the debts that they actually were, homeowners instead felt that high appreciation rates meant that their homes were allowing them to amass permanent wealth even if they had little or no equity in these homes. They were cash-poor, but they felt house-rich, and this feeling of wealth induced these negative equity owners to leverage and borrow against their homes.

Unlike the home envisioned in the Narrative, U.S. homes have come to be viewed as assets that can – and should – be converted into cash that an owner can use to make non-housing investments or finance purchases, or to repay or reduce non-housing debts. During the housing boom, homeowners increased – not retired – their mortgage debt by refinancing their mortgage loans or taking out "home equity" loans. Ironically, until homeownership rates stalled in the 1990s, home equity loans were called "second mortgages," and these loans were stigmatized so as to be avoided at all costs. Because mortgage debt was designed to go down – not up – only truly desperate homeowners would voluntarily increase their mortgage debt by taking out a second mortgage.

During the housing boom, however, financial institutions launched expensive advertising campaigns that were designed to remove the stigma associated with second mortgages and to rebrand these disfavored loans as products that helped homeowners free up cash that was trapped in their houses. Thus, flashy advertising campaigns extolled the virtues of home equity loans and encouraged homeowners to "Live Richly," "Make Dreams Happen," and "Seize your someday."[18] While second mortgages were considered to be for losers, home equity loans were branded as a way to give owners the financial freedom to make their dreams come true.[19]

[18] Louise Story, *Home Equity Frenzy Was a Bank Ad Come True*, N.Y. TIMES (Aug. 14, 2008).

[19] As an example of how second mortgages shifted in nomenclature: in 1999 the Harvard Joint Center for Housing Studies State of the Nation's Housing report used the term "second mortgage." By 2001, though, the report discussed how rising home prices and falling interest rates allowed homeowners "to tap into their home equity through refinancing and lines of credit." Joint Ctr. for Hous. Studies, Harvard Univ., *The State of the Nation's Housing* (2001), *available at* http://www.jchs.harvard.edu/sites/jchs.harvard.edu/files/son2001.pdf.

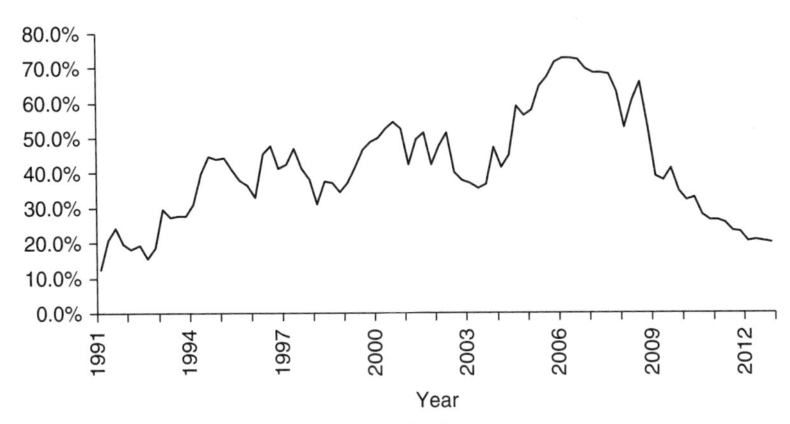

Figure 6.4. Percentage cash-out-share of refinances.
Source: Federal Housing Finance Agency.

Once owners stopped viewing mortgages as burdensome loans that should be repaid as soon as possible, homes stopped being "forced savings devices" and started to look more and more like automated teller machines. Far too many homeowners overdrew their "housing" accounts. As indicated in Figure 6.4, less than 25 percent of mortgage refinances were cash-out refinances in 1991. By 2006, however, more than 70 percent of all refinances were cash-outs. From 1991 to 2005, U.S. consumers extracted approximately $60 billion from their homes annually. During the housing boom, homeowners extracted an average of $700 billion in equity annually with $627 billion extracted in 2001 and a whopping $1.4 trillion extracted in 2005.[20]

Households with children, lower-income homeowners, and non-white households seemed especially likely to withdraw housing equity between 1998 and 2005. Studies indicate, however, that many of these homeowners appeared to have low levels of financial literacy and did not comprehend the risks the withdrawals from their "housing" accounts posed to their long-term financial and housing security. Just as reverse mortgages (or payday loans) can sometimes be a rational form of borrowing, there are sound reasons for homeowners to increase their mortgage debt by borrowing against their homes. For example, many homeowners sensibly use equity extractions to pay for home improvements and for medical or college expenses. Unfortunately, many households use the proceeds from home equity loans to pay down non-mortgage consumer debt – usually credit card debts – or to purchase other consumer goods. In

[20] Alan Greenspan & James Kennedy, *Sources and Uses of Equity Extracted from Homes*, 24–1 Oxford Review of Economic Policy 120–44 (2008).

effect, homeowners place their homes at risk in order to pay for stuff in the home, in their backyards, on their bodies, and in their driveways.[21]

Rather than discourage homeowners from treating their homes like an ATM and placing their homes at risk in order to pay for consumer goods or services, the United States gives homeowners a powerful incentive to borrow: homeownership tax benefits. As discussed earlier, the U.S. Tax Code places absolutely no restrictions on what homeowners can do with the proceeds of a home equity or cash-out refinancing loan. Banks' advertising campaigns during the housing boom made sure borrowers understood that the interest they paid on home equity loans is tax deductible just like interest payments on the mortgage loan they used to buy their homes. Given that U.S. tax laws let homeowners deduct the interest they pay on *all* mortgages regardless of how they used the loan proceeds, homeowners had an incentive to borrow against their homes to pay for medical or educational expenses (or to pay to install a swimming pool, finance Botox injections, buy a Harley, or pay their Visa or MasterCard bills).

Homeowners may not have realized that they were putting their shelters at risk by increasing the debt on their homes. The U.S. government knew what taxpayers were doing, however, and it did nothing to discourage people from jeopardizing the safety and security of their homes. Of course, U.S. leaders had an incentive to encourage homeowners to continue to extract equity from their homes: those risky transactions were propping up the U.S. economy and those second mortgages were good for the lenders who profited from the loan transactions.[22]

YOU OWN YOUR HOME . . .FOREVER

In the Narrative, thrifty young renters save for a down payment, buy a home using a low-cost, fifteen- to thirty-year, self-amortizing mortgage, and then repay the loan well before reaching retirement age. With no housing debt, the owners will be able to pay for ongoing living expenses with money saved while working or from a retirement pension. If the owners need to do major renovations to the home when they (and it) get older and they happen not to have enough money, in the Narrative they will have enough home equity to borrow against the house to pay for those renovations. Thus, in the Happy

[21] John V. Duca & Anil Kumar, *Financial Literacy and Mortgage Equity Withdrawals* (Dec. 16, 2010), *available at* http://www.kc.frb.org/publicat/events/research/2011DayAhead/DucaKumar.pdf.

[22] J. Comm. Tax'n, *supra* note 13; Joint Ctr. for Hous. Studies, Harvard Univ., *The State of the Nation's Housing* (2002), *available at* http://www.jchs.harvard.edu/sites/jchs.harvard.edu/files/son2002.pdf.

Homeownership Narrative, homeowners who save and sacrifice when they are young will be rewarded with a rent-free home for life. This was a likely scenario for most homeowners who purchased homes when the United States first started to subsidize home purchases after the Great Depression. But this part of the Narrative also portrays an outdated view of the economic reality most homeowners face.

While owners in the Happy Homeownership Narrative "own" their Home Sweet Home as soon as they sign the closing documents and move in, borrowers do not actually own their homes until they repay the mortgage loan. Unless homeowners pay for the house in cash, they will co-own the home with a lender for a number of years. Owners are especially likely to be in a long-term co-ownership relationship with a lender if they make a small down payment or if they increase and extend their mortgage debt by refinancing the loan or taking out a second mortgage. Furthermore, if the homeowners end up underwater (i.e., they owe more on the house than it is worth), they essentially enter in a long-term rent-to-own contract with the bank.

The Narrative also does not disclose that many owners, especially LMI homeowners, may never actually own their homes because they will be forced to move before they can recoup their initial buying costs and start accumulating equity. Nothing in the mound of required documents that buyers receive at closing warns them that one in eight homeowners move within three years of the time they purchase a home, one in three move within five years, and the average homeowner stays in a house for about eight years. Owners who are confident that they will own their homes for life do not perceive that there is always a possibility that they will need to move because of their jobs and that they may be forced to quickly sell their homes, potentially at a loss if the housing market is sluggish or sliding.[23]

The Happy Homeownership Narrative incorrectly portrays homeownership as a surefire way to have rent-free housing for life. Younger homeowners generally have higher delinquency rates than homeowners over the age of fifty. During the recent economic crisis, however, serious delinquency rates (which include mortgages that are ninety days or more delinquent and loans in foreclosure) for older Americans significantly outpaced rates for younger homeowners. The rates continued to soar even after the recession ended. The serious delinquency rates for prime loans for Americans over the age of fifty increased from .4 percent in 2007 to 2.5 percent in 2011, but the serious delinquency rate for subprime loans soared from approximately 7 percent in 2007 to

[23] Joint Ctr. for Hous. Studies, Harvard Univ., The State of the Nation's Housing (2006), *available at* http://www.jchs.harvard.edu/sites/jchs.harvard.edu/files/son2006.pdf.

25 percent in 2011. By the end of 2011, approximately 3.5 million loans held by older Americans were underwater, 600,000 of their loans were in foreclosure, and another 625,000 loans were seriously (ninety days or more) delinquent. During this five-year period, more than 1.5 million older Americans lost their homes, and the highest foreclosure rate during this period was for homeowners over the age of seventy-five. [24]

During the housing boom, older Americans withdrew equity from their homes at alarming rates and seemingly failed to understand that cash-out refinances endangered their long-term housing security. Older homeowners most often drained equity from their homes using reverse mortgages. As discussed in Chapter 5, reverse mortgages were marketed to seniors as a way to "unlock" cash from their homes that they could then use to pay bills – or travel to exotic locales. Unfortunately, many seniors took out reverse mortgages from brokers who misrepresented the nature of the loans or who engaged in other fraudulent behavior by, for example, keeping the loan proceeds and never giving the money to the homeowners.

Because so many older Americans lost their jobs during the recession or had shrinking retirement income, many seniors who used the proceeds from reverse mortgages to pay off other debts could not afford to pay property taxes or insurance. These senior Americans lost their homes even though they *were not* defrauded simply because they siphoned equity from their homes (at increasingly younger ages), and then could not afford to pay property taxes, insurance, or their other ongoing living expenses. While the older homeowners portrayed in the Narrative may live care-free and rent-free, actual housing security for older Americans has become decidedly insecure.

RENTERS PREFER SINGLE-FAMILY HOUSES

As noted earlier in this chapter, when renters decide to buy a home, they are making economic, investment, and consumption choices. Renters must first consider the cost of owning relative to the cost to renting, and then must decide whether to invest in a house or to place that money in another investment vehicle. They must then choose the particular type of house – either rented or owned – that suits their consumption preferences. In fact, renters who want to personalize their house in ways that a property owner might find objectionable may prefer to buy even if buying may not be the best investment or tax decision. For example, renters who want to paint the interior walls of their home salmon pink and apple green might be unwilling to rent a home

[24] Silver-Greenberg, *supra* note 4; Trawinski, *supra* note 4.

with beige walls – even if renting is the most sensible financial choice – if their idiosyncratic color preferences are more important to them than their monthly housing costs.

The housing consumption decision that renters can make is limited by the availability of particular types of dwellings. Most housing units in the United States are detached, single-family houses, and homes in the most desirable U.S. housing markets are overwhelmingly owner-occupied. Likewise, neighborhoods that have the most highly ranked schools consist primarily of single-family, detached housing. Given the limited stock of detached, single-family rental homes, renters who prefer to live in these types of homes are pushed toward homeownership simply because of the difficulty of finding their preferred housing on the rental market. Similarly, renters who want their children to attend highly ranked public schools in a well-respected school district may feel pressure to buy rather than rent.

Even if buying a home may not be in the household's overall economic or investment interest, the limited stock of single-family, detached rental homes in neighborhoods with highly ranked schools will push households with school-age children toward homeownership. Of course, single-family, detached houses can be rental properties and, as shown in the recent housing crisis, single-family, detached houses can easily vacillate between being owner- and renter-occupied properties. Renters who lack a strong economic or investment reason to buy a home ostensibly should not care whether they rent or buy a single-family home as long as it is located in a convenient, desirable neighborhood or school district. As long as U.S. tax laws and local zoning regulations favor owner-occupied housing, however, renters who can afford to buy a house will always be pushed toward homeownership.[25]

HOMEOWNER STABILITY IS AN ABSOLUTE GOOD

In the Happy Homeownership Narrative, being staked to real property gives the owner more housing security and makes the owner a more stable citizen. Without statutory rent controls or a written agreement with the landlord, a renter always faces the risk that the landlord will increase the rent. And, as

[25] David K. Ihrke & Carol S. Faber, *Geographical Mobility: 2005 to 2010: Population Characteristics*, U.S. Census Bureau (Dec. 2012); Edwin S. Mills & Ronald Simenauer, Homeownership as an Investment: Recent Trends and the Outlook for the 1990s (1991); U.S. Dep't of Hous. and Urban Dev. *American Housing Survey for the United States* (2009); Bipartisan Policy Ctr., *supra* note 3; Lewis M. Segal & Daniel G. Sullivan, Fed. Res. Bank of Chicago, *Trends in Homeownership: Race, Demographics, and Income*, Economic Perspectives (1998).

many renters discovered during the recent recession, a renter also faces the risk of eviction if the landlord fails to repay a mortgage loan or applicable property taxes on the rented housing. Given that they lack housing security, renters are assumed to be more mobile and less committed to their neighborhoods. U.S. leaders justify providing generous homeownership benefits because homeowner stability is viewed as good for families and is said to make neighborhoods safer and more secure.

As discussed later in this section, homeowners are considerably less mobile and are less likely to be planning to move than renters, and this appears to be true *even if neighborhood conditions are deteriorating.* When neighborhood conditions deteriorate, renters can leave when their lease term expires (or even earlier, if they can afford to make double rent payments for a few months). In contrast, homeowners cannot cut their losses easily, cheaply, or quickly because selling a house generally takes time. As a result, while homeownership gives an owner a financial stake *in* the house, homeownership also stakes the owner *to* the house. Renters may face housing *insecurity*, but they are spared from an unspoken and often overlooked negative consequence of homeowner stability: decreased mobility.

Because the homeowners depicted in the Narrative have stable employment and intend to remain in their homes for the long term, they do not need to consider whether homeownership prevents them from being able to reduce their living expenses if they lose a job or are forced to take a pay cut. Similarly, because all homes in the Happy Homeownership Narrative appreciate, a homeowner would never need to consider whether being anchored to a house makes it harder to accept a job in another city. Unlike this fictionalized view of homeownership, household income has become stagnant and the labor market has not provided reliably stable jobs for LMI workers for almost thirty years. Today's homeowners (unlike the mythical homeowners in the Narrative) need to be prepared to be unemployed at some point during their lifetime, and, increasingly, they need to be prepared to move to another city to accept a job.

It is hard for homeowners to sell their homes for a profit and move unless their homes are well-maintained and there is a supply of available buyers. While homeowners can always abandon their home or sell the home for a loss to reduce living expenses or to take a job in another area, most people are reluctant to do so, *especially* if they have accumulated equity in the house. If homeowners do not have accumulated home equity, being immobile and anchored to a house can have catastrophic consequences. Specifically, if housing markets are sluggish and the owners have little equity in their home or have an underwater mortgage, they can sell their homes and move only if they have enough disposable cash to pay off what is essentially a lump sum balloon payment. As was true for homeowners during the Depression, few underwater homeowners have enough spare disposable cash to pay off an underwater mortgage and they are especially unlikely to have cash if they need to move because they lost a job or their income dropped and they need to reduce their living expenses.

For many homeowners, the home has now become a burdensome albatross. Renters who are not staked to real property can more easily move to another region to accept a new job because the primary financial expense they face (other than the expenses all people face, such as moving expenses) is a potentially forfeited security deposit. In contrast, today's unemployed homeowner with an underwater mortgage continues to face the same choices unemployed homeowners had during the Depression: either remain unemployed in an unaffordable home (until the bank forecloses on the loan) or sell the home at a loss and accept employment in another area. Even if the homeowner abandons the house (or sells for a loss) and the lender repossesses the house, the owner is still liable for the mortgage debt. The homeowner can still be sued by the lender, and defaulting on the mortgage loan increases the risk that the homeowners' credit rating with be harmed.

While strategic defaults increased during the recession, data suggest that homeowners will not walk from their homes unless the amount they owe on the home is more than 60 percent higher than the value of the home. Moreover, owners generally resist selling their homes below a certain reservation price they have set, which is rarely lower than the amount of debt remaining on the home. Indeed, economic studies have found that individuals, especially those with a high degree of loss aversion, are simply unwilling to take a loss on the sale of their home, *even if* this decision may force them to forgo a better job opportunity in another city. As a result, most homeowners who have accumulated a significant amount of equity in their homes will not walk away from this investment unless the job they are offered in another area pays them enough to make mortgage payments on the loan for their existing home (which they cannot sell or can only sell at a loss) and also to pay for housing (be it rented or purchased) in the new location.[26]

[26] In addition to the 60 percent equity threshold, other factors that affect whether a homeowner will strategically default or will instead try to repay the mortgage include morality (the belief that it is wrong not to pay your bills) and whether the homeowner knows or lives near other owners who have strategically defaulted. Homeowners who are more financially literate also appear more likely to strategically default once they owe more than 50 percent of the home's value. Jeremy Burke & Kata Mihaly, *Financial Literacy Social Perception and Strategic Default* (Jun. 2012); John Leland, *Facing Default, Some Walk Out on New Homes*, N.Y. TIMES

Because of the significantly higher transaction costs associated with selling a home, homeowners are considerably less mobile than renters. During the recent economic crisis, many homeowners found themselves staked to property that they no longer wanted and that they could not afford. Census data show that fewer people moved in 2010 than any year since 1975. Other labor data show that U.S. workforce mobility is now at its lowest rate since World War II and that areas with decreased labor mobility because of high homeownership rates are statistically more likely to have high unemployment rates. Because so many unemployed and underemployed homeowners are tethered to homes that they cannot sell, it has become much harder for labor markets to match available jobs with workers who have the skills to perform those jobs. In short, while homeowner stability may be good for neighborhoods, having large numbers of unemployed or underemployed homeowners rendered immobile because a housing anchor is not good for labor markets. More importantly, being staked to a home they no longer want and can no longer afford is not good for owners.[27]

HOMEOWNERSHIP RATES WILL PLUNGE WITHOUT GOVERNMENT SUBSIDIES

U.S. housing policies subsidize homeownership, and politicians resist attempts to modify tax benefits based on the premise that eliminating or scaling back housing subsidies will depress homeownership rates. The United States is not alone in favoring homeownership over renting. Most developed countries support and often subsidize homeownership because of the role housing and consumer spending play in their nation's wealth and GDP. Similarly, homeownership is favored globally because of its perceived external benefits to communities and neighborhoods. Like in the United States, homeownership

(Feb. 29, 2008); Karl E. Case, *Land Prices and House Prices in the United States* 43 (1984). Although it is not a perfect analogy, unemployed, underwater homeowners currently face a dilemma similar to the one sharecroppers faced in southern farming states in the nineteenth and twentieth centuries. In a typical sharecropping arrangement, a sharecropper would plant crops on someone else's land and – in exchange for nominally "free" rent – would then be required to give the owner half the value of the crops. Sharecroppers usually bought seeds and farming equipment on credit from the owner (sometimes at exorbitant prices), and to repay this debt, sharecroppers would often need to work the land for an additional season. The largely uneducated sharecroppers usually lacked the ability to effectively market the crops to anyone other than the owner of the land, who usually determined the market value of the crop. Shareholders often found themselves trapped because they could not repay the debt to the landowner from the last season unless they stayed on the land to harvest a new crop the next season.

[27] Ihrke & Faber, *supra* note 25; Haughwout et al., *supra* note 11; David G. Blanchflower & Andrew J. Oswald, *Does High Home-Ownership Impair the Labor Market?* (Peterson Institute for International Economics, Working Paper No. 13–3, 2013).

is supported in other countries because it purportedly helps households accumulate wealth, makes owners more independent, more responsible, and better citizens, and provides social benefits for children. Citizens in other countries also view homeownership as a "dream," a path to a good life, and a way to avoid being a second-class citizen.[28]

As was true in the United States, homeownership rates increased in most European nations after World War II, and global homeownership rates have generally increased over the last thirty years. Before the housing market crashed in the mid-2000s, global homeownership rates ranged from less than 40 percent in Switzerland and Japan to 85 percent or higher in Ireland, Iceland, and a few Eastern European countries. As was also true in the United States, global housing prices soared from the 1990s through the mid-2000s largely because of strong global economies. This housing price appreciation increased household wealth, but it also made homeownership an increasingly elusive goal for LMI renters.[29]

Few nations had lending standards that were as lax as the U.S. underwriting standards during the housing boom. Still, borrowers in other countries were also approved for larger housing loans and were allowed to buy homes with smaller down payments. They were able to do this because of lower interest rates globally, financial market deregulation, and an increased reliance on financial intermediaries (like mortgage brokers) in housing transactions.

As was true in the United States, when the prime mortgage loan market became saturated in the early 2000s, the global financial community turned to the subprime mortgage loan market to maintain high levels of mortgage loan originations. Those subprime loans were also sold and packaged into securities, and the profitability and popularity of these securities (and the growth of

[28] Ownership, Control, and the Future of Housing Policy (R. Allen Hays ed., 1993); Ray Forrest & Ngai-Ming Yip, Housing Markets and the Global Financial Crisis (2011); Sarah Nettleton & Roger Burrows, *When a Capital Investment Becomes an Emotional Loss: The Health Consequences of the Experience of Mortgage Possession in England*, 15–3 Housing Studies 463–79 (2000).

[29] For example, ownership rates are lower in South American countries, in part due to relatively less developed mortgage markets and a limited housing supply. As is true in the United States, global homeownership rates generally increase with age, educational attainment, and income, and two-couple households with children are more likely to be homeowners than single-person households. Dan Andrews & Aida Caldera Sánchez, *Drivers of Homeownership Rates in Selected OECD Countries* (OECD Economics Department, Working Paper No. 849, 2011), *available at* http://dx.doi.org/10.1787/5kgg9mcwc7jf-en; Jón Rúnar Sveinsson, *Housing in Iceland in the Aftermath of the Global Financial Crisis*, in Housing Markets and the Global Financial Crisis 59 (Ray Forrest & Ngai-Ming Yip eds., 2011); Marc H. Choco, *Homeownership: From Dream to Materiality*, in Ownership, Control, and the Future of Housing Policy 9–10 (R. Allen Hays ed.,1993); Marc Hofstetter et al., *Effects of a Mortgage Interest Rate Subsidy: Evidence from Colombia* (IDB, Working Paper No. 257, 2011).

that market) gave lenders an incentive to originate more (and riskier) mortgage loans. When the U.S. housing crisis spread and triggered the global financial crisis in the mid-2000s, housing prices declined globally and homeowners abroad – like their U.S. counterparts – were often trapped with mortgages that were larger than their homes were worth.[30]

Despite higher homeownership and high house appreciation rates in the United States and globally over the last twenty years, homeownership subsidies vary wildly by country. A number of countries also give citizens incentives to purchase homes, but the United States stands alone in the price tag it places on the importance of homeownership. Other than Eastern European nations that had quasi-socialized or state-controlled systems of homeownership, no other country has ever provided homeownership subsidies that are as generous as U.S. tax benefits.

It is impossible to generalize the similarities and differences in the tax treatment of mortgage debt globally. Generally speaking, some countries give taxpayers a onetime grant when they purchase homes, while others give limited tax credits or let homeowners shield some of their income from tax when they sell their homes. Allowing homeowners to deduct mortgage interest, as is done in the United States, has been criticized globally because wealthier taxpayers are the main beneficiaries of this regressive tax subsidy, and the deduction encourages taxpayers to buy larger and more expensive houses. Likewise, critics in other countries note that the deduction is capitalized into real house prices, which increases overall housing costs and makes homeownership more costly for lower-income households.[31]

Because people buy homes for both financial and noneconomic – or personal – reasons, there is no reason to think that U.S. homeownership rates will plummet if U.S. politicians limit homeownership subsidies. Indeed, despite claims that people will stop buying houses if the United States reduces homeownership tax incentives and subsidies, there is no evidence that countries (like the United States) that provide a generous MID will necessarily have higher homeownership rates. For example, while homeownership rates in the United States and the

[30] Adam J. Levitin & Susan M. Wachter, *Information Failure and the U.S. Mortgage Crisis*, in THE AMERICAN MORTGAGE SYSTEM: CRISIS AND REFORM (Susan M. Wachter & Marvin Smith eds., 2011); Alan Murie, *The Changing Face of Homeownership in Britain: Divisions, Interests, and the State*, in OWNERSHIP, CONTROL, AND THE FUTURE OF HOUSING POLICY 110 (R. Allen Hays ed., 1993); Peter Mooslechner & Karin Wagner, *What Are the Relevant Issues Today?*, in HOUSING MARKET CHALLENGES IN EUROPE AND THE UNITED STATES chapter 2 (Philip Arestis et al., eds., 2010).

[31] Andrews & Caldera Sánchez, *supra* note 29. For example, before Hungary abolished its mortgage tax deduction in 2007, the top 20 percent of households with the highest income received 60 percent of the tax benefits from this housing subsidy. József Hegedüs, *Housing Policy and the Economic Crisis: The Case of Hungary*, in HOUSING MARKETS AND THE GLOBAL FINANCIAL CRISIS 119 (Ray Forrest & Ngai-Ming Yip eds., 2011).

Netherlands (countries that allow the MID) have exceeded 60 percent, other countries (like Switzerland) that allow the MID have relatively low homeownership rates (less than 30 percent). Likewise, national homeownership rates are high in some countries (including Canada, Australia, and Great Britain), even though the home buyers in those countries receive relatively limited subsidies to buy homes, and the subsidies they do receive are considerably less generous than the benefits that homeowners in the United States receive.[32]

As discussed earlier, U.S. homeownership tax subsidies disproportionately benefit higher-income households, and these subsidies encourage higher-income taxpayers to buy *more* houses, because larger interest payments allow them to shield more of their income from taxes. There is no clear evidence, however, that these subsidies give LMI households any incentive to buy homes, because most LMI households are not itemizers. While supporters of the MID argue that repealing or reducing the MID would make homeownership less desirable, reducing this tax subsidy could instead make homeownership more desirable (albeit for a different demographic group) by keeping housing affordable and accessible for homeowners from *all* income groups.

Even though higher-income homeowners might reduce their housing consumption and buy smaller homes if the United States were to scale back homeownership subsidies, the MID was never meant to encourage taxpayers to buy McMansions. Because, however, the real estate and financial services industries *need* people to buy homes and because these industries profit handsomely when McMansions are built and sold, U.S. housing policies have aggressively and persistently encouraged homeownership, even though those policies do not necessarily help LMI homeowners.[33]

U.S. HOUSING POLICIES ARE DESIGNED TO HELP HOMEOWNERS

U.S. housing policies that give people financial incentives to buy houses are justified by the Happy Homeownership Narrative's premise that homeowners are more stable and financially responsible than renters are, as well as

[32] J. Comm. Tax'n, *supra* note 13; Mooslechner & Wagner, *supra* note 30; Murie, *supra* note 30; Michelle Norris & Nessa Winston, *Housing Wealth, Debt and Stress before, during and after the Celtic Tiger*, in HOUSING MARKETS AND THE GLOBAL FINANCIAL CRISIS (Ray Forrest & Ngai-Ming Yip eds., 2011); ASHOK BARDHAN ET AL., GLOBAL HOUSING MARKETS: CRISES, POLICIES, AND INSTITUTIONS (2012). Homeownership rates in some nations exceed U.S. homeownership rates, but the quality of the amenities and services in owner-occupied homes varies, often dramatically, as some houses lack kitchens or have bathrooms that most U.S. households would find unacceptable. Dan Andrews et al., *Housing Markets and Structural Policies in OECD Countries* (OECD Economic Department, Working Paper No. 836); Marcela Cristini et al., *Argentina's Housing Market in the 2000s* (IDB, Working Paper No. 262, 2011).

[33] Eric Toder et al., *Reforming the Mortgage Interest Deduction* (Apr. 2010).

the belief that the United States benefits from having involved, civic-minded stakeholders. In years past, the Narrative may have accurately reflected the primary reason that U.S. political leaders encouraged taxpayers to go into debt to buy a home. But U.S. housing policies now encourage homeownership because it is good for the U.S. economy and *especially good* for the financial services and real estate industries.

Since at least the 1920s, the real estate industry has been one of the most politically influential interest groups in the United States and the industry has had a strong influence on U.S. housing policies. For example, when the United States shifted from an agrarian to an urban economy after World War I, the real estate industry foresaw a housing crisis because of the likelihood that urban dwellers would rent rather than buy their own homes. To avert that crisis, the real estate industry convinced the U.S. government to launch a public service campaign to persuade Americans that they had a patriotic duty to buy and own their own home. Urged in large part by then Secretary of Commerce Herbert Hoover, the U.S. Department of Commerce joined forces with realtors to establish housing policies that extolled the benefits of homeownership and encouraged Americans to buy homes. Since then, the real estate lobby's influence has thwarted all serious attempts to make U.S. housing policies favor multifamily or higher-density housing.[34]

Democratic and Republican leaders and the real estate and financial services industries all maintain that homeownership is good – indeed critical – for the United States because the housing sector plays such a critical role in stimulating economic growth. Personal consumption (i.e., consumer spending) is the largest component of the U.S. gross domestic product (GDP), and consumer spending on goods and services has consistently been the primary driver of U.S. economic growth. Indeed, until the 2007–2009 recession, personal consumption expenditures accounted for about two-thirds of all economic activity in the United States. Revenue from the housing sector (including actual home sales, home furnishings, real estate broker and agent fees and commissions, and state and local tax revenues) has consistently accounted for approximately 20 percent of consumer spending.[35]

[34] For example, efforts like the "Own Your Home" and the "Everyman's House" campaigns during the 1910s and 1920s admonished men to buy homes for their children's sake and to make their wives' dreams come true. JEFFREY M. HORNSTEIN, A NATION OF REALTORS®: A CULTURAL HISTORY OF THE TWENTIETH-CENTURY AMERICAN MIDDLE CLASS 123–32, 138–45 (2005).

[35] The 2002 Report of the Bipartisan Millennial Housing noted that "[t]he development of housing has a major impact on the national economy and the economic growth and health of regions and communities. Housing is inextricably linked to access to jobs and healthy communities and the social behavior of the families who occupy it. The failure to

A robust housing market is good for builders, banks, home improvement stores, and the U.S. economy. After major wars, economic downturns, and natural disasters, the United States has always relied on consumer spending, *especially housing expenditures*, to help revive an ailing economy. Building and selling homes boosts employment rates, increases the demand for consumer goods and services, and invigorates other economic activity (which is why local governments welcome builders of single-family housing, especially high-end homes, with open arms).

In addition to its profitability to banking institutions, mortgage lending also bolsters the U.S. economy. For example, while cash-out refinancing loans fell into disfavor after the recession, during the housing boom a congressionally appointed bipartisan housing commission looked favorably on cash-out refinance loans, observing that "homeowners cashed out more than $100 billion in equity through refinancing, using the proceeds for debt consolidation, home improvements, consumer purchases, investment, and other purposes *that helped to stimulate the economy*."[36] The U.S. economy remained sluggish for years after the recent recession ended largely because the residential housing construction sector struggled to recover from the financial crisis.

As noted earlier, lenders tightened lending standards even for borrowers who could qualify for prime mortgages, which made it harder for borrowers other than speculators and investors to qualify for low-cost prime mortgages. Tight credit hampered the recovery of the housing market, and the sluggish market contributed to higher unemployment rates because workers were not being hired to design or build homes or to produce the goods or provide the services (e.g., real estate agents, lawyers, and brokers) associated with building, buying, and selling homes.[37]

The U.S. government no longer subsidizes homeownership solely or even primarily because of idealized notions about how homeownership betters the lives of individual homeowners and their families. Political leaders no doubt support homeownership subsidies because of their desire to enact policies that improve the overall strength of the U.S. economy. Individual

achieve adequate housing leads to significant societal costs." *Meeting our Nation's Housing Challenges, available at* http://govinfo.library.unt.edu/mhc/MHCReport.pdf.

[36] *Meeting our Nation's Housing Challenges, supra* note 35, at 12.

[37] David Leonhardt, *Debt and Spending May Slow as Housing Falters, Fed Suggests*, N.Y. TIMES (Aug., 20, 2007), at C3; Fannie Mae National Housing Survey, *The Growing Demand for Housing* 2 (2002); Robert B. Avery et al., *The Mortgage Market in 2011: Highlights from the Data Reported under the Home Mortgage Disclosure Act*, Federal Reserve Bulletin, Bureau of Economic Analysis table 1.5.6 (Real Gross Domestic Product), available at http://www.bea.gov/national/nipaweb/TableView.asp?SelectedTable=36&Freq=Qtr&FirstYear=2007&LastYear=2009; *Meeting our Nation's Housing Challenges, supra* note 35.

political leaders have another, more personal, reason to support laws and policies that keep homeowners moored to homes: the real estate and financial services lobby *needs* those laws and *needs* people to buy houses.

The lobbying group broadly defined as the "financial sector" (which includes real estate interests and banks) is enormously influential and has consistently provided the largest source of campaign contributions to federal candidates and parties. Their contributions are bipartisan, although Republicans received higher contributions than Democrats until 2008. In the 2008 election cycle – when the recession had barely ended and the United States was still in the midst of an economic meltdown – these groups donated $468.8 million to federal campaigns and candidates. This was an 80 percent increase from the previous election cycle. The real estate industry alone gave $135 million to federal candidates and campaigns in 2008, with the National Association of Realtors leading the pack with $4.3 million in contributions.[38]

Public and private housing sector participants have always been intensely loyal to each other and have consistently rallied to defend each other from attack. For example, the Chair of the Senate Committee on Banking, Housing, and Urban Affairs has referred to realtors, home builders, and the financial services industry as "partners" in the government's attempts to expand homeownership opportunities for minorities.[39] Fannie Mae has viewed mortgage brokers, realtors, and lenders as unofficial partners in the effort to increase the number of Latino and black homeowners. Likewise, when Congress considered legislation that would have placed stringent regulations on Fannie Mae, Fannie Mae responded by employing seventy lobbyists to thwart those efforts.

Fannie Mae and Freddie Mac also made bipartisan contributions to political leaders and organization to ensure they would be protected. For example, in the 2002 election cycle, Freddie Mac contributed almost $1.7 million to the Democratic Party, more than $950,000 to the National Republican Congressional Committee (NRCC), and more than $660,000 to the Democratic Senatorial Campaign Committee, while Fannie Mae contributed more than $440,000 to the NRCC.[40]

The finance and housing sector (including the National Association of Home Builders and large mortgage lenders) have also protected Fannie Mae

[38] Opensecrets, *available at* http://www.opensecrets.org/industries/indus.php?ind=F10.

[39] *Hearing before the Committee on Banking, Housing, and Urban Affairs of the U.S. Senate, on Increasing Minority Homeownership, and Expanding Homeownership to All Who Wish to Attain It*, 108th Cong., 1st Sess. (Jun. 12, 2003) (statement of Sen. Richard Shelby, Chair of the Senate Committee on Banking, Housing, and Urban Affairs).

[40] Opensecrets, *available at* http://www.opensecrets.org/parties/contrib.php?cycle=2002&cmte=NRCC.

and Freddie Mac. In fact, the housing and financial services sector routinely joined with liberal Democrats, the Congressional Black Caucus, and the Congressional Hispanic Caucus to block attempts to regulate these GSEs from the early 2000s almost until the time they had to be placed in a conservatorship in 2008.[41] Moreover, in addition to receiving campaign contributions from the GSEs and the real estate sector, U.S. political leaders have also been the beneficiaries of low-cost, low-risk mortgage loans from private lenders. For example, a 2012 report disclosed that members of the U.S. House Oversight and Government Reform Committee and their staff members participated in a "VIP" program that allowed them to be approved for discounted mortgage loans.[42]

Given that political leaders have both political and personal interests in protecting the businesses who profit most from home sales, it is not surprising that, even when it became clear that mortgage banks and lenders were behaving recklessly and preying on certain low-income (and predominately minority) borrowers, U.S. leaders largely turned a blind eye to their behavior. And even when it was clear that many of the nontraditional subprime mortgage products that lenders were pushing were overly complex and unduly risky, political leaders resisted attempts to regulate lenders or to ban any of those risky loan practices and products.

When the United States encouraged lenders to innovate in the 1990s, those lenders acted with an exclusive profit-making motive. Their lending was not based on the altruistic, community-based model of mortgage lending depicted in the Christmas classic *It's a Wonderful Life*. Financing home sales, especially during the housing boom, was extraordinarily profitable, as the quote by the former chair of Fannie Mae that appears at the beginning of this chapter shows.

Ironically, the year 2013 looked remarkably like the year 2003: Corporate profits, the S&P 500 Index, and the Dow Jones Industrial Average bounced back from the recession and hit record highs. Nevertheless, U.S. household income remained sluggish, unemployment and underemployment rates remained high, and U.S. household finances remained as precarious as ever. Owning a home can, of course, increase an owner's net wealth. Given the political and financial influence of the financial services and real estate lobby, however, U.S. elected leaders have a political incentive to create, encourage, and subsidize home purchases. Despite the disconnect between what is good for U.S. households and what is good for the real estate and

[41] Johan Norberg, *Financial Fiasco: How America's Infatuation with Homeownership and Easy Money Created the Economic* Crisis (2009)

[42] Larry Margasak, *Report: Countrywide Won Influence with Discounts*, Associated Press (Jul. 5, 2012); Fannie Mae Foundation, African American and Hispanic Attitudes on Homeownership: A Guide for Mortgage Industry Leaders 8–9 (1998).

financial services sector, U.S. leaders continue to encourage people to buy homes without disclosing that homeownership is "good" for reasons that have more to do with the financial interests of influential lobbying groups than the financial well-being of the people who are being encouraged to buy homes. As the next four chapters show, this disconnect is vast, wide, and particularly harmful for blacks and Latinos.

7

The Burden of Home Buying While Black or Latino

After the Great Depression and again after World War II, the U.S. government engaged in aggressive efforts to increase overall homeownership rates. One early marketing and advertising effort, pushed by the powerful and politically influential real estate lobby, was the "Everyman's Home" campaign. This campaign emphasized that home buying was not just for the doctor and lawyer: *everyone*, including the wage-earning plumber or the electrician, could become a homeowner in the United States. This certainly was true for *some* doctors, lawyers, and wage earners.[1]

The Happy Homeownership Narrative neglects to mention that virtually all of the programs and initiatives the United States created to encourage and help Americans buy and remain in their homes, including the Everyman's Home campaign, were designed to help white households. Until homeownership rates stalled in the 1990s, U.S. political leaders engaged in few major efforts to make homeownership accessible or affordable for blacks or Latinos.

Black renters who have tried to become homeowners have been deemed "mud people" who do not pay their bills, their neighborhoods have been called slums, and the loans that banks offer to them have been called "ghetto loans." While such racist references and stereotypes might have been expected – and certainly would not have been shocking – in the 1940s or 1950s, loan officers referred to blacks using these derogatory terms in the 2000s, while they were steering blacks to higher cost mortgage products during the housing boom. Unlike the potential homeowners envisioned in the Everyman's Home campaign, blacks and Latinos have *always* faced significant, and at times almost insurmountable, burdens when they have tried to buy homes – whether they are doctors, lawyers, plumbers, or electricians.

[1] Jeffrey M. Hornstein, A Nation of Realtors®: A Cultural history of the Twentieth-Century American Middle Class 129–130 (2005).

REDLINING

As discussed in Chapter 3, the United States created the Home Owners' Loan Corporation (HOLC) to help stem the rising number of mortgage defaults and foreclosures during the Depression. The HOLC was authorized to buy short-term adjustable rate mortgages (ARMs) that were in default (or likely would be defaulted) from private banks and then refinance those ARMs with government-backed, fixed rate mortgages (FRMs) that were longer-term and self-amortizing. The HOLC also was authorized to grant loans to help owners recover homes they had lost to foreclosure. The HOLC's activities were largely financed by borrowing from the U.S. Treasury and from capital markets. The coordinated public-private venture succeeded in helping financially stressed homeowners to avoid foreclosure and remain in their homes. But only white homeowners were allowed to participate in the HOLC buy back/refinance program because of a racially biased loan rating system commonly known as redlining.

Although the HOLC did not create the racially biased redlining rating system, it systematized and legitimized redlining by using it to create an elaborate residential mapping series that divided neighborhoods based on their desirability, stability, and security. The color of the homeowners' skin was a central factor in the rating system, and race was used to determine whether a neighborhood was safe or desirable. The HOLC's rating system was derived in large part from the Realtors Code of Ethics. This Code, which was developed in the 1920s, admonished realtors not to engage in acts that would be "instrumental in introducing into a neighborhood a character of property or occupancy, members of any race or nationality, or any individuals whose presence will clearly be detrimental to property values in that neighborhood."[2]

Even though black *maids* and *servants* have lived in homes owned by whites throughout U.S. history, realtors deemed the presence of black *homeowners* in non-black neighborhoods to be detrimental to the property values of the homes owned by whites in those neighborhoods. The view that homeowners (or renters) of different races should be kept in separate U.S. neighborhoods and that all-black or racially mixed neighborhoods were high-risk were core elements of the Realtors Code. In fact, realtors were required to embrace redlining and adhere to these racist policies as a condition of membership in the National Association of Real Estate Boards.

Consistent with the view that the presence of members of certain racial groups (blacks) in certain neighborhoods (all-white) would harm property

[2] *Id.*, at 107.

values, the real estate industry developed a racial coding system to keep the races segregated. The HOLC's rating system gave neighborhoods occupied by higher-income whites the highest rating of "A". A neighborhoods were shaded green on the maps. In contrast, all-black neighborhoods received the lowest ranking of D and were shaded red. Because the real estate industry and the HOLC deemed homes in ethnically or racially integrated neighborhoods to be unstable, redlining made it virtually impossible for the few Depression-era blacks who owned homes to convert their short-term, high-cost loans into lower-cost and lower-risk HOLC loans.[3]

No one ever provided empirical data that proved that the mere presence of black homeowners in a white neighborhood would depreciate the values of white-owned homes. Instead, redlining's racist premises appear to have been derived from a prominent appraiser's "scientific evidence" that homes in white neighborhoods would automatically depreciate in value if blacks moved into those neighborhoods. This premise ignored existing stable, racially mixed neighborhoods that provided safe financial returns to owners. Despite the lack of objective evidence, realtors, local politicians, and the HOLC concluded that once blacks invaded a white neighborhood property values would drop.[4]

The government legitimized the discriminatory treatment of black and other non-white borrowers by using racist underwriting criteria to determine which mortgage loans it would approve or insure. As noted in Chapter 3, the Federal Housing Administration (FHA) was one of the many federal agencies that helped make homeownership more accessible and affordable to a broader swath of renters after the Depression. The FHA helped stabilize U.S. housing markets during the Depression by adopting policies that gave lenders an incentive to offer longer-term, lower-cost, and lower-risk loans. Lenders had an incentive to relax their underwriting criteria and offer long-term loans that had lower interest rates because the FHA guaranteed lenders that it (the government) would repay the loans if borrowers failed to do so. Because the risk

[3] John Kimble, *Insuring Inequality: The Role of the Federal Housing Administration in the Urban Ghettoization of African Americans*, 32 LAW AND SOC. INQUIRY 399 (2007); LEEANN LANDS, THE CULTURE OF PROPERTY: RACE, CLASS, AND HOUSING LANDSCAPES IN ATLANTA, 1880–1950 (2009); MEIZHU LIU ET AL., THE COLOR OF WEALTH: THE STORY BEHIND THE U.S. RACIAL WEALTH DIVIDE (2006).

[4] For example, the FHA reviewed a study prepared by an economist in San Francisco who found that when black residents moved into predominantly white neighborhoods in the San Francisco Bay Area there was no statistically significant impact on the values of the neighborhood's properties. While there was no valuation change in certain neighborhoods, some had a small property decline, while others actually had higher price valuations (which appears to have resulted from black home buyers' willingness to pay higher prices to live in white neighborhoods). Kimble, *supra* note 3.

of default for these loans shifted from lenders to the U.S. government, lenders were willing to expand credit and approve more mortgage loans because they knew they would be repaid even if the borrower defaulted.

This increased incentive to approve FHA-insured mortgage loans also made lenders considerably less willing to approve mortgage loans for potential homeowners who could *not* be approved for an FHA-insured loan. Lenders also had no incentive to approve loans that did not have FHA insurance because they faced significantly more restrictive federal regulations if they approved non-FHA loans. That is, to protect the financial stability of the banking industry, until the 1970s federal regulations essentially prevented banks from approving non-FHA-insured loans that included terms that were as favorable as FHA-insured loans. Because banks could not approve low-cost, low-risk, non-FHA-insured loans, *even if a private mortgage insurer had been willing to insure the loan*, the combination of federal regulations and redlining made it virtually impossible for blacks to buy homes (or for whites to buy homes in racially mixed neighborhoods) with low-cost mortgage loans.

Like the HOLC program, the FHA loan program's racist lending criteria and policies had the explicit goal and specific intent of keeping neighborhoods racially and economically segregated. The underwriting manual the FHA used starting in the 1930s favored neighborhoods that were stable and protected from "adverse influences," and the manual encouraged builders to include racially restrictive covenants in the subdivisions they built. As discussed in greater detail later in this chapter, these covenants were designed to prevent blacks from buying homes in predominantly white neighborhoods. Once the FHA lent its support to these racially biased covenants, developers routinely included the covenants in the homes they built in new (typically suburban) subdivisions. Moreover, the builders used subtle racial cues to signal that the subdivisions were racially exclusive by advertising that the homes in their developments met the FHA standards and could be purchased with a low-cost, FHA-insured loan.[5]

The FHA manual, like the Realtors' Code, concluded that it would be impossible for a neighborhood to retain stability unless the homes in the neighborhood would "continue to be occupied by the same social and racial classes."[6] The FHA imposed lending requirements to monitor whether a buyer

[5] Examples of restrictive covenants have been collected by the Seattle Civil Rights and Labor History Project, *available at* http://depts.washington.edu/civilr/covenants.htm ("No person of any race other than the white race shall use or occupy any building or any lot, except this covenant shall not prevent occupancy by domestic servants of a different race domiciled with an owner or tenant").

[6] Adam Gordon, *The Creation of Homeownership: How New Deal Changes in Banking Regulation Simultaneously Made Homeownership Accessible to Whites and Out of Reach for Blacks*, 115 Yale L.J. 186 (2005).

sought to use an FHA loan to buy a house in a non-white neighborhood or whether a black homeowner wanted to buy any home (be it in a black or white neighborhood). For example, the FHA would not insure mortgage loans unless the lender provided information about the borrower's characteristics, including his or her race. The FHA also required lenders to provide reports from architectural inspectors, risk examiners, and appraisers, and the FHA would not accept an appraiser's report unless the report disclosed whether the neighborhood was racially mixed. For all-white neighborhoods, the appraiser was required to disclose whether the neighborhood was at risk of being "infiltrated" or "invaded" by blacks or immigrants.[7]

As discussed in Chapter 3, borrowers who qualified for an FHA-insured loan had lower home buying costs, more predictable monthly payments, and lower risks of default because the loans had longer (typically thirty-year) repayment periods, were fully amortized, had smaller down payment requirements, and had lower interest rates. Because lenders generally would (or could) not approve low-cost loans unless the loans were federally insured, and because the FHA would not insure loans to purchase homes in racially mixed or homogeneous black neighborhoods, redlining increased housing costs for people who wanted (or were forced) to buy homes in racially or ethnically mixed neighborhoods.

The federal interventions in the mortgage finance market in the 1930s that made homeownership more accessible and affordable for whites who wanted to buy homes failed to provide the same benefits for potential black homeowners or for anyone who wanted to live in a non-white neighborhood. Unlike white potential homeowners, black renters who wanted to become homeowners were forced to save for a larger down payment in order to buy a home (often an older home in an urban area with lower appreciation rates) using higher-cost, non-FHA loans that had shorter repayment periods and above-market interest rates.

In addition to increasing the home buying and long-term housing costs for black households and making homeownership riskier for them relative to white borrowers, the FHA's racist underwriting policies helped maintain racially segregated neighborhoods. That is, even a white home buyer who *might* have been interested in living in a racially diverse area had a strong economic incentive to avoid the area, because it was virtually impossible for *anyone* to purchase a house in a racially mixed neighborhood with a low-cost, FHA-insured mortgage.[8]

7 *Id.*; Kimble, *supra* note 3.

8 LANDS, *supra* note 3; James H. Carr & Nandinee K. Kutty, *The New Imperative for Equality*, in SEGREGATION: THE RISING COSTS FOR AMERICA 1 (James H. Carr & Nandinee K. Kutty eds., 2008); Douglas S. Massey, *Origins of Economic Disparities: The Historical Role*

By the 1950s, the FHA had removed the discriminatory criteria from its underwriting manual, and during this same period the real estate industry removed the racially discriminatory language from its Code of Ethics. Then, in 1962 President John F. Kennedy made redlining illegal in Executive Order 11062 on Equal Opportunity in Housing. This order directed all federal agencies that insured or guaranteed housing loans to take all necessary and appropriate action to prevent discrimination in the sale or rental of property based on race. The order also outlawed housing discrimination by lenders who originated loans that were insured by the United States. While federal agencies, lenders, and realtors could no longer legally discriminate against black and Latino potential home buyers, as the next sections show, racial discrimination in real estate markets was far from gone.[9]

STEERING

It is now unlawful for real estate agents to restrict or attempt to restrict a potential purchaser's housing options in order to help perpetuate segregated housing patterns. But studies conducted over the last thirty years (and as recently as 2007) found that real estate agents continued to steer non-white (especially black) home buyers to less wealthy or to non-white neighborhoods and to steer white purchasers to white neighborhoods.

Even after real estate steering became illegal, blacks and Latinos who visited real estate offices received significantly less favorable treatment than white customers with comparable income and employment profiles. In general, non-white testers (especially Latinos) received less complete information about housing options, were shown fewer units, and generally received misleading information about available housing. Agents also gave blacks and Latinos less mortgage financing assistance and, as discussed in greater detail below, steered black and Latino borrowers to higher-cost mortgage products. For example, a recent study involving paired testers exposed how blacks and Latinos are treated relative to whites in the real estate market.

In the study, each team of white/black or white/Latino testers were given similar economic information (such as housing needs and job history), and researchers assigned the black and Latino testers slightly more favorable qualifications (for example, a larger down payment and higher income) to eliminate the possibility that any realtor discrimination might have been justified based on financial qualifications. In the investigation, two teams contacted the same

of Housing Segregation, in SEGREGATION: THE RISING COSTS FOR AMERICA 39 (James H. Carr & Nandinee K. Kutty eds., 2008); Gordon, *supra* note 6.

[9] Exec. Order No. 11,063, 27 Fed. Reg. 11,527 (Nov. 24, 1962).

real estate office to seek information about available housing opportunities. Researchers found that real estate agents steered black and Latino home buyers to racially integrated neighborhoods but steered white home buyers to white neighborhoods.[10]

Fortunately, the number of real estate agents who flagrantly refused to show blacks and Latinos properties in white neighborhoods appeared to have declined. But some real estate agents now appear to discriminate against potential tenants who they think seem "ethnic." Paired testing studies show that renters with ethnically sounding names or black- or Latino-sounding voices are treated worse (and often ignored) in rental markets compared to renters with white-sounding names or voices. Specifically, when realtors suspected that a potential tenant was not white, there was a higher likelihood that the realtor would refuse to schedule (or would cancel) an appointment, show the potential renter fewer houses, and give the renter limited or misleading information. Studies also show that agents continue to "editorialize" about certain neighborhoods and the public schools zoned for particular neighborhoods in ways that appear designed to discourage white buyers from purchasing homes in non-white areas.[11]

In addition to the harm steering imposes on black and Latino buyers who are not shown homes in white neighborhoods, it also imposes costs on black homeowners who try to sell the homes they own in non-white neighborhoods. As discussed in more detail in the next chapter, because whites have always had higher homeownership rates than blacks, steering them away from racially integrated neighborhoods creates a smaller pool of potential purchasers for homes in mixed-race neighborhoods. This decreased demand depresses the market value for these homes and simultaneously increases the demand for homes in all-white neighborhoods. Even though the color of the homeowner's skin should not affect the market value of the owner's home, creating and then

[10] Ingrid Gould Ellen, *Continuing Isolation: Segregation in America Today*, in SEGREGATION: THE RISING COSTS FOR AMERICA 261 (James H. Carr & Nandinee K. Kutty eds., 2008).

[11] Mary J. Fischer & Douglas S. Massey, *The Ecology of Racial Discrimination*, 3 CITY & COMMUNITY 221 (2004); Adrian G. Carpusor & William E. Loges, *Rental Discrimination and Ethnicity in Names*, 36 J. APPLIED SOC. PSYCH. 934, (2006) (discussing paired tests involving potential renters with ethnically sounding – Tyrell Jackson or Said Al-Rahman – or white-sounding – Patrick MacDougall – names). A recent lawsuit filed by a black owner of an exclusive co-op in Manhattan suggests that even wealthy black and Latino homeowners (including the singer Roberta Flack and a prominent black hedge fund manager) continue to face discrimination from their neighbors and that co-op boards may continue to quietly discriminate against potential black or minority purchasers (like Antonio Banderas, the voice of Puss in Boots in the widely popular Shrek movies). Peter Lattman & Christine Haughney, *Dakota Co-op Board Is Accused of Bias*, N.Y. TIMES (Feb. 1, 2011), *available at* http://www.nytimes.com/2011/02/02/nyregion/02dakota.html?pagewanted=all&_r=0.

maintaining all-white neighborhoods by steering whites away from racially mixed neighborhoods stigmatizes homes in racially diverse neighborhoods and, as discussed in more detail in Chapter 8, this negative stigma is capitalized in the prices of the homes.

CITIES VERSUS SUBURBS

FHA lending policies helped to create racially and economically cities and suburbs. During the 1930s and 1940s, the FHA expressed a clear bias in favor of loans that would be used to buy single-family homes in the suburbs. Given that the FHA (and later the VA) issued the vast majority of mortgage loans for suburban homes, they played an instrumental role in stimulating the suburbanization of the U.S. housing market and in excluding non-whites from those suburban markets. Although it is not uniformly true, homes in suburban neighborhoods are usually newer and have better and more amenities overall than homes in older, urban neighborhoods. For that reason, suburban homes generally have higher appreciation rates and market values relative to homes in urban areas. Because of redlining and other discriminatory lending policies, only whites could purchase suburban homes using low-cost, long-term, government-insured mortgage loans.

By making it easier for white borrowers to get low-cost financing to flee urban areas and buy homes in suburban areas, these federal housing policies facilitated the gradual decline of urban housing markets and the devaluation of homes in urban areas. Then, in the 1950s, U.S. transportation policies made it even easier for whites to live in the suburbs but continue to work in cities and these policies dramatically changed the landscape and demographics of urban U.S. cities.

The Federal-Aid Highway Act of 1944 designed a national system of interstate highways that would create a four-lane, interstate highway system to replace the existing two-lane, federal roads. Congress funded this expensive and comprehensive project in the Federal-Aid Highway Act of 1952 and the Federal-Aid Highway Act of 1954. Improving and expanding the federal highway system made it easier for Americans to flee inner cities and buy homes in the suburbs but still quickly get to inner cities for work. Even though it may not have been explicitly designed to create all-white suburbs, the highway system helped white households migrate to the suburbs, while black households remained in the urban core because they could not qualify for low-cost loans to buy suburban homes.

In addition to making it easier for whites to flee inner cities and buy homes in the suburbs, United States housing policies helped decrease the availability of homes in urban areas. The Housing Act of 1949 authorized federal urban renewal (often referred to as "slum removal") programs. These programs were designed to eliminate substandard and inadequate housing by clearing slums and blighted areas. Although the programs did not specifically target blacks, they were ostensibly meant to improve the housing conditions of blacks who lived in unsafe, rundown houses in inner cities. The programs succeeded in destroying substandard housing, but in the process they also destroyed many of the homes that blacks could afford given their limited employment, housing, and mortgage credit options. While whites who were displaced from dilapidated urban housing could move to the suburbs, few efforts were made to help displaced black residents find affordable housing in other areas. As a result, the displaced black residents were often relegated to other deteriorating, older homes in inner cities or they were crowded into public housing.[12]

As white residents continued to flee inner cities, suburban neighborhoods grew and increasingly provided better neighborhood amenities, like schools, parks, grocery stores, and other retail outlets. Eventually, jobs followed whites to the suburbs, and this made commuting even easier for white suburban homeowners. For decades, in fact, the fastest job growth has been in suburban communities. Because blacks and Latinos did not live in suburban neighborhoods and because few of those suburban areas were accessible by public transportation, it was harder for blacks to get to the jobs that were being created outside the urban core. While whites were able to move to these flourishing suburban communities, racial minorities (particularly blacks) remained concentrated in economically declining urban neighborhoods.

Blacks and Latinos are no longer excluded by law from owning homes in racially mixed or suburban neighborhoods. Still, de facto neighborhood segregation continues to exist largely because of the remaining vestiges of redlining and steering. Because of historical neighborhood segregation patterns, a disproportionate percentage of black and Latino renters and homeowners still live in urban areas that have concentrated levels of poverty. Blacks and other minorities have remained in inner cities while retail establishments and jobs have continued to migrate from the urban core to the inner and outer suburban areas that have welcomed the businesses and white homeowners but (until recently) not blacks or Latinos. Since 1990, the job growth in suburban areas has been almost five times larger than job growth in inner cities which is one reason that unemployment rates for blacks and Latinos have been higher than unemployment rates for whites.

[12] Massey, *supra* note 8; Liu et al., *supra* note 3; Stephen Grant Meyer, As Long as They Don't Move Next Door: Segregation and Racial Conflict in American Neighborhoods (1999).

Blacks and Latinos have consistently faced transportation and informational barriers in the labor market. Generally speaking, it is more costly for urban dwellers to work in the suburbs because of the lengthy and often automobile-dependent commute. In addition, a disproportionate percentage of blacks and Latinos live away from the neighborhoods that have the faster job growth, and they do not live near the employees who are getting the newly created jobs, so they are less likely to hear about job openings. Moreover, they often cannot get to interviews for those jobs unless they own cars, because most public transportation systems do not serve urban-to-suburban commuters well. This generally has caused what is commonly known as a spatial mismatch between jobs that were created in suburban areas and the housing that blacks occupy in urban areas, where job growth is declining.[13]

LAND USE LAWS

As discussed in Chapter 2, zoning laws are justified because of the assumption that municipalities need the authority to protect the health, safety, morals, comfort, convenience, and the general welfare of the community. In 1922, the U.S. Commerce Department's Advisory Committee on Zoning stated that zoning regulations "treat all men alike."[14] Just as "all men" were not created equally (or at least not viewed equally) in the U.S. Constitution, local zoning laws in U.S. cities did not treat all neighborhoods alike. Instead, zoning laws initially created and maintained racially segregated neighborhoods.

State and federal judges enforced laws that created and maintained racially segregated neighborhoods until the U.S. Supreme Court declared race-restrictive zoning laws to be unconstitutional in *Buchanan v. Warley*.[15] Local officials

[13] Edward L. Glaeser et al., *Why Do the Poor Live in Cities?* (Nat'l Bureau of Econ. Research, Working Paper No. 7636, 2000), *available at* http://www.nber.org/papers/w7636.pdf; Dolores Acevedo-Garcia & Theresa L. Osypuk, *Impacts of Housing and Neighborhoods on Health: Pathways, Racial/Ethnic Disparities, and Policy Directions,* in SEGREGATION: THE RISING COSTS FOR AMERICA 197 (James H. Carr & Nandinee K. Kutty eds., 2008); Stuart A. Gabriel & Stuart S. Rosenthal, *Homeownership in the 1980s and 1990s: Aggregate Trends and Racial Gaps,* 57 J. URB. ECON. 101 (2005); Margery Austin Turner, *Residential Segregation and Employment Inequality,* in SEGREGATION: THE RISING COSTS FOR AMERICA 151 (James H. Carr & Nandinee K. Kutty eds., 2008).

[14] Advisory Committee on Zoning of the Housing and Building Division, *The Zoning Law and Its Benefits,* N.Y. TIMES (Jun. 25, 1922), *available at* http://query.nytimes.com/mem/archive-free/pdf?res=F20613FC355B11728DDDAC0A94DE405B828EF1D3.

[15] 245 U.S. 60 (1917). The United States Supreme Court, in Corrigan v. Buckley, 271 U.S. 323 (1926), ruled that courts could enforce these *private* real property covenants because the covenants themselves did not violate the Fifth, Thirteenth, or Fourteenth Amendments of the U.S. Constitution. While the Court invalidated a racial covenant in Hansberry v. Lee, 311 U.S. 32 (1940), it refused to hold that racial covenants were unconstitutional.

argued that racially restrictive zoning laws were needed to prevent conflicts between the races and to preserve neighborhood peace. However, the main reason localities enacted and enforced racially discriminatory public land use laws was purely economic, and it was the same reason that was used to justify redlining and racially restrictive land covenants: the presence of black homeowners in white neighborhoods was deemed to harm the value of homes in white neighborhoods.

Even after race-restrictive public zoning laws were ruled to be unconstitutional in *Buchanan*, housing market discrimination and residential segregation remained the norm. A few cities in the U.S. South simply ignored the Supreme Court's ruling, some until the 1950s. Other cities enacted replacement ordinances that continued to maintain segregated neighborhoods by, for example, providing that no member of a race could occupy a house in a city block if the majority of the houses were inhabited by members of another race. Other ordinances provided that a member of one race could not live in a block if members of the other race were the only residents.[16]

While courts ultimately also struck down these replacement ordinances, many neighborhoods that were segregated by zoning laws remained segregated because of private, racially restrictive housing covenants. Racially restrictive covenants were private contractual agreements between property owners stating that neither they nor their heirs would sell, lease, or give their homes to blacks. These covenants were legal, and they were regularly enforced by state and federal courts until 1948, when the U.S. Supreme Court finally ruled that they were legally unenforceable in *Shelly v. Kraemer*.[17] Even after this unanimous ruling, national and local real estate organizations sought to maintain racially segregated neighborhoods, which included an attempt to amend the U.S. Constitution to make the race covenants constitutional. Moreover, these unenforceable restrictions remain in deeds, even though buyers and sellers may not even have realized that the covenants were in the deeds on their properties.[18]

VIOLENCE AND NO INSURANCE

Even when zoning laws and racially restrictive property covenants could not be used to keep blacks from buying homes in white neighborhoods, blacks often opted to avoid white neighborhoods because they worried about the

[16] Jackson v. Maryland, 132 Md. 311 (1918).

[17] 334 U.S. 1 (1948).

[18] For example, during his Supreme Court confirmation hearings in 1985, then Associate Justice of the United States Supreme Court William Rehnquist admitted that he had purchased two properties in 1961 and 1974 that had racially restrictive covenants in the deeds.

reception they might receive from their white neighbors. Blacks who were somehow able to finance home purchases in white neighborhoods often were greeted by white neighbors who tried to drive them out of the neighborhood by breaking windows, causing explosions, and sometimes even burning their houses to the ground. Many black homeowners – often at the suggestion of local law enforcement or city officials – abandoned their new homes after their neighbors threatened to bomb or burn their homes, or after they were "welcomed" to the neighborhood by a burning cross.

Rather than protect the black homeowners or prosecute the white neighbors, local officials sometimes offered to purchase the homes blacks bought in white areas, pay their moving expenses, and help them find suitable housing (in a segregated neighborhood), if they agreed not to live in an all-white neighborhood. To bolster the offer, some local leaders told the black homeowners – even if they already had been victimized by white mobs – that their families would no longer receive police protection if they remained in white neighborhoods.[19]

In addition to the risk of being physically injured or killed, blacks who bought homes in white neighborhoods were often unable to insure their homes because of the insurer's concern that the home might be torched or otherwise vandalized by angry white neighbors. In effect, insurance companies increased the black homeowners' housing costs and forced them to internalize the cost of their white neighbors' racist and violent conduct. In addition, blacks who owned older homes in older, all-black urban areas had higher insurance costs because insurance companies often refused to insure their properties because redlined neighborhoods were deemed to be high-risk. Even if the insurance company agreed to insure their homes, the homeowners were charged significantly higher premiums.

Although insurance companies no longer engage in redlining and cannot refuse to provide insurance for homeowners based on race, insurance costs for black and Latino households are still higher relative to white households. Research shows that, even after controlling for income, people who own homes in non-white areas tend to pay significantly higher home insurance rates than homeowners in white neighborhoods. Insurers are allowed to consider crime rates and the percentage of owner-occupied homes in the neighborhood when setting insurance premiums. Because blacks and Latinos are more likely to live in urban neighborhoods that have fewer owner-occupied homes, more lower-income families, and higher crime rates, they are still more likely to have higher insurance rates than whites.[20]

[19] LANDS, *supra* note 3; MEYER, *supra* note 12.

[20] Dana L. Kaersvang, *The Fair Housing Act and Disparate Impact in Homeowners Insurance*, 104 MICH. L. REV. 1993 (2006).

BLOCKBUSTING

Blacks who bought homes in formerly all-white neighborhoods and were not convinced to abandon (or scared into abandoning) those homes often saw the value of their housing investment drop when whites started to flee the now integrating neighborhood. While some whites undoubtedly chose to flee because they did not want to live near blacks, other whites were encouraged to flee – typically by realtors or investors who profited from the white exodus. The most well-known scheme that was used to induce white homeowner panic was a financially profitable scheme known as blockbusting.

In a typical blockbusting scheme, realtors would purchase homes in racially transitioning areas at discounted prices by notifying the current white residents that blacks had bought (or were rumored to be buying) homes in the neighborhood. Whites would panic and become convinced that they needed to flee the now diverse neighborhood because the impending black invasion would cause their property values to decline. The whites who sold their homes would often sell them at less than fair market value. Their flight would typically trigger other panic sales, which gave the realtors/speculators yet more opportunities to buy homes cheaply.

After buying the homes from panicked white sellers, the realtors (or their conspirators) would then advertise the availability of this neighborhood to blacks. Even though whites had sold their homes to realtors/speculators at below-market panic prices, the realtors/speculators would resell the homes to blacks at above-market prices. Because blacks had limited housing options, they were willing to pay a premium for a house that would allow them to escape a deteriorating urban neighborhood. Just as appraisers actively participated in steering and redlining by providing the scientific "evidence" that the presence of black homeowners would cause white-owned homes to depreciate, appraisers often participated in the blockbusting scheme by fraudulently inflating the value of the homes before the realtors/speculators sold them to blacks. As a result, blacks had higher home buying expenses than whites both because they were *willing* to pay more for the houses (because of their limited housing options) and because they were *forced* to pay more (due to fraudulent appraisals).

Because of the FHA's discriminatory underwriting criteria, black buyers rarely were able to obtain a mortgage loan from a traditional lender to finance their home purchases. Private market investors – often the same people who were involved with the blockbusting scheme – filled the void by agreeing to finance the home purchase with either a high-cost loan or a high-cost, equity-stripping mechanism known as a land installment contract. Land installment contracts, like traditional loans, gave the black purchaser the immediate use and possession of their homes. But the seller in a land installment contract retained title to the property until the purchaser paid a certain percentage of the contract price. Unlike white borrowers who were able to buy homes using low-cost, FHA-insured mortgage loans, blacks who bought homes using an installment contract had little housing security until they finished making most of the contract payments.

Many blacks bought homes on land installment contracts, even though they could not afford to make the monthly mortgage payments or to pay for routine maintenance. Because the seller retained title to the property, the seller could easily and quickly repossess the home and then resell it at an inflated price to another eager, cash-strapped black purchaser with limited housing options. In fact, homes in racially transitioning areas would often be sold multiple times in a year (i.e., flipped). Eager black buyers would buy these homes (at inflated prices), even though the homes were not well-kept. That the former owners neglected to make routine repairs is not surprising, of course, because many of them could barely afford to even make the monthly contract payments. And, as was common during the recent housing crisis, once the owners fell behind on their payments and knew they would soon be evicted, they had no incentive to invest their money in maintaining the homes.[21]

Both the white home sellers and the black home buyers were harmed by blockbusting. These arbitrageurs purchased the homes at distressed prices (often stripping home equity from the fleeing white homeowners), sold the homes they bought at below-market rates to blacks at above-market rates, and then often resold/flipped the homes once the cash-strapped black borrowers defaulted on their land contracts and were forced out of their homes. While the white sellers and black buyers were financially harmed by blockbusting, the realtors/speculators who induced the white panic and exodus earned enormous profits from blockbusting, ironically because some lenders agreed to help finance the blockbusting schemes.[22]

VOLUNTARY SEGREGATION: WHITE FLIGHT

Segregated neighborhoods were the norm in many U.S. cities until the 1960s. By the 1970s and 1980s, the enactment and enforcement of fair housing laws that banned housing discrimination in the housing and mortgage markets caused a marked decline in residential segregation. Still, white liberals who

[21] Anuj K. Shah et al., *Some Consequences of Having Too Little*, 338 SCIENCE 682 (2012).

[22] Lynne Beyer Sagalyn, *Mortgage Lending in Older Urban Neighborhoods: Lessons from Past Experience*, 465 ANNALS AM. ACAD.POL. & SOC. SCI. 98,(1983); Massey, *supra* note 8.

had willingly joined marches in the 1960s to ensure that blacks had the right to equal treatment in jobs and in schools were often ambivalent, and at times hostile, when blacks sought to move into their neighborhoods. Polls and surveys repeatedly indicate that most Americans value racially, ethnically, and politically mixed communities. Despite this stated preference for diverse communities and the increasing racial and ethnic diversity in the United States, U.S. cities largely remain segregated, and blacks and Latinos continue to live in hyper-segregated neighborhoods.

In general, Democrats, liberals, and college graduates place a higher value on diverse communities than Americans as a whole do. In addition to these demographic variations, studies show that the extent to which homeowners value integration and their reasons for this preference vary quite dramatically by race. Blacks appear to prefer living in racially integrated neighborhoods both because they perceive that homes in those neighborhoods are better and also because they place a high value on the concept of integration. They resist living in all-white neighborhoods because they fear their white neighbors might be hostile toward them.

Research has shown that neither blacks nor whites prefer to live in a neighborhood if their race is in the overwhelming minority, in part because they do not want their children to attend schools that have few children of the same race. Racial minorities do, however, appear much more willing than whites to live in neighborhoods where they are slightly in the minority. Whites, on the other hand, prefer to live in largely all-white neighborhoods and are willing to pay a premium to avoid living with too many blacks or Latinos. In fact, whites appear to prefer integrated neighborhoods only if they are sure that the neighborhood will remain stably integrated and that any non-white homeowner will be from their same socioeconomic class.[23]

A member of the George W. Bush administration captured the sentiment of many white parents in observing why suburban residents fail to support school choice:

> School choice is popular in the national headquarters of the Republican Party but is unpopular among the Republican rank-and-file voters who have

[23] Camille Zubrinsky Charles, *Neighborhood Racial-Composition Preferences: Evidence from a Multiethnic Metropolis*, 47–3 SOCIAL PROBLEMS (2000); James L. Vigdor & Jens Ludwig, *Segregation and the Test Score Gap*, in STEADY GAINS AND STALLED PROGRESS; INEQUALITY AND THE BLACK-WHITE TEST SCORE GAP (Katherine Magnusun & Jane Waldfogel eds, 2008); Raphael W. Bostic & Richard W. Martin, *Have Anti-Discrimination Housing Laws Worked? Evidence from Trends in Black Homeownership*, 31–1 THE JOURNAL OF REAL ESTATE FINANCE AND ECONOMICS 5–26 (2005); Turner, *supra* note 13; Gabriel & Rosenthal, *supra* note 13, at 57; Michael H. Schill & Susan M. Wachter, *The Spatial Bias of Federal Housing Law and Policy: Concentrated Poverty in Urban America*, 143 U. PENN. L. REV. 1285 (1995).

> moved away from the inner city in part so that their children will not have to attend schools that are racially or socioeconomically integrated.[24]

Opinion polls and surveys indicate that most people prefer to live in an integrated neighborhood and have their children attend integrated schools. Despite that, white owners rate non-white neighborhoods as less desirable and flee neighborhoods when they become too brown or black. Studies consistently show that white homeowners will flee neighborhoods once a certain percentage (sometimes as small as 5 percent) of black residents move in, and the neighborhood "tips" from white to non-white. Indeed, one study reports that white buyers generally will not purchase a home in a neighborhood with good schools and low crime rates that meets their requirements in terms of price, number of rooms, and other housing characteristics if that home is in a predominately black neighborhood.[25]

Recent census data show that blacks and Latinos at all income levels continue to live in largely non-white neighborhoods, although larger percentages of blacks and Latinos now live in suburban areas, the average white person lives in a neighborhood that is at least 75 percent white. In contrast, the average black or Latino lives in a neighborhood that is only 35 percent white. Even though many blacks continue to live in virtually all-black neighborhoods, the level of neighborhood segregation declined in the 1970s and 1980s when higher-income and college-educated blacks moved to all-white suburbs.

Neighborhood segregation continues to vary somewhat by income level, as lower-income blacks and Latinos remain more likely to live in segregated urban neighborhoods than higher-income blacks and Latinos. Suburban communities are now more diverse than they have ever been, and by 2010, almost 50 percent of blacks and Latinos lived outside of inner cities (up from 41 percent in 2000). The percentage of minority households living in inner cities also rose during that decade (from 45 percent to 50 percent), largely because of higher birth and immigration rates for those groups.

Because, however, blacks and Latinos have lower overall household incomes, they remain concentrated in non-white neighborhoods (be they urban or suburban). Moreover, relative to white households with comparable incomes, they are more likely to live in neighborhoods that have higher poverty rates. For example, a recent report found that middle-income black and Latino households who earn *more than* $75,000 live in neighborhoods where

[24] Peter W. Cookson, School Choice: The Struggle for the Soul of American Education 68 (1995).

[25] Gregory D. Squires, *Demobilization of the Individualistic Bias: Housing Market Discrimination as a Contributor to Labor Market and Economic Inequality*, 609 Annals of the American Academy of Political and Social Science 200 (2007).

the average household income is lower than the average household income in neighborhoods where white households who earn *less than* $40,000 live.[26]

Steering and other forms of overt racial discrimination may explain why some neighborhoods remain segregated. However, many segregation patterns appear to be the result of private, voluntary actions. That is, the process of "dynamic resegregation" keeps neighborhoods and schools segregated, because once the percentage of blacks and Latinos in predominately white neighborhoods reaches a tipping point, whites flee. Whites appear to fear and harbor biases against blacks (especially) and Latinos as neighbors, and they have continued to flee inner cities to live in mostly all-white suburbs, even though many of them have never had any direct personal experience with black or Latino neighbors.

By the mid-1990s, more than 50 percent of all whites lived in the suburbs. Since the late 1980s, though, more than 50 percent of the growth in the suburban population was due to an increase in the minority population. As blacks and Latinos moved to the suburbs, however, whites moved out. For example, the suburban areas that had the largest and fastest increases of minority residents also had the most rapid increases in segregation. In contrast, suburban areas that had stable (or declining) racial populations had the slowest increases in segregation. Additionally, as the inner ring of suburban communities became more diverse, whites fled to outer rings to get farther away from inner cities (and poor blacks and Latinos).

Because of the suburban flight, the percentage of white students who attend low-poverty, rural schools has increased over the last decade. Rural schools are now less likely to have a large concentration of poor students than suburban or urban areas. The overall percentage of white students in rural schools is now higher (71 percent) than in cities (30 percent) or suburbs (54 percent). Once whites flee to a suburban or rural area, they generally will not return to an urban core unless the inner city neighborhood is part of a gentrification effort and it appears that the neighborhood will become less brown, black, and poor.[27]

White flight appears to occur for a variety of reasons. Some whites may simply dislike blacks and Latinos and prefer not to be anywhere near them. Others may not have overtly racist views, but they may avoid moving into or

[26] John R. Logan & Brian Stults, *The Persistence of Segregation in the Metropolis: New Findings from the 2010 Census* (2011), *available at* http://www.s4.brown.edu/us2010/Data/Report/report2.pdf; Joint Ctr. for Hous. Studies, Harvard Univ., *The State of the Nation's Housing* (2012), *available at* http://www.jchs.harvard.edu/sites/jchs.harvard.edu/files/son2012.pdf.

[27] Susan Aud et al., *The Condition of Education 2013*, U.S. Department of Education, National Center for Education Statistics, NCES 2013–037 (2013), *available at* http://nces.ed.gov/pubsearch.; Sean F. Reardon & John T. Yun, *Suburban Racial Change and Suburban School Segregation*, 74 Soc. of Educ. 79 (2001).

remaining in a racially mixed neighborhood because of negative, race-based stereotypes. That is, whites might flee when blacks (especially) and Latinos move into their neighborhoods largely because of their perceptions about what *might* happen to their formerly all-white neighborhoods. For example, blockbusting tactics were effective because realtors/speculators were able to convince white owners that their property values (and the quality of the neighborhood schools) would *decrease* and that crime would *increase* when blacks bought homes in their neighborhoods. If white homeowners have explicit or implicit biases against blacks or Latinos they most likely will flee a racially transitioning neighborhood rather than wait to see whether the stereotype (that having black neighbors will cause the quality or safety of the integrating neighborhood to deteriorate) is actually true.[28]

White parents are especially likely to avoid or flee racially transitioning neighborhoods because of the perception of what will happen to the neighborhood schools if more black and brown children attend those schools. Where parents choose to buy a home – and remain – is often influenced by where their children will attend school. Realtors understand this, and they routinely provide information about the school district to clients when they are showing a home. While some white households with school-age children may simply dislike blacks and Latinos and may flee when the neighborhood starts to integrate, as will be discussed in more detail in Chapter 9, they are not wholly irrational in worrying that the public schools in non-white school attendance zones will be of lower quality. Household income obviously plays a role in the statistics, but data consistently show that inner-city schools and schools with large percentages of blacks and Latinos have lower test scores than schools that are mainly white.[29]

As was true when blockbusting was used to scare whites into fleeing the impending black invasion, whites continue to worry that if blacks or Latinos move into their neighborhood, their white neighbors will flee and leave them stuck in a predominately non-white neighborhood with neighbors who are from a different economic class. Polls and surveys consistently show that whites prefer to avoid living in non-white neighborhoods, *especially* if their neighbors are from a different socioeconomic class. White homeowners

[28] Kyle Crowder & Scott J. South, *Spatial Dynamics of White Flight: The Effects of Local and Extra Local Racial Conditions on Neighborhood Out-Migration*, 73 Am. Soc. Rev. 792 (2008).

[29] Turner, *supra* note 13; Chenoa Flippen, *Unequal Returns to Housing Investments? A Study of Real Housing Appreciation among Black, White, and Hispanic Households*, 82 Soc. Forces 1523 (2004); Crowder & South, *supra* note 28; Lisa Barrow, *School Choice through Relocation: Evidence from the Washington, D.C. Area*, 86 J. of Public Econ. 155 (2002).

(especially upper- and middle-income ones) leave neighborhoods when the first black or Latino moves in because of their fear that, even if the first neighbor shares their socioeconomic status, lower-income minority neighbors (or lower-income friends or family of the new neighbors) may soon join them.

While it is obviously irrational for white homeowners to believe that the color of other homeowners' skin could actually affect the value of their house, white fears and perceptions about the value of homes in racially integrated neighborhoods relative to homes in mainly white neighborhoods are not wholly irrational. As discussed in more detail in Chapter 8, data consistently show that homes in minority neighborhoods do in fact tend to appreciate less than comparable homes in non-minority neighborhoods and that neighborhoods that are transitioning from being all-white to racially mixed have slower rates of appreciation.

Additionally, it is irrational to believe that the color of a homeowner's skin determines whether a neighborhood will have a high crime rate, and not all black and Latino neighborhoods have high crime rates. Still, racially integrated neighborhoods with residents who have lower incomes generally have higher rates of poverty than all-white neighborhoods. Because drug use, higher crime rates, and out-of-wedlock births are more prevalent among lower-income populations, moderate- to higher-income homeowners (of all races) worry that an influx of lower-income residents to their neighborhoods will result in higher crime rates and that their taxes will increase if there is an increased demand for social and public services.

Homeowners typically will try to move when their neighborhoods experience rising crime rates. Therefore, if white neighbors have equity in their homes and they *can* move, they often will flee racially transitioning neighborhoods if they think that the new neighbors are lower-income, that their neighborhood will somehow become less desirable, and that this will cause their homes to have lower rates of appreciation. Blacks and Latinos, like whites, prefer to avoid neighborhoods with high crime rates. Although data show that white homeowners flee neighborhoods when crime rates are increasing, because of the constrained housing choices blacks and Latinos face in general, neighborhoods with rising crime rates appear to *attract* black and Latino residents.

Some white homeowners may conclude that the new black and Latino residents are the *cause* of the high crime rates. Given their limited housing choices, however, blacks and Latinos (especially if they are lower-income) appear more willing to purchase the homes of fleeing whites (just as blacks purchased the homes of whites who fled neighborhoods because of blockbusting tactics decades ago), even if the neighborhood has a rising crime rate, because the higher crime rate makes the neighborhood less desirable to whites and thus more affordable for them.[30]

In theory, people who own comparable homes should experience the same rate of appreciation regardless of the pigmentation of the homeowners' skin. This theory is not borne out in practice, and there is some basis for white homeowners' fears about buying a home (or remaining) in a predominantly non-white neighborhood, because potential buyers (or appraisers) continue to deem the homes in integrated neighborhoods to be less valuable.

REDLINING (REDUX)

By the 1950s, the FHA had revised its underwriting manual to remove the language requiring deeds to contain restrictive covenants and the language that encouraged redlining. In addition, redlining in connection with federally insured loans was officially outlawed in 1962. Even when courts could no longer enforce racially restrictive covenants and the FHA was required to offer government-insured mortgage loans that did not include these covenants, the FHA allowed developers to decide whether to sell new homes to black home buyers. Given the United States' racial past, and potentially because of fears that selling to blacks would deter white buyers, private developers routinely refused to sell new homes to blacks. This, again, allowed only whites to buy newer, more valuable homes using FHA-insured loans.[31]

It took until 1968 for Congress to finally pass the Fair Housing Act of 1968;[32] the same year, the Supreme Court finally ruled that private discrimination by home sellers was unconstitutional.[33] Throughout the 1970s, the United States continued to make efforts to eliminate the vestiges of redlining and overt discrimination in housing and mortgage finance markets. To help detect whether lenders were using discriminatory lending practices, Congress enacted the Home Mortgage Disclosure Act of 1975 (HMDA). HMDA requires lenders to provide data that disclose the geographic locations of mortgage loans they have approved.

While the HMDA reporting requirement does not specifically regulate redlining, these data show whether lenders are providing credit to poor, minority, and urban neighborhoods, and lenders must report information

[30] Glaeser et al., *supra* note 13. Lower-income households that have rental vouchers are more likely to move into neighborhoods when crime rates are increasing because those neighborhoods are less desirable and thus more affordable. John R. Hipp, *Violent Crime, Mobility Decisions, and Neighborhood Racial/Ethnic Transition*, 58 Soc. Probs. 410 (2011); Acevedo-Garcia & Osypuk, *supra* note 13; Ingrid Gould Ellen et al., *Memphis Murder Revisited: Do Housing Vouchers Cause Crime?*, U.S. Dep't of Hous. and Urban Dev. (2011).

[31] Exec. Order No. 11,063 27 Fed. Reg. 11,527 (Nov. 24, 1962); Meyer, *supra* note 12.

[32] Fair Housing Act, 42 U.S.C. §§ 3601–3619.

[33] Jones v. Alfred H. Mayer Co., 392 U.S. 409 (1968).

about the race and income of the loan applicants for loans with high-interest rates. In addition, partially in response to perceptions that blacks and Latinos were being denied credit for reasons that were not related to their risk of default, Freddie Mac and Fannie Mae urged lenders to use automated credit scoring as part of the mortgage underwriting process. Since 1995, lenders have relied on automated scoring devices in the mortgage approval underwriting process.[34]

Many people assumed that the mortgage origination approval process would become color-blind and less susceptible to lender bias, because credit scoring relies on the use of statistical models to evaluate a borrower's potential ability to pay based on their credit history. Others hoped that the HMDA reporting requirements would cause lenders to offer low-cost credit in a nondiscriminatory fashion. This did not happen. HMDA data reveal that lenders continued to engage in discriminatory practices that imposed higher housing costs on blacks and Latinos and that these practices were rampant during the housing boom. Unlike earlier redlining, though, during the housing boom lenders did not refuse to lend to blacks or to approve mortgages in racially mixed areas. Instead, lenders engaged in what is now referred to as reverse redlining by flooding non-white neighborhoods with high-cost, high-risk loans.

Even though it is economically or financially irrelevant when making a lending decision, the color of a borrower's skin played a predictive role in determining whether that borrower would be offered a low-cost loan. As an initial matter, HMDA data show that lenders regularly pushed buyers of *all* races into higher-cost mortgages. Before the recent recession, more than 60 percent of borrowers who accepted a higher-cost subprime ARM could have qualified for a lower-interest, fixed rate conventional loan. While all borrowers were pushed toward higher-cost loan products, blacks and Latinos received a disproportionately high percentage of the high-cost subprime loan products that were approved during the housing boom.[35]

Lenders conceded that blacks and Latinos received disproportionately more subprime loans. But, at least initially, lenders argued that credit risk – not race – explained why these groups received a disproportionate share of higher-cost subprime loans. Lenders also argued that HMDA data simply could not be used to support any claim that they engaged in reverse redlining or that prime loan mortgage applications were denied because of the race of the borrower, because the HMDA data do not analyze debt-to-income ratios

[34] Bipartisan Millennial Comm., *Meeting our Nation's Housing Challenges* 8 (2002), *available at* http://govinfo.library.unt.edu/mhc/MHCReport.pdf.; Mortgage Bankers Association, *Suitability. Don't Turn Back the Clock on Fair Lending and Homeownership Gains* (2007).

[35] Rick Brooks & Ruth Simon, *Subprime Debacle Traps Even Very Credit-worthy*, WALL. ST. J. (Dec. 3, 2007), at A1.

or the borrowers' credit histories. A recent study conducted by the Consumer Financial Protection Bureau confirmed an earlier Federal Reserve study that found that people who live in lower-income areas or predominately black and Latino areas generally have lower-than-average credit scores.[36]

Although the financial services sector attacked the validity of early studies, empirical data, paired testing results, and damning information uncovered during lawsuits filed against lenders as a result of the housing bust confirm that lenders and mortgage brokers disproportionately and illegally steered black and Latino borrowers to higher-cost loans simply because of the color of the borrowers' skin. For example, one study shows that more than 50 percent of all loans blacks received to purchase homes and 40 percent of the loans Latinos received were subprime loan products, but only 18 percent of home purchase loans issued to white borrowers were high-cost loans. Thus, blacks were almost three times and Latinos were almost twice as likely as white borrowers to receive a higher-priced loan. Another study found that subprime loans accounted for 51 percent of refinance loans in predominately black neighborhoods but only 9 percent of subprime refinance loans in white neighborhoods. In addition, analyses of the HMDA data revealed that blacks and Latinos were pushed into loan products that increased their housing costs regardless of their income levels. For example, while only 13 percent of low-income white buyers received high-cost subprime mortgages, almost 40 percent of low-income black buyers received subprime loans.[37]

The racial composition of the neighborhood, rather than the creditworthiness of individual borrowers, was the primary driver for subprime lending, and there was a higher density of subprime loans in black neighborhoods that had *low* poverty rates than in white neighborhoods with *high* poverty rates. Steering also occurred with higher-income borrowers, and low poverty black neighborhoods had considerably more subprime loans than low poverty white neighborhoods. While only 5 percent of higher-income whites received subprime mortgages, 23 percent of higher-income blacks and 17 percent of higher-income Latinos took out subprime mortgages. Perhaps most shocking is the disparity that exists between lower-income whites and higher-income blacks

[36] Consumer Financial Protection Bureau, *Analysis of Differences between Consumer- and Creditor-Purchased Credit Scores* (Sep. 2012); Fed. Res. Bd. of Governors, *Report to Congress on Credit Scoring and its Effects on the Availability and Affordability of Credit*, (Aug. 2007).

[37] Kathryn L. S. Pettit et al., *Housing in the Nation's Capital*, Urban Inst. 39 (2009). For example, in the District of Columbia and the surrounding area, neighborhoods that were more than 60 percent black and had low poverty rates had the highest density of subprime lending than any other neighborhoods in the area. The rate of subprime loans in higher-income black neighborhoods was 2.6 times higher than the loan density in low-poverty white neighborhoods.

and Latinos: 23 percent of *higher*-income black borrowers and 17 percent of *higher*-income Latino borrowers received a subprime, high-cost mortgage product, while only 13 percent of *lower*-income white borrowers received these high-cost loans.[38]

Blacks and Latinos were also more likely to be offered subprime loans that carried prepayment penalties. Generally speaking, this loan feature penalizes borrowers who attempt to refinance or prepay their higher-cost subprime loans within a specified period, typically the first two years of the loan term. Borrowers who could not afford to pay the penalty remain trapped in the higher-interest loan, even though refinancing the loan to a lower-interest rate could reduce the monthly loan payment. In addition to preventing borrowers from quickly reducing their monthly mortgage costs if they lose a job or have unexpectedly high monthly non-housing expenses, borrowers who cannot refinance a high-interest rate loan because of a prepayment penalty pay more in interest and relatively less in principal. Consequently, prepayment penalties make it harder for borrowers to accumulate equity in their homes.

HMDA data revealed that, while 2 percent of prime loan products contained prepayment penalties, more than 70 percent of subprime mortgages during the housing boom contained prepayment penalties. Moreover, the data show that the likelihood that borrowers would receive a loan product that had a prepayment penalty was 30 percent higher if the borrower lived in a zip code area that had high percentages of minority residents than if the borrower lived in a neighborhood that had a lower percentage of minority residents.[39]

In addition to the HMDA data, results from a paired testing study conducted before the housing crash also confirm the pattern of reverse redlining. In this study, white, black, and Latino testers posed as loan applicants who were seeking mortgage loans. Consistent with the HMDA data that researchers analyzed before the housing crash, white testers consistently were offered better loan terms than minority testers, even though the minority testers were given higher credit scores, slightly higher incomes, and longer employment records than the white testers. Minority testers were often steered to high-cost subprime mortgages despite having better credit profiles than white testers. Mortgage brokers also were more likely to seek ways to lower the housing costs of white testers. For example, white testers were told about lower-cost, FRMs 90 percent of the time but brokers discussed FRMs with minority applicants only 56 percent of the time.

[38] *Id.*; Debbie Gruenstein Bocian et al., *Race, Ethnicity and Subprime Home Loan Pricing*, 60 J. Econ. & Bus. 110, 110–11 (2008); National Fair Housing Alliance, *The Crisis of Housing Segregation: 2007 Fair Housing Trends Report* (2007).

[39] *Id.*

Although brokers rarely told testers that they could get a better mortgage deal at another location, 7 percent of white applicants – but no minority applicants – were told this, even though the white applicants all had lower incomes and credit scores than the minority applicants. Brokers also discussed loan fees, or "points," with white testers 74 percent of the time, but they only mentioned fees with minority shoppers 31 percent of the time, even though the total loan cost would increase based on the fees and points charged. Finally, mortgage brokers and loan officers presented white testers with twice as many loan options (including different rates, fees, and structures) as black and Latino testers.[40]

A recent $335 million settlement involving Countrywide Financial Corporation (currently a subsidiary of Bank of America) and the Civil Rights Division of the U.S. Department of Justice (DOJ) further confirms that lenders engaged in reverse redlining. After reviewing 2.5 million loan applications, the DOJ filed a complaint against Countrywide alleging that from 2004 to 2008 Countrywide systematically discriminated against black and Latino borrowers. The complaint argued that 200,000 black or Latino borrowers were steered to higher-cost subprime mortgages, while white borrowers with similar creditworthiness were placed in lower-cost, prime interest rate loans. The DOJ gathered data that showed that Countrywide's lending decisions were based on the borrowers' race, not because of their creditworthiness or any other objective risk factors (such as credit scores, loan-to-value (LTV) ratios, or debt-to-income ratios).

Countrywide's own underwriting criteria revealed that, even when income and applicable credit risk factors for black and Latino borrowers were comparable to those of white borrowers, black and Latino borrowers were steered to subprime mortgage products and away from lower-cost prime mortgage products. Evidence revealed during the litigation indicated that Countrywide decided to target black and Latino markets as part of a corporate business plan to expand its share of the subprime market, in part by increasing the volume of its subprime refinancing loans.

As part of its marketing plan, Countrywide loan officers convinced blacks and Latinos to refinance their high-cost loans before the artificially low "teaser" rates expired or to extract equity from their homes in cash-out refinancings. The loan officers "reminded" the black and Latino borrowers that their home would appreciate in price and that the increase would be adequate to compensate

[40] Bocian et al., *supra* note 38; National Fair Housing Alliance, *supra* note 38; Andra C. Ghent et al., *Race, Redlining, and Subprime Loan Pricing* 2 (Fed. Res. Bank of St. Louis, Working Paper No. 2011–033B, 2011), *available at* http://research.stlouisfed.org/wp/2011/2011–033.pdf.

for the larger mortgage debt. Countrywide never mentioned, of course, that their home – especially if they were located in a distressed or largely non-white neighborhood – might see little or no price appreciation. Nor did they explain that the housing market might crash and their home could plummet in value, leaving them trapped in a home with an underwater mortgage.

In addition to steering white borrowers *to* lower-cost, prime-interest rate loans, Countrywide steered white borrowers *away* from the same higher-cost products they were pushing on blacks. White borrowers had a higher rate of rejection for high-cost subprime loans than the rejection rates for blacks with similar credit histories. Thus, while lenders pushed blacks and Latinos into higher-cost subprime loans, these same lenders applied higher, stricter standards when whites with similar credit profiles applied for higher-cost subprime loans. By denying subprime loan applications for white borrowers at rates that exceeded the subprime loan denial rates for blacks, lenders prevented white (but not black) borrowers from making a costly credit decision that could have catastrophic, long-term financial consequences (including foreclosure and ruined credit).[41]

A number of cities (including Baltimore and Memphis) also sued lenders based on their lending practices involving minority borrowers during the housing bubble. The cities alleged that Wells Fargo Bank steered minority borrowers to subprime loans, even though many would have qualified for lower-cost loans. The cities argued that this racially discriminatory steering caused minority communities to have disproportionately high foreclosure rates and caused property values (and, thus, tax revenues) to plummet for other non-foreclosed homes in those neighborhoods.

Wells Fargo ultimately settled a lawsuit with the City of Memphis by agreeing to invest more than $400 million in loans to help generate economic development. That Wells Fargo agreed to settle in May 2012 is not terribly surprising given Countrywide's $335 million settlement in December 2011. But Wells Fargo had another strong incentive to settle: damning written testimony of former bank officials revealed a company policy to steer blacks and Latinos to higher-cost loans and to target their neighborhoods for higher-cost and higher-risk loans.

Affidavits provided by former Wells Fargo loan officers disclosed that Wells Fargo systematically steered black and Latino borrowers to higher-cost

[41] Press Release, U.S. Dep't of Justice, *Justice Department Reaches $335 Million Settlement to Resolve Allegations of Lending Discrimination by Countrywide Financial Corporation* (Dec. 21, 2011), *available at* http://www.justice.gov/opa/pr/2011/December/11-ag-1694.html; R. Glenn Hubbard et al., Analysis of Discrimination in Prime and Subprime Mortgage Markets (Nov. 22, 2011), *available at* http://ssrn.com/abstract=1975789.

subprime mortgage products and cash-out refinancing loans, and that the company systematically engaged in discriminatory lending practices. For example, all loan officers understood that their commissions would be higher and that they would receive bonuses if they steered borrowers who qualified for prime loans to subprime loans. Given this compensation structure, loan officers and mortgage brokers had a strong financial incentive to steer all borrowers (whether they had good or bad credit) to higher-priced loan products. Of course, borrowers with good credit never knew that they could qualify for a lower-cost mortgage product or that they had been steered to products designed for borrowers with blemished credit.

Wells Fargo loan officers did more, though, than just steer all borrowers to higher-cost loans: they were encouraged to misrepresent the risks associated with ARMs and other exotic loan products. For example, loan officers often failed to tell black and Latino borrowers that when the interest rates on their mortgage loan reset after the teaser introductory period ended, their monthly loan payments might dramatically increase. Likewise, loan officers often failed to explain that the borrowers might face substantial penalties if they attempted to refinance or prepay their higher-cost subprime loans.

The affidavits further revealed that the loan officers and mortgage brokers encouraged borrowers to accept higher-cost and higher-risk subprime loans by telling them that subprime loans had a quicker approval process, did not require as much documentation, and did not require a down payment. The loan officers also encouraged black and Latino borrowers to take out cash from their home equity, even though increasing their mortgage debt would make it less likely that they could refinance their subprime loan to a prime loan product.

Because the loan officer received a commission on each loan transaction and the amount of the commission increased based on the amount of the loan, the officer had a strong financial incentive to encourage the borrower to make an unwise borrowing decision. Although the loan officers accurately stated that subprime loans (but not prime loans) could be approved with little (or no) documentation or with low (or no) down payments, they never told the black and Latino borrowers that the loans were more expensive in the long run, were not in the borrowers' best interest, and could increase the likelihood that the borrowers would default on the loan and lose their home to foreclosure.

Even worse than the misrepresentations was the evidence that some Wells Fargo loan officers referred to black borrowers using racially derogatory language. For example, affidavits showed that loan officers called black borrowers "mud people" who did not pay their bills. Loan officers also referred to black neighborhoods as slums and "the hood," and they called the subprime loans that they were pushing on borrowers in black neighborhoods "ghetto loans."[42]

Lenders' unlawful steering practices unnecessarily increased home buying costs for black and Latino homeowners. One study found reverse redlining caused blacks and Latinos to be twice as likely to have mortgage loans with higher interests rates (of 9 percent or more) than whites and that, because of steering, blacks likely paid at least $5,000 more than whites for a thirty-year loan, while Latinos paid almost $3,500 more than whites. These amounts, if invested at a 5 percent rate of return, would increase the hypothetical black homeowner's net worth by almost $17,000 and would increase the hypothetical Latino homeowner's net worth by approximately $12,000.[43]

During and since the recession, blacks and Latinos do not appear to have been steered to higher-cost mortgage products. Instead, once lenders imposed tighter credit standards, black and Latino borrowers were more likely to be simply denied credit for a loan. Recent reports indicate that lending to those two groups has plummeted by more than 60 percent. That is, between 2004 and 2009, mortgage lending to Latinos decreased by 63 percent, while lending to blacks dropped by 60 percent. In contrast, lending to whites declined by only 17 percent.

Likewise, a recent survey conducted by the Federal Reserve reveals that the denial rate for conventional home purchase loan applications for black borrowers increased 15 percentage points (from 23 percent to 38 percent) from 2006 to 2012, when lenders tightened their underwriting standards, and denial rates for Latino borrowers rose from 19 percent to 27 percent during this period. In contrast, the denial rate for white borrowers who applied for conventional mortgages increased only 3 percentage points (from 12 percent to 15 percent). So, blacks and Latinos continue to face burdens in the mortgage finance market: they are *less* likely to be approved for a prime rate loan and are instead more likely to be offered a subprime product. This, again, increases

[42] Declaration of Tony Paschal, Mayor of Baltimore v. Wells Fargo Bank, 677 F. Supp. 2d 847, No. 1:08-cv-00062-JFM), Doc. 176–2 (2010), *available at* http://www.relmanlaw.com/docs/Baltimore-Declarations.pdf; Declaration of Doris Dancy, City of Memphis v. Wells Fargo Bank, No. 2:09-cv-02857-STA, Doc. 29–1 (W.D. Tenn. May 4, 2011), *available at* http://www.relmanlaw.com/docs/Declarations-Memphis.pdf; Declaration of Elizabeth M. Jacobson, Mayor of Baltimore v. Wells Fargo Bank, 677 F. Supp. 2d 847, No. 1:08-cv-00062-JFM, Doc. 176–1 (2010), *available at* http://www.relmanlaw.com/docs/Baltimore-Declarations.pdf. Other mortgage brokers have also admitted to charging black and Latino borrowers higher interest rates and fees than they charged white borrowers with similar financial backgrounds. And, during the housing boom, the compensation structure mortgage brokers used gave mortgage brokers and loan officers incentives to steer borrowers to higher interest rate products. Russ Buettner, $3.5 *Million Settlement in Mortgage Bias Case*, N.Y.TIMES (Aug. 28, 2012).

[43] Lauren J. Krivo & Robert L. Kaufman, *Housing and Wealth Inequality: Racial-Ethnic Differences in Home Equity in the United States*, 41 DEMOGRAPHY 585 (2004).

homeownership costs for blacks and Latinos and makes homeownership more burdensome and less financially beneficial for them.[44]

FRAUD

Lawsuits filed after the recent recession show that members of the lending community routinely engaged in what is commonly known as "affinity fraud." Affinity fraud occurs when minority loan officers or mortgage brokers target members of their race to induce them to participate in harmful financial transactions. Mortgage brokers were able to gain the trust of black and Latino borrowers by agreeing to simplify the loan application process by, for example, going door-to-door to market the lending products in minority neighborhoods and agreeing to meet in the borrowers' homes. Indeed, some reports revealed that brokers sent limousines to drive the gleeful (and unsuspecting) black and Latino borrowers to closing.

As the Wells Fargo settlement affidavits disclosed, brokers (including blacks and Latinos) routinely steered black and Latino borrowers to higher-cost, nontraditional mortgage products, even though many of them qualified for prime loan products. Elderly black and Latino borrowers and lower-income, first-time buyers were especially likely to fall prey to predatory or fraudulent lending practices when they bought homes or refinanced existing mortgages, or when brokers convinced them to take out mortgages to make often unnecessary home improvements. One common form of affinity fraud involved black churches.

During the housing boom, lenders targeted black churches and their members to gain access to black borrowers. Lenders sought to gain the trust of the potential black borrowers by holding events at the church and using black loan officers to push the high-cost loan products. For example, one lender created a "rebate" program where the lender agreed to donate money to a nonprofit (presumably the church) of the borrower's choice once the borrower's subprime loan was approved. Lenders also held workshops, sometimes entitled wealth-building seminars, at black churches to convince the parishioners to increase their wealth by buying a home using an alternative (i.e., subprime) lending product from the lender who sponsored the event.[45]

[44] Kenneth J. Cooper, *Lending to Blacks, Hispanics Plummets during Housing Crisis*, CHIC. SUN-TIMES (Feb. 14, 2011); Joint Ctr. for Hous. Studies, *supra* note 26.

[45] Elvin Wyly & C.S. Ponder, *Gender, Age, and Race in Subprime America*, 21 HOUSING POL'Y DEBATE 529 (2011); Jonathan Karp & Miriam Jordan, *How the Subprime Mess Hit Poor Immigrant Groups*, WALL. ST. J. (Dec. 6, 2007), at A1; Vikas Bajaj & Miguel Helft, *The Loan that Keeps on Taking*, N.Y. TIMES (Sep. 25, 2007), at C1; Nat'l Ass'n of Hisp. Real Est. Profs. & Nat'l Council of La Raza, *Saving Homes, Saving Communities: Latino Brokers Speak Out on*

Non-English speaking, Latino borrowers were frequent targets of predatory lenders and mortgage brokers, who often spoke Spanish. In a common affinity fraud transaction, the mortgage broker would persuade a non-English speaking, immigrant home buyer to apply for a nontraditional subprime mortgage but then would not properly disclose (or translate into Spanish) the loan terms to the borrower. The loans often did not ask the borrower to document income (thus, no-doc loans) and the brokers commonly asked the home buyers to sign blank documents. The brokers/lenders often misled the borrowers about the loan terms or convinced them to sign documents in English that contained features that the lender/broker never explained to the borrowers. Moreover, to improve the borrowers' credit scores, some brokers asked borrowers to get themselves added to the credit card account of a person with a better credit score.[46]

LIMITED CREDIT OPTIONS

Blacks and Latinos may have been willing to accept high-cost loans offered by neighborhood mortgage brokers because they did not have easy access to traditional lenders who offered low-cost mortgage products. Or they may also have been more willing to accept loan products that stripped their housing wealth because they had had prior unpleasant experiences with traditional banks and mortgage brokers. For years, traditional lenders refused to open bank branches in minority and lower-income neighborhoods. As a result, Congress passed the Community Reinvestment Act (CRA) of 1977, which requires banking regulators to examine whether lenders have complied with their obligation to serve the credit needs of borrowers who live in LMI neighborhoods.

Under the CRA, federal banking regulators must consider the total number and dollar amount of loans that banks approve for LMI borrowers. They then must rate the banks' performance and make the rating available to the public. The CRA makes the banks' lending decisions more transparent, but it does not have quantitative measures, nor does it establish minimum standards that banks must achieve in order to receive a satisfactory performance rating. Moreover, because borrowers have no right to sue banks based on their performance rating, banks face limited liability if they fail to increase their lending to LMI borrowers. The public can, however, comment on the

Hispanic Homeownership 9 (2007), *available at* http://www.nclr.org/index.php/publications/saving_homes_saving_communities_latino_brokers_speak_out_on_hispanic_homeownership/; Declarations of Elizabeth M. Jacobson and Tony Paschal, *supra* note 42.

46 Bajaj & Helft, *supra* note 45; Michael Powell & Janet Roberts, *Minorities Affected Most as New York Foreclosures Rise*, N.Y. Times (May 15, 2009), *available at* http://www.nytimes.com/2009/05/16/nyregion/16foreclose.html?pagewanted=all.

bank's performance if the bank files an application for a merger or attempts to acquire another lending institution.

As noted in Chapter 5, critics have blamed the CRA requirements for forcing lenders to engage in high-risk lending, and they contend that these federal mandates led to the unsound and reckless lending practices that caused the housing crash. The Federal Reserve considered these criticisms and examined the loan performance data for subprime mortgages that were made in LMI neighborhoods. The study found that CRA loans performed as well – if not better – than some subprime loans that lenders approved for borrowers in middle- or higher-income areas. Additionally, a loan program that helped lenders comply with the CRA showed that loans that lenders made in CRA areas had prime loan features and lower default risks than loans made in non-CRA areas.

Moreover, CRA loans, unlike most subprime loans, did not have prepayment penalties, adjustable-interest rates, the level of mortgage broker involvement, or the costs (and abuses) associated with most subprime loans. In fact, this research suggests that if there had been *more* CRA lending, there might have been fewer mortgage broker-initiated, subprime ARMs, and more CRA lending would have spared more home buyers (especially lower-income, black, and Latino borrowers) from being pushed into higher-risk, higher-cost subprime loans.[47]

Despite the CRA requirement that lenders notify regulators when they intend to close a branch, lenders continue to close branches in lower-income areas at disproportionately high rates, even while they continue to expand bank operations overall by opening branches in wealthier neighborhoods. Relative to white borrowers, it has always been harder for black and Latino borrowers to obtain mortgage loans from a highly regulated financial institution and, especially during the housing boom, they were more likely to borrow from a less heavily regulated mortgage company. Because blacks and Latinos have less access to highly regulated financial institutions and are less familiar with the home buying process, they are more likely to rely on information provided through churches or other community organizations and to rely on intermediaries, like mortgage brokers, to help them negotiate with lenders.

For example, before the recession, more than 44 percent of black borrowers received loans from smaller brokers and lenders who specialized in higher-interest rate mortgages and who were *not* subject to CRA requirements. In contrast, white borrowers were twice as likely as black borrowers to obtain a

[47] Glenn Canner & Neil Bhutta, *Staff Analysis of the Relationship between the CRA and the Subprime Crisis* (2008), *available at* http://www.federalreserve.gov/newsevents/speech/20081203_analysis.pdf; Roberto Quercia & Janneke Ratcliffe, *The Community Reinvestment Act: Outstanding, and Needs to Improve* (2009).

loan from a highly regulated financial institution subject to the CRA requirements. Unlike loan officers who are paid a salary by the lender, mortgage broker compensation is based on the amount of the mortgage loan: the larger (and more expensive) the loan, the higher the broker's compensation. The increased reliance on assistance from mortgage brokers, combined with a smaller presence of traditional lenders in LMI neighborhoods, is likely one reason that blacks and Latinos have disproportionately received higher-cost mortgage products and were steered to those loans by their friendly neighborhood mortgage brokers.[48]

Although the CRA may not have forced lenders to expand credit opportunities for LMI borrowers, the CRA does appear to have fostered greater competition among the banks that do serve lower-income neighborhoods. Moreover, the CRA has at least made it harder for lenders to engage openly in racial redlining. For example, because of the CRA reporting requirements, the U.S. Department of Justice sued two Midwestern banks for discriminatory lending practices. The investigation revealed that these lenders failed to provide lending services to black neighborhoods and then manipulated the reporting requirements to hide the fact that they made so few loans to households in black neighborhoods. The banks settled this lawsuit in 2011.[49]

FINANCIAL LITERACY

One reason that blacks and Latinos may not fit the profile of the homeowner portrayed in the Narrative and why they may have lower homeownership rates is because they have lower levels of financial literacy. Indeed, surveys show that approximately 30 percent of blacks and Latinos do not understand how to develop a better credit history, and they are less likely to know what type of credit they need to qualify for a mortgage. Likewise, research indicates that blacks, in particular, are unfamiliar with the various types of savings vehicles (including 401k and other retirement plans, or the stock market)

[48] Susan E. Woodward & Robert Hall, *Consumer Confusion in the Mortgage Market: Evidence of Less than a Perfectly Transparent and Competitive Market*, 100 AM. ECON. REVIEW: PAPERS AND PROCEEDINGS 511 (2010), *available at* http://www.aeaweb.org/articles.php?doi=10.1257/aer.100.2.511.

[49] Bostic & Martin, *supra* note 23; Jonathan Spader & Roberto G. Quercia, *CRA Lending in a Changing Context: Evidence of Interaction with FHA and Subprime Originations*, 44 J. REAL EST. FIN. & ECON. 505 (2012); Caroline Reid & Elizabeth Laderman, *Constructive Credit: Revisiting the Performance of Community Reinvestment Act Lending during the Subprime Crisis*, in THE AMERICAN MORTGAGE SYSTEM: CRISIS AND REFORM 159 (Susan M. Wachter & Marvin Smith eds., 2011); Nelson D. Schwartz, *Bank Closings Tilt Toward Poor Areas*, N.Y.TIMES (Feb. 22, 2011); Joint Ctr. for Hous. Studies, Harvard Univ., *The State of the Nation's Housing* (2002), *available at* http://www.jchs.harvard.edu/sites/jchs.harvard.edu/files/son2002.pdf.

and that they do not understand the relative advantages (or tax implications) of investing in stocks, employer-provided retirement plans, or other investment vehicles.[50]

Blacks and Latinos may be more likely to self-select subprime loans or other higher-risk and higher-cost, nontraditional loan products (even when they were not being illegally steered to those products) because they have more limited exposure to, and information about, the real estate and mortgage markets. For example, before the housing bust, two-thirds of all Americans preferred FRMs and appeared somewhat informed about the risk of ARMs. In contrast, lower-income homeowners and minority owners were more likely to *prefer* ARMs and were less likely to understand the risks of those products. Minority mortgage applicants also did not appear to understand the roles and responsibilities of the various players in the application process, which may explain why many of them assumed that the mortgage broker who steered them to higher-cost mortgage products that had onerous terms (like prepayment penalties) was unbiased, had a fiduciary duty to them, or was obligated to offer them a loan that had the least costly terms.[51]

Blacks and Latinos may also select higher-cost loans or avoid even attempting to buy a home because they systematically underestimate their creditworthiness and overestimate what is required to buy a home. Because of their overall lower homeownership rates, black and Latino households have less experience negotiating with mortgage lenders or brokers. Many blacks realize that they are perceived as poor credit risks, and even blacks with *good* credit incorrectly conclude that they in fact have *bad* credit. Latino and black borrowers also might be unwilling (or unable) to negotiate with lenders or mortgage brokers because of their perception (be it accurate or not) that they are not creditworthy, and this perception may cause them to accept products that are pushed on them by the lender.

[50] Fannie Mae Foundation, *National Housing Survey: Understanding America's Homeownership Gaps* (2003); Consumer Federation of America, *Lower-Income and Minority Consumers Most Likely to Prefer and Underestimate Risks of Adjustable Rate Mortgages* (Jul. 26, 2004); FANNIE MAE FOUNDATION, AFRICAN AMERICAN AND HISPANIC ATTITUDES ON HOMEOWNERSHIP: A GUIDE FOR MORTGAGE INDUSTRY LEADERS 10–12 (1998).

[51] Shelia D. Ards & Samuel L. Myers, Jr., *The Color of Money: Bad Credit, Wealth, and Race*, AM. BEHAV. SCIENTIST (2011); Irwin S. Kirsch et al., *Adult Literacy in America: A First Look at the Findings of the National Adult Literacy Survey*, U.S. Dep't of Educ. (2002), *available at* http://nces.ed.gov/pubs93/93275.pdf; Lauren E. Willis, *Decisionmaking and the Limits of Disclosure: The Problem of Predatory Lending: Price*, 65 MARYLAND L. REV. 707 (2006). Annamarie Lusardi & Peter Tufano, *Debt Literacy, Financial Experiences, and Overindebtedness* (Nat. Bur. Econ. Research Working Paper, 2009), *available at* http://www.nber.org/papers/w14808; Research Inst. for Hous. Am., *Insights into the Minority Homebuying Experience: The Mortgage Application Process* 4 (2003).

Of course, it is not surprising that black and Latino borrowers assume that they are not creditworthy and doubt their ability to negotiate better loan terms, because whites have historically been viewed (and treated) as more creditworthy than non-whites. Moreover, if potential black and Latino borrowers (like the mystery testers discussed earlier in the chapter) have been mistreated in the past by lenders who refused to approve their credit applications or to tell them of the availability of more favorable loan products, these borrowers may perceive that they have worse credit than other (white) consumers.[52]

As discussed in greater detail in Chapter 9, there are racial K–12 and college-education gaps, and because of those gaps, it is not surprising that blacks, Latinos, and LMI Americans are less financially literate overall than upper-income Americans, *especially* upper-income whites. As long as blacks and Latinos have relatively higher levels of financial illiteracy and relatively lower credit scores, though, their financial naïveté may make them more vulnerable and place them at greater risk for abuse in the real estate and financial services markets.[53]

CONSEQUENCES OF THE BURDEN

The Fair Housing Act, which was part of the Civil Rights Act of 1968, and other federal laws and policies prohibit discrimination in the sale, rental, and financing of dwellings. While U.S. laws no longer prevent minorities from purchasing their dream homes, governmental and private entities continued to engage in coordinated efforts to discourage blacks from buying homes in white areas well into the 1970s. Thus, even when the government and private lenders stopped engaging in overtly discriminatory practices, blacks and Latinos who tried to buy homes were burdened with the residual effects of years of government-sanctioned discrimination. They continue to face long-established residential segregation patterns, realtors who steer them away from the highest appreciating neighborhoods, and white neighbors who flee when they move into a neighborhood.

[52] Ards & Myers, *supra* note 50; Donald R. Haurin & Hazel A. Morrow – Jones, *The Impact of Real Estate Market Knowledge on Tenure Choice: A Comparison of Black and White Households*, 17 HOUSING POL'Y DEBATE 625 (2006); Ren S. Essene & William Apgar, *Understanding Mortgage Market Behavior: Creating Good Mortgage Options for All Americans*, Joint Ctr. for Housing Studies, Harvard Univ. (2007); Robert A. Avery et al., *Higher-Priced Home Lending and the 2005 HMDA Data*, FED. RES. BULL. A123, A127 (2006); Willis, *id.*

[53] Mark Wiranowski, *Sustaining Home Ownership through Education and Counseling* (Joint Ctr. for Hous. Studies, Harvard Univ., Working Paper No. W03–7, 2003).

Blacks and Latinos suffered catastrophic losses during the recent housing meltdown largely because they were steered to higher-cost, equity-stripping mortgage products. These losses vividly depict the burdens that blacks and Latinos continue to face when they try to become homeowners. As the next chapter shows, because of these burdens, it is virtually impossible for blacks and Latinos to reap the valuable homeownership benefits that the U.S. government has consistently lavished on whites.

8

The Benefits of Home Buying While Black or Latino

Blacks and Latinos have always placed a high value on homeownership, and they, like all Americans, believe that being homeowners will improve their lives and increase their household wealth. Civil rights and progressive housing groups also stress the benefits of owning a home and the importance of increasing black and Latino homeownership rates. For example, at the beginning of the recent recession, the Leadership Conference on Civil Rights stated that

> ... the right to the American Dream of homeownership has always been one of the most fundamental goals of the civil rights movement. It is vital because homeownership is the means by which most Americans build wealth and improve their own lives and the lives of their families, and homeownership is essential to the development of stable, healthy communities of which all Americans can be proud.[1]

Likewise, the National Council of La Raza noted at a congressional hearing in 2011 that

> [c]ommunities of color do not own homes at rates comparable to their White peers, which contributes heavily to the racial wealth gap. Civil rights institutions have fought for decades for policies that ensure that qualified borrowers of color are able to access the same homeownership opportunities enjoyed by the rest of the market.[2]

[1] *Strengthening Our Economy: Foreclosure Prevention and Neighborhood Preservation: Hearing before the Senate Committee on Banking, Housing, and Urban Affairs*, 110th Cong. 1 (2008) (statement of Wade Henderson, on behalf of the Leadership Conference on Civil Rights).

[2] *Commonsense Mortgage Origination Protections Empower Latino Homebuyers, Presented at Mortgage Origination: The Impact of Recent Changes on Homeowners and Businesses: Hearing before the House Subcommittee on Insurance, Housing, and Community Development of the House Committee on Financial Services* (Jul. 13, 2011) (statement of Janis Bowdler, on behalf of the National Council of La Raza).

As demonstrated in the last chapter, blacks and Latinos have always faced special obstacles and barriers – many placed by the U.S. government – when they have tried to buy homes. Even when these groups manage to overcome these obstacles and barriers, however, they receive fewer of the economic and noneconomic homeownership benefits that white homeowners with similar incomes and credit profiles receive. Despite having heavier burdens but fewer benefits, blacks and Latinos continue to be encouraged to do whatever it takes to buy a house. Given the demographic shifts in the U.S. population, though, it now appears that blacks and Latinos are being steered toward homeownership for reasons that likely have very little to do with *their* financial well-being.

HOMEOWNERSHIP RATES

Encouraging Americans to buy and remain in homes has been the primary goal of U.S. housing policies since the government intervened in housing markets after the Depression. Overall homeownership rates almost doubled during the twentieth century, and they have ranged from 64 percent to 69 percent since 1980. Indeed, overall homeownership rates in 2010 and 2011 (approximately 66 percent) remained high notwithstanding the record number of foreclosure sales during the 2007–2009 recession. As shown in Figure 8.1, however, just looking at the aggregate rate disguises the fact that homeownership rates vary – quite dramatically – by race, and overall rates hide the fact that there has always been a racial homeownership gap.[3]

At all relevant mobility phases, whites purchase homes at rates that exceed those of blacks and Latinos. That is, whites purchase homes at earlier ages and at higher rates as first-time home buyers who are establishing their households after they marry and start to raise a family than blacks or Latinos do. Likewise, white households sell their first homes and trade up to larger or more expensive homes at earlier ages and at greater rates than black and Latino households do. Black homeownership rates were less than 20 percent at the turn of the twentieth century largely because most blacks lived in the agricultural South and, as the descendants of former slaves, had little wealth and generally were unable to inherit property. Even when blacks left the rural South and migrated to cities in southern and northern states, though, their homeownership rates significantly lagged white homeownership rates.

[3] William J. Collins & Robert A. Margo, *Race and Home Ownership, 1900 to 1990* (Nat'l Bureau of Econ. Research, Working Paper No. 7277, 1999), *available at* http://www.nber.org/papers/w7277.pdf.

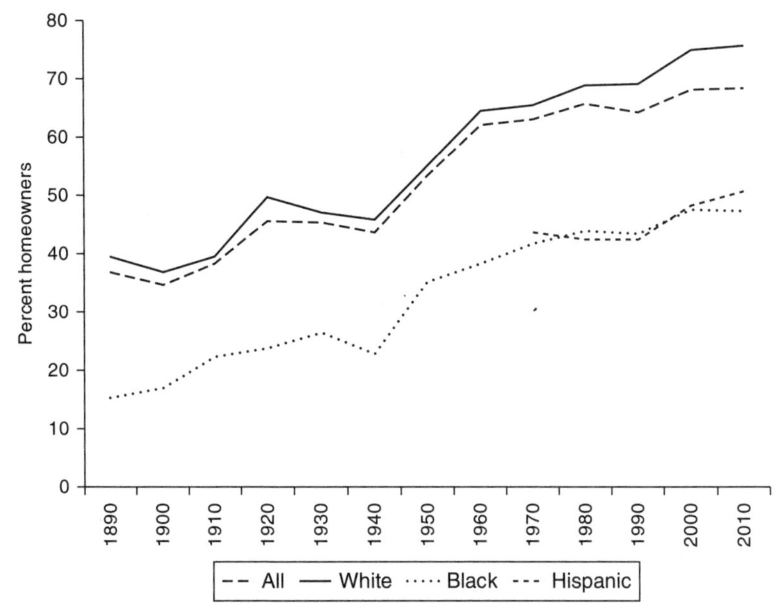

Figure 8.1 Homeownership rates by race.
Source: U.S. Census Bureau.

Overall homeownership rates dropped from 45.6 percent in 1920 to 43.6 percent in 1940 due to the economic crisis the Great Depression triggered. Once the United States agreed to buy and refinance short-term, high-cost private mortgage loans and then guaranteed mortgage payments for borrowers who qualified for FHA-insured loans, white homeownership rates soared. By 1950, white homeownership rates were more than 55 percent and overall homeownership rates were 53.4 percent, but black homeownership rates lagged behind white rates by almost 20 points (at barely 35 percent). Black homeownership rates largely remained the same throughout the 1940s and 1950s, likely because racially restrictive covenants were legally enforceable until the 1948 U.S. Supreme Court ruling in *Shelly v. Kraemer*.[4]

Overall homeownership rates continued to rise and reached 62 percent by 1960. Homeownership rates for white households were more than 64 percent that year while homeownership rates for blacks were 38 percent. Overall homeownership rates then started to rise again in the 1970s because of the influx of Baby Boomers who were establishing their own households. By 1980, the overall homeownership rate rose to approximately 66 percent, and the white homeownership rate that year exceeded 68 percent. In stark contrast, the homeownership rate for

[4] 334 U.S. 1 (1948).

blacks was 43.8 percent – just barely higher than *overall homeownership rates in 1940*. Homeownership rates for Latinos were even lower, at 42.4 percent.

Black and Latino rates may lag white homeownership rates for intergenerational reasons. Data show that the children of homeowners are more likely to become homeowners than renters' children, in part because homeowners discuss the benefits of owning a house with their children. Blacks and Latinos have lower overall homeownership rates and also generally have less experience with the home buying process. These two groups also are less likely to have family, neighbors, or close friends to consult with during the home buying process. In contrast, white renters tend to consult traditional sources of information, including real estate agencies or housing assistance agencies, when they are considering whether to buy a home. Because blacks and Latinos have less experience with the home buying process than whites do, they often rely more on newspaper ads or word-of-mouth information during the process. Relying on these less reliable sources is one reason black and Latino households are less informed about their financing options when they buy homes and about homeownership costs generally.[5]

As discussed later in this chapter, white birth rates have been declining since the 1990s relative to Latino and black birth rates. Less than 50 percent of all children born each year are white, and based on census projections, Latinos will soon constitute the largest percentage of potential new homeowners. For decades, U.S. leaders have acknowledged the difficulties blacks and Latinos have faced in housing and mortgage lending markets. Nonetheless, U.S. political leaders, Fannie Mae, and other housing entities did not engage in sustained or concerted efforts to find ways to make homeownership more accessible to black and Latino households until home sales stalled in the 1990s. When it became clear that the housing market would remain sluggish and might stagnate unless blacks and Latino households bought homes, U.S. leaders – encouraged by the politically powerful financial services and real estate industries – held summits, created commissions, and enacted programs and policies to increase black and Latino homeownership rates and, of course, home sales.[6]

[5] Donald R. Haurin & Hazel A. Morrow-Jones, *The Impact of Real Estate Market Knowledge on Tenure Choice: A Comparison of Black and White Households*, 17 HOUSING POL'Y DEBATE 625 (2006); Robert D. Dietz & Donald R. Haurin, *The Social and Private Micro-level Consequences of Homeownership*, 54 J. URBAN ECON. 401 (2003); *Successful Homeownership and Renting Through Housing Counseling: Hearing before the Subcommittee on Housing and Community Opportunity of the Committee of Financial Services, U.S. House of Representatives*, 108th Cong., 2nd Sess. (Mar. 18, 2004) (statement of Lautaro Diaz, deputy Vice President for Community Development, National Council of La Raza).

[6] The U.S. Census did not consistently record homeownership rates for Hispanics/Latinos until the 1970s. William J. Collins & Robert A. Margo, *Race and Home Ownership from the*

Both Presidents Clinton and George W. Bush made increasing minority homeownership rates a priority during their terms. For example, Henry G. Cisneros, who served as President Clinton's Secretary of Housing and Urban Development (HUD) from 1993 to 1997, worked with private lending groups, nonprofit agencies, and governmental agencies as part of the White House's *National Homeownership Strategy*. The Clinton *Strategy* recognized that black and Latino households had lower homeownership rates relative to whites with comparable incomes and sought to break down "racial and ethnic barriers" and "enable minority households to own homes in a much wider range of communities." The Clinton White House set a goal to increase overall homeowners by 8 million by 2000. The *Strategy* took "concerted actions" to help minority and low-income potential homeowners overcome the current barriers they faced when they attempted to become homeowners and focused on creating affordable and flexible financing arrangements.[7]

The George W. Bush administration set a goal of creating 5.5 million more minority homeowners by 2010. During the Bush administration, the U.S. Congress held a hearing on "Increasing Minority Homeownership, and Expanding Homeownership to All Who Wish to Attain It." During that hearing, Republican members of Congress, the Secretary of Housing and Urban Development, and representatives from the real estate industry all proclaimed their desire to increase the number of minority homeowners. To remove barriers to homeownership for minorities, Bush issued *America's Homeownership Challenge* to the real estate, mortgage, and banking industries.

The *Challenge* recognized that many LMI families, especially blacks and Latinos, could not realize the American dream of homeownership because they lacked the savings to make a down payment or pay closing costs. To make homeownership possible for them, Bush created the American Dream Down Payment Fund, which helped potential buyers who lacked savings. The *Challenge* also supported self-help homeownership programs (like Habitat for Humanity), gave builders an incentive to produce affordable homes, and expanded housing counseling programs.

A survey conducted in 1998 indicates that more than 70 percent of the black and Latino households surveyed perceived, rightly so, that mortgage lending discrimination and other barriers (including not having enough money

End of the Civil War to the Present, 101 AM. ECON. REV. 355 (2011); Hazel L. Morrow-Jones, *Black-White Differences in the Demographic Structure of the Move to Homeownership in the United States*, in OWNERSHIP, CONTROL, AND THE FUTURE OF HOUSING POLICY 39 (R. Allen Hays ed., 1993); Kerwin Kofi Charles & Erik Hurst, *The Transition to Home Ownership and the Black-White Wealth Gap*, 84 REV. ECON. & STAT. 281 (2002).

7 U.S. Dep't of Hous. and Urban Dev., *The National Homeownership Strategy: Partners in the American Dream* (1995).

for a down payment) made it harder for them to own homes.[8] During the Bush administration, HUD considered the barriers potential minority homeowners were facing and issued a report that identified the following as the primary impediments to minority homeownership: lack of affordable single-family housing; weak credit history; lack of capital for down payment; and, a lack of knowledge about the home buying process. HUD acknowledged that ongoing discrimination and segregation also contributed to the racial homeownership gap. Because it soon became clear that minority ownership rates would not increase without the help of the lending industry, the government challenged the real estate industry to work in conjunction with Wall Street to develop innovative loan financing options that facilitated a market approach to increasing minority homeownership.[9]

Because of the Clinton White House *Strategy*, overall homeownership rates increased from 64 percent to more than 67 percent between 1993 and 2000, and there were almost 2.5 million new black and Latino homeowners. While black and Latino homeowners accounted for only 13.8 percent of total homeowners, they represented almost 29 percent of the increase in the number of owners between 1994 and 1997. Likewise, the Bush *Challenge* helped increase overall homeownership rates, which hit an all-time high of more than 69 percent in 2004.

These increases, again, masked the persistent racial homeownership gap that has been fairly constant over the last thirty years despite repeated efforts, projects, and initiatives to close it. Since 1995, white homeownership rates have never been less than 70 percent, and they rose as high as 76 percent in 2004. In marked contrast, no racial group (blacks, Latinos, Native Americans, or Asians) had overall homeownership rates that exceeded 70 percent in 2004 (or in any other year). Even though black homeownership rates hit an all-time high of approximately 49.4 percent in 2004, and the highest Latino homeownership rate reached 49.8 percent in 2006, unlike white households, the majority of black and Latino households have *always* been renters.

One clear success of the Clinton and Bush efforts to close the gap was that minorities constituted approximately 40 percent of the net growth in new owners before the housing market collapsed. From the mid-1990s until the mid-2000s, the increase in the black homeownership rate (25 percent) was almost twice the overall homeownership increase (14 percent) and more than three

[8] FANNIE MAE FOUNDATION, AFRICAN AMERICAN AND HISPANIC ATTITUDES ON HOMEOWNERSHIP: A GUIDE FOR MORTGAGE INDUSTRY LEADERS 5 (1998).

[9] George W. Bush, *A Home of Your Own: Expanding Opportunities for All Americans* (Jun. 2002), *available at* http://georgewbush-whitehouse.archives.gov/infocus/homeownership/toc.html; U.S. Dep't of Hous. and Urban Dev., *Barriers to Minority Homeownership* (Jun. 17, 2002), *available at* http://archives.hud.gov/reports/barriers.cfm.

times the increase in white homeowners (7 percent). Latino homeownership increases were even more dramatic. During the housing boom, Latino homeownership rates increased by more than 60 percent – more than four times the overall homeownership rates. While some of the growth was due to the relatively younger ages of Latinos and blacks and to their larger birth and immigration rates, some of the growth occurred because lenders (at the urging of the government) adopted relaxed underwriting standards. Because, however, blacks and Latinos were disproportionately more likely to be steered to higher-cost mortgage products and because they had higher default and foreclosure rates, most of the increase in their homeownership rates – and the housing wealth created by those higher rates – was wiped out by the recent recession.

During and since the recession, blacks and Latinos had steeper homeownership rate declines and much higher foreclosure rates than whites. For example, black homeownership rates in 2010 (44 percent) were 28 percent lower than white homeownership rates, a larger gap than in 1990 (25 percent) or 2000 (26 percent). In fact, black homeownership rates in 2010 were lower than black homeownership rates in 1990 (45 percent). Similarly, despite the strong increase in Latino homeownership rates during the housing boom, their 2010 rates still lag white rates by almost 25 percent. In short, while black and Latino homeownership rates increased over time and rose faster from 1995 to 2005 than homeownership rates for white households, the homeownership gap between whites and other racial or ethnic minority groups has stubbornly hovered around 25 percent.[10]

STAKEHOLDER POWERS

In the Happy Homeownership Narrative, homeowners are more responsible and more involved in their communities than renters are. Because they are viewed as having a larger stake in their communities, they have been allowed

[10] Rolf Pendall et al., *Demographic Challenges and Opportunities for U.S. Housing Markets*, Bipartisan Policy Ctr. (Mar. 2012); Mark Wiranowski, *Sustaining Home Ownership through Education and Counseling* (Joint Ctr. for Hous. Studies, Harvard Univ., Working Paper No. W03–7, 2003); Kathleen C. Engel & Patricia A. McCoy, *From Credit Denial to Predatory Lending: The Challenge of Sustaining Minority Homeownership*, in SEGREGATION: THE RISING COSTS FOR AMERICA 81 (James H. Carr & Nandinee K. Kutty eds., 2008); Debbie Gruenstein Bocian et al., *Lost Ground, 2011: Disparities in Mortgage Lending and Foreclosures*, Ctr. for Responsible Lending (2011); Debbie Gruenstein Bocian et al., *Foreclosures by Race and Ethnicity: The Demographics of a Crisis*, Ctr. for Responsible Lending (2010); Latino Policy Forum, *Latinos and the Foreclosure Crisis: Its Impact in Cook County, Illinois* (2010); Kristopher S. Gerardi & Paul S. Willen, *Subprime Mortgages, Foreclosures, and Urban Neighborhoods*, Fed. Res. Bank of Boston (2008).

to employ local land use and zoning laws to influence how other properties in their neighborhoods can be used or developed. As noted in Chapter 7, white homeowners can use their stakeholder powers to exclude black home buyers from their neighborhoods. Because of federal housing laws and Supreme Court rulings, white homeowners can no longer use racially restrictive property covenants to exclude homeowners on the basis of their race, and local governments cannot use racially restrictive zoning codes to segregate neighborhoods by race. Starting in the 1960s and 1970s, however, local governments enacted facially race-neutral land use laws that still continue to segregate neighborhoods by income. This economic sorting has helped maintain the racially segregated U.S. neighborhoods that redlining and steering created.

Facially neutral exclusionary land use regulations fence out residents from neighborhoods by imposing minimum requirements that almost always increase housing prices. For example, many zoning laws exclude mobile homes, multifamily units, and high-density public housing projects from some single-family neighborhoods. Some communities, especially higher-income, suburban neighborhoods, fence out lower-income households by imposing large lot or minimum floor sizes.

Requiring developers to build larger houses and devote larger plots of land to each house both excludes renters and increases the overall price of land and housing. Other land use laws to restrict the number of occupants in a single-family home or mandate that all occupants in the house be from the same family. Ironically, even the largely progressive, environmentally "green" movement often fences out renters and affordable housing by preventing builders from constructing units on vacant, open spaces.

As was true with the very first zoning regulations, localities argue that exclusionary zoning ordinances are needed to preserve the character of the community and that placing multifamily units, like townhouses or apartments, and affordable housing projects in their neighborhoods will decrease the property values of the existing single-family homes and will increase the neighborhood's infrastructural costs. The homeowners who are most successful at fencing out multifamily housing or nondesirable public projects are the ones who live in higher-income, suburban neighborhoods. Black and Latino homeowners, however, have not been as successful in fencing out nondesirable (but socially beneficial) property uses. Instead, the homeowners who most often live in neighborhoods that have exclusionary zoning laws are disproportionately white. In contrast, the people most likely to be fenced out are LMI, black, and Latino. Even though some courts have struck down some ordinances for being overbroad, exclusionary zoning has largely succeeded in segregating neighborhoods by income, and in the United States income segregation nearly always creates (or perpetuates) racial segregation.

Suburban neighborhoods with upper-income residents tend to have higher-quality schools, parks, and other amenities. When these neighbors use their stakeholder powers to fence out LMI residents, they prevent those residents from having easy access to these higher-quality neighborhood services. Even more problematic are the external costs that fencing imposes on other neighborhoods. That is, fencing undesirable (but socially beneficial) projects or multifamily units out of higher-income, suburban neighborhoods protect the property values of the homes located in those neighborhoods. But fencing certain types of housing out of one neighborhood imposes costs on the homeowners who live in the neighborhoods that are then forced to accept those undesirable properties. The "losers" in the fencing battle are disproportionately lower-income and non-white neighborhoods. Thus, to the extent that multifamily housing or nondesirable property uses actually depress the value of other homes in the neighborhood, when upper-income homeowners fence out those properties, they impose costs on the LMI homeowners who cannot prevent those properties from being placed in their neighborhoods.[11]

HOUSING APPRECIATION

In the Happy Homeownership Narrative, homeownership is preferable to renting because homes always appreciate in value. This is true for some homes, but it has always been harder for black and Latino homeowners to own homes that appreciate in value. Discriminatory lending policies made it harder for blacks and Latinos to buy homes with low-cost, government-insured mortgages. Redlining and steering then made it harder for them to buy higher-appreciating homes in suburban neighborhoods. Even when redlining and other overt forms of housing market discrimination were banned, real estate agents continued to steer blacks away from higher-appreciating homes in white neighborhoods, and the vestiges of redlining created and perpetuated racially segregated neighborhood patterns. And, when blacks were finally able to buy homes in formerly all-white neighborhoods, blockbusting tactics in the 1950s and 1960s caused blacks to pay a premium for those homes.

Research spanning multiple decades and covering local, national, urban, and suburban housing consistently shows that homes in racially diverse neighborhoods (especially all-black neighborhoods) have lower appreciation rates

[11] Vill. of Belle Terre v. Boraas, 416 U.S. 1 (1974); Vill. of Arlington Heights v. Metro. Hous. Dev. Corp., 429 U.S. 252 (1977); Douglas S. Massey, *Origins of Economic Disparities: The Historical Role of Housing Segregation*, in SEGREGATION: THE RISING COSTS FOR AMERICA 39, 73 (James H. Carr & Nandinee K. Kutty eds., 2008); Tim Iglesias, *Our Pluralist Housing Ethics and the Struggle for Affordability*, 42 WAKE FOREST L. REV. 511 (2007).

and are not valued as highly as homes in white neighborhoods. Indeed, homes in non-white neighborhoods have lower appreciation rates even after controlling for multiple variables, including household structure and region, owner age and class, and the price range of the homes. The racial housing value and appreciation gap was sizeable until the 1940s, largely because a disproportionate number of black homeowners lived in southern states, and homes in that region had overall lower housing values. Once blacks started to migrate to northern states, though, many continued to own homes that had low appreciation rates, again, because of where those homes were located.

To avoid the inconvenience, humiliation, and time required to find and buy a home in a white neighborhood, many blacks chose to buy homes in predominately black, urban neighborhoods. Homes in those neighborhoods tended to be older, have higher maintenance costs, and lack many of the amenities found in newer or suburban homes in predominately white areas. As a result, because blacks and Latinos have been steered away *from* higher-appreciating suburban homes and *to* higher-cost mortgage financing, the homes they have owned usually have lower market values than those of whites.

Even though blacks were steered to (or chose to buy) lower-appreciating homes in urban neighborhoods, the racial home appreciation gap did close somewhat at the beginning of the 1960s. However, it stalled by the end of that decade when urban cities experienced riots and homeowners (white and black alike) fled to the suburbs. Prices for homes in urban areas dropped again in the 1970s when cities implemented school desegregation plans and even more whites fled to suburban schools. During this period, home appreciation rates increased and residential segregation decreased for the middle-class blacks who were able to flee urban neighborhoods and buy suburban homes.[12]

Homes in predominately non-white neighborhoods are also less valued in housing markets because whites have overall higher homeownership rates, are not willing to live in neighborhoods where they are in the minority, and will move whenever they perceive that the neighborhood is tipping. Some urban homes are objectively less valuable than newer suburban homes because of their smaller size and older features. Additionally, blacks and Latinos (and especially older black homeowners) have homes that are valued less than the homes that whites own because they are disproportionately more likely to own homes in lower-income, non-white neighborhoods that have a higher

[12] Deborah L. McKoy & Jeffrey M. Vincent, *Housing and Education: The Inextricable Link*, in SEGREGATION: THE RISING COSTS FOR AMERICA 125 (James H. Carr & Nandinee K. Kutty eds., 2008); W. J. Collins & R. A. Margo, *Race and the Value of Owner-Occupied Housing, 1940–1990*, 33 REGIONAL SCI. & URB. ECON. 255 (2003); Leah Platt Boustan, *School Desegregation and Urban Change: Evidence from City Boundaries*, 4 AM. ECON. J.: APPLIED ECON. 85 (2012).

percentage of undesirable (albeit socially beneficial) property uses, like higher-density rental properties, hazardous waste sites, group homes, and public housing projects. Older blacks are disproportionately more likely to live in neighborhoods that have undesirable properties. As a result, the homes they own are actually more likely to *depreciate* than appreciate. The presence of undesirable property uses partially explains why whites, who generally have greater housing options than blacks and Latinos, would avoid homes in urban or non-white neighborhoods. Not all whites avoided living in urban areas because of the objective market value of the homes.

Given the racial climate and social norms that existed in the United States until at least the 1950s, few whites would have elected to live in a predominately minority neighborhood. Additionally, it would have been economically irrational for white renters who were willing to live in black neighborhoods to purchase homes in those neighborhoods. As discussed in the last chapter, redlining made it virtually impossible for any buyer to get a low-cost mortgage loan to buy a home in a racially diverse neighborhood. Given their higher homeownership rates, when whites either avoid or are steered away from black or Latino neighborhoods, their decision decreases the demand and the market value for those homes.

The racial housing value gap does not exist solely because some LMI black and Latino homeowners live in urban neighborhoods: the gap exists regardless of the location of the house or the income of the homeowner. For example, data show that the owners of homes in predominately black, suburban areas have lower household incomes, and that the homes have lower values, and lower appreciation rates than similar homes in predominantly white suburban areas. Likewise, data show that the homes that higher-income blacks own have lower housing values relative to whites with similar economic profiles. Indeed, some data indicate that the racial gap in housing values actually widens with the owner's class because the gap between the housing values of higher-income black and white homeowners is often larger than the housing value gap for lower-income black and white homeowners.[13]

Obviously, the color of a homeowner's skin does not cause a home to be objectively more or less valuable. Whether the race of homeowners in a neighborhood objectively decreases the value of the homes is, of course, largely irrelevant if the market of potential buyers of those homes *perceive* that the homes are worth less than homes that whites own. Even though

[13] Hayward Derrick Horton & Melvin E. Thomas, *Race, Class, and Family Structure: Differences in Housing Values for Black and White Homeowners*, 68 SOC. INQUIRY 114 (1998); MELVIN OLIVER & THOMAS SHAPIRO, BLACK WEALTH/WHITE WEALTH: A NEW PERSPECTIVE ON RACIAL INEQUALITY (1995); Charles & Hurst, *supra* note 6.

there is no scientific basis for this belief, homes in minority neighborhoods in the United States are worth less because home buyers perceive those homes to be worthless, and these perceptions are capitalized in the value of homes. Perceptions that a community is "good" because it is safe or has highly rated schools or low taxes are capitalized into home values, as are perceptions that a community is "bad" because it has high crime rates or low-performing schools.

Because many Americans perceive that white neighborhoods are better and safer than non-white neighborhoods, the racial composition of a neighborhood affects the market value of the homes even if the homes in both neighborhoods are comparable in size and amenities. For example, the fact that a public school is racially diverse or is located in an area that has a desegregated school plan should not affect the value of the homes zoned for that school. Studies consistently show, however, that white homeowners will pay a premium to avoid school districts that are under a desegregation order or plan and that they will buy more expensive homes in neighborhoods that have less diverse schools.[14]

Ongoing realtor steering contributes to lower housing appreciation rates for homes in black and Latino neighborhoods by stigmatizing those neighborhoods. When potential white buyers are steered away from diverse neighborhoods, this act signals that there is something wrong with those neighborhoods. This steering, along with the implicit assumption that white buyers should avoid non-white neighborhoods, ultimately causes the homes to have less value in the housing markets simply because there will be fewer buyers seeking to purchase those stigmatized homes.[15]

[14] Lee Anne Fennell, The Unbounded Home: Property Values Beyond Property Lines (2009); James H. Carr & Nandinee K. Kutty, *The New Imperative for Equality*, in Segregation: The Rising Costs for America 1 (James H. Carr & Nandinee K. Kutty eds., 2008); Ingrid Gould Ellen, *Continuing Isolation: Segregation in America Today*, in Segregation: The Rising Costs for America 261 (James H. Carr & Nandinee K. Kutty eds., 2008); Katrin B. Anacker, *Still Paying the Race Tax? Analyzing Property Values in Homogeneous and Mixed-Race Suburbs*, 32 J. Urb. Aff. 55 (2010); Boustan, *supra* note 12.

[15] Margery Austin Turner, *Residential Segregation and Employment Inequality*, in Segregation: The Rising Costs for America 151 (James H. Carr & Nandinee K. Kutty eds., 2008); Lee Anne Fennell, *Homes Rule*, 112 Yale L.J. 617 (2002); Stephen Grant Meyer, As Long as They Don't Move Next Door: Segregation and Racial Conflict in American Neighborhoods 51 (2000). There is a huge demand for homes in Latino neighborhoods that consist primarily of recent immigrants. Although most non-black neighborhoods have appreciation rates that are lower than the rates in white neighborhoods, appreciation rates in immigrant Latino neighborhoods exceed both black and white neighborhood appreciation rates. Chenoa Flippen, *Unequal Returns to Housing Investments? A Study of Real Housing Appreciation among Black, White, and Hispanic Households*, 82 Soc. Forces 1523 (2004).

WEALTH ACCUMULATION

In the Happy Homeownership Narrative, homeownership is preferable to renting because homes appreciate in value, their appreciation increases household wealth, and that wealth can be used to pay college costs or to make a down payment on another (or second) house. The racial homeownership gap closed somewhat during the housing boom and black and Latino homeownership rates increased. Nonetheless, blacks and Latinos have never reaped the same financial benefits from homeownership as white households with comparable economic profiles, and they have been deprived of decades of accumulated household wealth because of the racially discriminatory housing policies and practices that were widespread (and legal) for most of the period from the Depression through the 1960s.

While the United States eased the path for white homeowners to buy homes and accumulate wealth after the Depression, federal housing policies that deemed homes in racially mixed neighborhoods to be unsafe and uninsurable caused those homes to be valued less than homes in non-redlined neighborhoods. In addition, redlining made it virtually impossible for blacks to buy homes with FHA-insured loans or with any other low-cost, longer-term loan. It was also harder for blacks to buy homes in white neighborhoods because of racially restrictive covenants, especially because the FHA encouraged developers to include these covenants in their new housing developments. And, until the 1950s, the FHA would not guarantee a private mortgage for a black renter who attempted to purchase a covenanted property.

Government-sanctioned obstacles in U.S. housing markets made it difficult for black households to buy homes – especially higher-appreciating suburban homes – in the 1950s and 1960s when housing prices in the United States were soaring. In addition, blacks were denied access to traditional low-cost mortgage loans, which meant that they paid more on average to buy homes that ultimately did not appreciate as much as homes in predominately white neighborhoods did. In contrast, whites were able to buy homes with lower-cost and lower-risk, FHA-insured loans, which reduced their overall home buying costs. Moreover, because these self-amortizing loans had lower interest rates and longer terms, white homeowners' risk of default (and, thus, of losing their homes) was lower. With lower mortgage debt, whites were able to accumulate more equity in their homes than blacks or Latinos with comparable incomes.

Research suggests that blacks may have paid twice the amount for homes they bought in the 1970s than they would have if they (or their parents) had been able to buy a home with a lower-cost, government-insured loan in the 1950s.[16] Although the United States finally decided to exert greater efforts to remove barriers to homeownership for blacks and Latinos in the 1990s, the past exclusion of blacks and Latinos from U.S. housing markets resulted in them having less home equity and lower overall household wealth.

Easier availability of mortgage credit during the housing boom increased minority homeownership rates, at least initially. These higher homeownership rates ostensibly could have helped blacks and Latinos accumulate more household wealth. But these higher homeownership rates came at a time when blacks and Latinos had stagnant income and high unemployment rates. Moreover, as noted in Chapter 7, blacks and Latinos were more likely to be offered (and to accept) nontraditional, subprime loan products to buy homes, and subprime loans have significantly higher default rates and are more likely to lead to a foreclosure sale than prime loans. Like millions of homeowners, many blacks and Latinos who were approved for these loans defaulted when interest rates reset and, because of stagnant (or no) income, they could not afford to make the monthly payments.

Black and Latino homeowners suffered devastating losses during the recent recession. At the beginning of the recession, black and Latino homeowners had mortgage debt that was more than 13 percent *higher* than comparable white homeowner mortgage debt, mainly because they had higher-cost mortgage loans and also because minority households are younger on average than white households. In addition to having higher overall mortgage debt, the amount of equity they had in their homes at the beginning of the recession was 26 percent *lower* than comparable white households. During the recession, the value of homes that minorities owned fell by 20 percent, while the value of white homes fell by 13 percent. As a result of higher mortgage debt, lower overall values, and steeper rates of depreciation, blacks and Latinos had disproportionately more underwater mortgages and higher default and foreclosure rates than whites with comparable economic profiles.[17]

While black and Latino homeownership rates increased during the housing boom, there was actually a net loss of ownership for these two groups because of their disproportionately higher foreclosure rates. For example, 7.9 percent of blacks and 7.7 percent of Latinos who received loans to buy a house (or refinance their mortgage loan) between 2005 and 2008 lost their homes to foreclosure between 2007 and 2009. During these relevant periods, only 4.5 percent

[16] John F. Kain & John M. Quigley, *Housing Market Discrimination, Homeownership and Savings Behavior*, AM. ECON. REV. 263 (1972).

[17] Joint Ctr. for Hous. Studies, Harvard Univ., *The State of the Nation's Housing* (2011), *available at* http://www.jchs.harvard.edu/sites/jchs.harvard.edu/files/son2011.pdf.

of white homeowners lost their homes to foreclosure. Even controlling for income, blacks and Latinos had higher foreclosure rates during the recession than white homeowners, and studies conducted before the recession indicate that blacks and Latinos have had higher foreclosure rates (especially for subprime mortgages) than whites since 1990. Two years after the recession ended, approximately 25 percent of Latino and black homeowners had either lost their homes to foreclosure or were seriously delinquent on mortgage loans that were approved between 2004 and 2008, while only 12 percent of white homeowners had lost their homes or were seriously delinquent.[18]

One reason that blacks and Latinos may have had higher foreclosure rates is because they had a disproportionate share of subprime loans, and the majority of subprime loans are refinance loans that are not used to purchase a home (and, thus, increase the homeowner's wealth). For example, data collected during the housing boom show that less than 10 percent of subprime loans were made to first-time home buyers to enable them to become a homeowner. During the housing boom, borrowers who purchased their homes with exotic mortgage products were encouraged to refinance those loans when interest rates reset on the loans. Rather than helping the homeowner increase equity in their homes, these loans drained equity from the homes. Just as blacks and Latinos were more likely to be steered to subprime loans originally, data confirm that they were also most likely to be steered to subprime refinance loans. Thus, while 16.7 percent of whites used subprime refinance loans, 30.9 percent of Latinos and 46.9 percent of blacks refinanced their mortgages (and thus removed equity from their homes) with a subprime product.[19]

The collapse of U.S. housing markets had a particularly devastating effect on black and Latino household wealth because home equity accounts for such a large share of their household wealth. Housing constitutes almost 60 percent of black overall wealth and approximately 65 percent of overall Latino wealth, but it constitutes only 44 percent of white household wealth. Black and Latino homeowners lost more than just their homes during the recession, though. As was true for all homeowners during the housing boom, blacks and Latinos often depleted any household savings they had to try to save their homes. While this is not true for all black and Latino homeowners,

[18] Ellen Schloemer et al., *Losing Ground: Foreclosures in the Subprime Market and Their Cost to Homeowners*, Ctr. for Responsible Lending (2006); Bocian et al. (2011), *supra* note 10; Bocian et al. (2010), *supra* note 10; Latino Policy Forum, *supra* note 10; Gerardi & Willen, *supra* note 10.

[19] Schloemer et al., *id.*; Press Release, Consumers Union, *Blacks and Hispanics Targeted by High-Cost Lenders: Texas' Midsize Cities Top List* (Oct. 28, 2002).

minorities in general appear more likely to deplete their savings or engage in other drastic acts if they believe that they (or their family members) are facing a foreclosure.[20]

HOMEOWNER SECURITY AND STABILITY

In the Happy Homeownership Narrative, homeowners buy homes with low-cost mortgages and then remain homeowners for the rest of their lives. In addition to having higher costs to acquire (and then remain in) homes and lower overall homeownership rates, blacks and Latinos are homeowners for shorter periods, spend less time overall as homeowners, rent (or live with relatives) for longer periods after losing their homes, and take longer to return to the status of homeowner than whites.

An HUD study examined homeownership tenure spells from 1980 to 2000, which includes the period just before homeownership rates stalled through the beginning of the housing boom. The study examined first-time homeowners who reverted to renter status because of divorce, job mobility, mortgage delinquency/foreclosure, or other factors. The HUD study confirms other research that has found that whites spend longer periods of time in homes they own and have shorter stays as renters when their homeownership spells end than blacks or Latinos.

Specifically, white first-time homeowners are estimated to remain in their homes for just over sixteen years, while black first-time homeowners are in their homes for nine-and-a-half years, and Latinos are in their first homes for twelve-and-a-half years. Blacks and Latinos have substantially higher rates of terminating spells of homeownership, and the rate at which blacks terminate homeownership and revert to being renters (or living with others) is 240 percent of the white rate. The rate at which Latinos revert to renter status is 168 percent of the white rate. Factors that contributed to the length of the ownership periods include marriage rates, family size (at the time of purchase), amount of formal education, unemployment rates, and whether the homeowner lives in an urban city.[21]

[20] *Straightening Out the Mortgage Mess: How Can We Protect Home Ownership and Provide Relief to Consumers in Financial Distress? (Part I): Hearing before the Subcommittee on Administrative & Commercial Law of the House Committee on the Judiciary*, 110th Cong. (2007) (statement of Hon. Marilyn Morgan, U.S. Bankruptcy Judge).

[21] Tracy M. Turner & Marc T. Smith, *Exits from Homeownership: The Effects of Race, Ethnicity, and Income*, 49 J. Regional Sci. 1 (2009). The HUD Study does not limit the definition of "termination" to foreclosures. Instead, homeownership terminations could result from any number of factors, including foreclosures, divorce, or a move to another city for a new job. U.S. Dep't of Hous. and Urban Dev., *The Sustainability of Homeownership: Factors Affecting the Duration of Homeownership and Rental Spells* 25 (2004).

The factors that likely contribute to blacks and Latinos having shorter homeownership tenures include that they have larger families, are less likely to attend college, have higher unemployment rates, and are more likely to live in urban areas. In addition, black households (especially low-income households) may have shorter homeownership tenures because they have higher mortgage debt levels, little equity in their homes, and little disposable income to provide short-term financial support if they lose their job or incur an unexpected household expense. While their income, education, and marital status contribute to blacks and Latinos having shorter homeownership tenures, the racial gap still remains after controlling for these factors, even though it is smaller for married, college-educated, and higher-income homeowners.

The HUD study also shows that homeowner households that lose their homes and revert to being renter households are much less likely to own again in the future. The estimated time that it takes for whites to become homeowners after losing a home for any reason is 10.7 years, but it is 14.4 years for blacks and 14.3 years for Hispanics. Relatively higher foreclosure rates and comparatively shorter homeownership spells make black and Latino households more likely to remain renters and not purchase another home again. Because they are less likely to sell a starter home and trade up to a nicer, more expensive home, they are less likely to benefit from the capital gains exclusion (which allows them to exclude up to $500,000 gains from the sale of their first home from taxes).[22]

In general, foreclosure and mortgage delinquency rates for prime mortgage loans and default and delinquency rates for loans for older (aged fifty and over) Americans are lower than rates for subprime mortgages or for loans made to younger Americans. The foreclosure rate for all mortgages (prime and subprime) for older black and Latino homeowners is significantly higher than the rate for white homeowners. Specifically, the foreclosure rate for older black homeowners who had prime mortgage loans was 3.5 percent, and the rate was 3.9 percent for older Latino homeowners. These rates are almost double the rates for older white homeowners (1.9 percent).

In addition to having higher foreclosure rates for prime loans (which have overall lower foreclosure rates than subprime loans), older blacks and Latinos are significantly more likely to have subprime loans than older white homeowners. Subprime loans account for 6.8 percent of all mortgage loans for white borrowers over the age of fifty, but account for 21.8 percent of loans for blacks and 12.9 percent of all loans made to Latinos. Since the recession ended, older Latino

[22] Thomas P. Boehm & Alan M. Schlottmann, *The Dynamics of Race, Income, and Homeownership*, 55 J. URB. ECON. 113 (2004); U.S. Dep't of Hous. and Urban Dev., *id.*

homeowners have had the highest foreclosure rate (14.1 percent) for subprime loans compared to the black (12.8 percent) rate and the white (11.5 percent) rate.[23]

Older blacks and Latinos may have higher default and foreclosure rates because they have less retirement income security than older whites. Data that was recently released by the Social Security Administration shows that one-third of white Americans over the age of fifty-five receive more than 50 percent of their retirement income in the form of social security benefits. In contrast, 75 percent of older black and Latino retirees rely on social security income for more than half of their retirement income. In addition, while 44 percent of whites receive income from an employer-provided pension, only 31 percent of blacks and 23 percent of Latinos receive retirement income from a private pension. Similarly, 57 percent of older whites receive income (dividends, royalties, trusts funds) from investments, while only 25 percent of blacks and 27 percent of Latinos receive investment income. Given the financial losses blacks and Latinos have suffered because of the housing crisis and the growing gap between the retirement income security of whites and that of blacks and Latinos, older black and Latino households do not receive the financial security that the Narrative promises for homeowners.[24]

TAX BENEFITS

In the Happy Homeownership Narrative, homeownership is preferable to renting because homeowners get to deduct from their income the interest they pay on their mortgage loans and the property taxes they pay on their homes. Homeowners can also avoid paying some of the taxes on the profits they earn when they sell their homes. As noted in Chapter 6, though, most taxpayers (even those who own homes) take the standard deduction and do not itemize their deductions. And, the taxpayers who itemize their deductions are significantly more likely to be higher-income. Because the home mortgage interest deduction (MID) only applies to homeowners and disproportionately benefits wealthy homeowners, it systematically disfavors blacks and Latinos.

As discussed earlier in this chapter, black and Latino households have lower homeownership rates than white households, and the values of the homes blacks and Latinos own are lower overall than the homes whites own. Furthermore, as discussed in greater detail in the next chapter, black and

[23] Lori A. Trawinski, *Nightmare on Main Street: Older Americans and the Mortgage Market Crisis*, AARP Public Policy Institute (2012).

[24] Social Security Administration, *Income of the Population 55 or Older, Income Sources* (2010), *available at* http://www.ssa.gov/policy/docs/statcomps/income_pop55/2010/sect02.pdf.

Latino households have lower overall household incomes relative to white households. Given these factors, blacks and Latinos are less likely to itemize their deductions or to have large, deductible interest payments. In addition, because blacks and Latinos have relatively shorter homeownership spells, they are less likely to sell their first homes, move up to a second (nicer or more expensive) home, and then take advantage of the homeownership benefit that lets taxpayers avoid paying capital gains taxes on up to $500,000 of the profits they make on the sale of their home (or $250,000 if they are unmarried). For example, data indicate that while only 32 percent of white homeowners remain in the first home they purchased, 65 percent of black and 55 percent of Latino homeowners over the age of sixty-five remain in the first home they purchased and never take advantage of the capital gains benefit.[25]

Homeownership's tax benefits are well-advertised and give homeowners an incentive to buy a more expensive home. The MID deduction is capitalized into the price of housing, and as a result increases the cost of housing for *all* homeowners but benefits only a select subset of homeowners. Because higher-income taxpayers are more likely to benefit from the homeownership tax subsidies, these subsidies redistribute income from renters and lower-income homeowners to existing higher-income homeowners. Given their lower homeownership (and thus higher rental) rates, lower overall household income, and lower home values, blacks and Latinos overall receive far less valuable homeownership tax subsidies than higher-income white households receive.[26]

COMMUNITY EXTERNALITIES

In the Happy Homeownership Narrative, living in a neighborhood with other homeowners has positive external benefits because homeowners are more stable and more involved in their communities than renters are. But, as noted in Chapter 5, people who lose their homes to foreclosure impose negative external costs on all other residents in their neighborhood. Even before the recent recession, black and Latino neighborhoods had significantly higher foreclosure rates than white neighborhoods in part because riskier, higher-cost subprime lending was concentrated in lower-income (and largely black and Latino) neighborhoods.

As early as 2003, the prestigious Joint Center for Housing Studies at Harvard accurately predicted what would happen to black and Latino

[25] Joint Ctr. for Hous. Studies, Harvard Univ., *The State of the Nation's Housing* (2002), *available at* http://www.jchs.harvard.edu/sites/jchs.harvard.edu/files/son2003.pdf.

[26] Roberta F. Mann, *The (Not So) Little House on the Prairie: The Hidden Costs of the Home Mortgage Interest Deduction*, 32 ARIZ. ST. L.J. 1347 (2000).

neighborhoods if the U.S. housing market stalled. In discussing the "growing number of [subprime] loans to borrowers with weak credit histories," the report observed:

> Though serving many borrowers who just ten years ago were denied access to credit, default rates on these loans are predictably higher than on standard loans. Because these loans are highly concentrated in low-income, primarily minority communities, *a wave of foreclosures could put a glut of homes on the market, lowering prices and threatening the stability of entire neighborhoods.* (Emphasis added)[27]

In general, living in a neighborhood with homeowners who are in financial distress harms neighbors who are not in financial distress because of the way distressed homeowners typically treat their houses.

Owners who have underwater mortgages or have already defaulted on their mortgage loans (and know they likely will lose their homes) have no economic incentive to take care of their homes by performing or paying for routine maintenance. Homes that are sold in a short sale or a foreclosure sale commonly have overgrown lawns and usually are visibly deteriorated. These homes may sit vacant or be boarded up until the bank completes the foreclosure process or from the time the bank buys the home until it is sold to a new owner. Moreover, homes that are sold in a foreclosure or short sale, especially abandoned blighted homes, are almost always sold at a discount. These lower sales prices impose negative costs and decrease appreciation rates for *all* homes in the neighborhood, and they especially harm owners who may be trying to sell their homes or take out a second mortgage against a home. In addition, abandoned houses can have negative social consequences for the entire neighborhood, because these homes create a haven for people seeking to participate in criminal activities.[28]

Of course, homeowners can protect themselves against some of the harm that results from living near an abandoned property by making sure they consistently perform routine and long-term maintenance on their own homes. Some owners who are not facing a foreclosure do not (or may choose not to) perform routine maintenance for a number of reasons. Generally speaking, household income affects whether a homeowner will have enough disposable income to do routine maintenance and repairs to their homes. Because there is a significant racial income gap, and blacks and Latinos have always had lower overall household incomes than whites, minority households typically

[27] Joint Ctr. for Hous. Studies, Harvard Univ. (2002), *supra* note 25.

[28] Dan Immergluck & Geoff Smith, *The External Costs of Foreclosure: The Impact of Single-Family Mortgage Foreclosures on Property Values*, 17 Housing Pol'y Debate 57 (2006), *available at* http://www.mi.vt.edu/data/files/hpd%2017(1)/hpd_1701_immergluck.pdf.

have less disposable income to use for routine home maintenance and major repairs. Black and Latino homeowners may also have less disposable income for repairs because mortgage lending steering has increased their housing costs relative to whites with comparable incomes. Once the cycle of disinvestment in homes starts and homeowners stop maintaining their homes (because they cannot afford to or because they choose not to), their neighbors may conclude that it also does not make sense for them to invest in their homes. Or, if homeowners live near rundown houses and conclude that remaining in the neighborhood is hopeless, they may flee (which further decreases the demand and value for those homes), rather than remain in a neighborhood where owners refuse to care for their homes.[29]

In addition to the external costs that living near foreclosed properties generally impose on other homeowners, recently uncovered evidence reveals significant disparities in how banks, lenders, investors, and other entities that manage Real Estate Owned (REO) assets have treated properties in black and Latino neighborhoods relative to REO properties in predominantly white neighborhoods. The substandard way that banks maintained and marketed REO properties in black and Latino neighborhoods after the recession imposed additional negative external effects on other homes in the neighborhoods by depressing their market values.

Specifically, the report found that foreclosed properties in predominately black and Latino neighborhoods were far more likely than properties in predominately white areas to be left in disrepair and to have visible maintenance problems, including chipped paint, broken or boarded-up windows and fences, trash strewn on the property, and overgrown (or dead) lawns. REO homes in black and Latino neighborhoods were also more likely to be left unlocked, which encourages thefts from the unsecured home and also encourages people to engage in criminal activities inside the home. In contrast, REO homes in white neighborhoods were more likely to have manicured lawns and be securely locked.[30]

[29] Shannon Van Zandt & William M. Rohe, *The Sustainability of Low-Income Homeownership: The Incidence of Unexpected Costs and Needed Repairs Among Low-Income Home Buyers*, 21 Housing Pol'y Debate 317 (2011); R. Glenn Hubbard et al., *Analysis of Discrimination in Prime and Subprime Mortgage Markets* (Unpublished Working Paper, Nov. 22, 2011), *available at* http://papers.ssrn.com/sol3/papers.cfm?abstract_id=1975789; Anuj K. Shah et al., *Some Consequences of Having Too Little*, 338 Science 682 (2012); Liu et al., The Color of Wealth: The Story Behind the U.S. Racial Wealth Divide 16–17 (2006).

[30] National Fair Housing Alliance, *The Banks are Back – Our Neighborhoods are Not; Discrimination in the Maintenance and Marketing of REO Properties* (2012); Danielle Douglas, *Wells Fargo Settles Complaint on Foreclosed Homes*, Wash. Post (Jun. 6, 2013), *available at* http://www.washingtonpost.com/business/economy/wells-fargo-settles-complaint-on-foreclosed-homes/2013/06/06/18e55954-ce24–11e2–9f1a-1a7cdee20287_print.html.

The study further found that foreclosed properties in black and Latino neighborhoods were less likely to have "For Sale" signs in the yards than homes in white neighborhoods. Failing to market a house obviously increases the likelihood that it will remain vacant longer than a home that is advertised and aggressively marketed to potential buyers. Given that real estate agents are less likely to market poorly maintained homes to their clients because of low "curb appeal," properties with substandard maintenance are less likely to be purchased by an owner-occupant and more likely to be purchased by an investor at a discounted price. In addition, because investors are more likely to use homes as rental property – especially in weak housing markets – by failing to adequately maintain and market REO homes, lenders make it less likely that a new owner-occupant will quickly purchase the home and provide the benefits that are associated with living near homeowners.

In April 2012, a housing advocacy group filed a complaint with HUD against lenders who failed to maintain and market homes in black and Latino neighborhoods. One lender, Wells Fargo, agreed to spend at least $42 million to settle allegations that it neglected the maintenance and marketing of foreclosed homes in black and Latino neighborhoods. Although it did not admit to wrongdoing, Wells Fargo agreed to provide $27 million to nonprofit groups to promote homeownership, neighborhood stabilization, and property rehabilitation. Wells Fargo also gave $11.5 million to the Department of Housing and Urban Development to help rehabilitation efforts in twenty-five U.S. cities.[31]

UNHAPPY, UNHEALTHY, AND IN DESPAIR

As noted in Chapter 2, homeowners consistently report that they are happier with their lives than renters and that they are happy with their status as homeowners. Despite the challenges that cash-strapped Americans continue to face in U.S. housing markets, homeowners overall continue to think that buying a home is the best long-term investment they can make. Recent Latino immigrants especially seem to view homeownership as key to achieving the American Dream, even though recent surveys show that black and Latino homeowners are much less happy with their status as homeowners than whites are.[32]

Blacks and Latinos (be they renters or homeowners) view homeownership as riskier and less secure than whites with comparable incomes. One survey found that only 20 percent of whites would not buy their current house if they

[31] National Fair Housing Alliance, *id.*; Douglas, *id.*

[32] Fannie Mae Foundation, *supra* note 8, at 13–14; Steven W. Bender, Tierra y Libertad: Land, Liberty, and Latino Housing (2010).

had to do it all over again. In contrast, Latinos were almost twice (39 percent) as likely to regret their decision to buy a home, and 35 percent of black homeowners also regretted their decision to buy their current home. A 2008 study found that black renters were more likely than whites to conclude that the risks of homeownership outweighed the benefits, and other recent studies continue to show that whites are more likely than blacks and Latinos to view owning as financially better than renting. More black and Latino *homeowners* viewed renting as financially better than owning relative to white homeowners, but black and Latino *renters* were just as likely as whites to want to buy a home in the future, and they viewed owning as financially superior to renting.[33]

In addition to deriving less happiness from being homeowners, blacks and Latinos who lose their homes seem more likely to have more foreclosure-related health problems than whites who lose their homes. As discussed in Chapter 5, losing a home in a foreclosure sale is stressful and harms everyone in the displaced household. Homeowners often neglect their personal health and forgo medical care in order to try to save their homes. Research conducted during the current foreclosure crisis indicates that blacks are more likely than whites to suffer from health-related foreclosure harms, to have higher hospitalization rates, and to have especially high rates of hypertension and asthma complications. The risk of losing a home also appears to pose greater risks to Latinos than whites, and they seem especially likely to avoid routine, preventive care visits with a doctor. With higher debt loads, fewer savings, and higher unemployment rates, foreclosures are particularly stressful for blacks and Latinos because of the increased difficulties they face due to their constrained resources when trying to prevent foreclosure.[34]

Because high-cost and high-risk lending was concentrated in black and Latino neighborhoods and because blacks and Latinos have disproportionately higher foreclosure rates than white households, black and Latino children are more likely to be forced to move because of a foreclosure. As noted in Chapter 5, moves – especially multiple moves – create instability and often lead to overcrowded housing conditions if the displaced family is forced to move in with friends or relatives. Blacks have always lived in more crowded situations than whites, and overcrowding has been found to have negative

[33] Rachel Bogardus Drew & Christopher Herbert, *Post-Recession Drivers of Preferences for Homeownership*, (Joint Ctr. for Hous. Studies, Harvard Univ. Working Paper No. W12–4, 2012); J. Michael Collins & Laura Choi, *The Effects of the Real Estate Bust on Renter Perceptions of Homeownership*, Federal Reserve Bank of San Francisco (2010).

[34] Dalton Conley, *A Room with a View or a Room of One's Own? Housing and Social Stratification*, 16–2 Sociological Forum (2001); *The Foreclosure Generation: The Long-Term Impact of the Housing Crisis on Latino Children and Families* (2010); Janet Currie & Erdal Tekin, *Is the Foreclosure Crisis Making Us Sick?* Nat'l Bureau of Econ. Research (2011).

academic effects on children. In addition, children who are forced to move because of foreclosure are sad, confused, and angry, and their feelings derive in part from their parents' inability to save their home. Children who must change schools lose many of their old friends and must adjust to a new school setting, so household disruptions negatively affect their academic performance, their behavior at school, and, often, their ability to make new friends and participate in extracurricular activities.[35]

BLACK AND LATINO HOMEOWNERS: THE FUTURE OF U.S. HOUSING

At the height of the housing meltdown, President Bush stated that making it easier for minorities to purchase homes would allow them to "save for the future, send their children to school," and help fuel the American economy.[36] Civil rights and progressive housing groups also advocate for housing policies that will help homeownership rates for blacks and Latinos. Civil rights groups believe that higher homeownership rates will ensure that more blacks and Latinos live in homes in neighborhoods that have higher-quality schools, lower crime rates, and better community amenities, like parks and recreational centers. These groups also support minority homeownership because homeownership generally helps increase overall household wealth, which then makes it more likely that owners can bequeath that wealth to their heirs.

While civil rights groups support homeownership for quite laudable reasons, the public and private housing sectors' support for increased black and Latino homeownership rates now appears to have little to do with the admirable goal of eradicating the vestiges of discrimination in housing or lending markets. Given the demographic shifts in the U.S. population, if blacks and Latinos do not purchase homes, there will be a crisis for the housing and financial services industries. The housing industry needs blacks and Latinos to have higher *homeownership rates* because of low white *birth rates.*

Since 1980, the population of minorities in the United States has grown from roughly 20 percent to just below 35 percent. From 2000 to 2010, more than 90 percent of the overall population growth in the United States came from minority groups. During that decade, the Latino population in the

[35] *Examining Lending Discrimination Practices and Foreclosure Abuses: Hearing before the Senate Committee on the Judiciary*, 112th Cong. (2012) (statement of Eric Rodriguez, Vice President of the Office of Research, Advocacy and Legislation, National Council of La Raza); Jennifer Comey & Michel Grosz, *Smallest Victims of the Foreclosure Crisis: Children in the District of Columbia*, Urban Inst. (2010);

[36] The White House, *Homeownership, available at* http://georgewbush-whitehouse.archives.gov/infocus/homeownership/ (archived website outlining President Bush's agenda to expand opportunities to homeownership).

United States increased by 43 percent (from 35.3 to 50.5 million). Latinos are the largest, as well as the fastest growing, individual minority group. Since the early 2000s, more than 40 percent of all Latinos were foreign-born (and more than 67 percent of Asians were foreign-born).

Latinos now constitute 16 percent of the U.S. population and almost 25 percent of all people under age eighteen. In sharp contrast, white birth rates are declining, and even with immigration crackdowns to prevent Mexicans from entering the United States, white households are projected to constitute only two-thirds of all U.S. households by 2020. Indeed, by 2013, whites accounted for less than 50 percent of all births in the United States, and deaths exceeded births for white Americans for the first time. By 2030, the U.S. population likely will be slightly more than 50 percent white, and that percentage is projected to drop to 46 percent by 2050.[37]

Young married adults who are forming their households are the ones who are most likely to transition from renting to owning. Because they are younger overall than whites, minorities likely will account for 70 percent of the households that are likely to buy homes during the next two decades. Latinos alone should represent 40 percent of the increase in new homeowners. In comparison, whites make up the largest percentage of older Americans, including the Baby Boomers who are selling homes to either live with relatives or rent housing. Without Latino births, there may not be enough future home buyers. If Latinos are able to buy homes, their birth rates should ensure that there are enough people to continue buying newly constructed houses and the houses that aging Baby Boomers are vacating.

U.S. politicians have known since the early 2000s that blacks and Latinos are crucial for the long-term stability of the housing market and that closing the homeownership gap is critical for the continued growth and profitability of the real estate and financial services industries. For example, Congress created the Bipartisan Millennial Housing Commission in 2000 to examine, analyze, and explore "the importance of housing, particularly affordable housing ... to the infrastructure of the United States" and "the various possible methods for increasing the role of the private sector in providing affordable housing."[38] The Commission's members included former elected officials, participants on previous national commissions, academic researchers, home builders, municipal planners and public administrators, and leaders of community development organizations.

[37] Angelina Kewal Ramini et al., *Status and Trends in the Education of Racial and Ethnic Minorities*, U.S. Dep't of Educ. 6 (2007).

[38] Bipartisan Millennial Hous. Comm'n, *Meeting Our Nation's Housing Challenges* (2002), *available at* http://govinfo.library.unt.edu/mhc/MHCReport.pdf.

The Commission's 2002 report acknowledged the importance of the housing sector to the U.S. economy and noted that, in addition to homeownership's "benefits to families and communities, housing is an engine of the national economy and crucial to its strength." The Report specifically acknowledged the importance of minority home sales to the U.S. economy:

> Lagging minority homeownership rates are a serious concern. Minority households are expected to account for two-thirds of household growth over the coming decade. Improving the ability of such households to make the transition to homeownership will be an especially important test of the nation's capacity to create economic opportunity for minorities and immigrants and to build strong, stable communities.[39]

Three years later, Congress held a hearing titled "Increasing Minority Homeownership, and Expanding Homeownership to All Who Wish to Attain It." During that hearing, Republican members of Congress, the Secretary of Housing and Urban Development, and members of the real estate industry stressed their desire to increase minority homeownership.

Buried in the prepared statements for that hearing, though, is an acknowledgment that the fulfillment of this vision of more minority homeowners is motivated by the possibility of adding billions of dollars to the U.S. economy. A prepared statement by the President of the National Association of Realtors starkly notes:

> [T]he biggest source of household growth ... will come from minorities and immigrants. Very simply, minorities will account for 64 percent of all new households.... The creation of these additional households will require more home construction as well as favorable economic conditions to lure potential homebuyers. The real estate industry and our Federal policy makers have a responsibility and obligation to ensure these groups are not ignored in their quests for housing opportunities.[40]

Finally, a 2012 report issued by the Bipartisan Policy Center confirms the importance of black and Latino births to the housing industry. This report noted that the next generation of home buyers, the Echo Boomer generation (the oldest of which turned thirty-two in 2013), is more racially diverse than any prior generation. More than 20 percent of the Echo Boomers that will soon be in their prime home-buying years are Latino, 14 percent were born

[39] Bipartisan Millennial Hous. Comm'n, *id.*

[40] *Hearing before the Committee on Banking, Housing, and Urban Affairs of the U.S. Senate, on Increasing Minority Homeownership, and Expanding Homeownership to All Who Wish to Attain It*, 108th Cong., 1st Sess. (Jun. 12, 2003) (statement of Rep. Katherine Harris); *Id.* (prepared statement of Cathy Whatley, President, National Association of Realtors).

outside the United States, and more than 10 percent have a parent who is an immigrant. This makes the Echo Boomer generation the largest group of first-generation citizens since the generation born to immigrants who came to the United States between 1890 and 1910.

In sharp contrast to the Echo Boomers, the generation over the age of sixty-five is generally whiter than subsequent generations. Eighty percent of Americans over the age of sixty-five and 70 percent of Americans between the ages of forty-five and fifty-nine are white, while only 7 percent are Latino. In contrast, less than 60 percent of all people between the ages of fifteen and twenty-nine are white, and only 55 percent of children under the age of eighteen are white.[41]

Blacks and Latinos may not realize it, but if they are not lured into homeownership, U.S. housing markets will collapse. The real estate industry and the government, though, are both fully aware that the future profitability of this industry and the financial services industry depend on black and Latino renters buying homes, even if they cannot afford to be homeowners. While the real estate and mortgage finance industries may no longer engage in blatant discrimination against blacks and Latinos, their desire to increase homeownership is not driven solely by an altruistic interest in rectifying their prior treatment of blacks and Latinos and finding ways to improve the lives of Latinos and blacks. Likewise, the U.S. government no longer supports homeownership simply because of the idealized view of the role homeownership plays in achieving the American Dream. Instead, U.S. politicians continue to enact laws and policies that induce blacks and Latinos to buy homes and keep financially strapped homeowners moored to mortgage loans because the financial services lobby *needs* those laws.

[41] Pendall et al., *supra* note 10.

9

Homeownership: Educational Disparities

Americans list inadequate education and financial insecurity as two obstacles that prevent them from achieving the American Dream.[1] As discussed in the last chapter, ongoing discrimination and the vestiges of redlining and steering continue to lower black and Latino homeownership rates. Past and present discriminatory practices and biases also make it harder for blacks and Latinos to buy high-appreciating homes with lower-cost financing. But racism alone does not explain why homeownership continues to be so elusive and fleeting for black and Latino households, why owning homes has not helped them close the racial wealth gap, and why the racial homeownership gap between whites and minorities has essentially remained the same for the last thirty years.

Most blacks, Latinos, and low- and moderate-income (LMI) Americans have had stagnant income for almost three decades, and they have been unable to consistently pay their bills – much less save enough money to make a down payment on a home. In sharp contrast, the top 10 percent of earners in the United States have received increasingly larger shares of the total income earned by workers in the United States, and these highly paid (and almost always college-educated) workers have amassed enormous wealth.

The racial homeownership gap persists and the income and wealth divide is widening principally because of the enormous gap between the earnings of college-educated workers and workers who do not have college degrees. Unless the United States finds a way to close the K–12 and college educational attainment gap, black and Latino homeownership rates will always lag white rates, and the homeownership rate for LMI Americans will continue to lag the homeownership rates of the highest-paid Americans.

[1] Robert Powell, *Holes in the Dream Catcher: Many Not Living American Dream; Older Folks Pessimistic*, CBS Market Watch (Oct. 13, 2004), *available at* http://www.marketwatch.com/story/dreameluding-many-americans-seniors-pessimist.

K–12 SCHOOLS: SORTING

In the Happy Homeownership Narrative, homeowners live in safe, stable neighborhoods that have high-quality schools, and their children generally have better grades and fewer disciplinary problems than the children of renters. What the Narrative fails to mention is that there is a strong correlation between the quality of neighborhood schools and the type and value of homes that whites own and those that blacks and Latinos own. As is true with neighborhood amenities in general, the perceived quality of a neighborhood school is capitalized in the price of neighborhood housing, and surveys and data consistently confirm that homeowners with school-age children consider the quality of the public schools their children would attend when they are deciding where to buy a home.

As discussed in the Chapters 7 and 8, blacks and Latinos now live in neighborhoods that are less segregated than they were in the 1970s, and blacks and Latinos are no longer confined to buying houses located in inner cities. Moreover, as noted in Chapter 8, black and Latino homeownership rates have increased since the 1970s, and their rates increased more than white homeownership rates during the housing boom. Nonetheless, because of redlining, steering, and white flight, black and Latino homeowners continue to live in homes in segregated neighborhoods. While neighborhoods can no longer be segregated by law, economic sorting is still legal and thriving. And, in the United States, economic sorting largely equates to racial sorting.

Parents, especially higher-income parents, will pay a premium for homes that are zoned for high-quality public schools. As a result, homes that are in attendance zones for lower-quality schools are less desirable, less valued in housing markets, and have lower appreciation rates. Neither elected officials nor the parents whose children attend higher-quality schools are willing to challenge the current school assignment model by suggesting that the United States should abandon educational policies that assign children to schools based on where they live. Given historical and ongoing neighborhood housing patterns, as long as public schools are sorted by economic status and race, black, Latino, and LMI children will continue to attend lower-quality schools, and this educational sorting ultimately will make it harder for them to become homeowners when they are adults.[2]

[2] Sandra Black, *Do Better Schools Matter? Parental Valuation of Elementary Education*, 114 Q. J. Econ. 577 (1999); Lee Anne Fennell, The Unbound Home: Property Values Beyond Property Lines (2009); Deborah L. McKoy & Jeffrey M. Vincent, *Housing and Education: The Inextricable Link*, in Segregation: The Rising Costs for America 128 (James H. Carr & Nandinee K. Kutty eds., 2008).

As discussed in earlier chapters, blacks and Latinos live in neighborhoods that have higher percentages of lower-income residents than white homeowners. Because of this, the typical white student attends a school where only 37 percent of his or her classmates are low-income. Neighborhood sorting makes it significantly more likely that black and (especially) Latino students will attend the K–12 public schools that have the highest concentration of poverty (i.e., schools where more than 75 percent of students are eligible for free or reduced-price lunches) and the schools they attend are becoming more economically segregated. For example, while slightly more than 50 percent of the students in the schools blacks and Latinos attended in the early 2000s were lower income, by 2010 a typical black or Latino student attended a school where lower-income students accounted for nearly 66 percent of his or her classmates.[3]

Black and Latino students are more likely to attend lower-income schools now than they were in the 1990s, and some data indicate that blacks are less likely to attend schools with white classmates now than they were before desegregation efforts began in the United States in the 1960s. For example, 80 percent of Latino students and 74 percent of black students still attend schools that have less than 50 percent white students. In addition, 43 percent of Latinos and 38 percent of blacks attend schools that have *less than 10 percent* white students. As noted in Chapter 8, because of declining white birth rates and rising black and Latino birth rates, whites now make up only slightly more than half of the students who are enrolled in public schools in the United States. Even though the population of school-age children in the United States is more diverse than it has ever been and white students now constitute only 50 percent of the overall student population, the typical white student attends a school where 75 percent of the student body is white.[4]

The concentration of poverty (rather than race or any other factor) in a school now appears to affect individual student achievement more than the student's own socioeconomic status. For example, studies show that lower-income students who attend higher-income, predominately white schools score significantly higher on standardized tests than lower-income students

[3] Using the percentage of students eligible for a free or reduced-price lunch (through the National School Lunch Program) as a proxy for the poverty level within a school, high-poverty schools are defined as schools in which more than 75 percent of the students are eligible. To be eligible for free lunch, a student must be from a household with an income at or below 130 percent of the poverty threshold. To be eligible for reduced-price lunch, the student must be between 130 percent and 185 percent of the poverty threshold. See Susan Aud et al., *The Condition of Education*, Nat'l Ctr. for Educ. Statistics, U.S. Dep't of Educ., (2013), *available at* http://nces.ed.gov/pubs2013/2013037.pdf; Gary Orfield et al., *E Pluribus Separation: Deepening Double Segregation for More Students* (2012).

[4] Orfield, *supra* note 3.

who remain in higher-poverty, predominately black or Latino schools. Studies also show that black students who attend higher-income schools are more likely to graduate from high school and to attend and graduate from college than black students who remain in segregated, lower-income schools.[5]

Because students at low-poverty schools consistently score higher on standardized tests than students who attend high-poverty schools and blacks and Latinos disproportionately attend high-poverty schools, it is not terribly surprising that black and Latino students' overall achievement rates are positively correlated with the achievement rates of students who attend the highest-poverty schools. For example, in 2011 the average eighth-grade reading score was 274 for white students and was 279 for students who attend the lowest-poverty schools. In contrast, the average score was 249 for black students, was 252 for Latinos (and for students who received free or reduced-price lunches), and was 247 for students who attend the highest-poverty schools.

Reducing the poverty levels in the schools that blacks and Latinos attend would improve their achievement rates. As long as neighborhoods remain economically and racially segregated and street addresses determine school attendance zones, however, schools will remain segregated by income, by race, and by student achievement rates.[6]

Neighborhood sorting also creates disparities between the high school graduation rates for black, LMI, and Latino students. Fortunately, many of the educational disparities between white children and black and Latino children have improved significantly since the days of separate and unequal schools. White, black, and Latino students all have lower dropout rates and higher high school completion rates than they did in the 1970s. As shown in Figure 9.1, the overall high school completion rate in 1975 was 62.5 percent then rose to 87.6 percent by 2012.

While high school graduation rates for blacks and Latinos appear to have increased and dropout rates have dropped, graduation and dropout rates (which are calculated based on the percentage of sixteen- to twenty-four-year-olds who are not in school and have not earned a high school diploma or equivalent) continue to vary by race and by income.[7] For example, the overall

5 Orfield et al., *supra* note 3.

6 Aud et al., *supra* note 3, at table A-23–2.

7 Because of federal reporting laws, some school districts are reported to engage in practices that encourage (or force) lower-achieving students to leave their campuses before the school is required to report them as dropouts. As a result, the data on graduation and dropout rates is easily manipulable.

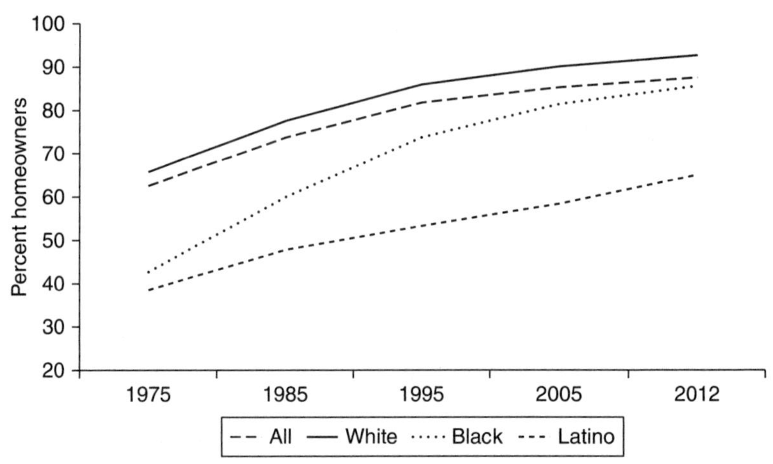

Figure 9.1. High school completion rates for people over age 25.
Source: Nat'l Ctr. for Educ. Statistics.

dropout rate in 1980 was 14.1 percent, and the dropout rate for whites was 11.4 percent. But the dropout rate for blacks in 1980 was 19.1 percent, and the Latino dropout rate was 35.2 percent – more than three times the white dropout rate. By 2011, the overall dropout rate had fallen to 7.1 percent, and the white dropout rate was 5 percent. The dropout rate for blacks remained higher (7.3 percent) than white or overall rates, and the Latino dropout rate (13.6 percent) was still significantly higher than the white dropout rate.[8]

That dropout rates for blacks and Latinos are higher than overall or white dropout rates is disconcerting but not particularly surprising: whites have higher overall income, and household income is now the best predictor for whether students will graduate from high school. Just as they are more likely to have higher standardized test scores, students who attend schools that are low-poverty (and more than 50 percent white) are significantly more likely to graduate from high school than students who attend schools that are high-poverty (and more than 50 percent black or Latino). For example, in 2010 schools that had the fewest number of students who received free or reduced-price lunches

[8] Nat'l Ctr. for Educ. Statistics, U.S. Dep't of Educ., *Fast Facts* (2012), *available at* http://nces.ed.gov/fastfacts/display.asp?id=16. While some Latinos (including Cubans and South Americans) have dropout rates that are similar to white dropout rates, the Latino rate remains high largely because the immigrant dropout rate (44 percent) is significantly higher than the rate for first-generation Latinos (15 percent). John Michael Lee Jr. & Tafaya Ransom, *The Educational Experience of Young Men of Color: A Review of Research, Pathways and Progress*, College Board Advocacy & Policy Ctr. (2011); Charmaine Llagas & Thomas D. Snyder, *Status and Trends in the Education of Hispanics*, Nat'l Ctr. for Educ. Statistics, U.S. Dep't of Educ. 40 (2003).

had the highest graduation (and lowest dropout) rates, while schools that had the greatest percentage of students who received free or reduced-price lunches had the lowest graduation (and highest dropout) rates. Similarly, schools with a student body that was more than 50 percent white had the highest graduation and lowest dropout rates, while schools that had mostly black or Latino students had the lowest graduation and highest dropout rates.[9]

EXPLAINING THE K–12 GAP: INCOME

Just as homes in non-white neighborhoods are valued less in U.S. housing markets than homes in white neighborhoods, schools in racially and economically segregated neighborhoods are likewise valued less than schools in mainly white and higher-income neighborhoods. While it is not uniformly the case, racially segregated schools in black and Latino neighborhoods have relatively fewer educational resources and overall lower test scores, rank lower on outcome-based assessments, and are less desirable than schools in white neighborhoods. For a number of reasons, students who attend high-poverty schools consistently perform worse on K–12 student achievement tests and have lower high school graduation rates than students who attend low-poverty schools.

Recent budget cuts have forced many school districts to reduce non-core classes (or to cut extracurricular activities) in order to fund the day-to-day operation of the schools. High-poverty schools can supplement their budgets by applying for Title I federal funding to provide enhanced educational support for struggling students. This funding is limited, however, and rarely enough to pay for the resources schools need to help disadvantaged students meet the increasingly challenging state academic standards. As a result, high-poverty schools are forced to divert funds from non-academic activities to pay for tutoring and other core academic programming. In contrast, wealthier public schools routinely offer enrichment activities (like sports, arts, and music programs) that poorer schools increasingly cannot afford to provide. Unlike higher-income parents, parents of the children who attend high-poverty schools are unable to subsidize the school's budget by donating funds and they often cannot volunteer during the school day to give the schools additional educational support.[10]

[9] Aud et al., *supra* note 3, at table A-16–2

[10] Elementary and Secondary Education Act, 20 U.S.C. §§ 6301 et seq. (2012); McKoy & Vincent, *supra* note 2; Sean P. Corcoran & William N. Evans, *The Role of Inequality in Teacher Quality*, in Steady Gains and Stalled Progress: Inequality and the Black-White Test Score Gap (Katherine Magnuson & Jane Waldfogel eds., 2008).

In addition to having fewer athletic and fine arts activities and a larger percentage of students who need additional tutoring to meet the state academic standards, non-white, high-poverty schools typically provide a more limited range of educational resources (such as fewer books and limited or older technology), higher teacher, principal, and superintendent turnover rates, and fewer experienced and certified teachers compared to students who attend wealthier schools.[11]

Students who attend high-poverty schools are also at a social disadvantage relative to students who attend low-poverty schools. Students at high-poverty schools are not exposed to as many contacts and networks that reaffirm the importance of achieving academic success, attending college, or engaging in other activities that might help them out of poverty. Students who attend lower-income schools are also less likely to have a large peer group that consistently completes homework or regularly attends school. Additionally, students in lower-income schools often feel pressured into engaging in socially unacceptable behavior (such as committing crimes, dropping out of school, or having unprotected sex), especially if peer groups in their schools deem those activities to be acceptable or if students who attend the schools have concluded that there is little reward to excelling academically.[12]

While school resources and social pressures within the school contribute to lower test scores in high-poverty schools, parental educational attainment and household income now seem to be the main reasons that children who attend low-poverty schools perform better than children who attend high-poverty schools. Since the 1970s, the children of highly educated parents (regardless of income) have consistently performed better overall in school than the children of parents with lower educational levels. Indeed, the black-white achievement gap has substantially narrowed over the last thirty years for black children

[11] A recent study funded by the Congressional Black Congress found that students who attend high-poverty and non-white schools are 70 percent more likely to have teachers who are not certified or who lack a college major or minor in the courses they teach. See Ivory A. Toldson & Chance W. Lewis, *Challenge the Status Quo: Academic Success among School-Age African-American Males* (2012).

[12] *Id.*; Katherine Magnuson et al., *Inequality and Black-White Achievement Trends in the NAEP*, in STEADY GAINS AND STALLED PROGRESS: INEQUALITY AND THE BLACK-WHITE TEST SCORE GAP (Katherine Magnuson & Jane Waldfogel eds., 2008); Margery Austin Turner, *Residential Segregation and Employment Inequality*, in SEGREGATION: THE RISING COSTS FOR AMERICA (James H. Carr & Nandinee K. Kutty eds., 2008). For example, a study of low-income children who lived in relatively affluent Montgomery County, Maryland, showed that students who attended higher-income schools in the county performed better than lower-income students who attended lower-income schools in that county. See Heather Schwartz, *Housing Policy Is School Policy: Economically Integrative Housing Promotes Academic Success in Montgomery County, Maryland* (2010).

whose parents have college degrees. While the racial achievement gap may have narrowed somewhat, the income achievement gap has widened.

As discussed in greater detail later in this chapter, there is now an ever-widening income gap between workers who have college degrees and workers who lack college degrees, and this gap has created an income achievement gap between the children from families at the 90th percentile of income and children from families at the 10th percentile of income. In fact, household income may now predict student achievement better than a student's race or the parent's educational level. Recent data indicate that the income achievement gap is wider than the black-white achievement gap. That is, by 2010 the income achievement gap was twice as large as the black-white achievement gap.

Children from higher-income families perform better academically than children from lower-income families for a number of reasons. Lower-income households with children often spend up to 50 percent of their income just on housing expenses. Because lower-income parents are frequently forced to reduce what they spend on other basics, like health care and retirement savings, these resource constraints make it difficult for their children to participate in after-school, weekend, or summer enrichment programs. Children from resource-constrained households also are less likely to attend or participate in social or cultural activities (like soccer, gymnastics, drum lessons, tennis, karate, etc.) that would enrich their lives, help improve their academic achievement, and potentially prevent them from participating in high-risk, socially undesirable behaviors.[13]

Higher-income parents are generally more involved in their children's education, and they have the finances to support their children in ways that will help them excel academically. Higher-income parents are more likely to invest in their children's cognitive development even before they enter K–12 by, for example, spending more time reading to them and placing them in high-quality preschools. These parents also tend to have more free time to devote to helping their children at home or can pay for tutors or others to help with their children during the school year. Research shows that upper-income families spend up to seven times more on their children's extracurricular activities than lower-income families do and that their income allows them to place their children in summer enrichment activities and programs that will ensure that their children retain the knowledge they learn during the academic year. These activities help their children avoid the "summer slide" and make it

[13] Corcoran & Evans, *supra* note 10; Sean F. Reardon, *The Widening Academic Achievement Gap between the Rich and the Poor: New Evidence and Possible Explanations*, in WHITHER OPPORTUNITY? RISING INEQUALITY, SCHOOLS, AND CHILDREN'S LIFE CHANCES (Greg J. Duncan & Richard J. Murnane, eds., 2011).

more likely that they are prepared to advance to higher achievement levels when the new school year starts.[14]

EXPLAINING THE K–12 GAP: MARRIAGE AND CHILDREN

In addition to differences in their parents' income and educational attainment, children who attend high-poverty schools perform worse academically and have lower high school graduation rates than children who attend low-poverty schools because of differences in their parents' marital status. Blacks, Latinos, and lower-income mothers have lower marriage rates than whites, higher-income women, and college-educated mothers. Almost fifty years ago, a congressional report (the "Moynihan Report") discussed the profound disadvantages that lower-income black children who were reared in single-mother households had relative to children who were raised in middle-class households.[15] The Moynihan Report, though controversial at the time, noted:

> This dependence on the mother's income undermines the position of the father and deprives the children of the kind of attention, particularly in school matters, which is now a standard feature of middle-class upbringing.[16]

Although marriage rates overall have dropped over the last fifty years, more than 50 percent of Americans overall are married, and a recent survey reaffirms that a desire to be married remains the norm in the United States for all income groups, educational levels, and races.[17] Despite this desire, marriage rates for all income groups have steadily declined for the last three decades, and people are getting married at older ages.

Generally speaking, most people marry within their socioeconomic group. Higher marriage rates for women with college degrees appear to be related, in

[14] Joint Ctr. for Hous. Studies, Harvard Univ., *The State of the Nation's Housing* (2011), *available at* http://www.jchs.harvard.edu/sites/jchs.harvard.edu/files/son2011.pdf; David Grissmer & Elizabeth Eiseman, *Can Gaps in the Quality of Early Environments and Noncognitive Skills Help Explain Persisting Black-White Achievement Gaps?*, in STEADY GAINS AND STALLED PROGRESS: INEQUALITY AND THE BLACK-WHITE TEST SCORE GAP (Katherine Magnuson & Jane Waldfogel eds., 2008).

[15] Office of Policy Planning & Research, U.S. Dep't of Labor, *The Negro Family: The Case for National Action* 5 (1965) [hereinafter *The Moynihan Report*] (The Moynihan Report observed that "[a]t the heart of the deterioration of the fabric of Negro society is the deterioration of the Negro family. It is the fundamental source of the weakness of the Negro community at the present time." Many criticized the Moynihan Report for painting an unfavorably unflattering portrait of the black family).

[16] *Id.*

[17] Frank Newport & Joy Wilke, *Most in U.S. Want Marriage, but Its Importance Has Dropped; Young Adults More Likely Not to Want to Get Married*, Gallup Poll (Aug. 3, 2013).

part, to the grim employment prospects for men who lack college degrees. The relationship between marital and unemployment rates has existed for a long time: the Moynihan Report observed a positive correlation between higher unemployment rates and lower marriage rates (and higher divorce rates) for blacks almost fifty years ago.[18] Lower marriage rates for younger women now also appear to be related to their relatively higher college attendance rates. That is, relative to men, women have enrolled in college and attained college degrees at higher rates over the last thirty years, and these higher educational attainment rates seem to have caused highly educated women to delay marriage and childbearing.

Marriage rates for women of most races also seem to be affected by higher job instability for men. Labor market prospects for men – especially LMI men – have worsened over the last thirty years, and their decreased earnings potential appears to affect current marriage rates for LMI Americans. Indeed, some LMI women report that they now explicitly choose to remain unmarried (and be single mothers) due to of the unavailability of what they perceive to be "marriageable" males. Similarly, because the college graduation rate for men now lags the graduation rate for women, and income for LMI males has been stagnant for several decades, many women now choose to delay marriage, and – in some instances – to avoid marriage altogether, even if they have children.

Marriage rates appear to be particularly lower for LMI blacks because over the last thirty years, income for young black males has dramatically declined, college attendance and graduation rates have declined, and incarceration and homicide rates have increased.[19] Almost fifty years ago, the 1965 Moynihan Report reported that "[n]early a quarter of Negro women living in cities who have ever married are divorced, separated, or are living apart from their husbands."[20] The report found that number to be shockingly high compared to the 8 percent unmarried rate for white women. Now the overall marriage rate

[18] *The Moynihan Report*, *supra* note 15. ("During times when jobs were reasonably plentiful (although at no time during this period, save perhaps the first 2 years, did the unemployment rate for Negro males drop to anything like a reasonable level) the Negro family became stronger and more stable. As jobs became more and more difficult to find, the stability of the family became more and more difficult to maintain.").

[19] Daniel Schneider, *Wealth and the Marital Divide*, 117 AM. J. SOCIOLOGY 627 (2011); Mindy E. Scott et al., *Young Adult Attitudes About Relationships and Marriage: Times May Have Changed, But Expectations Remain High*, in CHILD TRENDS: RESEARCH BRIEF NO. 2009–30 (2009), *available at* http://www.childtrends.org; Thomas E. Trail & Benjamin R. Karney, *What's (Not) Wrong With Low-Income Marriages*, 74 J. MARRIAGE & FAMILY 413–27 (2012); Francine D. Blau et al., *Understanding Young Women's Marriage Decisions: The Role of Labor and Marriage Market Conditions*, 53 INDUS. & LABOR RELATIONS REV. 624 (2000).

[20] *The Moynihan Report*, *supra* note 15.

for whites is 51 percent, while the Latino rate is 50 percent, and the black rate lags well behind at 28.5 percent. Ironically, the overall *marriage* rate for black women is now almost identical to what the *unmarried* rate for black women was in 1965.

Some Americans, especially if they are lower-income, are avoiding marriage because of financial considerations. Studies show that unmarried people now feel that certain baseline economic standards should be met before marriage. Those standards include a stable job, steady income, savings, and other sources of personal wealth (including cars and homes). Lower-income adults appear to have more traditional values about the roles men and women should play in a marriage, which may be one reason why lower-income women are more concerned about whether a potential mate has the financial capacity to be a traditional breadwinner and why lower-income men may be unwilling to marry the mothers of their children if they do not think they can support their families.[21] Black women seem especially likely to avoid marriage when labor market conditions for males are weak, and data show that as the adult male unemployment rate *increases* – especially for males who work in layoff-prone industries, like construction – the marriage rate for black women *decreases*.[22]

Lower marriage rates have dramatically increased the number of children who are reared in single-parent homes over the last thirty years. For example, while less than 20 percent of children overall were reared in single-parent households in the 1980s, that number has now more than doubled, even as overall teen birth rates have dropped. In fact, despite the decline in teenage mothers having children, more children are now being reared in single-parent households. Just as there are a number of reasons to explain why women are delaying (or avoiding) marriage, women are also choosing to have children but remain single for various reasons.

Obviously, some mothers are forced to rear their children in single-parent households because the fathers of their children refuse to marry them or provide financial or emotional assistance with their children. In addition, as was true when no-fault laws destigmatized divorce, the increase in the number of divorced women rearing children may have destigmatized single mothers rearing children. But, a growing number of women, especially those under the age of thirty, appear to now make the choice to have children but not wait to marry Mr. Right, especially given the grim employment prospects that some men face.

[21] Scott et al., *supra* note 19; Trail & Karney, *supra* note 19.

[22] Blau et al., *supra* note 19; Martha J. Bailey & Susan M. Dynarski, *Inequality in Postsecondary Education*, in Whither Opportunity? Rising Inequality, Schools, and Children's Life Chances (Greg J. Duncan & Richard J. Murnane, eds., 2011).

While more women overall are choosing to have children and not marry, the incidence of single-parent households varies by the age, college attainment, income, and race of the mother. Thus, although almost 60 percent of mothers are married when they have children, nearly two-thirds of women under the age of thirty are unmarried when they choose to have children.[23] Women with college degrees are more likely (92 percent) to be married when they have children. Only 62 percent of women who attended college but did not receive a degree and less than half (43 percent) of women who have only a high school diploma or equivalent are married when they have children.[24] The most stark disparity is the gap between the marital rates for white and black mothers.

The Moynihan Report discussed the increase in single-parent families and the growing racial gap by observing that

> [b]oth white and Negro illegitimacy rates have been increasing, although from dramatically different bases. The white rate was 2 percent in 1940; it was 3.07 percent in 1963. In that period, the Negro rate went from 16.8 percent to 23.6 percent.

The report further observed, with alarm, that

> [a]s a direct result of this high rate of divorce, separation, and desertion, a very large percent of Negro families are headed by females. While the percentage of such families among whites has been dropping since 1940, it has been rising among Negroes.
>
> The percent of nonwhite families headed by a female is more than double the percent for whites. Fatherless nonwhite families increased by a sixth between 1950 and 1960, but held constant for white families.
>
> It has been estimated that only a minority of Negro children reach the age of 18 having lived all their lives with both of their parents.
>
> Once again, this measure of family disorganization is found to be diminishing among white families and increasing among Negro families.[25]

The 23.6 percent rate had nearly tripled by 2010. Now, 73 percent of black children are born outside of marriage compared with 53 percent of Latinos and 29 percent of white children.[26]

Just because marriage rates have dropped and more women are choosing to have children and rear them in single-parent households does not mean,

[23] Blau et al., *supra* note 19.

[24] Child Trends, *Births to Unmarried Women: Indicators on Children and Youth* (2013), *available at* http://www.childtrends.org/wp-content/uploads/2012/11/75_Births_to_Unmarried_Women.pdf.

[25] *The Moynihan Report*, *supra* note 15.

[26] Child Trends, *supra* note 24.

of course, that all children reared in single-parent households are destined to perform poorly academically. Still, lower overall marriage rates for all races appear to have contributed to the fact that the racial K–12 achievement gap has narrowed (but still has not closed). Because marriage rates are higher for college-educated and higher-income women, the income achievement gap is now growing because of the profound advantages that children reared in two-income households have over children reared in one-income households.

Generally speaking, children who live with two parents receive more nurturing, care, and attention, although many single mothers are also deeply involved with their children's academic performance. Not all single mothers are poor, and there has been an increase in the number of higher-income women who are choosing to have children but not marry the fathers of their children. Still, as discussed in more detail later in this chapter, lower-income children are disproportionately more likely to be reared by lower-income single mothers who lack college degrees and, because of these resource constraints, they are less likely to graduate from high school, attend and graduate from college, and become homeowners.[27]

THE COLLEGE ATTENDANCE GAP

Surveys indicate that almost 90 percent of all white, black, and Latino high school seniors expect to attend college right after they graduate from high school and that 80 percent of all high school seniors expect to receive a bachelor's degree. These expectations vary slightly depending on whether the student's parents graduated from college. Thus, while 92 percent of female and 85 percent of male students with college-educated parents expect to attain a college degree, only 82 percent of female and 70 percent of male students whose parents who do not have a bachelor's degree expect to graduate from college.[28]

[27] Blau et al, *supra* note 19. While not all children of single mothers were unintended, since the 1980s black women and women with less education or income are much more likely to experience unintended births than married, white, college-educated, and higher-income women. The percentage of white women who have unplanned births is 20 percent, while the rate for Latino women is 35 percent, and the rate for black women is more twice (45 percent) the white rate. William D. Mosher et al., *Intended and Unintended Births in the United States: 1982–2010*, Nat'l Health Stats. Reps (Jul. 2012).

[28] Brian A. Jacob & Tamara Wilder Linkow, *Educational Expectations and Attainment*, in Whither Opportunity? Rising Inequality, Schools, and Children's Life Chances (Greg J. Duncan & Richard J. Murnane eds., 2011).

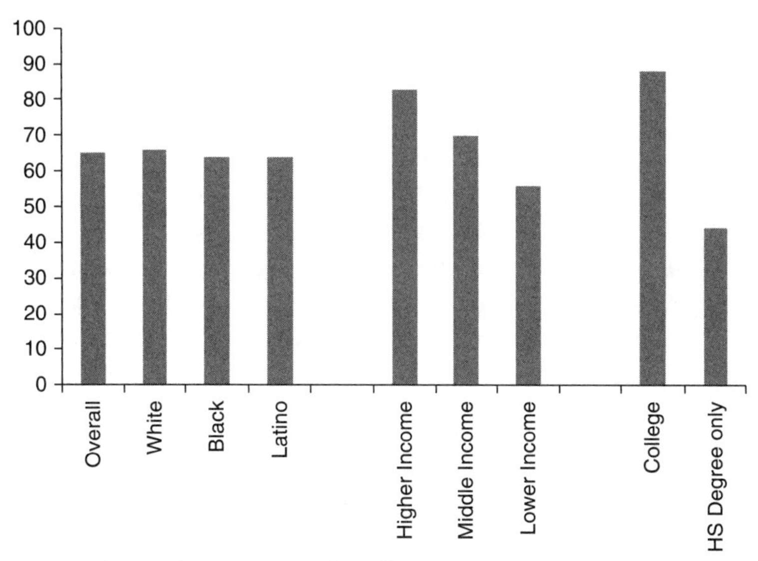

Figure 9.2. Parental expectations for college.
Source: Nat'l Ctr. for Educ.Statistics.

Most parents also expect that their children will attend college. A recent survey indicates that more than 90 percent of parents with students in grades six through twelve expected their children to attend college, and 65 percent expected the students to earn at least a bachelor's degree. These expectations vary only slightly by race: as shown in Figure 9.2, the percentage of white, black, and Latino parents who expected their children to attend college was virtually the same (66 percent, 64 percent, and 64 percent respectively). The expectations vary dramatically, though, depending on the parents' income and educational levels.

Parents who earned more than $75,000 annually were significantly more likely to expect their children to attend college (83 percent) than parents who earned between $50,000 and $75,000 (70 percent) and those who earned between $25,000 and $50,000 (51 percent). Similarly, parents who had a college degree were significantly more likely (88 percent) to expect their children to finish college than parents who graduated from high school but did not attend college (44 percent).[29]

[29] Laura Lippman et al., *Parent Expectations and Planning for College*, Nat'l Ctr. for Educ. Statistics (2008). Research has shown that students' learning and achievement may be affected by their perceptions of their family's economic standing and that resource-deprived students may feel that it is harder for them to succeed at school, which may then cause them to exert less effort to achieve by, for example, not doing homework, watching too much

The children of college graduates and children from higher-income households are significantly more likely to attend college than children with similar test scores and class ranks who are lower-income or whose parents do not have college degrees. As noted earlier, data consistently show that children who live in two-income households are statistically more likely to graduate from high school. Because overall black and Latino household income is lower than white household income and black and Latino students are more likely to be reared in lower-income households by a single parent who does not have a college degree, their college attendance rates are correspondingly lower.[30] One study found that 85 percent of high school seniors whose parents had a least a bachelor's degree enrolled in college compared to 45 percent of high school seniors whose parents had less than a high school education. Likewise, in 2010, 52 percent of all lower-income high school graduates immediately enrolled in college compared to 82 percent of upper-income high school graduates and 67 percent of students from middle-income families.[31]

The college attendance income gap is especially pronounced at the most selective four-year colleges. Almost 75 percent of the students who enroll in selective four-year colleges and universities live in households from the richest economic quartile. In contrast, less than 15 percent of students who attend the fifty wealthiest colleges and universities receive Pell Grants (a need-based financial aid program that guarantees that every student who economically qualifies for a grant will receive one). Lower-income students who receive Pell Grants are more likely to attend public colleges. Indeed, largely because of concerns about the increased economic polarization of postsecondary education, a number of elite private universities permit lower-income students to attend for free, while others take students' socioeconomic background into account when making their admissions decisions. Because of mounting costs, though, many of these schools are now scaling back financial aid for lower-income students, have abandoned need-blind admissions policies that accept students regardless of their financial need, and are aggressively pursuing wealthy students.[32]

TV, not reading for pleasure, skipping school, or dropping out altogether. Magnuson et al., *supra* note 12; Meredith Phillips, *Culture and Stalled Progress in Narrowing the Black-White Test Score Gap*, in STEADY GAINS AND STALLED PROGRESS: INEQUALITY AND THE BLACK-WHITE TEST SCORE GAP (Katherine Magnuson & Jane Waldfogel eds., 2008); Su Jin Gatlin Jez, *The Influence of Wealth and Race in Four-Year College Attendance* (2008).

[30] Rearing boys in a lower-income, single-family home seems especially likely to depress their college attendance rates, *especially* if their fathers are absent from their lives.

[31] Bailey & Dynarski, *supra* note 22.

[32] Robert Haveman & Timothy Smeeding, *The Role of Higher Education in Social Mobility*, THE FUTURE OF CHILDREN (Aug. 2006); Anthony P. Carnevale & Stephen J. Rose, *Socioeconomic*

One reason that black, Latino, and LMI students fail to attend college is college preparedness, which is not surprising given the lower K–12 test scores and high school graduation rates that these students have relative to white and higher-income students. For example, a recent study found that the public schools that serve the most black and Latino students in the United States are less likely to offer algebra (only 65 percent), physics (40 percent), or calculus (29 percent). Other data show that white high school graduates are three times more likely to have taken calculus than black graduates, and whites are twice as likely to have taken calculus as Latino graduates. Higher percentages of white (31 percent) graduates also had completed a combination of biology, chemistry, and physics courses than had their black and Latino peers (22 percent and 23 percent, respectively). Because of those deficiencies, many black, Latino, and LMI students cannot satisfy the admissions requirements for flagship public state universities or elite private colleges.[33]

In addition to lacking the necessary courses to be admitted to college, LMI, black, and Latino children often do not receive guidance during the college preparation process and, because of their overall lower household income, they cannot depend on receiving financial assistance as they prepare for college. For example, a recent report found that while 87 percent of white parents planned to help pay for their children's college costs, only 76 percent of black parents and 72 percent of Latino parents stated that they planned to help pay for their children's college expenses. Black and Latino students who attend high-poverty schools and have actually taken the required college preparatory courses in high school often cannot afford to pay for the expensive college examination preparation courses that wealthier students routinely take to help raise their college entrance scores. LMI, black, and Latino children may have lower college attendance rates because their parents are not as informed about the college application process, likely because of the parents' lower overall college attendance rates and because the children do not live in communities where attending college is the norm.

As shown in Figure 9.3, the parents of white students were more likely (72 percent) to report that they had enough information about college costs to

Status, Race/Ethnicity and Selective College Admissions, in AMERICA'S UNTAPPED RESOURCE: LOW-INCOME STUDENTS IN HIGHER EDUCATION (Richard D. Kahlenberg ed., 2004), at table 1.1.; Beckie Supiano & Andrea Fuller, *Elite Colleges Fail to Gain More Students on Pell Grants*, CHRON. HIGHER EDUC. (Mar. 27, 2011); Awilda Rodriguez, *At Elite Colleges, No Room at the Dance for Low-Income Students*, CHRON. HIGHER EDUC. (Sep. 9, 2013); Catharine Hill, *We Cut Student Aid at our Own Peril*, CHRON. HIGHER EDUC. (Sep. 25, 2011).

[33] Aud et al., *supra* note 3.

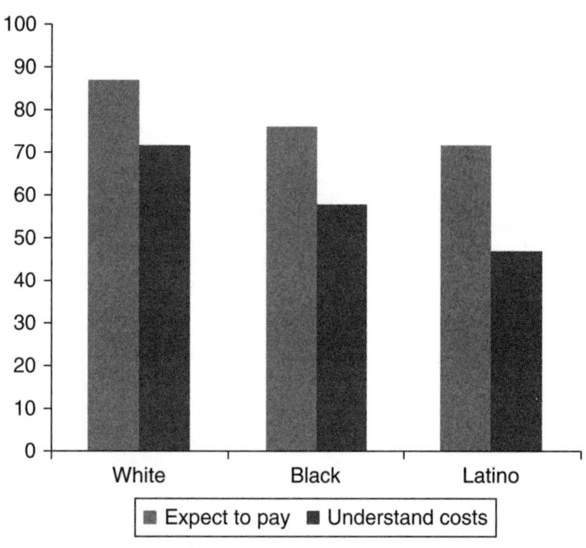

Figure 9.3. Parental expectations and understanding of college costs.
Source: Nat'l Ctr. for Educ.Statistics.

start planning for their children's postsecondary education than black (58 percent) or Latino (47 percent) parents.[34]

Black, Latino, and LMI students overall are less prepared for college and have lower college attendance rates because they live in communities where fewer people attend college. Students who live in communities where high school graduates are expected to attend college are more likely to enroll in college (especially in elite colleges and universities). These students also have access to college graduates (be they their parents, neighbors, or other family members) who can explain the college application process to them. Because black and Latino students are more likely to have parents who did not attend college and they often lack family members, neighbors, or friends who are familiar with the college education process, the college application process may be alien to them. If their teachers and school counselors do not tell them about the application process and financial aid options, black and Latino

[34] Lippman et al., *supra* note 29; Lindsey E. Malcom et al., *Tapping HSI-STEM Funds to Improve Latina and Latino Access to STEM Professions* (2010); Toldson & Lewis, *supra* note 11. Ironically, while black men are underrepresented on college campus, they are overrepresented in profitable revenue generating college sports. For example, while they make up approximately 5 percent of undergraduate students, they account for more than 55 percent of football and basketball players at NCAA Division I colleges and universities. Shaun R. Harper, *Black Male Student Success in Higher Education: A Report from the National Black Male College Achievement Study* (2012).

students may miss out on financial aid opportunities that would help finance their college education.

THE COLLEGE DEGREE ATTAINMENT GAP

High school students are completing high school and attending and graduating from college in record numbers. In 2012, for the first time ever, almost one-third of all U.S. adults between the ages of twenty-five and twenty-nine had at least a bachelor's degree. That year, 63 percent of adults between the ages of twenty-five and twenty-nine attended some college, while 90 percent of that age group received a high school degree or equivalent. The college attendance rate for recent high school graduates has increased for all racial groups over the last twenty years – *especially* for women. Women in all racial groups except Asians continue to have higher college attendance rates relative to men. Despite higher overall high school graduation and college attendance rates, high school seniors' expectations that they will graduate from high school and attain a college degree do not always match actual college graduation rates, and these expectations go largely unmet for black, Latino, and LMI Americans.

More than 50 percent of the children from the wealthiest families attain at least a bachelor's degree. In sharp contrast, more than 34 percent of the children from the poorest families do not even graduate from high school. Just as the overall household income gap has widened dramatically over the past several decades, the increase in the college completion rate between the top income quartile over the last fifty years is four times larger (18 percent) than the growth for lower-income students (4 percent).[35] Even though overall college attendance rates have steadily increased for all groups over the past two decades, the college graduation rate for blacks and Latinos still lags the white graduation rate. Thus, while 39 percent of all white adults between the ages of twenty-five and twenty-nine had a bachelor's degree in 2011, only 20 percent of blacks and 13 percent of Latinos in that age group had at least a bachelor's degree.[36]

[35] Bailey and Dynarski, *supra* note 22; Su Jin Gatlin Jez, *The Differential Impact of Wealth vs. Income in the College-Going Process* (2011).

[36] Aud et al., *supra* note 3; Lee Jr. & Ransom, *supra* note 8; Richard Fry & Kim Parker, *Record Shares of Young Adults Have Finished Both High School and College*, Pew Research Ctr. (2012). College attainment rates for Latinos vary. While recent immigrants from Mexico and Central America have relatively low college attendance and graduation rates, Latinos from South America (and high-income Latinos) have rates that equal or exceed overall college attainment rates. Stella U. Ogunwole et al., *The Population with a Bachelor's Degree or Higher by Race and Hispanic Origin: 2006–2010*, Am. Cmty. Survey Briefs, U.S. Census Bureau (2012).

The college graduation racial gap is not surprising, given that black, Latino, and LMI high school students exhibit more of the risk factors associated with not completing college. Research indicates that the following factors decrease the likelihood that high school graduates will attain a college degree: being academically underprepared, not attending directly from high school, attending part-time, having no parental financial support, being financially responsible for children, working more than thirty hours a week, and being a first-generation college student. Black, Latino, and LMI students attain college degrees at lower rates than whites for a number of reasons.

First, they may underestimate the difficulty of completing college, *especially* if they were academically underprepared or if they have less time to study because they must work to pay for college. Similarly, white children overall attend low-poverty schools that provide greater educational benefits and better prepare them for college than the schools that black and Latino children attend. Given this, black and Latino children are less likely to take the courses that will prepare them academically for college, and they often arrive at college academically underprepared. Often, students who graduate from high-poverty high schools are required to take remedial courses (because they either did or could not take college prep courses in their secondary schools) before they can take college-level classes.

Blacks and Latinos also report that they continue to face hostile campus climate issues, including subtle putdowns and questions about whether they were admitted to college because of academic merit or because of a racial quota. Many black and Latino students may fail to perform as well as white college students because of what is commonly referred to as the "stereotype threat" – the threat of being viewed negatively based on racial stereotypes. Thus, an overall inhospitable campus environment and psychological impediments may prevent them from succeeding in college and attaining a college degree. The major reason that blacks and Latinos appear to have lower college graduation rates, especially at more selective institutions, is because of money.

While it is unclear whether household income or wealth determines whether (and where) children will attend college, education experts agree that the cost to attend college is now serving as an almost insurmountable barrier for lower-income students. Indeed, just as income is now the best predictor of a students' K–12 success, when controlled for academic competence, family income and the students' socioeconomic status is the best predictor of whether the student will earn a bachelor's degree. Largely because states have reduced funding for higher education, college costs have skyrocketed since the 1990s and have generally outpaced inflation. For example, between 1990 and 2000, tuition at private colleges and universities increased by 70 percent, tuition at public universities increased by 84 percent, and two-year college tuition rates increased by 62 percent. Because income has largely been stagnant for the last thirty years, higher college tuition and fees, coupled with the markedly decreased availability of need-based financial assistance, have created a higher education system that is polarized by income.[37]

Stagnant household income combined with soaring college costs cause black and Latino students to have relatively high levels of financial need. Colleges have increased tuition, but the financial aid scholarships they are awarding based on need have not kept pace with those tuition rate increases. Instead of increasing their need-based financial aid, colleges are increasingly providing merit-based financial aid and are awarding a disproportionate share of those merit-based scholarships to wealthy students. For example between 1995 and the beginning of the recession in 2007, the share of students who received merit-based financial aid more than doubled (from 8 percent to 18 percent) at public colleges and from 24 percent to 44 percent at private colleges.[38]

Because they have lower parental contributions and there is less need-based financial aid, Latino, black, and LMI students often need to work more than fifteen hours each week to finance their education. Students who work longer hours are at a greater risk of failing to attain a college degree, and students who work long hours also tend to perform worse in college than study who are not required to work. Working off-campus is especially harmful to students' academic performance in college, as confirmed by a recent study that examined the college experiences of black males who graduated in six years or less. This study noted that black males are more likely to withdraw from college if they work off-campus.[39]

COLLEGE: ECONOMIC SORTING

As is true with neighborhoods and K–12 schools, household income now appears to be sorting students into the type of college they will attend and the amount of educational loan debt they will have when they graduate. Although, as discussed in more detail later in this section, the student loan debt burden and default rates are particularly high for students who attend for-profit colleges, an increasing number of students overall are now amassing

[37] The College Board, http://www.collegeboard.org/.

[38] Stephen Burd, *Undermining Pell: How Colleges Compete for Wealthy Students and Leave the Low-Income Behind* (May 2013).

[39] Jacob & Linkow, *supra* note 28; Mary Nguyen, *Degreeless in Debt: What Happens to Borrowers Who Drop Out*, Education Sector (2012), *available at* http://www.educationsector.org/publications/degreeless-debt-what-happens-borrowers-who-drop-out; MALCOM ET AL., *supra* note 34; Bailey & Dynarski, *supra* note 22; Jez, *supra* note 29; Harper, *supra* note 34; Haveman & Smeeding, *supra* note 32.

massive student loan debt because of soaring tuition rates and stagnant overall household income. Blacks (in particular) and Latinos have higher educational debts relative to whites, and blacks with bachelor's degrees have especially high student loan debt levels.

At the beginning of the recent recession, 27 percent of black college graduates had loan debt that exceeded $30,000, while only 16 percent of white and 14 percent of Latino college graduates had that level of student loan debt. By the end of the recent recession, only 10 percent of white college graduates had loan debt that exceeded $70,000, while 14 percent of Latinos and 27 percent of blacks graduated from college having accrued more than $70,000 in student debt. While 42 percent of white students finish their postsecondary education with *no* student loan debt, only 23 percent of black students and 32 percent of Latinos graduate debt-free. In addition to having higher student debt loads, many students fail to even receive a college degree. Almost 30 percent (a 5 percent increase from a decade ago) of college students take out student loans to attend college but drop out of school before they earn a degree.[40]

Whether students can attend college and graduate with manageable student loan debt levels affects their future buying capacity, including whether they can afford to buy a house. Data now indicate that student loan debt levels are depressing homeownership rates. For example, a 2013 Federal Reserve study found that Americans in their twenties and thirties who have student loan debt are less likely to have mortgages than people the same age who lack student loans, despite the fact that most people who have student loan debt are better-educated and likely will have higher lifetime earnings.

While college graduates have overall higher income than workers who lack a college degree, young college graduates are now struggling to buy homes largely because of the instability of the labor market and higher-than-normal unemployment rates for younger people. As noted earlier in this chapter, unsteady and uncertain income has caused younger Americans to delay marriage, and this same income instability is now causing them to delay buying cars and homes, often because they cannot save enough money to make a down payment.[41]

[40] Lynch et al., *supra* note 40; Lee Jr. & Ransom, *supra* note 8; Gov't. Accountability Office, *Proprietary Schools: Stronger Department of Education Oversight Needed to Help Ensure Only Eligible Students Receive Federal Student Aid* (2009); Sandy Baum & Patricia Steele, *Who Borrows Most? Bachelor's Degree Recipients with High Levels of Student Debt*, College Board Advocacy & Policy Ctr. (2010); Algernon Austin, *Graduate Employment Gap Students of Color Losing Ground*, Econ. Policy Inst. (2010).

[41] Stuart A. Gabriel & Stuart S. Rosenthal, *Homeownership in the 1980s and 1990s: Aggregate Trends and Racial Gaps*, 57 J. Urb. Econ. 101 (2005); Nguyen, *supra* note 39; Meta Brown & Sydnee Caldwell, *Young Student Loan Borrowers Retreat from Housing and Auto Markets*, Fed. Res. Bank N.Y. (2013), *available at* http://libertystreeteconomics.newyorkfed.org/2013/04/young-student-loan-borrowers-retreat-from-housing-and-auto-markets.html.

Given the stagnant household incomes, soaring college tuition rates, and higher overall student debt loads they now face, students need to attend colleges that increase the likelihood that they will graduate and that they will be employed after they graduate. Employers place a significantly higher value on employees who have a bachelor's degree, and students who receive an associate's degree earn less overall than students who receive degrees from four-year colleges. Soaring college costs for the last two decades combined with lower overall household income have increasingly caused black, Latino, and LMI students to attend two-year colleges.

Ironically, soaring tuition and fees at four-year colleges and university, have also caused more middle- and higher-income students to attend community colleges, although many of these students ultimately attend (and graduate from) four-year colleges. Specifically, while only 12 percent of students from high-income families attended community colleges in 2009, that number increased to 22 percent in 2010. Because community college enrollments have increased in recent years, the increased competition for fewer seats in community college classrooms has now made it harder for lower-income students, many of whom are black and Latino, to attend the one type of college that has historically been affordable and accessible to them.[42]

Larger percentages of black, Latino, and LMI students are also attending for-profit colleges and universities. As shown in Figure 9.4, 26 percent of the students at for-profit colleges are black, while only 12 percent of students at private, nonprofit colleges and 13 percent of students at public colleges are black. Similarly, while Latinos represent 19 percent of the students at for-profit colleges, they represent only 11 percent of students at private nonprofit colleges and 13 percent of students at public colleges. While whites (who have higher overall college attendance rates) constitute 50 percent of all students at for-profit colleges, they constitute 70 percent of all students at private colleges and 66 percent of all students at public colleges.[43]

The dropout rate for students who attend for-profit colleges exceeds 40 percent, and the graduation rate is less than half the graduation rate for not-for-profit four-year colleges. Although college-educated workers earn considerably

[42] Although college costs overall have steadily increased over the last decade, higher-income parents actually paid less (15 percent) for college for their children in 2011 than they did in 2012, which may be because more high-income children attended community colleges or may also be because colleges are awarding more merit-based scholarships. MALCOM ET AL., *supra* note 34; Gary Rhoades, *Closing the Door, Increasing the Gap: Who's Not Going to (Community) College?* (2012); Sallie Mae, *How America Pays for College* (2011), *available at* https://www1.salliemae.com/NR/rdonlyres/BAF36839-4913-456E-8883-ACD006B950A5/14952/HowAmericaPaysforCollege_2011.pdf.

[43] Gov't. Accountability Office, *supra* note 40.

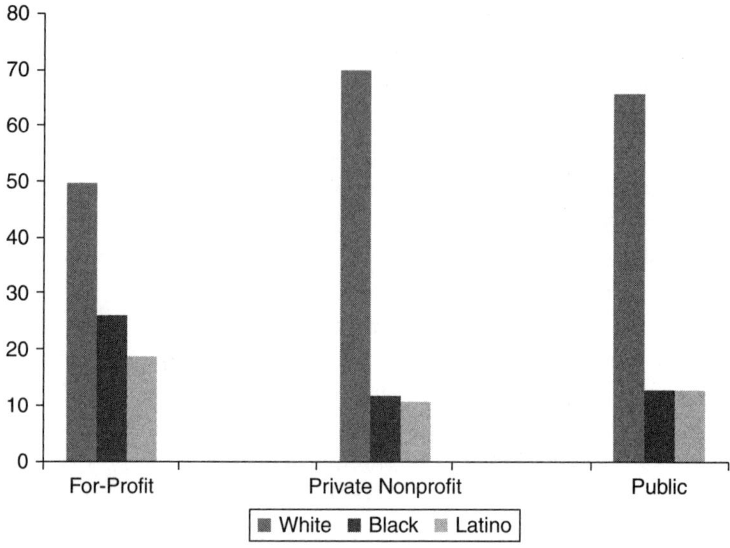

Figure 9.4. College attendance by type and race.
Source: Government Accountability Office.

more than workers who have only a high school degree, students who attend college (especially for-profit colleges) but fail to earn a degree have unemployment rates that are 10 percent higher than people who graduate from college. They are also significantly more likely to default on student loans than students who receive a college degree. Students who attend for-profit colleges fund their education largely through student loans. In fact, some for-profit colleges receive the majority of their income from federal loans and grants, and they take a disproportionate share of the total amount of student loan dollars used at educational institutions.[44]

Students who attend for-profit colleges often do not know that the educational benefits they receive from these schools are not worth the massive student loan debt they incur by attending the school. Moreover, students often do not realize the likelihood that they will incur student loan debt at these colleges but never receive a degree, or the likelihood that their debt loads will make it difficult (if not impossible) for them to buy homes in the future. While for-profit colleges have been heralded as low-cost alternatives to traditional four-year or public community colleges, these colleges have been criticized for accepting students (and their financial aid), even though many of those students are not academically prepared to attend and succeed in college.

[44] Nguyen, *supra* note 39.

In addition, for-profit colleges have been criticized for spending a disproportionate amount of their budgets (23 percent) on marketing and advertising compared to not-for-profit colleges (1 percent) and for making deceptive or misleading claims to prospective students.[45]

Over the last decade, state and federal regulators have increased their scrutiny of for-profit colleges because of the relatively higher debt loads students at for-profit colleges incur relative to students at not-for-profit, four-year, or community colleges. The government also has investigated the marketing and operating practices of for-profit colleges, because students at these colleges are significantly less likely to graduate and significantly more likely to default on their student loans. For example, the Government Accountability Office (GAO) conducted undercover tests at fifteen for-profit colleges. The GAO investigation found that all of the colleges made deceptive or questionable statements to the GAO's applicants.

Some applicants were encouraged to falsify their financial forms in order to qualify for federal financial assistance, and others were pressured into enrolling before they had time to consider other financing options. The investigation also disclosed that college representatives exaggerated the applicants' expected salary after graduation, mischaracterized the total cost to complete the degree, and failed to disclose their graduation rates. A former admissions representative of a for-profit college admitted that prospective students were referred to as "leads" and that representatives were assigned a quota of students they needed to enroll in the college each week.[46]

Most Americans believe that in order to get ahead in life, you need to have a college degree. Likewise, most Americans – especially blacks and Latinos – believe that a college education is necessary for success in life. Because of labor market changes and soaring tuition rates, black, Latino, and LMI students are more likely to attend two-year and for-profit colleges, even though students who graduate from those colleges have lower lifetime earnings, and students who attend for-profit colleges are less likely to graduate and will have relatively higher student loan debts whether or not they graduate. A college education, especially one from a four-year college, is even more important now than it was thirty years ago. As discussed in greater detail in

[45] Baum & Steele, *supra* note 40; Mamie Lynch et al., *Subprime Opportunity: The Unfulfilled Promise of For-Profit Colleges and Universities*, Educ. Trust (2010).

[46] Gov't. Accountability Office, *For-Profit Colleges: Undercover Testing Finds Colleges Encouraged Fraud and Engaged in Deceptive and Questionable Marketing Practices: Testimony Before the Committee on Health, Education, Labor, and Pensions, U.S. Senate* (2010) [hereinafter *For-Profit Colleges*] (statement of Gregory D. Kutz, Managing Director Forensics Audits and Special Investigations, GAO); *Id.*, (statement of Joshua Pruyn, Former Admissions Representative, Alta College, Inc.).

Chapter 10, college graduates now have considerably lower unemployment rates, better jobs, higher lifetime earnings, and greater overall household wealth than people who lack college degrees. College graduates also are now significantly more likely to become homeowners. As long as black, Latino, and LMI Americans have low college graduation rates, they will continue to have lower homeownership rates.[47]

[47] John Immerwahr & Jean Johnson, *Squeeze Play: How Parents and the Public Look at Higher Education Today*, Public Agenda (May 31, 2007), at 9, 21.

10

Homeownership: Income Disparities

Homeowners in the Narrative need steady employment to be able to save money for a 20 percent down payment. The hypothetical homeowner also needs steady income to qualify for a low-cost mortgage and to then repay the loan over fifteen to thirty years. Chapter 9 shows why black, Latino, and LMI Americans enter the workforce less educated and with higher debt loads. Because K–12 and college sorting puts them at a disadvantage in labor markets, black, Latino, and LMI workers have higher unemployment rates and lower credit scores, income, and wealth than white and upper-income workers. These disparities make it harder for them to buy homes, and until the income and wealth gaps close, they will never reap the Narrative's homeownership benefits.

EMPLOYMENT

Even though state and federal laws protect employees from overt discrimination in the workforce, recent charges filed with the United States Equal Employment Opportunity Commission (EEOC) and suits that the EEOC has filed against employers expose the employment discrimination that blacks and Latinos – particularly black males – continue to face in U.S. labor markets. For example, the number of charges employees filed with the EEOC in the last decade has ranged from a low of approximately 26,000 in 2005 to more than 35,000 a year in both 2010 and 2011. Despite these somber numbers and ongoing discriminatory practices in the workforce, employment conditions for black and Latino workers have improved, and employers are less likely to engage in the blatantly discriminatory practices that were commonplace until the 1970s. However, studies show that implicit or explicit negative biases that employers have against black and

Latino workers continue to make it harder for blacks and Latinos to succeed in labor markets.[1]

Some employers continue to assume that white workers are more professional, are more intelligent, have better skills, and are better caliber workers than blacks and Latinos.[2] Other employers discriminate against black and Latino job applicants because of the employer's perception that their *customers* may hold racially biased views against blacks or Latinos. In addition, recent paired testing investigations reveal that some employers engage in "name discrimination"; that is, they make employment decisions based on the names of potential employees.

These investigations showed that potential employees with ethnic-sounding names, like Lakisha and Jamal, are less likely to be asked to interview for a job than applicants with names like Emily and Greg. Another subtle form of discrimination that exists involves "street address discrimination," where employers make employment decisions based on where the potential employee lives. Employers who discriminate against job applicants who live in lower-income, predominately minority neighborhoods do so based on the perception that these potential employees are not as good as the potential employees who live in white neighborhoods.[3]

The Moynihan Report noted that in the 1960s "[t]he fundamental, overwhelming fact is that Negro unemployment, with the exception of a few years during World War II and the Korean War, has continued at disaster levels for 35 years."[4] Unemployment rates soared after the housing market crashed, but for the two decades before the crash it generally had remained low. Despite relatively lower overall rates, though, there has always been a significant gap between the unemployment rates of white, black, and Latino workers, and the gaps are particularly large during economic downturns. As shown in Figure 10.1, black and Latino overall unemployment rates during the recent recession exceeded white unemployment rates and remained higher than national averages after the recession ended.

[1] http://www.eeoc.gov/.

[2] Employers do seem to prefer hiring recent Latino immigrants because of the perception that recent immigrants have a stronger work ethic than native-born workers. PHILIP MOSS & CHRIS TILLY, STORIES EMPLOYERS TELL: RACE, SKILL, AND HIRING IN AMERICA (2001).

[3] *Id.*; Marianne Bertrand & Sendhil Mullainathan, *Are Emily and Greg More Employable Than Lakisha and Jamal? A Field Experiment on Labor Market Discrimination*, 94 AM. ECON. REV. 991, 992 (2004); James H. Carr & Nandinee K. Kutty, *The New Imperative for Equality*, in SEGREGATION: THE RISING COSTS FOR AMERICA (James H. Carr & Nandinee K. Kutty eds., 2008); Margery Austin Turner, *Residential Segregation and Employment Inequality*, in SEGREGATION: THE RISING COSTS FOR AMERICA (James H. Carr & Nandinee K. Kutty eds., 2008).

[4] Office of Policy Planning & Research, U.S. Dep't of Labor, *The Negro Family: The Case for National Action* 5 (1965) [*The Moynihan Report*].

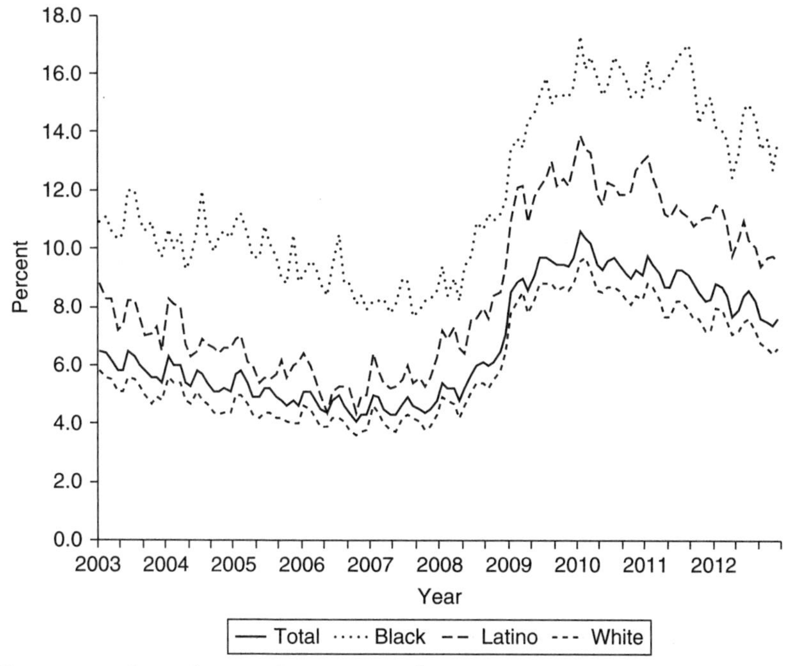

Figure 10.1. Annual unemployment rates by race.
Source: U.S. Bureau of Labor Statistics.

While the highest unemployment rate (9.3 percent) occurred in October 2009, the highest Latino rate (13.1 percent) occurred over a year later in November 2010, and the black unemployment rate did not peak until August 2011 – fully two years after the recession ended. In fact, the *lowest* black unemployment rate since the recession is still higher than the *highest* white unemployment rate during the recession (and, in fact, throughout the last decade). Similarly, the *lowest* Latino unemployment rate since 2009 is almost equal to the *highest* post-recession white unemployment rate. By the time the economy improved in April 2013 and unemployment rates declined, the overall unemployment rate for all workers was 7.5 percent, and it was 6.7 percent for white workers. The unemployment rate for black workers was (at 13.2 percent) almost double the white unemployment rate, while the Latino unemployment rate was 9 percent.[5]

Blacks and Latinos have higher overall unemployment rates in part because they are (and have always been) overrepresented in certain segments of the

[5] U.S. Dep't of Labor, *The Employment Situation – July 2013* (2013), *available at* http://www.bls.gov/news.release/pdf/empsit.pdf; Algernon Austin, *No Relief in 2012 from High Unemployment for African Americans and Latinos*, Econ. Policy Inst. (2012).

labor market. For example, Latino male unemployment rates exceed overall and white male unemployment rates largely because recent immigrant Latino workers are often less skilled and more poorly educated than native workers. Because recent immigrants are overrepresented in the construction industry, which is cyclical and was hard-hit by the recent recession, these immigrant workers lower the overall Latino male unemployment rates.

Black workers, especially males, have relatively higher unemployment rates (and, as discussed in the next section, lower overall income) because many of the low-skilled but high-wage unionized jobs they historically held have either been eliminated or now pay significantly less than they did in the 1970s. As discussed in Chapter 4, until the 1980s the manufacturing sector accounted for a large percentage of total jobs in the United States, and those jobs paid higher-than-average hourly wages for lower-skilled workers. While all U.S. workers are now less likely to have these jobs, black workers have especially been harmed by the reduction in the number of these higher-wage, lower-skilled jobs. Indeed, black workers are now 15 percent less likely than white workers to have high-wage manufacturing jobs.[6]

One reason that blacks and Latinos are overrepresented in lower skill jobs and have higher unemployment rates is because they are less likely to have a college degree than whites. As discussed in Chapter 4, employers place a premium on college degrees, and some now refuse to hire employees who lack a college degree, even for low-skilled jobs (like receptionists or file clerks) that traditionally did not require a college degree. Because employers are now demanding higher skills (often college degrees) from workers who are hired for lower-skilled jobs, workers who do not have a college degree fare poorly, *especially* in weak labor markets. In fact, given the changes in the labor market and the premium employers currently place on college degrees, approximately 60 percent of jobs in the United States require some postsecondary education or training. The percentage of jobs available to non-college graduates has drastically decreased over the last thirty years from 72 percent in 1973 to 44 percent in 1992. The percentage is expected to drop to 22 percent by 2020.[7]

[6] EEOC, *2011 Job Patterns for Minorities and Women in Private Industry (EEO-1), available at* http://www1.eeoc.gov/eeoc/statistics/employment/jobpat-eeo1/2011/index.cfm#select_label; Algernon Austin et al., *Whiter Jobs, Higher Wages: Occupational Segregation and the Lower Wages of Black Men*, Econ. Policy Inst. (2011); John Schmitt & Ben Zipperer, *The Decline in African-American Representation in Unions and Manufacturing*, 1979–2007 (2008); Peter S. Goodman, *A Hidden Toll on Employment: Cut to Part Time*, N.Y. Times (Jul. 31, 2008).

[7] U.S. Bureau of Labor Statistics, U.S. Dep't of Labor, *A Profile of the Working Poor* 2 (2006); David Autor, *The Polarization of Job Opportunities in the U.S. Labor Market: Implications for Employment and Earnings* 5 (2010); Harry J. Holzer & Marek Hlavac, *An Uneven Road and Then a Cliff: U.S. Labor Markets since 2000*, Project U.S. 2010 (2011), *available at*

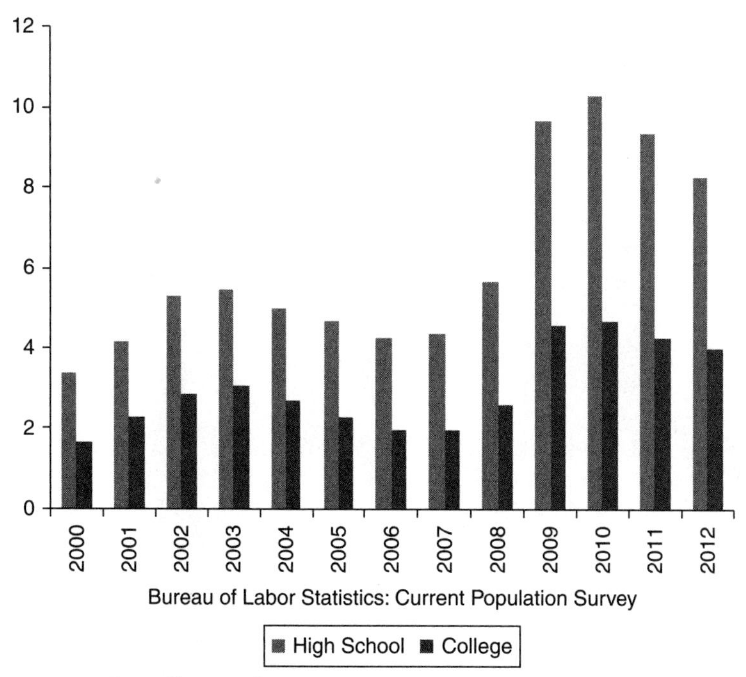

Figure 10.2. Overall unemployment rate 2000–2012.
Source: U.S. Bureau of Labor Statistics.

As shown in Figure 10.2, throughout the housing boom and the recession, college-educated workers had lower unemployment rates relative to less educated workers. The unemployment rate for high school graduates soared during the two years after the recession. By the first quarter of 2013, the unemployment rate for colleges graduates was still higher than it had been during the housing boom but was almost half (3.9 percent) the 7.5 percent overall unemployment rate. In addition to having lower unemployment rates, college graduates have lower underemployment rates and shorter unemployment stints.[8]

Because they are less educated and less well-educated, underemployment and unemployment rates for younger black and Latino (especially male) workers have consistently been higher than for white workers, and the recent recession widened this gap. For example, before the recent recession,

http://www.s4.brown.edu/us2010/Data/Report/report4.pdf; Anthony P. Carnevale et al., *Career Clusters: Forecasting Demand for High School Through College Jobs*, 2008–2018 (2011).

[8] U.S. Bureau of Labor Statistics, *Earnings and Unemployment Rates by Educational Attainment*, *available at* http://www.bls.gov/emp/emptab7.htm.

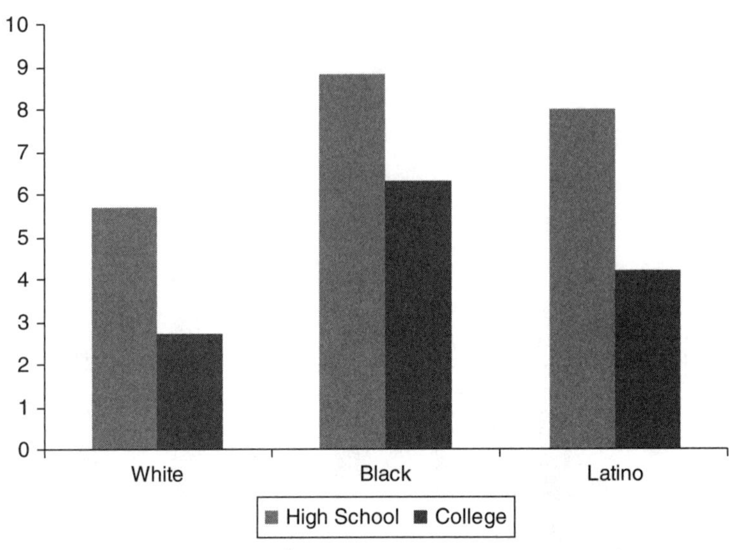

Figure 10.3. Increase in unemployment rate 2007–2011.
Source: Current Population Survey.

20 percent of all black high school graduates who were not attending college were unemployed, while only 9.5 percent of white and 8.8 percent of Latino high school graduates were not working. By 2010 (after the recession officially ended), less than half (49.7 percent) of recent black high school graduates had jobs while more than 62 percent of white high school graduates and almost 59 percent of Latinos had jobs.

The unemployment rates for recent college graduates, while lower than the rates for non-college graduates, also vary dramatically by race. For example, in 2012 (three years after the recession ended), the unemployment rate for black college graduates was 6.3 percent, while the Latino unemployment rate for college graduates was 5.1 percent. Black and Latino college graduates were unemployed at rates that exceed the white (3.7 percent) and overall (4.0 percent) unemployment rates. In fact, their rates were most comparable to the unemployment rate for whites who had degrees from two-year colleges (5.4 percent). Additionally, as shown in Figure 10.3, from the start of the recession until two years after it had ended, blacks and Latinos had significantly higher increases in their unemployment rates than white workers did. In fact, the unemployment rate increased more for blacks who graduated from college (6.3 percent) than it did for whites who lacked college degrees (5.7 percent).[9]

[9] *Id.*

With lower college graduation rates, blacks and Latinos are more likely to have unsteady jobs and higher unemployment rates. As long as they continue to have higher unemployment rates relative to whites, this wage instability will always depress their long-term homeownership rates.

CREDIT SCORES

Blacks and Latinos overall have higher home buying costs, in part because they are more likely to buy homes with higher-cost subprime loans. Even if they are not illegally steered to higher-cost loans, however, higher unemployment rates and, as discussed in the next section, lower overall income will cause blacks and Latinos to have disproportionately higher mortgage default and foreclosure rates. When any homeowner loses a home in a foreclosure sale, the homeowner loses more than just accumulated equity and shelter: mortgage defaults and foreclosures damage credit scores, and having a lower credit score then makes it harder to qualify for a future mortgage loan, *especially* a low-cost loan. In fact, the increased reliance on automated credit scoring as a means to ration high versus low cost credit has now sorted borrowers into two groups: borrowers with high scores qualify for low-cost loan products, while borrowers with lower scores are relegated to higher-cost, higher-risk mortgage products. A recent Federal Reserve report found that the credit scores of mortgage borrowers who are in a foreclosure process drops so low that they would be eligible only for subprime loans, *even if* they had a prime credit score before they defaulted on their mortgage loan.[10]

Mortgage foreclosures harm credit scores for years, and foreclosures and lower credit scores have lasting, harmful collateral effects. For example, landlords increasingly use credit scores as a screen for potential tenants. Renters with lower credit scores pay higher security deposits for residential utility services in states that permit landlords to rely on credit scores and data when setting prices. Similarly, people with lower credit scores pay higher insurance premiums in states that permit companies to rely on credit scores and data to price insurance.[11]

Automated credit scoring now affects the labor market, and unemployed workers may now be haunted by their bad credit, because credit reporting bureaus are selling their services to employers. Almost 50 percent of all employers now report using credit data to screen their potential employees, which may be one reason that it became harder for Americans who lost their

[10] Kenneth P. Brevoort & Cheryl R. Cooper, *Foreclosure's Wake: The Credit Experiences of Individuals Following Foreclosure* (Nov. 8, 2010).

[11] Geoff Smith & Sarah Duda, *Bridging the Gap: Credit Scores and Economic Opportunity in Illinois Communities of Color* (2010).

jobs and could not pay their bills during the recession to get a job (which would allow them to pay their bills). Because of this increased reliance on credit checking in the labor markets, since 2010 seven states have enacted laws that restrict how employers can use credit reports in the hiring process.[12]

Some low-income housing policy groups and Latino housing groups are now suggesting that lenders should decrease their reliance on automated credit scoring. These groups maintain that blacks and Latinos are harmed by automated credit scoring because many of the demographic variables that are used to assign scores rely on unfair and potentially discriminatory procedures and processes. For example, Latinos (especially recent immigrants) often lack credit histories, have unsteady income (or are paid in cash), and cannot verify their income. This causes them to have relatively lower credit scores because they have thin (or no) credit histories and may not even have bank accounts.

In addition, not owning a home decreases a borrower's credit score because homeownership is used as a factor to indicate that a borrower is stable. Because of lower homeownership rates, black and Latino renters have lower credit scores, which then makes it harder for them to be approved for low-cost mortgage loans. Even though loan officers have discriminated against blacks and Latinos in the past by subjectively concluding that they posed higher credit risks because of where they lived (or wanted to live), and even though blacks and Latinos have never fared particularly well in subjective mortgage underwriting processes, some housing advocates now suggest that lenders should return to the old model of approving loan applications face-to-face and using a manual, relationship-based underwriting process.[13]

INCOME

The Happy Homeownership Narrative assumes that all homeowners will have reliably predictable income over a fifteen- to thirty-year period to repay their mortgage loans. This assumption is no longer true for black, Latino, and LMI Americans because they have not received a fair share of the aggregate income increases that U.S. workers have received over the last thirty years. Indeed, as noted in Chapter 4, although aggregate personal income in the United States has increased over the last thirty years, overall income has been stagnant for LMI workers for almost thirty years.

[12] Gary Rivlin, *The Long Shadow of Bad Credit in a Job Search*, N.Y.TIMES (May 11, 2013).

[13] Eric Rodriguez, *Assessing the Damage of Predatory Lending by Countrywide: The Fallout for Latino Families, Hearing on Examining Lending Discrimination Practices and Foreclosure Abuses of the Senate Committee on the Judiciary* (Mar. 7, 2012); Smith, *id.*; Cassandra Jones Havard, *On the Take: The Black Box of Credit Scoring and Mortgage Discrimination*, 20 BOSTON U. PUBLIC INTEREST L.J. 241 (2011).

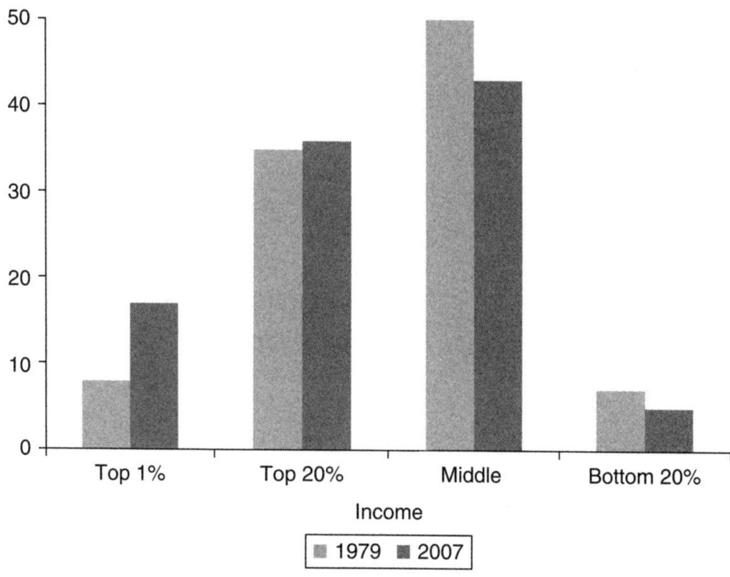

Figure 10.4. Share of total income earned.
Source: Congressional Budget Office.

Data analyzed by the Congressional Budget Office show that, since the 1980s, higher-income households have received a disproportionate percentage of income gains, and income for the top 1 percent of earners has grown at astronomical rates. Specifically, income for the top 1 percent grew by 275 percent between 1979 and 2007. Income for the next highest earners (the top 80–99 percent) increased by 65 percent, although this rate obviously pales in comparison to the top 1 percent. Income increases for the remaining 80 percent of the population over this period ranged from 40 percent (for the middle class) to 18 percent (for the bottom 20 percent of earners).

In addition to having the largest absolute income increases, the *share* of total income for higher-income earners also increased, while the share accruing to LMI households decreased. As shown in Figure 10.4, while the top 1 percent of earners received 8 percent of total income in 1979, by 2007 that share had more than doubled (to more than 17 percent). The rest of the top 20 percent of earners received substantially the same share of income in 1979 (35 percent) as they did in 2007 (36 percent). Middle-income workers lost significant shares of total income during this period. While they received 50 percent of total income in 1979, that share had dropped to 43 percent in 2007. People in the bottom 20 percent, who only had 7 percent of total income in 1979, had an even smaller share (5 percent) by 2007.

While household income for all groups in the United States declined during the recent recession, the income drop for top earners was not as steep as the income drop for the bottom 99 percent. In addition, while income for the top 1 percent dropped largely because of stock market losses, household income for the bottom 99 percent dropped because of high unemployment rates. Household income for lower-wage earners has remained flat throughout the five years after the recession ended. In contrast, income for top earners rebounded by 2013 – principally because the stock market has rebounded since the recession.[14]

Obviously, if the share of total income over the last thirty years had been more evenly distributed between earning groups, the income gap would not be as great. Indeed, if LMI homeowners had received even close to proportional shares of the income gains over the last thirty years, they probably would look more like the homeowners envisioned in the Happy Homeownership Narrative. A fair distribution of income would have allowed more homeowners to save and buy a home yet not be forced to rely on high-cost subprime mortgage products to finance the purchase.

Certain demographic groups in the United States are consistently among the highest earners, and those same groups also have the highest homeownership rates. Overall household income is consistently higher in two-income households and households headed by a married couple. The households that are most likely to be lower income are single-parent (notably, female) households and, as discussed in Chapter 9, there has been an increase in the number of female-headed households over the last thirty years. While lower income levels in single-parent households do not completely explain the income and wealth gap between the top 1 percent and the other 99 percent, researchers have calculated that up to 25 percent of the overall income gap may be because of the increase in single-parent households.[15]

Additionally, white households have always had higher incomes than black and Latino households. The racial income gap is especially large for male workers. For example, the average wage disparity between white and black male workers in 2008 (before unemployment rates started to soar) was almost $6/hour. The disparity was largest for workers who had a high school diploma

[14] Cong. Budget Office, U.S. Cong., *Trends in the Distribution of Household Income between 1979 and 2007* (2011); Richard Fry & Paul Taylor, *A Rise in Wealth for the Wealthy; Declines for the Lower 93%: An Uneven Recovery, 2009–2011*, Pew Research Ctr. (2013), *available at* http://www.pewsocialtrends.org/2013/04/23/a-rise-in-wealth-for-the-wealthydeclines-for-the-lower-93/.

[15] Meizhu Liu et al., The Color of Wealth: The Story Behind the U.S. Racial Wealth Divide 2 (2006); Zhu Xiao Di, *Growing Wealth, Inequality, and Housing in the United States* 3 (Joint Ctr. for Hous. Studies, Harvard University, Working Paper W07–1, 2007); Robert Haveman & Timothy Smeeding, *The Role of Higher Education in Social Mobility*, The Future of Children (Aug. 2006), at 130–33; Nat'l Ctr. for Educ. Statistics, U.S. Dep't of Educ., *Persistence and Attainment of 2003–04 Beginning Postsecondary Students: After 6 Years* (2010); Nat'l Ctr. For Educ. Statistics, U.S. Dep't of Educ., *The Condition of Education* (2006).

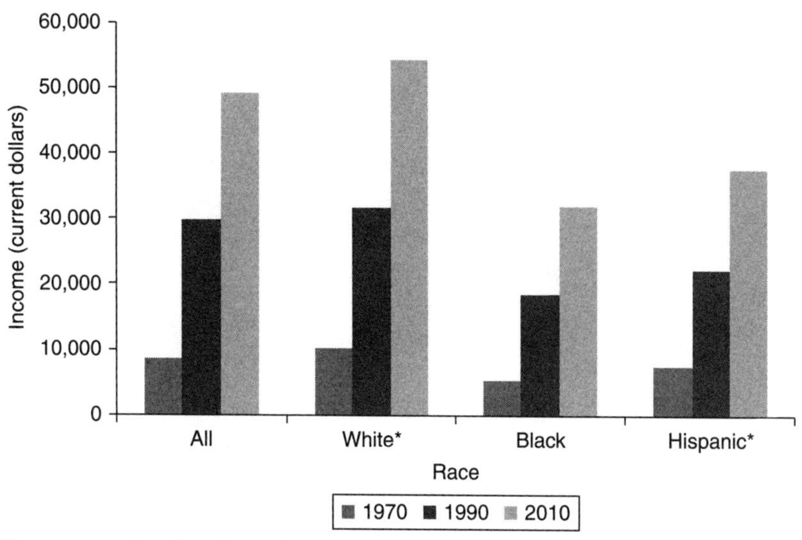

Figure 10.5. Median household income by race.
Source: Current Population Survey.

(or less), but the wage disparity remains even controlling for educational attainment. Specifically, black male workers with college degrees earned 74 percent of what white male workers earned.[16] As shown in Figure 10.5, by 2010 (when unemployment rates rose to more than 10 percent) black household income was approximately 65 percent of white household income, and Latino household income was about 70 percent of white household income.

Overall black household income was especially affected by the recent recession. For example, during the three-year period after the recession ended (June 2009 to June 2012), median household income for whites dropped 5.2 percent, while household income for blacks dropped more than twice as much (11.1 percent). Latino households fared better, with income dropping only 4.1 percent during the three years after the recession ended. Indeed, as shown in Figure 10.5, median household income for blacks in 2010 was significantly lower than median white income in 2010 and, in fact, was essentially the same as median household income for whites *in 1990*.[17]

[16] Austin et al., *supra*, note 6.

[17] Jesse Bricker et al., *Changes in U.S. Family Finances from 2007 to 2010: Evidence from the Survey of Consumer Finances*, 98 FED. RES. BULL. (2012); Michael A. Fletcher, *Household Income is Below Recession Levels, Report Says*, WASH. POST (Aug. 23, 2012); Hazel L. Morrow-Jones, *Black-White Differences in the Demographic Structure of the Move to Homeownership in the United States*, in OWNERSHIP, CONTROL, AND THE FUTURE OF HOUSING POLICY 47 (R. Allen Hays ed., 1993).

A number of factors contribute to lower overall black and Latino household income. Household income has always been higher overall in households that have income from two spouses or partners. As discussed in Chapter 9, blacks have lower marriage rates, and there are more black single-parent households relative to whites with comparable incomes. While Latino households are more likely than black households to be married, blacks and Latinos (particularly) have larger families compared to whites. And, even though Latinos have higher marriage rates than blacks, Latino households are more likely than other households to have only one spouse who earns income, and this depresses their overall household income. Additionally, while white household net worth generally increases if there is more than one child, black and Latino households appear to experience substantial financial harm if the couple has more than one child.[18]

In addition to having higher unemployment rates and lower marriage rates, blacks and Latinos also have lower overall income because of the occupational segregation of the U.S. workforce. A recent report found that, even controlling for educational attainment, most U.S. occupations remain racially segregated. Blacks and Latinos are significantly underrepresented in higher-skilled and higher-wage professional industries (like investment banking) but are overrepresented in lower-wage service jobs (like home health aid). Latino men (especially recent immigrants) have disproportionately high representation in the construction industry, while Latino women are overrepresented in laborer and service jobs. Similarly, black males are overrepresented in service, laborer, and lower-wage sales jobs, while black females are overrepresented in lower-wage sales, service, and clerical jobs.[19]

The main reason black and Latino household income lags white income, though, is because blacks and Latinos are less likely to have a college degree. Workers with a college degree are more likely to have a higher-paying

[18] U.S. Census Bureau, 2010 *Census: Hispanic Origin and Race of Coupled Households, available at* http://www.census.gov/population/www/cen2010/briefs/tables/tab05.pdf; Chenoa Flippen, *Unequal Returns to Housing Investments? A Study of Real Housing Appreciation among Black, White, and Hispanic Households*, 82 Soc. Forces 1523 (2004); Matthew A. Painter II & Kevin Shafer, *Children, Race/Ethnicity, and Marital Wealth Accumulation in Black and Hispanic Households*, 42 J. of Comparative Fam. Studies 145 (2011); Daniel Schneider, *Wealth and the Marital Divide*, 117 Am. J. Sociology 627 (2011); Tracy M. Turner & Marc T. Smith, *Exits from Homeownership: The Effects of Race, Ethnicity, and Income*, J. Regional Sci. (Feb. 2009), at 1–32.

[19] In addition, as was true forty years ago, many young black males choose not to even participate in the official labor force, and recent research show that the reported unemployment rate for low-skilled black males might be even higher if the data did not exclude incarcerated males. Rebecca Blank, *Economic Change and the Structure of Opportunity for Less-Skilled Workers*, in Changing Poverty (Maria Cancian & Sheldon H. Danziger, eds. 2009).

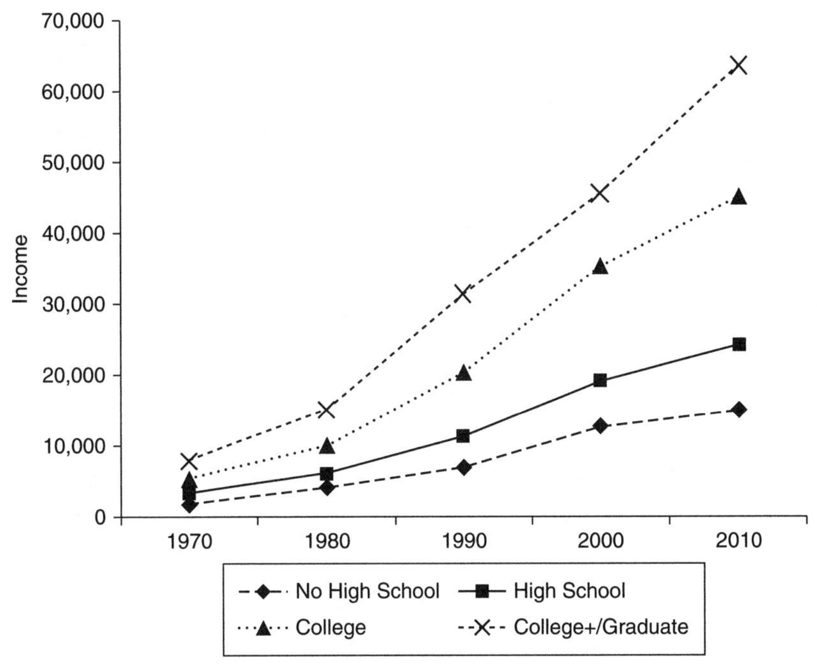

Figure 10.6. Mean income by educational attainment, females.
Source: Current Population Survey.

management and professional job than workers who lack a college degree. Just as college graduates have lower unemployment rates relative to workers who lack a college degree, for the last thirty years college graduates have experienced high job and wage growth and have earned increasingly larger shares of overall U.S. income. As Figures 10.6 and 10.7 show, income and educational attainment are positively correlated: the more education the worker has, the more income the worker receives.

It is still possible, of course, for a worker who does not have a college education to be successful in the labor market. And some critics of the "college is good for all" mantra question whether the United States is now overinvesting in college education. These critics correctly note that many Americans with college degrees do not achieve the economic gains traditionally associated with having a postsecondary degree because they are working in jobs that historically were held by people who lack a college degree. Although today's college graduate may not have the same type of higher-prestige job that a 1970s graduate might have had, the relevant comparison is not between a college graduate today and a college graduate thirty years ago.

At least from the perspective of homeownership rates, the only relevant comparison is between the financial position of college graduates and the

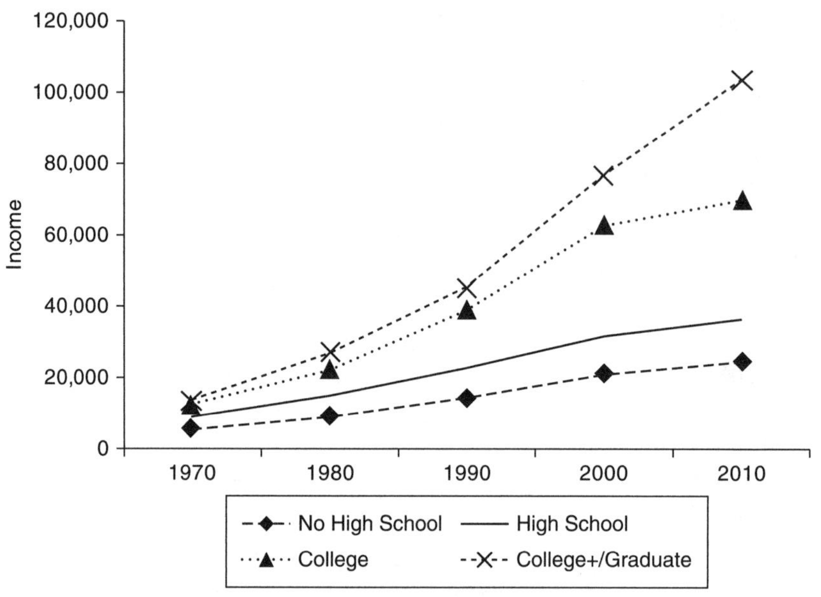

Figure 10.7. Mean income by educational attainment, males.
Source: Current Population Survey.

financial position of people who lack college degrees. That is, while many U.S. workers could successfully perform the tasks associated with low-skilled jobs if they received only on-the-job training or postsecondary training, employers consistently use the attainment of a college degree as a signal of the employer's intelligence, ambition, drive, or talent. As long as employers refuse to hire workers for even low-skilled positions unless they have a college degree, Americans will need to graduate from college in order to succeed in U.S. labor markets.

In the 1970s, Americans who had only a high school diploma or equivalent could reasonably expect to be employed, earn enough to support their families, and buy a house. That is no longer true. Because of the virtual disappearance of high-wage, lower-skilled jobs and because of employers' increased demands for workers who have advanced technology skills, wages for workers with less than a high school degree (or who graduated from high school but did not graduate from college) have grown little over the last thirty years, and the income gap between those who have and those who lack a college degree is widening. Between 2000 and 2010 median earnings for male workers with less than a high school education (adjusted for inflation) dropped, while median earnings for men with at least a college education rose. Similarly, while college graduates earned 30 percent more than workers with a high school diploma in 1980, by 2010 college graduates on average earned 70 percent more than workers with only a high school degree.

A recent Congressional Budget Office report shows that the median wage for male workers with a college degree was 72 percent higher than the wages for men with only a high school or equivalent degree in 2009. This wage differential dramatically exceeds the 27 percent wage differential in 1979. A similar pattern exists for women. That is, the 2009 median wage for female workers with a college degree was 68 percent higher than the median wage for women who have only a high school or equivalent degree, and this wage differential is almost twice the 36 percent wage differential in 1979.[20] Similarly, the expected earnings over a forty-year time period for a male college graduate is $2.4 million compared to $1.3 million in lifetime earnings for a male high school graduate, while women with college degrees should expect to earn $636,000 more than female high school graduates. In addition to having higher expected lifetime earnings, college-educated workers are substantially more likely to have professional or managerial jobs with fringe benefits than lower-skilled, lower-educated workers historically received from their jobs in the manufacturing sector.[21]

Historically, American workers with just a high school diploma could earn enough to buy a home and join the middle-class. Since the 1980s, a college degree has essentially been a prerequisite to stable, high-wage employment and the American Dream of homeownership, and income mobility is now slipping out of the reach of Americans who do not have college degrees. As shown in Figure 10.8, homeownership rates for all races generally increase as income increases. Black, Latino, and LMI Americans have lower college graduation rates, which causes them to have lower overall household income. Lower overall income then makes it harder for these household to save money to make a down payment on a home. Given their relatively lower incomes and relatively higher home buying costs, it is not surprising that they are largely consigned to buy homes in neighborhoods that have older, less well-maintained homes that do not appreciate as much as the homes that whites own.

[20] Joint Ctr. for Hous. Studies, Harvard University, *America's Rental Housing: Homes for a Diverse Nation* 6 (2006). Bureau of Labor Statistics, *supra* note 8; Nat'l Ctr. for Educ. Statistics, U.S. Dep't of Educ., *Digest of Education Statistics* (2000), at table 382. That gap is even higher in some areas of the country. *See* Christopher H. Wheeler, *Wage Gap Widens, Especially in Cities*, Fed. Res. Bank St. Louis (2005), *available at* http://www.stlouisfed.org/publications/re/articles/?id=376 (reporting that workers in one federal reserve district who have four-year degrees earned 80 percent more than high school graduates in 2000).

[21] Michael Hout, *Social and Economic Returns to College Education in the United States*, 38 ANN. REV. SOCIOL. 379 (2012); Julian Tiffany, *Work-Life Earnings by Field of Degree and Occupation for People With a Bachelor's Degree: 2011*, American Community Survey Briefs (Oct. 2012); Autor, *supra* note 7; Holzer & Hlavac, *supra* note 7.

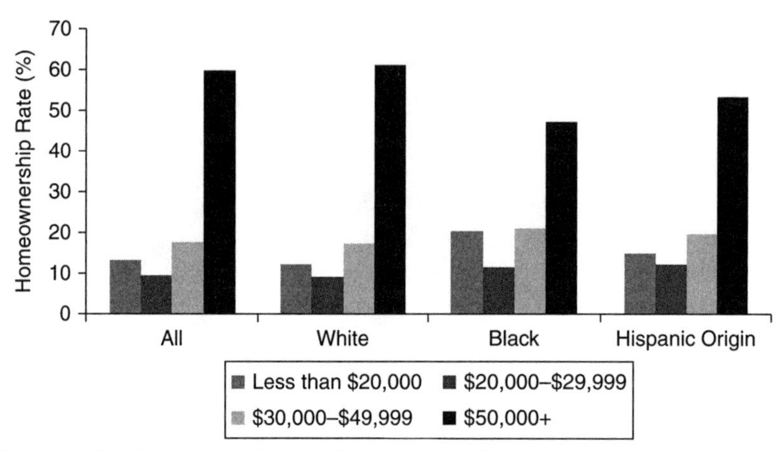

Figure 10.8. Homeownership rate by income and race, 2010.
Source: Current Population Survey.

Chapter 7 describes the recent multimillion dollar settlements involving lenders and mortgage brokers who illegally steered black and Latino borrowers to higher-cost subprime loans reveal. These settlements show that relatively lower household income is not the *only* reason that black and Latino homeowners have higher purchasing costs relative to whites. But even without illegal and discriminatory steering, black and Latino renters and homeowners are less competitive in housing and lending markets because of the ever-growing income gap. In addition, because of lower income but higher unemployment levels, blacks and Latinos often have limited resources to use to make repairs to their homes, and letting their homes deteriorate affects the market value of their homes, especially if those homes are already older and less well-maintained. Finally, because they have lower household income but higher overall unemployment rates, blacks and Latinos are at higher risk for defaulting on future mortgage payments and losing their homes.[22]

WEALTH

Finally, the homeownership gap between whites and minorities has not closed, and likely will never close, until the racial wealth gap closes. Household wealth is generally defined as the sum of assets minus the sum of debts. The most common forms of wealth are savings, stocks, bonds, home equity, and business ownership interests, and the largest debts that most households have are

[22] Morrow-Jones, *supra* note 17.

mortgages and student loans. Wealth encompasses both earned and inherited wealth, and people with financial wealth are generally better off and more financially secure than people who have a high income but lack wealth.

Wealth provides long-term financial security and flexibility primarily because it can be liquidated and serve as an income replacement if a person loses a job or incurs a large unexpected expense (like medical bills) or a large, expected but non-routine expense (like college tuition). Unlike income that is earned in the present, whether a person has wealth is largely determined by past events, tends to change slowly over time, and often involves ancestors. The richest Americans inherited or were given most of their private financial wealth from parents or grandparents, and Americans routinely rely on inherited or earned wealth to help them acquire more wealth, start businesses, or pay college expenses.[23]

There has never been a time in U.S. history – not before or after the Civil War, the Depression, or the recent recession – that white household wealth has not significantly exceeded black and Latino household wealth. White households have always owned significantly more real property and financial assets, including certificates of deposit, savings, bonds, and stocks (either owned directly or in a mutual fund or retirement accounts) than black and Latino households. While the gap is smaller for higher-income households and for people with college degrees, there is a gap at all income levels. As shown in Figure 10.9, the median household net worth for whites in 2000 was $79,400 and was $55,000 for all groups.

In stark contrast, median household wealth for blacks was smaller by tenfold, at $7,500, and Latino household wealth was $9,750. For families in the lowest earning quintile, the gap is especially pronounced. While overall median net worth for the lowest earning quintile, including home equity, was $7,396, white families in this group had a median net worth of $24,000 (three times larger than *overall black household wealth*), compared to $57 for black families and $500 for Latino families. The racial wealth gap has either remained the same or has increased notwithstanding substantial increases in black and Latino homeownership rates.[24]

The racial wealth gap partially results from the fact that blacks and Latinos are less likely to diversify their investment assets and are more likely to be LMI

[23] Schneider, *supra* note 18.

[24] Bricker et al., *supra* note 17; Shawna Orzechowski & Peter Sepielli, *Net Worth and Asset Ownership of Households: 1998 and 2000*, U.S. Census Bureau, at 2, 6, 12 (Current Population Reports, P70–88, May 2003), *available at* http://www.census.gov/prod/2003pubs/p70–88.pdf; Lauren J. Krivo & Robert L. Kaufman, *Housing and Wealth Inequality: Racial-Ethnic Differences in Home Equity in the United States*, 41 Demography 585 (2004).

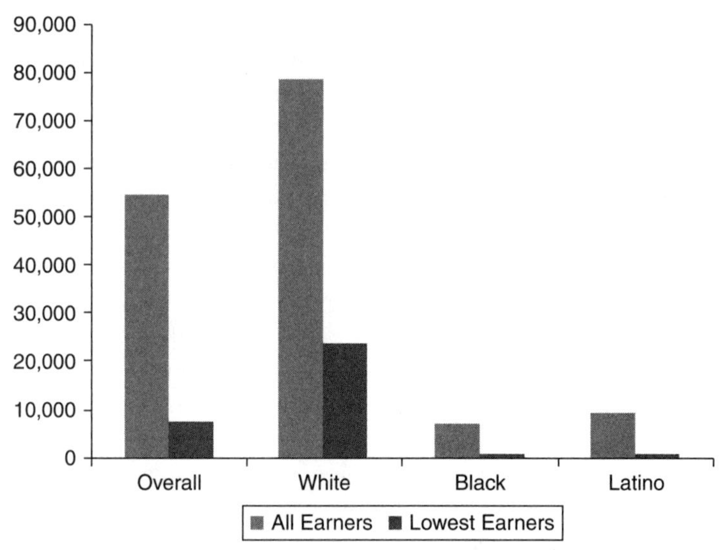

Figure 10.9. 2000 U.S. median net worth.
Source: U.S. Census Bureau.

households. Lower-income households hold almost 70 percent of their household wealth in home equity, while higher-income homeowners hold less than 40 percent of their net wealth in home equity. Because housing constitutes a significant part of overall household wealth for most black, Latino, and LMI Americans and they generally do not invest in different types of assets, they are at a measurably higher risk of losing their wealth if they lose their homes or if those homes fail to appreciate in value. But the primary cause for the current racial wealth gap is that whites inherit more from their families than blacks or Latinos.[25]

Whites are at least three times more likely to receive an inheritance than blacks and Latinos. Additionally, the inheritance that blacks and Latinos receive is about one-third less than the average inheritance that whites receive. While only large inheritances appear to increase the homeowner's overall wealth, receiving an inheritance helps renters purchase homes earlier, gives them money to use for a down payment, and lowers their overall home buying costs. Research shows that – regardless of the size of the inheritance – people who inherit money are more likely to own a home and can purchase a larger

[25] Bricker et al., *supra* note 17; Carr & Kutty, *supra* note 36; Signe-Mary McKernan et al., *Do Assets Help Families Cope with Adverse Events*, Urban Inst. (2009); Joint Ctr. for Hous. Studies, Harvard Univ., *The State of the Nation's Housing* (1999), *available at* http://www.jchs.harvard.edu/sites/jchs.harvard.edu/files/son99.pdf.

home than people who do not receive an inheritance. At least 20 percent of first-time home buyers receive money from a relative or friend to make the down payment, and this gift or loan often constitutes more than 50 percent of the down payment.[26] One study found that 15 percent of white homeowners received their entire down payment from their families, and another 27 percent received part of their down payment from family members. While 54 percent of white renters paid for the down payments solely with their own savings, almost 90 percent of black home buyers used only their savings to make the payment, and only 6 percent received all of their down payment from family members.[27]

The ability to make a down payment (especially a sizeable one) lets potential owners borrow less, qualifies them for lower-cost mortgage loans, prevents them from having to purchase costly private mortgage insurance (PMI), and generally lets them start accumulating equity sooner. Because they have less inherited wealth, lower overall household (and largely stagnant) income, and few opportunities for inter-generational wealth transfers, black and Latino parents are not able to give or loan their children money for a down payment, and they are not in a position to help them make their mortgage payments after they buy their first home. Likewise, the wealth gap makes it harder for blacks and Latinos to purchase assets (including homes) that would allow them to accumulate wealth in their lifetimes that they could then pass on to their heirs.

The recent recession has wiped out years of accumulated wealth for U.S. households. All races and income groups (except the very highest earners) from all educational attainment groups experienced significant declines in

[26] Melinda C. Miller, *Land and Racial Wealth Inequality,* 101 Am. Econ. Rev.: Papers & Proceedings 371 (2011), *available at* http://www.aeaweb.org/articles.php?doi=10.1257/aer.101.3.371; Joint Ctr. for Hous. Studies, Harvard Univ., *The State of the Nation's Housing* (2001), *available at* http://www.jchs.harvard.edu/sites/jchs.harvard.edu/files/son2001.pdf; Joint Ctr. for Hous. Studies, Harvard Univ., *The State of the Nation's Housing* 13 (2007), *available at* http://www.jchs.harvard.edu/sites/jchs.harvard.edu/files/son2007.pdf; Liu et al., *supra* note 15, at 171; Lewis M. Segal & Daniel G. Sullivan, Fed. Res. Bank Chi., *Trends in Homeownership: Race, Demographics, and Income,* Econ. Perspectives (1998); Flippen, *supra* note 18; Christopher J. Mayer & Gary V. Engelhardt, *Gifts, Down Payments, and Housing Affordability* (Fed. Res. Bank of Bos., Working Paper No. 94–4, 1994); Matthew Hall & Kyle Crowder, *Extended-Family Resources and Racial Inequality in the Transition to Homeownership,* 40 Soc. Sci. Res. 1534 (2011).

[27] The Transition to Home-Ownership and the Black–White Wealth Gap. While blacks and Latinos are less likely to receive inter-generational transfers of wealth, black and Latino renters are more likely to provide limited financial support to members of their extended families than white renters are. They are often asked to help family members pay their routine living expenses, and they themselves have relatively lower income and wealth, which may partially explain why black and Latino renters buy homes later than whites do and also why it is harder for them to save to make a down payment.

household wealth during the recession. While median wealth for all households dropped by 28 percent between 2005 and 2009, the recession had a particularly devastating effect on black and Latino wealth. Average white household wealth dropped 16 percent to $113,149 (in 2009) from $134,992 (in 2005). In stark contrast, average black household wealth dropped more than 50 percent to $5,677 (from $12,124 in 2005) and Latino household wealth dropped a whopping 66 percent to $6,325 (from $18,359 in 2005).

A recent Federal Reserve study examined the devastating effect the recent recession has had on black and Latino household wealth and found that, between 2007 and 2012, white household wealth declined 10 percent, while Latino wealth declined almost 27 percent and black household wealth fell 30 percent. Overall household wealth for higher-income blacks decreased more than wealth for higher-income whites even after the recession. In addition to an increase in the racial wealth gap in general, there also is a growing racial gap between the number of households that have absolutely *no* wealth, due in large part to the recent recession. That is, while 15 percent of white households had zero or negative wealth in 2009, 35 percent of black households and 31 percent of Latino households had no wealth.[28]

Higher foreclosure rates and plummeting home values, combined with stock market losses in the recession, have eliminated the wealth gains that blacks and Latinos had made since the 1980s, and their wealth levels are now at the lowest levels in twenty-five years. Because of the recession, the wealth gap between white households and black and Latino households has reached record levels and is wider now than it has been since the United States started to focus on closing the racial homeownership gap in the 1990s. Of course, the racial wealth gap is not terribly surprising given the ever-widening wealth gap between the top 1 percent of the U.S. population and the rest of U.S. workers.

The Occupy Wall Street movements in 2011 and 2012 dramatically revealed the wealth and income differences between the top 1 percent and everyone else. Since 2000, the top 1 percent of U.S. households have held more than one-third of total U.S. household net wealth. By 2013, the richest 1 percent of the U.S. population owned approximately 40 percent of total U.S. wealth, and the top 25 percent of U.S. households now own 87 percent of all wealth. After the recession ended, wealth for the richest 7 percent of Americans rose

[28] Rakesh Kochhar et al., *Twenty-to-One: Wealth Gaps Rise to Record Highs Between Whites, Blacks and Hispanics*, Pew Research Ctr. (2011); Rolf Pendall et al., *Demographic Challenges and Opportunities for U.S. Housing Markets*, Bipartisan Policy Ctr. (Mar. 2012); Bricker et al., *supra* note 17; Shaila Dewan & Robert Gebeloff, *Among the Wealthiest 1 Percent, Many Variations*, N.Y. TIMES (Jan 14. 2012).

by 28 percent, while the net worth for the bottom 93 percent of Americans dropped by 4 percent between 2009 and 2011. As long as household wealth is disproportionately held by the richest Americans, the racial wealth gap will not close, because – given their overall income and wealth levels – blacks and Latinos are largely missing from the top 1 percent (and top 25 percent). Until that wealth gap closes, the racial homeownership gap will not close.[29]

[29] Fry & Taylor, *supra* note 14.

11

Outlook and Prescription for the Future

This book has presented a somber narrative of the road to homeownership for low- and moderate-income (LMI), black, and Latino Americans. The sobering statistics concerning their K–12 and college graduation rates, income and wealth levels, overall homeownership rates, and lower home appreciation rates contradict the rosy picture depicted in the Happy Homeownership Narrative. The Narrative's portrayal of renters and homeowners matched the economic profiles of renters from the 1940s until the 1960s, who were encouraged and allowed to purchase homes with low-cost, government-insured mortgages. But homeownership is no longer easy, low-cost, or low-risk for LMI Americans. And the Happy Homeownership Narrative has *never* really applied to blacks and Latinos.

Homeownership is constantly pitched as the best way for LMI families to build wealth, and civil rights and housing advocacy groups view homeownership as the best way for blacks and Latinos to have financial stability. But it is now time for everyone – renters, homeowners, and U.S. politicians alike – to acknowledge and accept that the Happy Homeownership Narrative is based on false myths and assumptions and that many Americans should delay or avoid buying homes. Rather than encouraging renters to behave recklessly simply to elevate their status to homeowners, the United States needs to develop a coherent housing policy that enables LMI families to have affordable housing (be it owned or rented) and that acknowledges the link between housing and educational policies.

CHANGING THE NARRATIVE

Despite efforts to increase black and Latino homeownership rates for the last thirty years, the only entities that have consistently benefited from these efforts have been the groups that profit from home sales: realtors, home builders (and the companies that sell them supplies), home improvement stores, and lenders. As noted in earlier chapters, these politically powerful industry groups and the politicians who received financial support from them have fought to keep homeownership as the focal point of U.S. housing policies. The National Association of Realtors, the Mortgage Bankers Association, and the National Association of Home Builders – all of which tend to support Republican politicians – are among the loudest cheerleaders who extol the benefits of homeownership and who encourage cash-strapped homeowners to do whatever it takes to continue paying the mortgage loans for homes. These moneyed industry groups are not cheering alone, however, and support for home sales does not come just from the right side of the political spectrum.

Grassroots housing advocacy groups, community-action groups, the Congressional Black Caucus, La Raza, and most civil-rights organizations join banking and real estate groups to extol the benefits of homeownership for black, Latino, and LMI renters. These groups, who are most often aligned with Democratic politicians, consistently oppose tight lending practices or any policies that make it harder for blacks and Latinos to buy homes. In addition, they are largely mute when critics note that high-income homeowners are the ones who primarily benefit from the enormously generous federal tax benefits. These left-leaning groups generally support relaxed credit standards because of their belief that greater access to mortgage credit is the best way to remedy the harm caused by decades of discriminatory lending policies in black and Latino communities. These groups also welcome credit opportunities for blacks and Latinos because their communities were abandoned and were largely ignored by traditional lenders.

Although homeownership has helped some LMI, black, and Latino households increase their wealth, it is imperative that U.S. political leaders abandon their relentless and, increasingly, reckless efforts to propagate the outdated myths associated with homeownership. The assumption that owning a home is largely risk-free and low-cost is no longer true for the vast majority of black, Latino, and LMI households in the United States. Leaders should instead accept and acknowledge the dire economic conditions facing LMI homeowners and potential home buyers. Even though housing is crucial for the U.S. economy and owning a house has tremendous benefits for some owners, Congress and other U.S. leaders should rethink *all* of the direct and indirect benefits that homeowners receive and should work to create a new housing narrative that reflects that buying a home no longer provides the same benefits for renters or U.S. neighborhoods as home buying did from the 1940s through the 1980s.

The new narrative needs to clarify that, for many, homeownership is no longer a forced savings device nor an unequivocally good investment, and that most of the economic and psychological benefits associated with homeownership are now enjoyed only by a small group of upper-income (and mostly white) homeowners. The narrative must acknowledge that, for blacks and Latinos, homeownership has always been high-risk, high-cost, and hard to attain, and that homeownership often imposes significant negative external costs on predominately black or Latino neighborhoods. Finally, the new narrative needs to disclose how U.S. laws have allowed upper-income homeowners to fence out certain properties and certain people from their neighborhoods under the guise of protecting their housing investments. The new narrative should expose the fact that fencing has created educational sorting, which has long-term harmful effects on the children who are sorted out of those neighborhoods and their higher-ranked schools.

HOMEOWNERSHIP: NOT ALWAYS A FORCED SAVINGS DEVICE

As discussed in Chapter 3, before the Depression, Americans were forced to save enough money to make a 50 percent down payment on their homes. This onerous savings requirement gave potential homeowners an incentive to be financially responsible, but it also made it hard for most younger Americans to buy homes. When the United States intervened in the mortgage finance markets after the Depression and helped create the long-term, fixed rate mortgage (FRM), more renters were able to buy homes. Although these interventions allowed renters to buy homes but make only a 20 percent down payment, renters had an incentive to remain thrifty savers, because they still had to make the down payment and then repay the fifteen- to thirty-year mortgage. By the 1990s, lenders relaxed the down payment requirement and let borrowers buy homes but make smaller down payments of 5–10 percent. While this smaller requirement gave borrowers less of an incentive to be thrifty, they still had at least *some* incentive to save.

Once lenders created the exotic mortgage products that renters used to buy homes during the housing boom, borrowers could buy homes without making *any* down payment. Moreover, some of those exotic products were "interest only" mortgages that did not require borrowers to make full payments of principal, while others were "option payment" loans that let borrowers choose monthly payments that resulted in the loan negatively amortizing. Given these loan features, borrowers had no real incentive to save to make the monthly payments, at least until interest payments reset and monthly payments increased. Similarly, because homeowners were encouraged to remove equity from their homes with second mortgages (or reverse mortgages, for older homeowners), even existing homeowners during the housing boom had virtually no incentive to be thrifty savers.

Renters now have an incentive to save because, after the recent housing market crash, lenders predictably tightened mortgage lending standards, and it is harder for LMI Americans to obtain a loan to buy a house. Because most of the legislative responses to the housing crisis involved programs that were designed to help existing homeowners refinance their mortgage loans, lenders were inundated with requests from existing homeowners to refinance their high-cost mortgage loans. Since 2008, lenders have largely focused on loan refinancings mostly because those transactions require less documentation, are easier to complete, and are less risky to the lenders. Because of the relative ease and profitability of loan refinancings, lenders currently have little incentive to relax their lending standards to increase the volume of purchase money mortgage loan originations.

Even though most U.S. housing markets were stronger by 2013, the housing market will not fully recover until individual renters and homeowners start buying homes. The combination of tighter credit standards and decreased lender interest in approving loans that borrowers use to buy homes has made it harder for cash-strapped borrowers to qualify for mortgages to buy homes, which is likely why home purchases by investors and all-cash buyers fueled the housing recovery in 2013. By mid-2013, political leaders, progressive housing groups, and the real estate industry had become concerned that first-time homeowners were being shut out of the home buying market by cash-flush investors. If the future bears any resemblance to the past, these groups will soon clamor for programs, policies, or innovations to make it easier for cash-strapped homeowners to buy a home.

Before repeating the costly mistakes of the past, political leaders and housing advocates should rethink the basic income assumptions about homeowners in the Happy Homeownership Narrative and ask whether Americans who have not (or cannot) save should be encouraged to buy homes. The Narrative assumes that younger Americans will have the capacity to save money from their present income to make a down payment and then use their future income to repay the mortgage loan over a fifteen to thirty-year period. Because income has been stagnant or declining for LMI workers for almost thirty years, borrowers likely have felt compelled to purchase homes using exotic, high-interest rate loans that do not require a down payment. LMI Americans did not save to buy homes during the housing boom because they *could* not save.

Many U.S. workers can no longer exhibit the financial virtue of thrift portrayed in the Narrative because their future income has become unstable and unpredictable. Indeed, in a 2013 national poll, 77 percent of participants stated that, compared to thirty years ago, is it less likely that Americans now have enough money to make a 20 percent down payment on a home.[1] Even if most potential homeowners *could* save enough money to make a down payment and pay closing costs, since 2009 U.S. unemployment rates have been higher than they have been in thirty years, and U.S. workers now experience longer periods of unemployment when they lose their jobs.

As discussed in Chapter 6, younger Echo Boomers who have college degrees and are the demographic group that should be forming households and buying homes can no longer reliably predict whether they will have a full-time job after they graduate from college. Given these grim and sobering income and employment statistics, it has become virtually impossible for most black, Latino, and LMI workers to model the attributes of the thrifty homeowner in the Narrative who saves for the future. Many do not save for the future because they are struggling just to pay their current bills. And none of the current economic indicators suggest that their economic affairs will appreciably improve any time soon.

HOMEOWNERSHIP: NOT ALWAYS A GOOD INVESTMENT

The sobering statistics presented in this book show why homeownership can no longer be viewed as a guaranteed, surefire investment for LMI, black, and Latino homeowners. The people who have consistently had the greatest return on their housing investments are homeowners or investors who were able to buy homes in neighborhoods with high appreciation rates. Owning was especially lucrative for people who were able to buy high-appreciating homes using government-insured, low-risk mortgage loans. The "winners" in the housing market investment venture have disproportionately been white and higher-income. Blacks and Latinos overall have failed to reap the financial benefits that homeownership has promised – and largely delivered to – whites.

Many people who bought a home from the 1940s until the 1980s with low-cost, government-insured mortgages were able to capitalize on that investment, and they received a large return on their investment because of housing price appreciation during that period. Homeownership was also a lucrative investment for some people who bought homes during the housing boom, especially investors who flipped properties and homeowners who were able to sell their homes before the housing market crashed.

Black and Latino homeowners were largely prevented from buying homes with low-cost mortgage loans for most of the twentieth century, and many

[1] Hart Research Associates, *How Housing Matters: Americans' Attitudes Transformed by the Housing Crisis & Changing Lifestyles* (2013).

of them who bought homes during the housing boom lost their housing investments and a sizeable portion of their wealth when the housing market crashed. As noted in Chapter 8, houses in predominately white neighborhoods appreciate at rates that far exceed the rates for homes in predominately black or Latino neighborhoods. Blacks and Latinos overall have owned fewer higher-appreciating homes because they have been routinely steered *away from* these homes and, to make matters worse, steered *to* higher-cost mortgage loans.

LMI, black, and Latino homeowners also are more likely to be losers in the housing market investment game because they buy homes in neighborhoods that have more foreclosed homes, and the presence of these homes imposes negative costs on the other homeowners in the neighborhood. Blacks, Latinos, and LMI borrowers are also more likely to live in neighborhoods that have a higher percentage of undesirable (though socially beneficial) property uses, like half-way houses and commercial properties, because upper-income homeowners almost always succeed in fencing out those types of properties from their neighborhoods.

Finally, the homes in predominately black or Latino neighborhoods and in racially transitioning neighborhoods are valued less in the market because white homeowners continue to resist living in neighborhoods that are becoming too brown or black. Because whites have higher homeownership rates than blacks and Latinos, their refusal to purchase homes in black and Latino neighborhoods (or to remain in those neighborhoods if the neighborhood's racial makeup tips) decreases the demand for those homes. This reduced demand renders those homes less valuable but simultaneously increases the value of homes in predominately white neighborhoods that white potential buyers favor.

In addition to the discriminatory treatment they have received (and continue to receive) in the real estate and mortgage lending markets and to the aversion some whites have to living in black and Latino neighborhoods, certain demographic factors make it harder for blacks and Latinos to receive the same type of return on their homeownership investment. As noted in Chapters 8 and 9, because blacks and Latinos have higher home buying costs, relatively lower overall income, relatively higher debt levels, and higher unemployment rates, they have shorter homeownership tenures and increased risk that they will lose their home to foreclosure. Because blacks and Latinos are in homes for shorter periods of time, they accumulate significantly less equity overall, which, in turn, reduces their overall household wealth relative to whites. In addition, having shorter homeownership tenures but higher foreclosure rates makes it is less likely that they will move up to a second (nicer or more expensive) home.

Even though some investors and homeowners have always been able to earn huge profits by buying high-appreciating or expensive homes or by treating their houses like tradable commodities that they bought and sold (i.e., flipped) every two years, U.S. housing policies should not favor homeownership because it can produce high investment returns similar to the rates that investors would receive from a hedge fund. If U.S. housing policies are based on the premise that homeownership is good and builds wealth for ordinary Americans and that it creates stable citizens and communities, homeownership benefits should be designed to ensure that the people who intend to live in the homes they purchase – rather than just lenders, home builders, high-income homeowners, or investors – are the ones who actually receive those benefits.

Whether or not they benefit financially from owning homes, recent surveys show that Americans continue to believe in at least some of the Narrative's depiction of the financial benefits of homeownership. More than two-thirds of the people polled in a 2010 Fannie Mae survey agreed that homeownership provides a safe place to live and a good place to raise children. Survey results also show that Americans felt that owning a home is preferable to renting because homeownership generally gives families more space and gives owners more control over their living space. In addition, despite the problems many cash-strapped and often underwater homeowners had encountered due to the recent recession, most of the people who participated in this survey continued to believe that renting is a bad investment.[2]

A more recent 2013 poll conducted on behalf of the MacArthur Foundation indicates that Americans' views about the benefits of homeownership have started to shift. While 70 percent of those surveyed wanted to become homeowners, almost 60 percent stated that buying a home was less appealing than it was thirty years ago. Additionally, almost 70 percent of the respondents believed that, compared to the last three decades, it is less likely that households will build wealth through homeownership, and almost 80 percent felt that homeowners today are at greater risk of losing their homes to foreclosure than they were thirty years ago. Although Americans do not appear to have completely abandoned the view that the American Dream necessarily includes owning the home you live in, more than 60 percent of owners and 67 percent of renters now believe that renters can be just as successful as homeowners in achieving the American Dream. This view is especially prevalent among the eighteen- to thirty-five-year-old age group that should be forming households and buying homes.[3]

[2] Fannie Mae National Housing Survey (2010–2011).

[3] Hart Research Associates, *supra* note 1.

Americans' views about the financial benefits of homeownership seem to be shifting, but U.S. political leaders still seem unwilling to develop housing policies that de-emphasize homeownership and instead focus on ways to provide more affordable housing opportunities, whether they are owned or rented. This is unfortunate because, unless and until U.S. housing policies dispense with the romanticism associated with homeownership, it will be virtually impossible to convince most LMI, black, and Latino home buyers that there are significant opportunity costs associated with the decision to buy a house, that the investment is risky, and that buying the only home they can afford (as soon as they possibly can) could imperil their children's future if the home forces their children into lower-quality public schools.

TOUCHING THE THIRD RAIL: THE MORTGAGE INTEREST DEDUCTION

The mortgage interest deduction (MID) is one of the most well-known tax benefits, and likely is *the* most well-known tax benefit for homeowners. Most renters and homeowners continue to believe that buying a house is generally better than renting because homeownership provides valuable tax benefits. But individual renters and homeowners are not the ones who lead the charge to protect the MID whenever it appears that Congress *might* modify this tax expenditure. Of course, this is not terribly surprising given that, as noted in earlier chapters, only one-third of U.S. taxpayers actually take the MID. Instead, the groups that lobby most vigorously and testify regularly before Congress whenever it appears that Congress may eliminate – or even modify – the MID are the ones who consistently benefit from high homeownership rates: realtors and the financial services industry.

President Obama created a bipartisan "National Commission on Fiscal Responsibility and Reform" ("Fiscal Commission") that was tasked to propose recommendations to help balance the budget and improve the country's long-term fiscal situation. The Fiscal Commission considered revising the MID, which caused the National Association of Realtors (NAR) to create a "Home Ownership Matters" campaign. The "Call to Action" on the NAR website urged realtors to call their representatives and defend the MID. The NAR website included a "Home Ownership Matters" widget that the NAR urged realtors to add to their web sites. Realtors heeded the call to action, publicized the NAR's campaign to protect the MID, and warned of dire consequences if Congress revised the MID.[4] As an example, one realtor website contained the following:

[4] http://www.realtor.org/topics/home-ownership-matters?wt_mc_id=rd0093.

> Have you heard that one of the solutions to resolve the federal budget deficit is a proposal to eliminate … mortgage interest tax deduction for home owners?
>
> That's true. This was one of the proposals included in suggestions from President Obama's deficit commission. Its preliminary report was released to the media in November.
>
> Now, the government needs to balance the budget but there's a question whether eliminating home loan interest deduction will help the economy.
>
> According to the NAR (National Association of REALTORS®), Mortgage interest has been deductible for nearly 100 years, and the proposed changes will affect 75 million home owners in the United States.
>
> When purchasing a home, buyers compute the tax benefits. Without the tax deductions on mortgage, many families would not be able to afford their homes.
>
> The NAR asks Realtors to contact Congress and urge them to oppose any efforts to reduce or eliminate the Mortgage Interest Deduction.[5]

To further engage local realtors, the NAR created a "Realtor Action Center" Facebook page, which describes the REALTOR® Party as "[a]n energized movement of real estate professionals fighting to keep the dream of homeownership alive for this country."[6] This Facebook page presents the following as the NAR mission statement:

> The NATIONAL ASSOCIATION OF REALTORS® strives to be the collective force influencing and shaping the real estate industry. *It seeks to be the leading advocate of the right to own, use, and transfer real property*; the acknowledged leader in developing standards for efficient, effective, and ethical real estate business practices; and valued by highly skilled real estate professionals and viewed by them as crucial to their success.
>
> Working on behalf of America's property owners, the NATIONAL ASSOCIATION OF REALTORS® provides a facility for professional development, research and exchange of information among its members and to the public and government *for the purpose of preserving the free enterprise system, and the right to own, use, and transfer real property* (emphasis added).[7]

These lobbying efforts no doubt benefit some individual homeowners. The main reason, however, the NAR seeks to preserve the free enterprise system and the right to own property is because without home purchases and sales, the NAR would cease to exist.

5 http://www.domarealty.com/blog/do-not-eliminate-mortgage-interest-deduction/.

6 https://www.facebook.com/realtoractioncenter.

7 *Id.*

U.S. politicians are largely sympathetic to the needs of the real estate industry, even though their needs may not always be good for the individuals who are being encouraged to buy homes. For example, during an April 2013 hearing on "Tax Reform and Residential Real Estate," the Chair of the House Ways and Means Committee stated:

> Homeownership is an integral part of the American dream, and the tax code has long provided a variety of incentives to make it easier for families to buy and own a home. *We also know that the real estate industry plays a large role in our economy. So, this is an area that needs careful, thoughtful review* (emphasis added).[8]

The range of witnesses who testified at this hearing included economists and housing experts who debated whether (and by how much) the tax preferences for owning homes affect the demand for homes, home prices, or homeownership rates. The witnesses expressed widely divergent views concerning whether people would be willing to rent the same type of home they would choose to buy, or whether people buy larger homes because of the MID. While experts may not have reached an agreement about the role tax benefits play in encouraging renters to buy homes, no one disputes that the homeownership tax benefits disproportionately favor certain homeowners, that these homeowners are mostly higher-income, and – given the income gap between whites and racial minorities – that these taxpayers are disproportionately white.[9]

Because of the influence of the mortgage finance and real estate industries, U.S. politicians have no economic or political incentive to repeal or even modify the MID (or the favorable capital gains treatment of the profits from the sale of homes), and they routinely reject calls to eliminate homeownership benefits for upper-income Americans. Unlike higher-income Americans, LMI renters are less likely to buy homes, and for that reason they are the taxpayers who need financial incentives to become homeowners. Indeed, if the purpose of providing tax benefits is to encourage Americans to buy homes, U.S. tax and housing policies need to be drastically revised to give more than just a small percentage of upper-income homeowners an incentive to buy a house.

[8] *Hearing before the Committee on Banking, Housing, and Urban Affairs of the U.S. Senate, on Tax Reform and Residential Real Estate*, 108th Cong., 1st Sess. (Apr. 25, 2003) (prepared statement of Rep. Dave Camp), *available at* http://waysandmeans.house.gov/news/documentsingle.aspx?DocumentID=331534.

[9] http://waysandmeans.house.gov/calendar/eventsingle.aspx?EventID=330283. Witnesses included economists from the private and public sectors, consultants from think tanks, university professors, the representatives from NAR, and the National Association of Home Builders.

To align housing policies with the purported goal of those policies (which is to increase homeownership rates), at a bare minimum, Congress should adopt the recommendations of the Fiscal Commission that proposed lowering the MID (to $500,000 instead of the current $1 million), and the MID should be restricted to mortgages that are used to purchase primary residences.[10] Because second mortgages on homes and mortgages for second homes do not help renters become homeowners, taxpayers should not be allowed to deduct interest on those loans. Additionally, to discourage reckless borrowing (and lending), federal tax laws should not allow homeowners to deduct interest on exotic mortgage loans (e.g., negatively amortizing, interest-only, liar, and no down payment loans), like the ones lenders approved for borrowers during the housing boom.

Realtors argue that families would not be able to afford their homes without the tax deductions. However, as noted in Chapter 6, high-income renters in other countries have high homeownership rates even though their governments do not provide tax benefits as generous as the ones in the United States. Academic research does not support the claim that limiting or eliminating the MID would drastically affect current homeownership rates, because higher-income taxpayers (the ones who are most likely to use the MID) have always had the highest homeownership rates, and people who buy houses view homeownership as both an investment and a consumption activity.

Given the cultural significance of homeownership, there is no reason to assume that most Americans will stop buying homes and choose to rent if Congress modifies the MID or if more of the gains from the sales of homes is taxable. While most research finds that high-income buyers may choose to purchase less expensive homes if homeownership benefits are less generous, subsidizing McMansions has never been the stated goal of U.S. housing policies. Neither tax nor housing policies should subsidize those purchases, especially given that current housing policies benefit so few LMI Americans.

DECREASING EXTERNALITIES IN BLACK AND LATINO NEIGHBORHOODS

U.S. housing policies should also be revised to provide additional financial support for homeowners who live in neighborhoods that have been disproportionately harmed by the recent foreclosure crisis and neighborhoods that

[10] National Commission on Fiscal Responsibility and Reform, *The Moment of Truth*, (2010), *available at* http://www.fiscalcommission.gov/sites/fiscalcommission.gov/files/documents/TheMomentofTruth12_1_2010.pdf.

primarily house the undesirable (albeit socially useful) properties that politically powerful homeowners fenced out of their more affluent neighborhoods. Neighborhoods with a high percentage of neglected, abandoned, and foreclosed homes (or homes that were sold in short sales) often attract criminal activity. The resulting higher crime rates are capitalized in the value of homes in the neighborhoods. In addition, because of higher foreclosure rates in black and Latino neighborhoods, the property values of homeowners in those neighborhoods who did *not* have risky mortgages, were *not* in default on those mortgages, and did *not* behave recklessly dropped, even though they had been financially responsible, because they were forced to live in homes that had overgrown lawns or were in a visibly deteriorated condition. Living near abandoned or rundown properties made it harder for responsible homeowners to sell their homes or borrow against those homes.

If the United States is serious about finding ways to maintain high homeownership rates for black, Latino, and LMI Americans, then the government must increase the amount of financial assistance it gives to homeowners who live in neighborhoods that have high foreclosure rates. As discussed in Chapter 4, the U.S. Department of Housing and Urban Development's Neighborhood Stabilization Program (NSP) agreed to provide grants to state and local authorities to help them address the problems that result from having abandoned and deteriorated homes in a community. Cities that receive NSP grants can use those funds to buy land or houses, to demolish or rehabilitate abandoned properties, or to provide down payment or closing cost assistance to LMI families who seek to purchase the rehabilitated homes. The NSP also allows local governments to provide grants to nonprofit organizations that seek to buy the abandoned, foreclosed homes in targeted areas. While this program could counteract the problems homeowners have when they live near empty, deteriorating homes that drag down a neighborhood's property values when left unabated, the NSP has had only limited success because of insufficient funding.

Congress initially appropriated $5.9 billion for the NSP program. Because housing markets collapsed in many cities and foreclosure rates rose to record high levels during and after the recession, the budgeted amount was simply not enough to respond to the dire needs of cities. Funding was especially inadequate to help black and Latino neighborhoods, which had relatively greater numbers of vacant and deteriorated properties than white neighborhoods. To maintain homeownership rates and help increase overall household wealth for black, Latino, and LMI homeowners, Congress should either provide additional funding for the NSP program or develop new programs to help rehabilitate neighborhoods that have been ravaged by high foreclosure rates.

Additionally, while it is politically naive to assume that politicians will ever enact zoning laws that place undesirable property uses in higher-income neighborhoods, U.S. housing policies should acknowledge that black, Latino, and LMI homeowners are harmed financially when upper-income homeowners are allowed to fence out undesirable projects. To help offset any house price depreciation because of the presence of the undesirable uses, neighborhoods that house undesirable properties that benefit the entire community should be compensated for this harm. Compensation could be in the form of additional funding to improve neighborhood schools, parks, community centers, or other neighborhood amenities that might increase the desirability of the homes in those neighborhoods.

REDEFINING THE GOVERNMENT'S ROLE IN THE MORTGAGE MARKET

When foreclosures skyrocketed during the Depression and Americans lost their homes in record numbers, the United States intervened in the mortgage finance market and helped create the long-term, self-amortizing FRM that has defined and dominated the mortgage lending market ever since. This intervention transformed the mortgage lending market and caused homeownership rates (at least for whites) to rise. When overall homeownership rates stalled in the 1990s, the United States intervened again. This time, the United States encouraged lenders to "innovate" mortgage products to make it possible for more renters to buy homes. The United States also permitted Fannie Mae and Freddie Mac to provide liquidity in the mortgage finance market by purchasing or securitizing high-cost subprime loans instead of the lower-risk conforming mortgages the GSEs had been allowed to buy or securitize until then. This innovation caused homeownership rates to rise for *all* races.

Unlike the low-cost, low-risk mortgage products that resuscitated housing markets after the Depression, however, the exotic mortgage loan products that borrowers used to buy homes during the housing boom did little to make it possible for struggling, cash-strapped renters to become long-term homeowners. Homeownership rates (especially for blacks and Latinos) plummeted once the housing market collapsed; millions of homeowners lost their houses, while others found themselves trapped in homes that were worth less than the amount of the outstanding mortgage debt.

The United States is at another critical junction. As they did after the Depression, U.S. political leaders need to act decisively and boldly to ensure that federal housing policies help, not exacerbate, the economic plight of struggling homeowners. Even if homeownership remains the focal point of U.S. housing policies, political leaders need to ensure that U.S. housing policies are consistent with the goal of encouraging renters to be financially responsible, thrifty savers who buy homes using low-cost, low-risk mortgage products that allow them to live in safe, stable neighborhoods for the rest of their lives. To ensure the long-term stability of U.S. housing markets and to protect American households from high-cost and high-risk mortgage products, leaders must craft housing policies that do more than simply find ways to help cash-strapped homeowners modify – and then continue to repay – their mortgage loans. U.S. housing policies must focus on helping the renters who *should* be buying (but cannot afford to buy) houses: young LMI, black, and (especially) Latino renters.

Housing policies cannot continue to encourage buyers to purchase houses with costly or risky mortgage products. Even if the United States continues to insure, purchase, or securitize mortgage loans, the loans should be limited to mortgage products that are long-term, self-amortizing FRMs that Americans use to purchase homes. Just as homeowners should not be allowed to deduct interest on the high-cost and high-risk exotic mortgage loans that triggered the recent economic crisis, the U.S. government should not insure, purchase, or securitize high-cost and high-risk mortgage products (like interest-only, no- or low-doc, and no down payment loans). These exotic loans discourage borrowers from being thrifty and also discourage lenders from carefully determining whether the borrower can actually afford to buy the home.

Likewise, because reverse mortgages and second mortgages/home equity loans do not increase homeownership rates or make homeownership more accessible to renters, U.S. housing and tax policies should not subsidize or otherwise encourage these loans. Second mortgages, reverse mortgages, and the exotic high-cost and high-risk loan origination products that lenders innovated before the housing boom generate income for the financial services and real estate industries and help bolster the U.S. economy generally. Unfortunately, these loans discourage households from exercising the qualities that homeownership is said to create (i.e., thrift and financial responsibility), and the foreclosure rates for these loans (*especially* reverse mortgages) make it harder for Americans to have housing security as they age.

MAKING HOUSING AFFORDABLE

Our country's leaders also need to shift their views of the role that renting should play in the United States, as many Americans have already done. While no single housing initiative will close the racial homeownership gap or make it possible for cash-strapped LMI renters to buy homes, U.S. leaders need to craft policies that support cash-strapped Americans who prefer to remain renters. Thus, rather than continue to focus on increasing home sales, affordable housing (be it rented or owned) should become the centerpiece of U.S. housing policies. As discussed in earlier chapters, homeownership subsidies make homeownership more financially attractive and give renters less of an incentive to rent because the subsidies decrease the relative cost of owning a home as a pure consumption good and also increase its value as an investment. These subsidies reduce the attractiveness and demand for rental housing, especially for the middle- and upper-income taxpayers who benefit the most from homeownership's tax benefits.

Given the persistence of racial homeownership, education, income, and wealth gaps, U.S. political leaders need to consider ways to make it easier for black, Latino, and LMI households to find affordable housing in safe neighborhoods that have good schools, even if those initiatives encourage black, Latino, and LMI Americans to remain renters. Again, while none of the following proposals will singlehandedly close the racial gaps, the proposals can at least start to narrow some of those gaps. First, rather than providing homeownership tax benefits in the form of deductions, Congress should adopt the recommendation of the Fiscal Commission and convert the deduction to a tax credit that would provide more benefits for LMI homeowners who do not itemize their deductions.

Congress should also consider creating other ways to provide tax credits for renters who are trying to save money for a down payment. For example, just as existing tax laws encourage workers to save for retirement by investing in employer provided retirement plans (like 401ks), Congress should explore ways to encourage employers to provide a housing savings plan that lets LMI workers accumulate money for a down payment. Likewise, just as the United States has sponsored down payment assistance programs to encourage renters to save to buy a home, U.S. housing policies should also sponsor and subsidize programs that help renters save money for a rental security deposit or for other expenses associated with moving into rental housing. The United States should also consider ways to give landlords an economic incentive to help LMI renters use part of their monthly rent as a credit for a down payment on that (or a different) home.

Rather than providing tax benefits for higher-income taxpayers who have large mortgage loans, the United States should consider ways to provide subsidized mortgages for LMI homeowners. As an example, the United States could provide grants that could be used to subsidize the interest rate on a mortgage loan (up to a certain amount) for LMI Americans who want to buy a home. Assuming the borrower is financially responsible and makes payments on the mortgage loan for a specified period of time, the borrower could receive an annual lump sum payment that could be renewed for a specified number of years early in the loan term (e.g., three–five years). Such a program would give LMI borrowers an incentive to save and be financially responsible before they bought a house and would encourage them to develop good spending habits during the first few years of the mortgage term because the interest subsidy would be available only if the borrower is current on the loan payments.

Housing policies also need to focus on ways to encourage developers, builders, and existing property owners to provide more rental housing. Admittedly, the current Section 8 low-income rental voucher program is controversial, and many suburban homeowners lobby to fence out affordable housing from their neighborhoods. If, however, LMI parents could find subsidized rental housing in safe neighborhoods that have high-quality schools, they would have less of an incentive to buy a home (*any home*) in a neighborhood with high-poverty schools. Moreover, if the pool of rental units in neighborhoods that are zoned for higher-quality schools was larger, fewer black, Latino or LMI renters would need to buy homes in neighborhoods that are zoned for lower-quality schools.

Finally, the United States should seriously consider the possibility of giving tax subsidies to Americans who own houses jointly, communally, or cooperatively. A form of ownership that allowed owners to, for example, have a shared equity interest in a house or have a long-term lease of property that is owned by a community trust, would not give individual homeowners the same type of benefits they would have if they owned their home outright in a fee simple ownership. But shared ownership would give individuals more housing security than those who remained renters and also would provide some of the wealth-building features associated with homeownership.[11] Although the

[11] Low-income housing advocates have suggested a variety of ways for LMI renters to have a shared ownership interest in the homes they live in. For example, renters could be encouraged to purchase shares of stock in a cooperative organization that gives their members the right to occupy a housing unit. Or renters could join a not-for-profit entity that allows the resident members to live in housing that is owned and managed by the entity. Innovative financing that involves equity sharing is another option. Finally, renters should be encouraged to have a shared equity interest in a home. Individual owners will accumulate a smaller amount of wealth than they would if they owned the home, solely because they would need to share the profits of the home at resale. But under a properly drawn shared equity model, the homeowners could at least recoup their initial investment and any improvements they made to the property. Given the difficulties that black, Latino, and LMI homeowners have faced when they have tried to save enough money for a down payment, under certain circumstances it might be in their best interest financially for them to receive only a portion of the sales proceeds to ensure that they have lower costs in what is essentially privately subsidized housing. For a fuller discussion of these, and other proposals, see J. Peter Byrne & Michael Diamond, *Affordable Housing, Land Tenure, and Urban Policy: The Matrix Revealed*, 34 FORDHAM URBAN L.J. 527 (2007); Rick Jacobus & Jeffrey Lubell, *Preservation of Affordable Homeownership: A Continuum of Strategies* (2007), *available at* http://www.ncbcapitalimpact.org/uploadedFiles/downloads/JacobusLubelloptions4–07.pdf; John Emmeus Davis, *Shared Equity Homeownership: The Changing Landscape of Resale-Restricted, Owner-Occupied Housing* 65 (2006).

idea of cooperative or shared equity ownerships has never been embraced by U.S. policymakers, mortgage loan innovations that created forty- to fifty-year mortgages essentially created a long-term co-ownership between the lender and the borrower. In fact, although most borrowers may feel that they "own" their home as soon as they sign the closing documents and unpack the moving boxes, until they repay the mortgage loan, borrowers *always* co-own the home with the entity that owns the mortgage loan.

TEACHING HOMEOWNERSHIP 101

In addition to reducing tax subsidies for homeownership and increasing the availability of affordable housing (be it rented or owned), U.S. leaders need to review and revise the message that is being delivered in government housing education programs. Currently, most education programs are financial literacy or home buyer assistance programs that are designed to explain the benefits of homeownership and to help renters save for a down payment or generally prepare to become homeowners. Housing and financial literacy programs should not be designed to discourage renters from buying houses. But these programs should explain that buying a home is both an investment and a consumption decision and that buyers should carefully balance the costs and risks of owning with those of renting (including the opportunity costs of investing in a home instead of stocks, bonds, etc.). Moreover, given what now appear to be permanent changes in the structure of the U.S. labor markets, potential homeowners especially need to be told that they likely will have an extended period of unemployment, that they may need to move because of a job, that being staked to a house may decrease their mobility, that losing their job may cause them to lose their home to foreclosure, and that losing one home in a foreclosure may make it nearly impossible to become a homeowner again.

Housing programs that provide information based on outdated assumptions about homeownership should be revamped to ensure that renters receive clear and explicit information about the risks associated with buying a home, *especially* if they are black or Latino. For example, housing education programs need to clearly explain the importance of comparison shopping for mortgage products to avoid being steered to higher-cost mortgage products. Black and Latino renters in particular need to understand the risks associated with buying a home in a high-poverty, non-white neighborhood with low-performing schools. All renters should be told that renting housing in a higher-income neighborhood with higher-performing schools is better for their children long-term because attending higher-performing schools increases the likelihood that children will graduate from high school, receive a college degree, and, as a result, have higher potential future earnings and better employment prospects.

Rather than simply explaining the importance of saving for a down payment and the importance of creating a household budget that ensures they have enough money to repay a mortgage loan, housing programs should stress why homeowners need to budget for short- and long-term maintenance costs. Renters also need to be told that failing to properly maintain a home harms their housing investment by reducing the value of the home and decreasing the desirability of their neighborhood. Given the importance of maintenance and the evidence that suggests that LMI homeowners underestimate the costs of routine and long-term maintenance expenses, government housing programs should explore ways to give potential homeowners hands-on practice with simple home repairs and basic home maintenance. Similarly, homeownership programs should explain the process of working with independent contractors to ensure that LMI, black, and Latino homeowners avoid some of the predatory schemes that mortgage brokers over the last twenty years have concocted to convince older homeowners to take out second mortgages to make home repairs that were often unnecessary and overpriced.

Finally, housing policies should give lenders an incentive to tie the interest rate on mortgage loans to the borrowers' participation in financial literacy training and counseling. That is, rather than relying almost solely on a credit scoring system that currently prefers borrowers with wealth and especially favors borrowers who already own homes, the United States should consider ways to give financial incentives to lenders who agree to offer discounted interest rates to borrowers who voluntarily participate in training sessions that might help them become the homeowners envisioned in the Narrative: long term, financially responsible, thrifty savers who take care of their homes and are concerned and involved neighbors.

Of course, it is unclear whether financial education programs actually increase financial literacy and change an individual's financial behavior. In addition, even a successful financial education program will not, standing alone, eliminate the homeownership gap between white, higher-income homeowners and LMI, black, and Latino renters. Still, most research indicates that financial literacy is positively correlated with better financial behavior, including retirement planning, saving, investing in stocks, and accumulating wealth. Conversely, studies show that people with low levels of financial literacy typically accumulate too much debt, engage in high-cost borrowing, and are more likely to default on their mortgages or lose their homes to foreclosure.[12]

CHANGING THE HOMEOWNERSHIP PARADIGM

In the Narrative, as soon as a couple marries and has children, they save to buy a home to ensure that their children receive the benefits that purportedly flow (automatically) to the children of homeowners. While leaders are the only ones who can change U.S. housing policies, actual and potential homeowners can and should rationally develop their own views about whether (and when) homeownership is best for them.

Americans live longer now than they did when the parents of Baby Boomers bought homes just after World War II. In addition, unsteady employment, stagnant income, and crushing debt (especially student loan) loads now force younger Americans to live at home with their parents for longer periods. Americans overall are also getting married and having children at later ages. Younger LMI women (and now even more higher-income, college-educated women) are choosing to have children but not marry the fathers of their children for a variety of reasons.

The new homeownership narrative should reflect the demographic changes in U.S. households. Renters should understand that, even if they delay homeownership until they are forty or fifty, they can live in their homes for a long time with (or without) their children. Postponing homeownership for a decade will give them more time to save for a down payment and hopefully will give them time to find a job that will provide reliably stable income during the term of the mortgage loan. Black and Latino renters, in particular, need to ignore the romanticism associated with homeownership and should rationally assess whether the net benefits they might derive from owning a home exceed the benefits they would receive from renting – *especially* if they can rent a home in a neighborhood that is zoned for a higher-quality public school.

Despite the myths associated with homeownership and the U.S. government's relentless push to get more people to buy houses, individual Americans need to write their own homeownership narrative that includes a personal pledge to avoid homeownership until they are financially stable and can afford the short- and long-term costs associated with owning a home. Black and Latino personal homeownership narratives should reflect that they are at

[12] For a review of financial literacy studies and surveys, see Justine S. Hastings et al., *Financial Literacy, Financial Education and Economic Outcomes*, 5 ANN. REV. OF ECON. 347 (2013).

a significant disadvantage in U.S. housing markets because they have lower overall incomes, low or negative wealth, larger student loan debts, lower credit scores, and lower educational attainment levels. Their homeownership narratives also should reflect that they have lower marriage rates, are more likely to be single parents, and have higher unemployment rates. Given the problems blacks and Latinos have had (and continue to have) in the mortgage finance and real estate markets and the fact that their neighborhoods have a disproportionate number of public property uses and foreclosed homes, it is critically important for blacks and Latinos to carefully document the benefits they likely will receive if they buy a home against the burdens they likely will encounter if they can only afford to buy a home in a lower-income neighborhood using a higher-cost mortgage product.

Compared to the post–World War II home buyers and their Baby Boomer children, there are considerably fewer Echo Boomers and, thus, fewer potential homeowners who make up the demographic group that historically would be the most likely to buy homes (i.e., married couples over the age of thirty who are starting their own households). Moreover, declining white birth rates will decrease the number of new households that likely will buy houses, *unless* homeownership rates for blacks and (especially) Latinos dramatically increase and are maintained. If younger Americans continue to delay marriage, having children, and buying a home, or if their college debts remain high but their income remains stagnant, the decreased demand to buy homes will continue to depress housing values absent another intervention in housing markets. But, even though lower house values harm existing homeowners and longer rental stints harm the home building and mortgage lending industries, lower market values can actually help cash-strapped renters once they rewrite their homeownership narrative and delay buying a home until they can afford to be homeowners.

LINKING EDUCATION AND HOUSING POLICIES

Surveys consistently show that Americans think that one of the best reasons to buy a home is because it provides a good and safe place to live and raise children. As noted earlier, though, zoning and other land use laws, combined with the vestiges of discrimination in the real estate and lending markets, fence out most black and Latino children from higher-quality schools. Even though homeowners in LMI, black, and Latino neighborhoods with a disproportionate number of undesirable (albeit socially beneficial) properties in their neighborhoods appear happy with their decision to buy a home, the grim statistics presented in Chapter 9 indicate that black and Latino parents are undermining their children's economic future by buying houses in segregated neighborhoods with high-poverty, segregated schools.

While home buying is always good for the real estate and financial services industries, renting a home in a neighborhood that has better public schools would be better for most LMI, black and Latino households. Repeated efforts, policy initiatives, and the like have not closed the homeownership gap between races and between upper-income and LMI Americans, and this gap has remained fairly constant for over thirty years. Despite the myths associated with owning the home you live in, black and Latino households should avoid homeownership if the only home they can afford is in a neighborhood that will consign their children to attend the worst-performing schools in the city or region.

Blacks and Latinos must end their love affair with homeownership and instead fall in love – again – with education. Black and Latino owners, more than LMI owners, must realize that a short-term housing decision will have a long-term effect on their children's educational opportunities and that investing in a house may not be the best use of limited investment funds given the true costs of and likely return on that investment. Just as white homeowners with school-age children avoid neighborhoods that have low-performing schools, black and Latino homeowners with school-age children must take extreme caution when selecting the home they will live in.

There are now, and there always have been, chronic problems in the housing market, especially for LMI and minority homeowners. Given a choice between making a high-risk investment in a house in an area with low-performing schools or renting a home in an area that has good schools, LMI, black, and Latino households should invest in their children's education by renting for a longer period (perhaps until their children graduate from high school). Likewise, given their relatively higher foreclosure rates and relatively lower homeownership rates, black, Latino, and LMI Americans should invest in college for themselves or their children rather than investing in a home they may lose before they recoup their investment and that might not appreciate in value as much as homes in predominately white, upper-income neighborhoods do.

Black, Latino, and LMI households must understand and accept that delaying (or avoiding) homeownership will have long-term benefits – especially for their children – if renting a home in a neighborhood that has better public schools increases the likelihood that their children will graduate from high school, attend a postsecondary institution, and increase their potential for higher paying jobs and increased household wealth in the future. Data show that children who attend high-poverty schools are statistically less likely to graduate from high school, attend college, and graduate from college. Moreover, K–12 economic sorting imposes costs on the children who attend high-poverty schools because, even if they receive a quality education, they are deprived of contact with higher-income classmates who one day might be able to help them get a better job.

While it is not possible to verify the accuracy of the phrase "It's not what you know, it's who you know," employers still rely on referrals from their current employees when they are looking to hire. In addition to being segregated from personal contacts that might lead to better jobs in the future, children who live in segregated neighborhoods and attend segregated, high-poverty schools are excluded from social networks that might provide information about the college application process and opportunities for financial assistance to attend college.

It is possible, of course, for black and Latino children to obtain a quality education at a racially segregated, high-poverty school, and black and Latino parents with school-age children might reasonably choose to have their children attend predominately non-white schools because of the social benefits their children might derive from attending schools where they are not in the minority. Still, before parents reflexively buy a house, they should consider whether they could rent a home in a neighborhood that has a higher-performing, lower-poverty school.[13]

Although black and Latino renters need to individually consider how their housing choices are affecting their children's educational options, U.S. housing policies also need to acknowledge the link between education and homeownership. Just as national transportation policies after the Depression redesigned the federal interstate highway system and, in the process, facilitated the suburbanization of the United States, political leaders now need to find better ways to link housing policies to educational policies. Instead of continuing to push housing policies that largely ignore the link between neighborhoods and their schools, the United States should adopt policies that recognize the relationship between housing choices and school choices and that acknowledge that blacks and Latinos often make housing choices that have negative educational consequences for their children.

Political leaders should create a joint education-housing task force that is tasked to find ways to prevent housing policies from perpetuating K–12 economic sorting. For example, the United States could provide financial assistance to cities that implement socioeconomic K–12 school integration plans or could give financial incentives that encourage individual public schools to accept transfer requests from low-income students.[14] Some students who attend

[13] Rachel Garshick Kleit, *Neighborhood Segregation, Personal Networks, and Access to Social Resources*, in SEGREGATION: THE RISING COSTS FOR AMERICA (James H. Carr & Nandinee K. Kutty eds., 2008).

[14] These plans will be controversial, because they run counter to wealthy homeowners' views that they have the right to exclude residents of other parts of the city from "their" schools. The federal No Child Left Behind policy theoretically accomplishes this, as it gives students

high-poverty schools cannot attend college right after graduation because they could not take required courses, so the United States should also find ways to help high-performing students who attend low-performing schools have easy access to higher-track or AP courses. Finally, just as U.S. housing policies encouraged builders to include racially restrictive covenants in their housing developments, U.S. housing policies should encourage developers (and cities) to build affordable housing in neighborhoods that are in attendance zones for higher-quality schools.[15]

Partnerships, task forces, or other coordinated efforts between, for example, the U.S. Departments of Education and Housing and Urban Development cannot singlehandedly solve the problems LMI Americans face when they attempt to become and remain homeowners. Still, requiring federal agencies to study and propose solutions to the looming educational/housing crisis that faces black, Latino, and LMI Americans would fundamentally shift U.S. housing policies and signal the government's recognition that economic and educational sorting are principally responsible for the persistent racial, wealth, income, and homeownership gaps.

who attend a Title 1 school (which, by definition, has a high percentage of low-income students) the right to transfer to another school in the district with the district providing busing if the school fails to make "adequate yearly progress" for two consecutive years. 20 U.S.C. § 6316(b)(1)(A), (E) (Supp. II 2002). Recent data show, however, that only small percentages of the students who are eligible to transfer take advantage of this opportunity. Richard D. Kahlenberg, *Socioeconomic School Integration*, 85 N.C.L. Rev. 1545 (2007).

[15] As an example, developers who want to build residential high-rises in downtown Austin, Texas, must offer public benefits in return. Those benefits include renting or selling units at affordable spaces, paying fees that can be used to build affordable housing in other parts of the city, or providing a day care center in the new housing development. Sarah Coppola, *High-Rise Housing Plan to Require Public Benefits*, AUSTIN-AMERICAN STATESMAN (Jun. 29, 2013), at B1.

Index

Adjustable interest rates (ARMs), 10, 40, 45, 78, 79, 80, 83, 99, 105, 108, 146, 165, 170, 174, 176
Affordable housing projects, 186
  Habitat for Humanity, 183
American Dream, 5, 12, 113, 114, 121, 179, 183, 200, 205, 258
Automated credit scoring, 74, 165, 237, 238
Automated teller machine, 129

Baby Boomers, 28, 65, 68, 120, 121, 125, 181, 203, 270
Bankruptcy, 77, 96, 110
Blockbusting, 157, 158, 162, 163, 187
Buchanan v. Warley, 154

Civil Rights groups and organizations
  La Raza, 179, 253
  Leadership Conference on Civil Rights, 179
Clinton Administration, 23, 72. *See also* Homeownership Initiatives—U.S. Government
College
  Community College, 227, 229
  For-profit, 225, 227, 228, 229
  Four-year, 220, 227
  Labor market prospects for graduates, 226, 234
  Pell Grant, 220, 221n32
  Preparedness, by race, 221
  Tuition, 67, 224, 225, 227
Congressional Acts
  1968 Fair Housing Act, 13, 164, 177
  Community Reinvestment Act (CRA), 107, 108, 173
  Federal Housing Enterprises Financial Safety and Soundness Act of 1992, 72
  Federal-Aid Highway Act of 1944, 152
  Federal-Aid Highway Act of 1952, 152
  Federal-Aid Highway Act of 1954, 152
  GI Bill, 44
  Housing Act of 1949, 152
  National Housing Act of 1934, 43
  Tax Reform Act of 1986, 51
Consumer Debt
  Credit card debt, 28, 51, 90, 118, 129
  Deleveraging, 120
Consumer Financial Protection Bureau, 110, 166

Demographics, by race
  Birth rates, 182, 203, 208, 271
  College graduation rates, 223, 224, 237, 245, 252
  High school dropout rates, 209, 210, 211
  High school graduation rates, 105, 209
  Inheritance, 248, 249
  Marriage rates, 17, 194, 214, 215, 216, 217, 218, 242, 271
Department of Housing and Urban Development (HUD), 43, 102, 184, 194, 195, 200
Discrimination, by race or ethnicity
  Paired testing, 151, 166, 167, 232
  Wells Fargo Settlement, 172

Echo Boomer, 120, 121, 204, 205, 256, 271
Employment rates
  Blacks and Latinos, 15, 17, 153, 194, 195, 201, 215, 232, 233, 234, 236, 237, 242, 246, 257, 271
  College graduates, 230, 235, 236, 243
  The Great Depression, 38
  Overall, 71, 88
  Permanent part-time positions, 88
  Since 2007–2009 Recession, 86, 88, 116, 117, 119, 121, 141, 232, 233, 240, 241, 256

Employment rates (*cont.*)
  Whites, 153, 232
  Younger Americans, 121, 226, 270
Equal Employment Opportunity Commission, 231
Euclid v. Ambler Realty, 56, 57, 58
Executive Order 11062 on Equal Opportunity in Housing, 150

Fannie Mae
  Conservatorship, 46, 110, 143
  Franklin Raines, 114
Federal Home Loan Bank system, 42
Federal Home Loan Mortgage Corporation, 43
Federal Housing Administration (FHA)
  FHA-insured loans, 181, 191
  Underwriting manual, 148, 150, 164
  Underwriting standards, 46
Federal Housing Finance Agency (FHFA), 110
Federal Reserve, 4n3, 28n11, 50n13, 73n12, 78n18, 83n23, 86n1, 87n3, 92n9, 94n10, 101n22, 102, 103, 106n30, 108, 109, 109n35, 110, 112n39, 113n41, 118f6.1., 119f6.2., 126, 133n25, 141n37, 166, 166n36, 171, 174, 185n10, 201n33, 226, 237, 250
Federal tax benefits
  Mortgage interest deduction, 3, 51, 123, 196, 259
  Real estate taxes, 123
  State and local real estate taxes, 52
  Untaxed, imputed rental income, 4, 53, 54
Financial Institutions
  Bank of America, 103, 168
  Wells Fargo, 169, 170, 172
Fixed interest rates (FRM), 9, 45, 46, 48, 66, 73, 80, 83, 254, 264
Foreclosure externalities (negative)
  Abandoned and dilapidated properties, 93, 112
  Emotional and physical distress, 95, 96, 97
  Lower property values, 169, 263
Foreclosure sales, 86, 87, 103, 180
Freddie Mac
  Conservatorship, 46

Generation Xers, 120
George W. Bush administration, 72, 183. *See also* Homeownership initiatives–U.S. Government
Government Accountability Office (GAO), 229
Government National Mortgage Association (Ginnie Mae), 43
Government-sponsored enterprise (GSE), 43, 44, 46, 47, 48, 49, 50, 51, 72, 76, 78, 101, 108, 109, 143, 264

The Great Depression, 1, 2, 7, 17, 19, 23, 38, 39, 40, 41, 42, 45, 48, 50, 64, 72, 73, 74, 75, 76, 79, 80, 85, 99, 105, 131, 135, 145, 146, 147, 180, 181, 191, 247, 254, 264, 273
Gross domestic product (GDP), 54, 140
GSE Act, 72, 107
GSE debt, 110

Homeowner's association (HOA), 36, 55
  George Lucas and Marin County, 62
  Regulations, 55, 56
Homeownership Externalities (negative)
  Abandoned property, 93, 94, 112, 198, 263
  Criminal activity, 93, 198, 199, 263
  Fencing out residents or property types, 186, 257
  Household disruption, 202
Homeownership Initiatives—U.S. Government
  2008 Hope for Homeowners program, 110
  America's Homeownership Challenge, 183
  Down payment assistance programs, 266
  Everyman's Home campaign, 145
  Home Affordable Modification Program (HAMP), 111
  Home Affordable Refinance Program (HARP), 111
  Increasing Minority Homeownership, and Expanding Homeownership to All Who Wish to Attain It, 183
  Making Home Affordable Program (MHA), 111
  The National Homeownership Strategy, 72, 183
  Neighborhood Stabilization Program (NSP), 112, 263
Homeownership rates
  Black homeownership rates, 180, 181, 184, 185
  Latino homeownership rates, 14, 15, 179, 182, 185, 191, 192, 202, 206, 207, 247, 252
  Overall homeownership rates, 9, 15, 17, 44, 64, 72, 86, 145, 180, 181, 182, 184, 185, 194, 252, 264
  Racial gap, 14, 180, 184, 185, 191, 195, 203, 206, 246, 250, 251, 265, 269, 272
  White homeownership rates, 15, 180, 181, 184, 185, 207
Household income, 9, 11, 26, 28, 47, 68, 81, 116, 143, 162, 197, 213, 224, 239, 240, 242
  Black, 241
  Black and Latino, 15, 17, 197, 198, 220, 242, 245, 249

LMI workers, 11, 68, 81, 92, 215, 238, 246, 255
Racial gap, 198
Stagnant, 1, 9, 10, 11, 17, 28, 47, 68, 72, 81, 85, 88, 90, 92, 113, 116, 134, 192, 206, 208, 225, 270
White, 198, 220, 241
Household wealth
Blacks and Latinos, 179, 192, 193, 247, 248, 250, 257, 263, 272
Changes over time, 83, 118, 250
College graduates, 230
LMI, 248
Overall, 27, 28, 64, 65, 202, 246
Racial gap, 251
Whites, 193, 247
Housing prices
Appreciation rates, 3, 8, 10, 24, 28, 101, 137
Bidding wars during boom, 82, 124, 126
Boom, 3, 29, 64, 82, 114, 127
Decline in 2007–2009 Recession, 15, 83, 84, 109, 125, 127, 138

K–12 Schools
Economic sorting, 272, 273
Extracurricular activities, 32, 97, 202, 211, 213
Income achievement gap, 213, 218

Labor trends
Labor markets, generally, 135, 136, 231, 232, 234, 238, 268
Manufacturing sector, decline over time, 69, 70, 234, 245
Mobility, 136, 180, 245
Occupational segregation, 234, 242
Permanent part-time positions, 88
Unemployment or under employed, 136
Land installment contracts, 158
Land use and zoning laws
Exclusionary zoning laws, 5, 126
Racially restrictive convenants, 148, 155, 155n18, 164, 181, 191
Racially restrictive zoning, 155, 186
Variances, 5, 58, 59, 62
Loan servicers, 111
Loan to value (LTV)
Loan, 44, 76, 77, 78, 83, 85, 99
Ratio, 39, 40, 44, 45, 99
Low to moderate income (LMI)
Homeowners, 125, 131, 139, 240, 253, 263, 264, 266, 269
Households, 72, 81, 87, 108, 123, 139, 239, 248, 253, 266
Neighborhoods, 108, 173, 174, 175
Renters, 9, 68, 253, 261, 265, 266, 267

Millennial Housing Commission, 203
Mortgage Bankers Association, 253
Mortgage brokers, 101, 137, 142, 166, 168, 170, 172, 173, 174, 175, 176, 246, 269
Mortgage fraud, 101, 102, 104
Affinity fraud, 172, 173
Inflating borrowers' incomes, 101
Inflating home values, 101, 104, 157
Mortgage innovation, 10, 126
Relaxed lending standard, 24
Teaser interest rate, 10
Mortgage interest deduction (MID), 51, 123, 196, 259. *See also* Federal tax benefits
Mortgage interest rates
Interest rate reset, 10, 40, 78, 170, 192, 193, 254
Mortgage loan, features
Balloon payment, 39, 40, 135
Cash-out refinance, 83, 85, 129, 130, 132, 141, 168, 170
Default rate, 11, 83, 192, 198, 225
Interest Only (IO), 79, 265
Jumbo loans, 49
Liar loan, 262
Loan modifications, 102, 103
Low documentation loan (lo doc), 75
No documentation loan (no doc), 75, 99, 170
Non- or negative amortization, 14, 79, 80, 83
Piggyback loan, 99
Prepayment penalty, 167
Refinancing, 27, 42, 82, 87, 102, 106, 114, 128, 131, 141, 167, 168, 255
Self-amortizing, 2, 3, 23, 26, 46, 68, 80, 130, 146, 191, 264, 265
Underwriting standards, 2, 23
Mortgage-backed securities (MBS), 47. *See also* Fannie Mae; Freddie Mac
Foreign investors, 101
Private label securities (PLS), 48, 49, 100, 101
The Moynihan Report, 214, 215, 217, 232

National Association of Home Builders, 142, 253
National Association of Real Estate Boards, 146
The National Association of Realtors, 142, 204, 259
National Bureau of Economic Research, 82
National Commission on Fiscal Responsibility and Reform (Fiscal Commission), 259
Neighborhoods
And, antagonism toward halfway houses, 5, 58, 59, 62, 187

Neighborhoods (*cont.*)
And, antagonism toward homeless shelters, 5, 58, 59, 62, 98n18
Segregation, 13, 153, 155, 158, 160, 161, 186
Suburban, 13, 46, 56, 61, 152, 153, 186, 187
Urban, 13, 153, 157, 164, 188
White flight, 157, 161, 207
New Deal, 1, 47
Not in My Backyard (NIMBY), 4, 59

Obama Administration, 111
Occupy Wall Street, 250

Piggyback loan, 76, 77, 99, 100
Price-to-Rent ratio, 121
Public schools
Quality and effect on home prices, 36, 133, 207

Realtors Code of Ethics, 146
Redlining, 12, 13, 146, 147, 148, 149, 150, 152, 153, 155, 156, 157, 164, 165, 167, 168, 171, 175, 186, 187, 189, 191, 206, 207
Retirement income, 27, 89, 90, 91, 92, 132, 196
Reverse mortgage, 89, 90, 91, 129, 132, 255, 265. *See also* Mortgage loan, features

Second mortgage, 26, 28, 76, 83, 89, 92, 94, 100, 128, 130, 131, 198, 255, 262, 265, 269
Secretary of Housing and Urban Development (HUD), 22, 183, 204
Henry G. Cisneros, 72
Herbert Hoover, 140
Securitization, 46, 47, 48, 49, 109. *See also* Mortgage-backed Securities (MBS)
Short sale, 87, 93, 94, 198, 263
Single-parent household, 216, 217, 218, 220, 240, 242
Spatial mismatch, 154
Steering, 12, 13, 102, 145, 151, 152, 153, 157, 169, 171, 186, 187, 190, 199, 206, 207, 246
Student loan, 92n9, 121, 225, 226, 228, 247, 270, 271
Subprime loan, 12, 14, 48, 49, 50, 75, 77, 78, 83, 89, 90, 91, 99, 100, 101, 102, 103, 108, 109, 131, 137, 165, 166, 166n37, 167, 169, 170, 171, 172, 174, 176, 192, 193, 195, 196, 237, 246, 264

Too Big To Fail, 109
Top 1%, 68, 69, 81, 239, 240, 250, 251

U.S. Congress
Campaign contributions, 142, 143
Congressional Black Caucus, 143, 253
Congressional Budget Office (CBO), 124
Congressional Hispanic Caucus, 143
House Ways and Means Committee, 261
National Republican Congressional Committee (NRCC), 142
U.S. Government
Department of Commerce's Advisory Committee on Zoning, 56, 154
Department of Treasury, 111
Intervention in mortgage market, 149, 254, 264
Transportation policies, 152, 273